OXFORD MONOGRAPHS ON
LABOUR LAW
*General Editors*: Paul Davies,
Keith Ewing, Mark Freedland

LEGISLATING FOR CONFLICT

*Oxford Monographs on Labour Law*

*General Editors*: Paul Davies, Fellow of Balliol College, Oxford, and Reader in Law at Oxford University; Keith Ewing, Professor of Public Law at King's College, London; and Mark Freedland, Fellow and Tutor in Law at St John's College, Oxford.

This series is the first new development in the literature dealing with labour law for many years. The series recognizes the arrival not only of a renewed interest in labour law generally, but also the need for a fresh approach to the study of labour law following a decade of momentous change in the UK and Europe. The series is concerned with all aspects of labour law, including traditional subjects of study such as industrial relations law and individual employment law, but it will also include books which examine the law and economics of the labour market and the impact of social security law upon patterns of employment and the employment contract.

Forthcoming titles in this series

*The Right to Strike*
KEITH EWING

*The Law Relating to Dismissal from Employment*
HUGH COLLINS

# Legislating for Conflict

SIMON AUERBACH

CLARENDON PRESS · OXFORD
1990

Oxford University Press, Walton Street, Oxford OX2 6DP
Oxford New York Toronto
Delhi Bombay Calcutta Madras Karachi
Petaling Jaya Singapore Hong Kong Tokyo
Nairobi Dar es Salaam Cape Town
Melbourne Auckland
and associated companies in
Berlin Ibadan

Oxford is a trade mark of Oxford University Press

Published in the United States
by Oxford University Press, New York

© Simon Auerbach 1990

British Library Cataloguing in Publication Data
Auerbach, Simon
Legislating for conflict. – (Oxford monographs in labour law, 1).
1. Great Britain. Industrial relations. Strikes. Law
I. Title
344.1041892
ISBN 0–19–825275–7

Library of Congress Cataloging-in-Publication Data
Auerbach, Simon.
Legislating for conflict/Simon Auerbach.
—(Oxford monographs on labour law)
Includes bibliographical references and index.
1. Trade-unions—Law and legislation—Great Britain. 2. Labor
disputes—Great Britain. I. Title. II. Series.
KD3050.A98    1990    344.41'0189—dc20    [344.104189]    90–39510
ISBN 0–19–825275–7

Typeset by Pentacor PLC, High Wycombe, Bucks.

Printed in Great Britain by
Bookcraft Ltd, Midsomer Norton, Avon

*Dedicated to my father
and to the memory of my mother*

# Editors' Preface

It is our aim as editors of this new series to promote the publication of books which will make a distinctive contribution to the study of labour law. For this purpose we have adopted a deliberately open-ended view of the subject. Consequently we expect to deal with topics which straddle the frontiers between labour law and other areas of law, whether it be social security law, pensions law, or company law. We expect also that books in the series will not necessarily adopt a formal or legalistic approach, for we would wish to encourage authors to draw upon the contributions made by other disciplines, whether it be industrial relations, political science, or economics. And we would expect, finally, that books in the series will not concentrate exclusively on legal developments in Britain. We are conscious of the importance of EEC law, and aware of the growing interest in the labour laws of EEC member states, as well as in comparative labour law generally.

The first title to appear in the series is in our view a distinguished example of what, we hope, the series will achieve. Simon Auerbach offers a fresh approach to labour law scholarship by combining law and politics to provide a detailed examination of the origins and enactment of major legislation. His study examines the development of government policy and the legislative history of the industrial conflict legislation of the 1980s. He also examines the provisions in the legislation which at least ostensibly were more concerned with the internal regulation of trade unions than with industrial conflict. His study makes an important contribution to our understanding of why the legislation was introduced in the first place and why it took its present shape. Above all, Simon Auerbach provides valuable insight into the theoretical bases which are thought to underpin much of modern labour law. As such, his work is in our submission an important and definitive addition to the literature of recent labour law history.

P.L.D.
K.D.E.
M.R.F.

*31 July 1990*

# Acknowledgements

THIS book was researched and written in Oxford and London between 1985 and 1990. Over that period, many people have given me interviews, provided me with documents, or contributed information, ideas, advice, or assistance. I can mention only some of them here.

Paul Davies has seen the project through from start to finish, as supervisor of my doctoral thesis, co-editor of this book, and with unerring and unfailing advice and support given far beyond those roles. Colin Crouch was, particularly as a non-lawyer, an invaluable co-supervisor at Oxford. Roy Lewis examined my thesis, and subjected it to some searching criticism. Mark Freedland also examined the thesis, and has since as co-editor offered much guidance in the development of the book. Keith Ewing, as co-editor, also provided welcome guidance and encouragement. A previous collaboration, and many discussions, with John Bowers helped me to formulate my ideas, particularly on the 1988 Act and more recent developments. Numerous conversations with Michael Seifert have sharpened my analysis, and I am grateful also to him and to his partners for allowing me the time needed to see the book through to completion. As for so many before me, Bill Wedderburn has inspired and encouraged my understanding of, and my writings on, labour law.

Thanks go also to my editor at Oxford University Press, Richard Hart, and to all his colleagues for their work. Thanks too to the staff at the Bodleian Law Library, and at all the other libraries which I used, for their great help.

Finally, heartfelt thanks to Julie George, who gave unfailing personal support, and literally made completion of the book possible, by her own commitment both to me and to it.

*March 1990*                                                                                     S. J. A.

# Contents

# Abbreviations

| | |
|---|---|
| AC | Law Reports Appeal Cases |
| ACAS | Advisory Conciliation and Arbitration Service |
| ACPO | Association of Chief Police Officers |
| AER | All England Law Reports |
| AIB | Association of Independent Businesses |
| APAP | Association of Professional Ambulance Personnel |
| APEX | Association of Professional Executive and Clerical and Computer Staff |
| Aslef | Associated Society of Locomotive Engineers and Firemen |
| AUEW | Amalgamated Union of Engineering Workers |
| BALPA | British Airline Pilots Association |
| BIM | British Institute of Management |
| *BJIR* | *British Journal of Industrial Relations* |
| CA | Court of Appeal |
| CAC | Central Arbitration Committee |
| CBI | Confederation of British Industry |
| CCO | Conservative Central Office |
| Ch. | Law Reports Chancery Division |
| Ch. D. | High Court Chancery Division |
| *CLJ* | *Cambridge Law Journal* |
| *CLLJ* | *Comparative Labour Law Journal* |
| *CLP* | *Current Legal Problems* |
| CO | Certification Officer |
| CPC | Conservative Political Centre |
| CPPA | Conspiracy and Protection of Property Act |
| CPS | Centre for Policy Studies |
| CS | Court of Session |
| CSEU | Confederation of Shipbuilding and Engineering Unions |
| CTU | Conservative Trade Unionists |
| DC | Divisional Court |
| DE | Department of Employment |
| DEP | Department of Employment and Productivity |
| *DULJ* | *Dublin University Law Journal* |
| EA | Employment Act |
| EAT | Employment Appeal Tribunal |
| EEF | Engineering Employers' Federation |
| EETPU | Electrical Electronic Telecommunications and Plumbing Union |
| *EG* | *Employment Gazette* |
| EPA | Employment Protection Act |
| EP(C)A | Employment Protection (Consolidation) Act |
| FSR | Fleet Street Law Reports |

| | |
|---|---|
| GMBATU | General Municipal Boilermakers and Allied Trades Union |
| HC | House of Commons |
| HL | House of Lords |
| IALS | Institute of Advanced Legal Studies |
| *ICLQ* | *International and Comparative Law Quarterly* |
| ICR | Industrial Cases Reports |
| IEA | Institute of Economic Affairs |
| IER | Institute of Employment Rights |
| *ILJ* | *Industrial Law Journal* |
| ILO | International Labour Organisation |
| IOCCAUS | Inns of Court Conservative and Unionist Society |
| I.o.D | Institute of Directors |
| IPCS | Institution of Professional Civil Servants |
| IPM | Institute of Personnel Management |
| IR | Irish Reports |
| IRA | Industrial Relations Act |
| *IRJ* | *Industrial Relations Journal* |
| *IRLIB* | *Industrial Relations Legal Information Bulletin* |
| IRLR | Industrial Relations Law Reports |
| *IRRR* | *Industrial Relations Review and Report* |
| ISTC | Iron and Steel Trades Confederation |
| ITF | International Transport Workers' Federation |
| *JBL* | *Journal of Business Law* |
| *JLS* | *Journal of Law and Society* |
| KIR | Knight's Industrial Reports |
| *LQR* | *Law Quarterly Review* |
| *LS* | *Legal Studies* |
| *MLR* | *Modern Law Review* |
| MSC | Manpower Services Commission |
| NCT | National Chamber of Trade |
| NEDC | National Economic Development Council |
| NGA | National Graphical Association |
| NICA | Northern Ireland Court of Appeal |
| NIRC | National Industrial Relations Court |
| NUJ | National Union of Journalists |
| NUM | National Union of Mineworkers |
| NUR | National Union of Railwaymen |
| NUS | National Union of Seamen |
| *OJLS* | *Oxford Journal of Legal Studies* |
| OR | Official Report (Hansard) |
| *OREP* | *Oxford Review of Economic Policy* |
| *PL* | *Public Law* |
| POEU | Post Office Engineering Union |
| QB | Law Reports Queen's Bench |
| QBD | High Court Queen's Bench Division |
| RSC | Rules of the Supreme Court |
| SCR | Supreme Court Reports (Canada) |
| SDP | Social Democratic Party |

| | |
|---|---|
| SI | Statutory Instrument |
| SLADE | Society of Lithographic Artists, Designers, Engravers and Process Workers |
| SLT | Scottish Law Times |
| TDA | Trade Disputes Act |
| TDTUA | Trade Disputes and Trade Unions Act |
| TGWU | Transport and General Workers' Union |
| TLR | Times Law Reports |
| TUC | Trades Union Congress |
| TULRA | Trades Union and Labour Relations Act |
| TULR(Am)A | Trade Union and Labour Relations (Amendment) Act |
| UCW | Union of Communications Workers |
| UDM | Union of Democratic Mineworkers |
| UIC | Union of Independent Companies |
| UPW | Union of Post Office Workers |
| WLR | Weekly Law Reports |

# Table of Cases

# Table of Statutes

*When the general-secretary of the TUC gave evidence to the Select Committee on employment he said:*

*We only claim three rights: the right to combine in order to pursue the collective interest of our members, the right to be recognised by employers for collective bargaining purposes and the right to withdraw labour, that is to say the right not to work except on terms and conditions which have been agreed with an employer. These are the characteristic rights of free trade unions in all democratic countries.*

*I have no quarrel with that statement. If these are the rights that trade unions need to function effectively, they have nothing to fear from the Bill.*

Mr Tebbit, to Parliament, 8 February 1982

*. . . I do not believe that people who go on strike in this country have a legitimate cause. Throughout the period of the Labour Government and this one, I have never supported any strikes in this country.*

Mrs Thatcher, to Parliament, 22 June 1982

*Public opinion, so far as I can tell, unquestioningly concedes the right of men in a free society to withdraw their labour. It just draws the line at strikes.*

Michael Frayn, A Perfect Strike, 1967

# [1]

# Introduction

## (1) A DECADE OF CHANGE

In 1978, four years into a Labour Government, the development of collective labour law in Britain had reached a point at which it seemed possible that a new era of stability might be ahead. To many academic commentators, all the signs were that a sustainable settlement, at least regarding the broad legal framework in areas such as industrial conflict, had been achieved.[1] The dramatic upheavals in labour law and industrial relations of the early 1970s, associated with Mr Heath's Conservative Government, and in particular its Industrial Relations Act 1971, had given way to the reinstatement—'but stronger and clearer than it was then'[2]—of the framework of industrial-conflict law first established some seventy years before in the Trade Disputes Act 1906, a framework which had itself stood intact until only a few years earlier when it was dismantled to make way for the 1971 Act.

While the Labour Government had thus committed itself unequivocally to the 'voluntarist' approach to industrial-conflict law which the 1906 Act had expressed, the Conservative Opposition was for its part in no mood for strong dissent. The Industrial Relations Act was widely perceived as an almost unmitigated failure and a major contributor to the downfall of the Heath administration in 1974.[3] In the major review of industrial relations and labour law policy which followed, the Conservative employment spokesman, the then Mr James Prior, soon concluded, and was happy to reiterate in 1978 a frequent pledge, that 'when we return to office we shall not undertake sweeping changes in the law.'[4]

In 1988, after almost ten years of unbroken Conservative rule, the state of industrial-conflict law in Britain had been transformed by a series of measures which to many indicated a change of Government philosophy far more fundamental than had the Act of 1971. If the essence of the voluntarist approach had been that the conduct of peaceful industrial action should be unrestricted and unregulated by law, the consistent pattern of the 1980s was the introduction of increasingly deep and detailed restrictions and regulations,

---

[1] See e.g. Wedderburn (1978: p. 458); Davies (1979: pp. 33–4).

[2] Per Lord Scarman *NWL Ltd.* v. *Woods* [1979] ICR 867, 886G–H.

[3] See e.g. Weekes *et al.* (1975).

[4] OR HC vol. 942 col. 1847 (27 Jan. 1978). For earlier pledges in a similar vein, see CCO (1976: p. 45); Howe *et al.* (1977).

so that 'the law in force [in 1988] would have been both unrecognisable to and unimaginable by the trade unions of the mid–1970s' (Ewing 1988*a*: p. 11).

Today, we find that peaceful industrial action is liable to be unlawful if it is secondary or sympathetic action,[5] concerns a union membership or recognition issue,[6] involves persons picketing away from their place of work,[7] lacks the support of a majority of those involved in a ballot,[8] or possibly one of a set of ballots,[9] is regarded as politically inspired, or otherwise falls outside a narrow range of legitimate topics for dispute.[10] New measures will attack 'unofficial' action, of every type.[11] Codes of Practice add nearly one hundred paragraphs of regulation to the framework.[12] Nor is it merely employers and other 'outsiders' who are now to act as the regulatory agencies. Dissentient union members, equipped with the 'right to work' regardless of any ballot,[13] now find the weapons of injunction and receivership at their disposal,[14] and a new and ready source of official funding, through the Commissioner for the Rights of Trade Union Members.[15] For unions which fall foul of the new laws, the punishments include massive fines, which readily run into six figures, and sequestration of assets, a particularly draconian measure which has become an established feature of the bitterest disputes.[16]

How and why has this revolution in industrial-conflict law come about? What were the policies and strategies underlying the new laws, and how were they developed? Much has already been written about the Conservative Governments of the 1980s; and among writers of almost all disciplines and political persuasions it has become something of a trite axiom that 1979 marked a watershed: a decisive break with the values and approach of the post-war consensus which for more than thirty years before had enjoyed cross-party support.[17] Whether in other areas of policy that judgement is indeed sound, is not an issue for this book; but critics and supporters of the 1980s Governments alike have argued that such a momentous change was crucially reflected in the policy towards labour law and industrial relations.

[5] Employment Act 1980, s. 17. See now, Employment Bill 1990, cl. 4.

[6] Employment Act 1982, s. 14; Employment Act 1988, s. 10.

[7] Trade Union and Labour Relations Act 1974, s. 15, as amended by Employment Act 1980, s. 16.

[8] Trade Union Act 1984, ss. 10 and 11; Employment Act 1988, s. 1.

[9] Employment Act 1988, s. 17.

[10] Trade Union and Labour Relations Act 1974, s. 29, as amended by Employment Act 1982, s. 18.

[11] Employment Bill 1990, cls. 6 and 7.

[12] Employment Act 1980, s. 3, as amended by Employment Act 1988, s. 18; Code of Practice on Picketing (1980); Code of Practice on Trade Union Ballots on Industrial Action (1990). Employment Bill 1990, cl. 10.

[13] Employment Act 1988, ss. 3–5.

[14] Ibid. ss. 23 and 9, respectively.

[15] Ibid. ss. 19–21. Employment Bill 1990, cls. 8 and 9.

[16] On sequestration, see Jacob (1986); Kidner (1986).

[17] See e.g. Crouch (1982*b*: ch. 5); Holmes (1985*b*: esp. pp. 34–40); Middlemas (1983); Lawson (1980: p. 1).

Writers differ as to which areas of this policy were most significant, but among labour lawyers a widely shared critique of the relation of labour law changes to broader policy objectives has been developed.

The leading and most prolific exponent of the 'new politics of labour law' is undoubtedly Lord Wedderburn.[18] He has identified a common thread running through the changes in industrial-conflict law, namely that: 'The collective strength of workers is to be limited by the boundaries of the employment unit . . . '(Wedderburn 1985a: p. 43)—boundaries which are set by capital, alone or together with the state. The explanation for this change, he argues, lies in the fact that the Conservative Government of the 1980s 'is the first British Government since the war to pursue a policy on industrial relations law which is integrally geared into its overall economic policies' (p. 36). Those policies are themselves said to be set by the agenda of the so-called New Right—of Friedman and in particular of Hayek—in essence requiring that the labour market work free of the obstacles created by trade unions: 'a rigged market in which combination laws price labour into such jobs as there may be' (p. 43).

Lawyers who make out a similar critique from a standpoint sympathetic to the 1980s Governments are rather harder to find, but a noteworthy account was offered at an early stage by Richard Tur (1982). He too identifies Hayek as a key inspiration behind the new legislation. The presupposition upon which it rests, he argues, is 'simplicity itself': the unrestrained market of individualistic, self-motivated competition, the operation of which is both just and efficient (pp. 157–8). Tur reasons that it is logically impossible at once to reject economic laissez-faire and to embrace free collective bargaining, and that '[e]ither one allows market forces to determine wages or one seeks to regulate wages' (p. 160).[19] Tur concludes, contrarily to Wedderburn, that far from being incompatible with trade unions' activities, the free market economy is 'ultimately the only economy which can sustain them' (ibid.).[20]

The writings of both these commentators involve observations of three kinds about the legislation, about only—but crucially—the third of which they disagree: first, that the driving force behind the legislation is *economic* policy; secondly, that the ideas which inspire that policy are exemplified in the writings of people such as Hayek; thirdly, that the implementation of this policy is either wholly incompatible with unions' activities, or the only system which can genuinely offer them a role. The arguments of both suggest a legislative regime which is both consistent and deliberate in its intent: a regime upon which a particular theoretical outlook or objective can be seen as the most pervasive influence of all.

[18] See esp. Clark and Wedderburn (1983); Wedderburn (1984), (1985a), (1985b), (1986b: pp. 68–96), (1989b).

[19] Tur does not consider the possibility of intermediate strategies.

[20] Cf. Holmes (1985b), arguing that the Thatcher Government restored 'genuine' free collective bargaining.

It is hard to imagine anyone who has lived through the 1980s in Britain, of whatever political persuasion, wanting to quarrel with the suggestion that the period witnessed a steady move to the right in Conservative and Government policies, closely identified in all quarters with the ideas and aspirations of the Prime Minister of the period, Mrs Thatcher. Nor could the development of industrial-conflict law—especially when set alongside the series of measures removing all props to collective bargaining and maintenance of wage levels, and the steady erosion of employment protection legislation—be intelligibly viewed as an exception to that rule. Yet even within the context of those essential premisses, there is still room for a difficult and vital debate. In particular, this book will argue that the 'New Right' critique alone presents an incomplete and insufficient account of the industrial-conflict legislation of the 1980s. Whilst persuasive and incisive in the broad sweep of its analysis, the 'New Right' critique fails among other things to take sufficient account of the greater and more varied complex of influences and events which shaped the legislation. This fact, combined with the excessive simplicity of the traditional analysis in marking 1979 as the point of abrupt transition from a voluntarist to a post- or anti-voluntarist era, ultimately serves to blur our understanding, and blunt our evaluation, of developments both before and after that date. The analysis put forward in this book will in particular lead to two key conclusions which should supplement and build upon the New Right thesis. First, that a greater range and sophistication of influences and considerations must be seen as having determined the industrial-conflict laws of this period, than are to be found in the preachings of the Hayekian New Right alone. Secondly, that to obtain a more complete understanding of the legislation and its origins, it is necessary to recognize the degree to which the 'voluntarist consensus' had in fact already largely broken down before 1979, and hence to recognize the extent of the continuity and overlap between the preoccupations and priorities of the Governments of the 1980s, and those of the administrations which preceded them in the 1960s and 1970s.[21] How, then, will this book present such an analysis?

## (2) SOURCES AND METHODS

Kahn-Freund argued, over twenty years ago, that the law student should be taught to consider each concrete situation from two different angles: 'He should learn to look at it in a strictly and rigidly dogmatic way and he should also learn to look at it as a social situation requiring the solution of a social problem' (1966: p. 129). He regarded the two approaches as mutually indispensable. More recently, Lord Wedderburn has concluded that '[t]he battle for socio-legal studies has been largely, though not entirely, won in British law faculties' (1985a: p. 22). Today it is indeed considered a

---

[21] For the full argument, see chs. 10 and 11 below.

commonplace if not a necessity for lawyers to widen their concerns beyond a mere acquaintance with the law itself, and to seek to view the law, as it is said, in its 'social context'. This is pre-eminently true of labour law, for 'industrial relations' as a subject of interest has become a focal point around which scholars from a very wide range of disciplines within the social sciences have gathered and exchanged ideas, a fact reflected in the body of learning which they have produced.[22]

In a field as politically controversial as that of labour law today, it is hard to see how it could be otherwise; yet this very fact raises an immediate and difficult challenge. Having once left the home base of pure legal analysis, how far ought the lawyer to range? Few can expect to command any great level of expertise or sophistication of knowledge very far beyond the field of their own area of specialization, and perhaps most would have no great desire to attempt to do so. Such considerations give rise to practical and intellectual limitations on the pursuit of the potentially all-embracing goals of socio-legal studies. An understanding and acceptance of these constraints is surely eminently advisable. Nevertheless, it is also arguable that, although lawyers have already contributed a significant body of writing on the post-1979 legislation, there is yet one particular line of enquiry into the subject which has not so far been pursued in any systematic or thoroughgoing fashion—and that this is one which is particularly well suited to be pursued by a lawyer. Hepple and Brown perceptively diagnosed the source and nature of the lacuna, in 1981. In essence, the problem is that—notwithstanding Kahn-Freund's attempts to redress the tendency—the common lawyer's approach to the study of law through the case-law still dominates the legal literature. Thus, even when statute law is itself the subject, the primary method of analysis tends to be discussion of how the statutory provisions might be, or have been, interpreted in the cases.[23]

Why not instead take the legislation as it appears on the statute-book, less as the starting-point, and more as the finishing point of our analysis? Some might argue that such a methodology, whatever its merits, is one which non-lawyers are better placed to adopt. But Hepple and Brown suggested not only that this was an essential approach for all those concerned to understand the social operation of statute law, but also that traditional legal skills could be brought to bear upon the task in important ways. For bound up with the problems of pure legislative policy are those deriving from such matters as the constraints and principles governing statutory drafting, and the rules and judicial practice of statutory interpretation (Hepple and Brown 1981: pp. 59–62 and 67). This book will attempt to show that there are a number of important benefits to be gained from taking this sort of approach to the industrial-conflict legislation of the 1980s. The preferred methodology has naturally guided the choice of source materials and the uses to which they

[22] A useful assessment of the labour lawyers' input is Wedderburn (1986*a*).
[23] See Hepple and Brown (1981: pp. 56–9). See also Atiyah (1987: pp. 29–32).

will here be put. Some initial discussion of this topic may therefore be helpful.

Perhaps the most obvious primary source for any lawyer studying legislation to turn to is the pages of Hansard. The existing legal literature certainly makes use of Hansard, but usually for one of two fairly limited purposes. First, the Parliamentary debates invariably generate a host of memorable and often controversial quotations which are bound to enliven and so improve almost any academic account. There is a more serious aspect to this fact, too, for such quotations and catch-phrases, sometimes by design of the utterer, sometimes not, may easily attain the status of symbolic embodiment of the very essence of legislative policy. Certainly, as we shall see, this was a feature on more than one occasion of the legislation with which we are concerned. The second main occasion of resort to Hansard is when a provision seems to be too obscure or ambiguous for clear sense to be made of it on its face. Of course, this ought not ever to happen, but the unfortunate reality is, as Holt CJ put it, that though 'an Act of Parliament can do no wrong, . . . it may do several things that look pretty odd.'[24] Whilst the courts are not supposed to have recourse to Hansard, others may naturally turn to it in such instances in search of enlightenment—though whether or not they can be sure of finding it is of course another matter.

There are, however, also more general and substantial reasons for lawyers to consult Hansard. Obviously, it may prove instructive to examine the form in which a bill is presented to Parliament, and the source and nature of the amendments by which it is transformed into the final Act. Against this it must be noted that many bills survive the Parliamentary process largely unscathed. The IRA 1971 provides an appropriate example. One study of its legislative history concludes that whilst 'in formal terms Parliament lies at the centre of law-making', in fact: 'The formal institutions of Parliament are in most cases peripheral to the shaping of legislation, and this is especially the case when a party is as committed as were the Conservatives to a particular line of action' (Moran 1977: pp. 97–8). Nevertheless, this writer still maintains that the Parliamentary process performs an important function which is 'not to scrutinise legislation but to publicise the views of the main antagonists in a debate' (p. 99).

Griffith's study of the Parliamentary process, while also highly sceptical of its value as a method of scrutinizing and improving bills, makes the latter point particularly forcefully. In particular, the scrutiny to which ministers are subjected is in his view 'One of the most important aspects of Parliamentary democracy in the United Kingdom, and certainly one of the most valuable' (Griffith 1974: p. 232 and ch. 8 generally). Certainly, the formal function of the committee stages is 'to go through the text of the bill clause by clause and, if necessary, word by word' (Gordon 1983: p. 549)

---

[24] *City of London* v. *Wood* 12 Mod 669, 687–8 (1701).

and ministers may therefore be called upon to explain and defend the Government's desired course in corresponding detail. Whilst Parliament may be a—to some—surprisingly ineffectual forum in which to try and *change* Government policy, it nevertheless has much potential to be one in which it is *discovered*.

The extent to which the debates on a particular bill in fact discharge this function is dependent in no small measure upon the standard of the briefings, general knowledge of the field, and debating skills of the participants on all sides. Additionally, a skilful Opposition can turn to its own use, aspects of Parliamentary procedure itself.[25] For example, debate on any aspect of a bill cannot finally be 'closed' until it actually becomes law. So it is possible for different amendments touching the same issue to be tabled at several points as the bill passes through both Houses of Parliament. Sometimes this does no more than make the debates rather tedious reading, but it does provide the opportunity for the Opposition to probe into the Government's position on a particular issue. It may, for example, be revealing if an amendment which has been carefully redrafted to take account of the Government's originally stated objections, is retabled but again refused. Again, pure 'drafting amendments', which seek to remove perceived defects in the structure of a clause, or to achieve its stated goals in a more elegant or efficient way, may be tabled by Government or Opposition. But of course, no two different forms of wording will achieve *precisely* the same legal effect, and it may transpire that what the Opposition puts forward as a drafting amendment is regarded by the Government as involving a substantive change of approach which it is not prepared to adopt.

Procedural considerations may also significantly affect the form in which a bill is first published. In particular, amendments may only be tabled which are relevant to the subject-matter, and do not go beyond the scope, of the bill as a whole, and of the particular clause to which each amendment relates. This means that the sponsor of the bill (here, the Government) has some scope for setting the agenda of the debate, in terms of the issues which the bill raises and the manner in which it treats them (Gordon 1983: pp. 506, 528, and 549).[26] This political weapon is unlikely to be neglected by a Government operating in an area as controversial and complex as industrial-conflict law. To this one must add a number of other 'preparational' and 'operational' constraints which will further bind the drafter. Lawyers accustomed to anatomizing individual provisions at retrospective leisure, may need to become adjusted to the feel of how such factors can impinge upon the form which legislation takes.[27]

[25] The 'bible' of Parliamentary procedure is Gordon (1983), but a useful short account of public bill procedure is Miers and Page (1982: pp. 113–30).

[26] The Opposition may still widen the debate somewhat, e.g. by tabling a new clause, which though beyond the scope of any existing clause, is within that of the whole bill (Gordon 1983: p. 555).

[27] On this topic, see e.g. Bennion (1983: ch. 3); Miers and Page (1982: ch. 4).

Considerations such as these suggest that a careful reading of Hansard may yield some fruit, even when a bill is little altered by its progress through Parliament. Nevertheless, that yield must be in essence in the nature of a revelation of the details of policy already formed. For the Government, the presentation of the bill is all but the end of the policymaking process, which may have had its beginnings anything from weeks to years earlier. More fully to understand legislative policy, we must therefore dig back further. In the case of the legislation of the 1980s, the genesis of its development is, as we shall see, to be found in the demise of the previous Conservative Government in 1974, and of its Industrial Relations Act (IRA) the same year, which necessitated a wholesale review of Conservative policy on labour law and industrial relations.[28] This critical debate will be set against the background of the much wider tensions which had already become evident in the voluntarist system, and had already made their impact felt upon the policies of the Labour Party. Within Conservative ranks, the controversy generated by this debate was great, and the apparent resolution of the policy debate by the late 1970s thinly concealed continuing tensions and deep differences within the party. The IRA had been preceded by an intensive internal party debate which was essentially resolved while the Conservatives were in opposition, permitting the groundwork to be very thoroughly laid by the time of their return in 1970.[29] But much of the policy behind the post-1979 legislation was—as will be shown—the product of the ongoing internal party debate during the period of Government, and the legislation continued to be developed piecemeal, at times on the hoof, throughout the 1980s.

A discussion of only the finished legislation, by definition does not consider another source, namely those measures which were at one time canvassed, but ultimately rejected. Often, a number of possible avenues are openly explored by Government itself in 'consultative' papers, public speeches and interviews, and so forth. Here again, subject to the investigative skills of the media, Government itself chooses how far the options which it is considering shall be the subject of public knowledge. Proposals are however also invariably put forward (whether requested or not) by a variety of other sources, most notably by the many interest and pressure groups, particularly the various employers' organizations, as well as by lawyers and other academic experts in the field. Their views are imparted to Government and to the public at large through a number of different channels, notably by the publication of 'policy documents' and responses to Government consultations, and of letters and articles in the press. Some organizations may also reach arrangements with MPs or members of the House of Lords whereby their desired amendments to legislation are tabled, in effect on their behalf, during the actual course of Parliamentary debates. Members of both Houses may of

---

[28] See further the discussion in ch. 2 below.
[29] See e.g. Moran (1977: chs. 1–4); Barnes and Reid (1980: chs. 7–8).

course themselves form factions and pressure groups independently or regardless of any such association.

So once again, whilst a Government which is sufficiently single-minded may not be divertable from a chosen policy course, it will rarely be for want of trying on the part of all these persons and organizations. Their aspirations and representations, expressed both inside and outside of Parliament, provide a potentially illuminating standpoint from which to assess and evaluate the Government's own particular concerns.

A further potential source of enlightenment is the work of the Select Committees—here usually that on Employment. These committees exist in order generally to investigate and report upon matters and issues within their field, and frequently concern themselves with the legislation or legislative policy of the departments with which they are identified. As well as interviewing ministers and other interested parties in person, they also customarily receive written evidence and opinion from a wide range of sources. Reports on topics directly related to a department's activities will usually elicit a ministerial reply in some form, but notwithstanding reforms strengthening the committees' powers introduced in 1979, and their not insignificant influence in some cases, ministers are still in no sense legally bound to accept their recommendations. As with some of the other sources which have been discussed, we may therefore find that the work of the select committees has little impact on the actual shape of legislation, but is nevertheless an illuminating source to turn to when seeking to understand it.[30]

So far, the focus has been on the primary sources which it is suggested have not previously been exploited to the full; but a further aspect of much existing work in this field deserves mention, namely the fact that existing analyses of the new legislation have tended to take as their bench-mark for evaluation, the previous legislative structure which it reshaped. This need not necessarily be a result of ideological or doctrinal influences, for at a more mundane level, it may be the easiest if not the only logical way in which to approach analysis and exposition of the new law. Whatever the reason in a particular case may be, however, such approaches have an important limitation, for, as will be argued, the abstentionist perspective is itself a peculiarly narrow one on the subject, and to view the new legislation solely through its window therefore precludes the possibility of seeing the relationship of each to the other within a broader landscape.

## (3) SCOPE AND LAYOUT

There are few, if any, areas of labour law which the legislation of the 1980s has left untouched. Whilst changes in the field of industrial conflict must

---

[30] On select committees generally, see Gordon (1983: pp. 681 ff.). On the work of the employment committee from 1979 to 1983, see Johnson (1985).

ultimately be viewed in the context of the wider programme of legislation, there is nevertheless still some necessity to address the question: what do we mean when we talk of 'the law of industrial conflict'? The answer given by labour lawyers to that question was for many years clear and consistent: the focus of concern in Britain was on the position of those who *organize* industrial action, which dictated an analysis of the common-law doctrines tending to render such activity unlawful, and of the statutory protections designed to neutralize the common law and so have the opposite effect. The study of the development of industrial-conflict law up to any particular moment was in essence the study of the ever developing dynamic between these two forces, although the roles of judiciary and legislature were occasionally reversed.[31]

At the start of the 1990s, to answer this question has become a rather more tantalizing task, a problem to some extent of the chicken and egg variety. In the early years of the 1980s the traditional approach could be relatively readily adapted to accomodate the new legislation. The consistent technique used by the legislation at the outset was the selective removal or repeal of statutory protections. Thus to the two questions: 'is there any common law liability?', and: 'is there any statutory protection?', one had only to add a third: 'has that protection been removed?'[32] As the decade wore on, however, things became more complicated. As the Government shifted its approach from the technique of restriction to that of regulation, so a prejudgement of what ought to be regarded as part of industrial-conflict law became more hazardous, importing the risk of neglecting measures which, if in fact examined, might be found to owe their existence largely to Government concerns about industrial conflict. This broadening of approach, from policies of pure restriction, to a combination of policies of regulation and restriction, will be a central and correspondingly developing theme of this book.

Whilst the lawfulness of the activities of the organizer of industrial action has traditionally been at the centre of the labour lawyer's concerns, many other questions have of course always arisen. The law and procedures affecting sanctions and remedies is of crucial practical significance and became an increasingly complex and critical area in the 1980s.[33] In addition, issues may arise as to how the employer may treat the individuals who participate in industrial action, or other employees, customers, or suppliers. The answer to each of these questions will often depend in part on that to one or more of the others. Again, these are all issues which have tended to find greater prominence in recent years. All these topics will therefore be encountered during the course of and incidental to the main discussion. It is

[31] See e.g. Davies and Freedland (1979: ch. 8, esp. at pp. 600–6).
[32] The approach of Lord Diplock in *Merkur Island Shipping* v. *Laughton* [1983] 2 AC 570, 604F-H.
[33] See Kidner (1986); Auerbach (1987); Wedderburn (1989*a*); Lightman (1987).

perhaps as well to remind ourselves at the outset of the extensive backcloth into which the new legislation was woven. The discussion will touch more than once upon the implications of its being patched as a series of pieces into such a complex fabric.

A word of qualification is in order, with which to conclude this introduction. While it is an integral part of this enterprise to consider and comment upon the major 'external' sources of argument or policy considerations which have tended to influence Government proposals for changing the law of industrial conflict, the book is emphatically not an essay on that subject in its own right. The reader who hopes to find an answer to the so-called 'strike problem' in these pages will therefore be disappointed. Nevertheless, it is suggested, what labour lawyers can and should seek to do is to recognize and understand the significance of the major arguments—be they derived from economics, politics, or whatever discipline—in terms of their *implications* for Governmental approaches to the law of industrial conflict, and the ways in which the consequences of different arguments interact with one another. These are matters which are given particular attention in chapters ten and eleven.

The book proceeds as follows. After an opening assessment of the broader context of developments prior to 1979, chapters two to nine go on to present a chronological account of the legislative history of the new law, drawing chiefly on primary sources of the types which have been discussed. In addition, this account is used as the medium through which to initiate a critique of the legislation, drawing upon more diverse secondary sources. Initial assessments of the measures introduced in each of the four Acts of 1980, 1982, 1984, and 1988, conclude chapters three, five, seven, and eight. The measures destined to reach the statute-book in the Employment Act 1990 are considered in chapter nine. Chapter ten analyses more closely the elements of the voluntarist consensus, and puts forward a broader analytical framework within which the new legislation may be located. It considers within such a framework a selection of possible policy approaches towards the major issues of industrial-conflict law, which have been widely canvassed as alternatives to a purely voluntarist approach. Chapter eleven draws on this exercise, and upon the conclusions of earlier chapters, in order—through the medium of a response to the New Right thesis—to put forward the book's own concluding assessment of the legislation.

# [2]

# The Breakdown of the Voluntarist Consensus (I):
## Conservative Policy before 1979

### (1) INTRODUCTION

Writing in the 1950s, Kahn-Freund developed a brilliant analysis of the state of labour law in Britain, the essence of which he captured in a single notion: 'collective laissez-faire'.[1] The concept had many meanings and applications, but undoubtedly its central import and most perfect realization was found in the field of industrial conflict. Here its meaning was simple: that the peaceful exercise of collective economic sanctions in the field of industrial conflict should be completely lawful.[2] This was the doctrine otherwise known as abstentionism or voluntarism. It was first a descriptive theory, articulating the legislative stance embodied in the Trade Disputes Act 1906, but it was also strongly prescriptive, the degree of absence of law being held out as a direct measure of a system's state of 'maturity' (Kahn-Freund 1954a: p. 43).

Clearly, at the heart of this approach was a commitment to the importance of the right to strike. But, as chapter ten will explore, there are many arguments as to what the right to strike is, why it is so important, and what legal structures are necessary to secure it. For Kahn-Freund the right was vital, first because it was the only source of workers' *economic* power faced with the universal fact of subordination to the power of the employer, and secondly and more specifically because it was an essential element in the exercise of that economic power to the social advantage of workers, through a system of collective bargaining.[3] In the 1950s Kahn-Freund could also without hesitation assert that the social value of collective bargaining was something about which all major political parties were agreed (1954a: p. 52).

Nevertheless, industrial conflict clearly was and is not without its harmful effects. Above all there is the sacrifice made by individual workers who

---

[1] See Kahn-Freund (1954a), (1954b), and (1959).

[2] This did not therefore extend to actual physical harm to person or property, although the abstract line between physical and economic harm may sometimes prove to be hard to draw in practice.

[3] See Kahn-Freund and Hepple (1972: ch. 2); Kahn-Freund (1977: ch. 1); Lewis (1979: pp. 208–10).

engage in industrial action themselves, most immediately felt in terms of loss of wages. For the employer and customers and suppliers there will also be disruption and inconvenience, the very thing which renders industrial action an effective economic weapon for workers.[4] Apart from these direct 'frictional' effects of conflict, Governments charged with running the capitalist economy may have wider concerns about less direct consequences. Chief among these will be the implications which a particular conflict, or the terms upon which it is resolved, may have for Government policies in relation to incomes or inflation, unemployment or other economic indicators. These may be regarded as the 'structural' effects of industrial conflict.[5] Nor, for some, is this the end of the story. Critics on the right are apt to see dire constitutional and political implications in a system which permits the free interplay of collective forces, underpinned by laws of the style of 1906, and such 'constitutional' arguments formed the basis of bitter attacks on the 1906 Act from the very moment of its enactment.[6]

What was the view taken of these potential frictional, structural, and political effects, under the doctrine of collective laissez-faire? The fact that collective bargaining was inevitably wedded to the causing of frictional harms much perturbed the early exponents of its virtues, the Webbs;[7] but Kahn-Freund suggested a solution to this dilemma which they had perhaps not fully anticipated. This stemmed from the fact that the mature system was characterized by, as much as anything, the existence of sophisticated and well-established systems of dispute resolution which tended to minimize the incidence of overt conflict, keeping it at levels sufficiently low for the trade-off between frictional effects and social benefits to remain eminently and unquestionably desirable.[8]

What of structural and political effects? These receive little attention in traditional voluntarist accounts, a fact which may suggest a deficiency in their analysis. Traditional labour lawyers may for example have been remiss in their failure in the past to consider the mutual implications of labour law and incomes policy/anti-inflation strategies each for the other.[9] One can observe too that the existence of the post-war consensus which prevailed throughout the period of the high point of voluntarism, tended to take such matters outside of the range of political controversy and debate.[10] But we should not therefore conclude that the traditional voluntarist position did not contain an

[4] Cf. Davies and Freedland (1984a: p. 693).

[5] See Friedman (1951) who coined the designations 'frictional', 'structural', and 'political', which have been adopted and adapted here.

[6] See e.g. Dicey (1914: pp. xliv-xlvii), and Pollock (1908: pp. v and 96–7), and generally Phelps Brown (1986: ch. 3).

[7] See e.g. Webb (1906).

[8] On this, see esp. Kahn-Freund (1954b). It did not follow that the mechanisms in question needed the backing of legal sanctions (ibid. pp. 64–7).

[9] For an assessment, see Davies and Freedland (1983: Introduction).

[10] See Crouch (1982b: ch. 1 and generally).

implied view regarding political and structural effects. Indeed, the very existence of such a strong consensus points towards the opposite conclusion. For the persistence of consistent cross-party support for a set of policies— which included the high level incorporation of trade-union leaders and the pursuit of Keynesian economic policies designed to preserve full employment and promote growth—surely reflects the fact that no serious incompatibility between, or fundamental flaw in, such policies was perceived to exist by those who supported them at the time.

Traditional voluntarism as expounded by Kahn-Freund in the 1950s may then indeed have appeared to be both a complete and a workable doctrine; but whether developments of the 1980s can still be accommodated within this analytical framework has today become 'a matter for debate' (Simpson 1986: p. 798). In general terms this is because the continued value and adequacy of a model first developed in the 1950s has fallen increasingly into question in the changed circumstances of succeeding decades. This fact was to some extent masked by the continuing commitment of Labour Governments of both the 1960s and 1970s to the maintenance of a voluntarist legislative framework in the field of industrial conflict, a stance reinforced by the conclusions of the Donovan Commission on which Kahn-Freund was a key influence.

In reality, notwithstanding the continuity of form of the structural legal framework through this period, the continued tenability of voluntarism as the sole basis for Government policy was already a pressing issue on the agenda by the time of the return of a Labour Government in 1964. Set in a longer term perspective, the golden age of the post-war consensus can be seen as a more fragile and transitional (Wedderburn 1985b: p. 498) phase in a development of long-run national economic decline, accelerated by the break-up of empire in the decades immediately following the war.[11] Thus: 'The record of the 1960s and 1970s was of a slow, tentative but cumulatively profound politicisation of industrial relations. For much of the period, this process involved half-hearted and precarious efforts at concertation' (Hyman 1989a: p. 206). As increasing levels of conflict and national and international economic pressures began to undermine the assumptions upon which the voluntarist consensus had been founded, the Labour Government of the 1960s felt impelled to set up the first Royal Commission on Trade Unions since the 1906 Act, to introduce a statutory incomes policy, and finally to propose trenchant reforms of labour law, including the introduction of restrictions in the field of industrial conflict.[12]

[11] For assessments which set the post-war consensus, and its breakdown, in such a context, see Fox (1985b: esp. at pp. 167–8 and chs. 7–9); Gamble (1985), (1988b); MacInnes (1987: esp. ch. 2); Sked and Cook (1984). It is arguably possible to trace the process, and its implications for the voluntarist consensus, back at least into the last century, but to do so would be a task beyond both the scope and the needs of the present work.
[12] See Donovan (1968) (established 1965), Prices and Incomes Acts 1966–8, and *In Place of Strife* (DEP 1969), respectively.

It was surely these measures, spanning the period of Donovan's investigations and report, rather than the conclusions of the Donovan report itself, which characterized the nature and extent of the preoccupations of the Government of the day.[13] Speaking in 1967, Kahn-Freund did not conceal his awareness of the magnitude of the threat which such developments presented to the old traditions. The newly introduced statutory incomes policy provisions, he thought 'express the crisis in our labour law, even if (as may well be the case) they will be applied in practice only rarely and most certainly with great hesitation and even reluctance' (1968: p. 21). The persistence of conflict and economic problems through the 1970s deepened Kahn-Freund's anxieties. On rereading in 1978 his paper of the 1950s concerned specifically with dispute resolution, he considered he had then anticipated neither the resurgence of 'spontaneous action' over 'organised group behaviour', nor the increased centrality of the contradiction between 'group autonomy' and anti-inflation strategies (1978: pp. 75–7). His parting conclusion was that '"collective laissez-faire" may be in need of adjustment more than any other part of the British heritage' (1979: p. 88).

As in the 1960s, so in the middle and late 1970s, following the return of Labour to power, the stability and strengthening of the legal framework for industrial conflict proved a poor guide to the nature of the major preoccupations of the Government of the day. With regard to the frictional effects of conflict, the main concern of the 1960s, articulated by Donovan, had been the resurgence of small-scale, unofficial, 'wildcat' disruptions, which it argued might be tackled through reforms in the framework of collective bargaining itself. In the 1970s, however, the disruption caused by large-scale, official, frequently public-sector action became the issue of the day, and one which presented a more direct challenge to the Government itself.[14]

The tension between free collective bargaining on the one hand, and incomes policy and anti-inflation strategies on the other, also remained a persistent feature, a failure to find an adequate solution to this problem contributing in part to the eventual downfall of the Labour Government in 1979. Indeed, the twistings and turnings in their closing years of both Governments of this decade, as they found themselves impaled on this problem, suggested the truth of the maxim that 'as long as Governments are concerned with unemployment and inflation they cannot accept whole-heartedly the principle of non-intervention' (Prondzynski 1985: p. 186).

The debate over political effects also grew more intense during this period. The social contract policies of the Labour Government provoked a strengthening and broadening of the concern within Conservative ranks about the post-war consensus approach to relations between unions and Government. Some Conservative commentators argued that the influence of

---

[13] Cf. Davies and Freedland (1983: pp. 4–5).
[14] See Durcan *et al.* (1983: ch. 12).

certain union leaders over the shaping of Government policy was such that they functioned almost as additional cabinet members, thus implying a threat to Parliamentary sovereignty and to democracy itself. Of course, this was not a view shared by the Labour Government itself, which made it a key element of its strategy to promote such involvement. Furthermore, the critique presented a singularly one-sided view of our political system in which a range of pressure groups and organizations—of which trade unions are only one—may be able to threaten persuasive sanctions against, and curry fluctuating levels of favour with, changing Governments.[15]

Nevertheless, the 1970s also saw the resurgence of a vigorous and continuing tradition on the left which criticized social contract-type arrangements, arguing that union leaders should not be distracted from, or hampered in the pursuit of, their primary and overriding function of representing and pursuing their members' interests.[16] This viewpoint not only mistrusts the ability of any (capitalist) Government to act informedly in the interests of workers,[17] but also argues that it is of the essence of the value of trade unionism in a democratic pluralist society, that unions should actively pursue their own factional interest.[18] The social contract therefore came under political attack by a pincer movement from both left and right.

Finally, the debate intensified in the 1970s as to the nature of the social benefits of collective bargaining itself, and here once again the criticism was not confined to the attacks of the most fundamental nature coming from the right. Elsewhere, the concern did not amount to a questioning of the essential economic imbalance between labour and capital—which it was a primary aim of collective bargaining to redress—nor of the view that no accommodation can be reached as long as the social conditions of production are regarded as subordinate to the maintenance of consumption (Prondzynski 1985: p. 183). Rather, the debate focused on the wider problems of distribution attributable ultimately to 'the general human problem of the scarcity of desired resources' (Crouch 1982a: p. 37). Once again, issues of distribution *within* the ranks of labour did not perhaps press as visibly in the 1950s when Kahn-Freund first promulgated the ethic of collective laissez-faire, but the Webbs themselves had suggested that it was an in-built feature of the method of collective bargaining that stronger unions would achieve more by it, weaker ones less.[19] In the 1970s, commentators, including Kahn-Freund, expressed concern at what they saw as the spread of *internecine* conflict between different sections of the work-force (Kahn-Freund 1979: p. 76, 1981: p. 202; Taylor 1982b: p. 160). This issue surfaced again in the 1980s in debates within the labour

[15] See Fox (1985a: pp. 166–7); for a survey which covers the role of other pressure groups as well as unions, see Gamble (1980).

[16] See the many well-known sayings of Frank Cousins, e.g. quoted in Goodman (1979: pp. 369 and 382). For a modern critique of the social contract along these lines, see Benn (1981).

[17] As expressed by the TUC (1968: p. 140) in evidence to Donovan.

[18] See e.g. Flanders (1970: pp. 37–47).

[19] This point is taken up by Phelps Brown (1986: p. 52).

movement over issues such as a minimum wage, an example of the 'method of legal enactment' which the Webbs saw as one of the alternatives to collective bargaining, on the basis that, once established, legal entitlements may be made available to all, regardless of relative or fluctuating bargaining power (Webb and Webb 1920: pp. 796–806).

It is against the background of these continuing debates and Governmental preoccupations that the development of the debate inside the Conservative Opposition during this period must be set, and it is to this that we can now turn our attention.

## (2) THE PROPOSED SETTLEMENT OF 1974

Hard though the fact may be to recall, or even quite to believe at the beginning of the 1990s, the fall of the Heath Government in 1974, and the widely perceived failure of the IRA 1971, had a catastrophic impact on the Conservative Party in general, and its labour law and industrial relations strategy in particular. At the risk of over-simplification, the party can be seen as having split into two remarkably distinct and opposed camps.[20] In one group were those who considered that a comprehensive and firm policy on labour law and industrial relations had been proved to be all the more necessary by the events of 1970–4. This group was identified most closely with Sir Geoffrey Howe, the architect of the IRA, and with Mrs Thatcher who became party leader in 1975, and set the tone for her leadership by promising that the mistakes and about turns of the Heath era would never be repeated.

The other, far more cautious, view, was at this time most closely identified with Mr James (now Lord) Prior, who became the party's shadow employment spokesman from 1974–9 and Employment Secretary from 1979–81. He was a close adviser to and staunch supporter of Mr Heath, and has acknowledged in retrospect the overwhelming influence on his approach of his experiences prior to 1974:

It's almost inconceivable to someone like myself who did actually see the passage of the Industrial Relations Act and all that happened subsequently in '71 to '74 to recognise the difference [in] mood [by 1979] . . . the mood was right for rather more legislation . . . than I ever thought would be justified or politically acceptable.[21]

Notwithstanding the intensity of the internal party dispute in this period, it was Prior's views which at this stage prevailed. He rapidly concluded that to reintroduce anything approaching another Industrial Relations Act would be a fatal error.[22] Instead, he sought to establish a common approach with

[20] Generally on this period of development in Conservative policy and strategy, see Behrens (1977); Moran (1979); Gamble (1980); and Behrens (1980: esp. ch. 6).

[21] Prior quoted in Whitehead (1985: p. 371); see too Prior (1985).

[22] The idea had been abandoned by the time of the second election of 1974: see *Conservative Party Manifesto*, October 1974, in Craig (1975: p. 425).

Labour, now in Government. In the field of industrial conflict, he offered the Labour Government the opportunity to establish an agreed framework of law—that is, one which the Conservatives would undertake to support in opposition, and not to alter if returned to power themselves. This offer was first spelled out during debates on the Trade Union and Labour Relations (TULR) Bill 1974. The terms of settlement were that Labour's planned restoration of the trade-disputes immunities along the lines of the Trade Disputes Act (TDA) 1906, should in one particular respect follow exactly the terms of that Act. This was that the pivotal protection—against the tort of inducing breach of contract—should apply only in respect of contracts of employment.[23]

This formulation was attractive to the Conservatives for at least two reasons. First, it might allow the courts the opportunity to restrict some forms of secondary and more widespread forms of industrial action. That such activity might without protection be actionable at common law had been clear at least since the decision in *Thomson* v. *Deakin*.[24] Secondary and sympathetic action had been longstanding Conservative preoccupations, and the subject of regulation in the 1971 Act.[25] In this way, then, something approximating to that Act's approach might be revived. Secondly, there was a simple and superficially appealing argument which could be employed in favour of drawing the line at this point: this was exactly what the 1906 Act had done—and no Labour Government had previously altered that. This was technically true, although it of course overlooked Labour's argument that the extension was now necessary merely to keep pace with the developing common law.[26]

Because the Labour Party at this time lacked an overall majority in the House of Commons, the Conservatives were able to carry this amendment, and the pledge to stand by the 'settlement' thus secured was repeated in their October 1974 manifesto.[27] So it is worth noting—indeed it is with hindsight quite striking to note—that at this point the Conservative Party was proposing no alteration in the basic framework of industrial-conflict law at all. Although, as we shall see, certain specific concerns did arise in the years up to 1979, Prior made a point of regularly stressing the pledge not to revive the Industrial Relations Act, encouraging the optimism of many commentators which was noted at the start of chapter one.

However, the official stance on the legal framework was accompanied by a deep concern about the same wider policy issues which confronted the Labour Government. Prior thought it essential to overturn the impression that the Conservative Party simply could not 'work' with the trade unions,

---

[23] See OR St. Cttee. E TULR Bill 9th sitting (18 June 1974) cols. 453 ff.

[24] [1952] Ch. 646 (CA). Treatment of the intricacies of the case-law, and of its interaction with the TULRA s. 13 protections, is deferred to ch. 3 below.

[25] IRA 1971 s. 98. See the further discussion in chs. 3, 9, and 10 below.

[26] See generally the discussion in Donovan (1968: paras. 878–901).

[27] See n. 22 above.

for it was his view, and the widely received opinion at the time, that a Government which could not work with the unions could not work at all. If the Conservatives could not dispel this myth, they might not even be returned to office.[28] Prior therefore supplemented his attempt to forge a consensus intended to 'depoliticize' the issue of labour law with a carefully considered approach to the trade unions.[29] His strategy was two-pronged.

First, he attacked Labour's 'Social Contract', in part arguing that it was not to the advantage of union leaders themselves. It was Government that remained in control of the big decisions such as on the economy, but the unions might still be held responsible by 'public opinion' for matters which it was not within their power to affect; to add to this, they might find that their commitment to support Government initiatives, particularly on pay restraint, severely compromised their duties to, and standing with, their members. Prior advocated that Government should certainly have dealings with the unions, but it would be better for all concerned if those dealings took place at arms' length.[30] Secondly, he developed and canvassed widely the alternative notion of an 'annual economic assessment'. This would be neither a social contract nor an incomes policy, but a high-level, high profile forum at which unions, management, Government, and MPs as well as others would participate in open discussion of past trends and possible future developments in the economy.[31] The strategy in essence would be not to restrain the unions by law or by incomes policy, but to mobilize the forces of 'rational' open argument and of public opinion against excessive or unrealistic pay claims, as well as to 'educate' trade unionists about the likely impact of their individual claims, and hence where their 'best interests' lay.[32] A variation on this proposal was canvassed at this time by the CBI, and versions were subsequently supported by other organizations.[33]

Whilst representing the official policy of his party during this period, Prior's whole approach to these issues was severely at odds with the instincts of Mrs Thatcher and other key figures, both on the issue of economic policy and on the role of the unions. Once again, the elements of cross-party consensus at official policy level were perhaps more superficial and fragile than they appeared to be at the time. Furthermore, while Prior's approach required involvement from union leadership, and support from union membership (1979b: p. 9), nevertheless, changes to labour law did not have to be completely ruled out. Rather, Prior's strategy, and the lessons he drew

[28] For an illustration of how low some leading Conservatives had got, see Biffen (1976); see too Behrens (1977: pp. 9–10).

[29] See Wigham (1982: p. 210).

[30] See e.g. Prior (1976).

[31] See Prior (1977b).

[32] See Prior (1977a), (1977b).

[33] On the CBI proposals, see *Financial Times* (19 May 1977); (1977) 15 *BJIR* pp. 420–1; and on their proposed 'bargaining calendar' into which the forum would fit, see Arnold (1981: pp. 146–7). For similar proposals by the BIM, see *Management Today* (Feb. 1980: p. 97), (Aug. 1980: p. 73).

from the IRA experience, suggested that reforms should be limited and specific, piecemeal, and above all, the subject of full consultations, and responsive to the mood of 'public opinion', not least among trade unionists themselves.[34] Perhaps somewhat unrealistically, Prior hoped that limited changes might be achieved within the context of a continuing Government–union dialogue (1979c: p. 17).[35] In relation to industrial conflict three specific issues of concern to Conservatives emerged in the period up to 1979, namely, secondary action, picketing, and a particular recruiting tactic practised by the art union, SLADE. We can consider each in turn.

## (3) THREE ISSUES

### (a) Secondary Action

Mr Prior's victory of 1974 on this issue was to prove shortlived. Returned with an increased majority at the October election, Labour put through amending legislation which ensured that immunity in relation to interference with contracts was no longer restricted to contracts of employment.[36] Prior called it a 'sad day' and a matter of 'great regret' that what could have formed 'the basis of industrial relations law without party division for a number of years . . . a prize for which it would have been well worth fighting' had thereby been lost,[37] words which convey some sense of how this particular legal issue was central to his whole approach to the area. So the possibility of further legislation to reamend the 1974 Act in this respect remained on the Conservative agenda; but other developments between 1976 and 1979 suggested that '[t]here was, however, a chance that the courts themselves would effectively restrict union immunities' (Prior 1986: p. 158). This chance arose from a series of judgments spearheaded by Lord Denning MR in the Court of Appeal, in which the courts interpreted the statutory protections, so as to restrict their otherwise 'blanket' coverage.[38]

Davies and Freedland's study of Lord Denning's influence on labour law reveals the approach which lay behind these developments. They show how Lord Denning's judgments of the 1960s and 1970s displayed a commitment to a 'right to strike', provided that it was subject to some limitation by reference to the extent of disruptive harm caused. While the pivotal immunity was in the 1960s confined to contracts of employment, Lord

---

[34] See Prior (1979a), (1979b).

[35] For details of the early talks in 1979, see Dorfman (1983: pp. 112–123).

[36] TULR(Am)A 1976, s. 3(2).

[37] OR HC vol. 882 col. 1390 (3 Dec. 1974).

[38] The key cases were *BBC* v. *Hearn* [1977] ICR 685; *Beaverbrook Newspapers* v. *Keys* [1978] ICR 582; *Associated Newspapers Group* v. *Wade* [1979] ICR 664; *Star Sea Transport Corporation* v. *Slater* [1978] IRLR 507; *PBDS (National Carriers) Ltd.* v. *Filkins* [1979] IRLR 356; *Express Newspapers* v. *MacShane* [1979] ICR 210. For full analysis, see Ewing (1979) and Kerr (1980: pp. 59–74).

Denning therefore pursued a two-pronged strategy of resisting developments which might undermine this basic statutory protection, while at the same time promoting the development of the common law in other ways. When, however, the statutory immunity was widened in 1976, Lord Denning soon set out to 'work back' towards his ideal balance, by attacking the width of the immunities in general, in particular by various narrow interpretations of the limbs of the so-called 'golden formula' (Davies and Freedland 1984*b*: pp. 377–411).[39] The cases illustrate that this approach was not easy to translate into one simple legal test, and the courts experimented with a variety of different techniques. Yet at the same time, Lord Denning homed in very precisely on the *point* at which—by whatever test happened to be appropriate—the line ought properly to be drawn: action should remain protected in so far as it affected the immediate or first customers and suppliers of the primary employer, but no further (Denning 1983: p. 182).[40] The consonance with Mr Prior's approach was indeed striking, as we shall see. However, there was a risk that the Court of Appeal's approach might not prevail, as by spring 1979 their most recent judgment had been appealed and awaited hearing in the House of Lords.[41] The Lords might yet with their authority either consolidate the earlier line of cases, or overturn them at a single stroke. Mr Prior decided to await the Lords' judgment, and the 1979 manifesto included no specific promise to legislate on the matter. However, he was already conscious that should the Lords reverse the Court of Appeal's approach, legislative action might be necessary (Prior 1986: p. 158). In the mean time he concentrated his attention on another issue which had come very much to the fore: picketing.

### (b) Picketing

In 1965 Lord Wedderburn commented that the 'right to picket' was 'not used so extensively in modern practice' (1965: p. 223); the Donovan Commission dwelt briefly on the topic (Donovan 1968: pp. 227–31). Statistically it remains true that the incidence of picketing of any sort is low, and that most of it is generally small-scale, peaceful, and uneventful.[42] Nevertheless, as the result of a series of specific events, the 'picketing problem' grew to be a major issue of Conservative concern during the 1970s. The task here is only to explain the nature of the specific response adopted in the EA 1980, but this nevertheless requires some detailed and cautious analysis, for the debate over the issue is a complex and therefore difficult one through which to navigate a clear and illuminating path of discussion.

---

[39] For discussion by Lord Denning himself, see Denning (1983: sec. 6, chs. 3–4).

[40] Cf. IRA 1971, s. 98's definition of an 'extraneous party'.

[41] *Express Newspapers* v. *MacShane* [1979] ICR 210.

[42] See Daniel and Millward (1983: pp. 242–52 and 292–3); Millward and Stevens (1986: pp. 282–94).

The most basic reason for this complexity is that 'picketing' is a term which is used to describe a wide variety of different activities. This has been effectively conveyed by Bercusson:

The pickets may limit themselves to merely observing scabs; they may attempt to communicate information to them as to the existence of a strike; they may go beyond this and attempt to persuade them not to aid the employer by working for him (or in the case of customers, doing business with him)—using placards, speaking, shouting, and persisting despite refusals to attend. They may go beyond persuasion to where their behaviour amounts to a threat—through their mere presence, by physical violence, social ostracism or economic boycott; or they may engage in actual assaults, destruction of property or the physical blocking of entrances and interference with traffic. Picketing activity may range from one extreme to the other on this spectrum (1977: pp. 271–2).

Bercusson was concerned with industrial picketing, but the summary which he gave points also to a further source of complexity: where 'picketing' describes behaviour intended to communicate or inform, it may equally occur in non-industrial contexts. The common feature, however, is that the participators are seeking to exercise a freedom to communicate or inform in a public place. This dimension of industrial picketing has been recognized in countries such as the United States, where freedom of speech is protected under the Constitution, and is therefore easily capable of arising as a positive issue in industrial picketing litigation.[43]

In this country, by contrast, the freedom of speech issue is usually thought relevant, if at all, not to 'picketing' but to 'demonstration'. While there have been a number of English cases involving protest or demonstration over non-industrial issues, where this dimension has been given some weight,[44] no similar trend is to be found in the industrial picketing cases. When the court perceives that it is dealing with 'picketing' and not 'demonstration', it will then ironically usually adopt the simpler approach that '[i]t does not matter what people are called. What is relevant is what they do.'[45] Although picketing is not per se unlawful, there is then little basis upon which technical illegalities may be overcome by the assertion of a 'right to picket'; and the supplementation of the usual trade-disputes immunities by the protection granted in section 15 of TULRA 1974 has signally failed to fulfil any such role.[46] This is perhaps ironic, for this protection has never extended to

[43]  See Bellace (1981: pp. 134–6); Summers, Wellington, and Hyde (1982: pp. 487–8).

[44]  e.g. *Hubbard* v. *Pitt* [1976] 1 QB 142, in the striking dissent of Lord Denning MR; *Hirst* v. *Chief Constable of West Yorks, The Times* 19 Nov. 1986 (Div. Ct.); *UK Nirex* v. *Barton, The Times* 14 Oct. 1986 (Henry J); *Hipperson* v. *Newbury District Electoral Registration Officer* [1985] 1 QB 1060 (CA).

[45]  Per Stuart-Smith J *News Group Newspapers* v. *SOGAT* [1986] IRLR 337, 342 para. 34 and 124 para. 350.

[46]  See *Kavanagh* v. *Hiscock* [1974] 1 QB 600; *Broome* v. *DPP* [1974] ICR 84 HL. Although May LJ in *Rayware Ltd.* v. *TGWU* [1989] IRLR 134, 135 para. 17 held that s. 15 conferred 'the right to peaceful picketing within certain limits', the decision of a different Court of Appeal in *Union Traffic Ltd.* v. *TGWU* [1989] IRLR 127 is more characteristic of the courts' approach to the section.

anything more than the peaceful communication or obtaining of information, or peaceful attempts at persuasion—the type of activity in which the freedom of speech aspect is most prominent.[47]

The narrowness of the TULRA protection has accentuated the actual and perceived divide whereby the task of regulating industrial picketing has been divided up between labour law and the law of public order in general; but public-order law, which focuses on criminal rather than civil sanctions, has never allowed anything much more than the types of action comprehended in the first sentence of Bercusson's summary, and probably a good deal less. In particular, at least since the decision in *Piddington* v. *Bates*,[48] it has been clear that the police have a wide discretion to control the numbers gathering at any one place, under the general umbrella of their duty to maintain the peace. That discretion also operates through the wide range of criminal offences with which pickets and demonstrators may potentially be charged.[49] The state of the criminal law means that in practice almost any form of picket may be conducted at the discretion of the police. This may have a positive aspect where the organization of picket lines occurs in conjunction and close co-operation with the police,[50] but as we shall see, it has for other reasons been criticized from the right as well as from the left.

The development of the Conservative Party's proposals on picketing law was closely tied up with a number of events of the 1970s. We need first briefly to identify these events and their impact on the general public debate concerning picketing, before turning to consider how they influenced Conservative policy. The key events were as follows.

1. The miners' strike of 1972 featured a novel development: the highly organized deployment of so-called flying and mass pickets at a variety of carefully chosen locations. The culmination was the legendary episode in which a mass picket succeeded in securing the closure of the Saltley coking plant.[51]

2. In 1974 there was another miners' strike around which, as is well known, Mr Heath called a general election. On this occasion, however, there was no repetition of events of the kind which occurred in 1972. This seemed to be chiefly due to the NUM's decision—the reasons for which need not concern us—to issue a 'code of practice' dealing with the general conduct of picket lines, and in particular stipulating that the number of pickets deployed at any one location should not exceed six.[52]

---

[47] Cf. the analysis in the Canadian case of *Retail Wholesale and Department Store Union* v. *Dolphin Delivery Ltd.* [1986] 2 SCR 573.

[48] [1961] 1 WLR 162.

[49] For argument that mass picketing is inherently unlawful, see Bennion (1985). For recent affirmation of 'pre-emptive powers', see *Moss* v. *McLachlan* [1985] IRLR 76.

[50] See Kahn *et al.* (1983: pp. 86–91) whose research also suggests that in many cases the police have no involvement at all.

[51] See Clutterbuck (1978: pp. 73–4) and Geary (1985: pp. 70–8).

[52] See Clutterbuck (1978: p. 112); *The Times* (8 Feb. 1974); *Guardian* (8 and 9 Feb. 1974).

3. The Labour Government returned in 1974 reviewed the law. Concern now focused on the recent decision in *Broome* v. *DPP*[53] which had confirmed unequivocally that pickets had no statutory right to stop vehicles and were in the identical legal position to a hitch-hiker.[54] It appeared to some that the right peacefully to communicate and persuade—if there ever was one—had in effect been undermined by the rise of the internal combustion engine. One solution, it was argued, would be to create a limited right to stop vehicles for the purposes of communication. This would have a double advantage, because as well as restoring a more effective right to picket, it would also remove what was often the very cause of escalating trouble where it occurred on picket lines. This reasoning appealed to the then Employment Secretary, Mr Michael Foot, but in the face of the complications and controversy to which the proposal gave rise, no such right ever reached the statute-book.[55]

4. The lengthy dispute at the Grunwick processing laboratories in London in 1976–7 refuelled the concern over violence on picket lines and the problems of mass demonstrations. The dispute was for many months a peaceful one but began to escalate as more and more outside groups gathered to demonstrate their support for the workers involved, and others gathered to oppose them.[56]

5. In the so-called winter of discontent of 1978–9, there were extensive strikes, secondary and flying pickets, in actions involving among others road haulage and public-service employees, and consequent high levels of disruption.[57] Under Government pressure, the TGWU issued a code of conduct which stressed the importance of maintaining essential supplies, and recommended that picket lines should 'be composed only of employees of employers in dispute and union officials who have been authorised by the regional secretary'.[58]

The eventual settlement of most of the disputes was marked by the issue of a joint TUC–Government statement, known as the Concordat. This had three TUC guides, including one on the conduct of industrial disputes, attached to it.[59] Again, this addressed the problems of flying picketing and maintaining essential supplies. Unions were encouraged 'save in exceptional circumstances' to confine picketing to the premises of the parties to the dispute or their customers or suppliers, within the context of the general aim of

[53] [1974] ICR 84 (HL).

[54] Ibid. at 89F per Lord Reid.

[55] For the debate on 'right to stop' proposals in the Employment Protection Bill 1975, see OR St. Cttee. F 28th sitting (17 July 1975) col. 1485.

[56] Clutterbuck (1978: ch. 16); Geary (1985: pp. 83–8), who notes that an 'official' APEX picket was allowed in front of the police cordon which held back demonstrators.

[57] For useful accounts on which this section draws, see Dorfman (1983: ch. 3); Holmes (1985a: ch. 8); Whitehead (1985: ch. 13).

[58] TGWU code of practice—text reproduced in the *Financial Times* (19 Jan. 1979, para. 3(*b*)).

[59] *The Economy, the Government and Trade Union Responsibilities* (DE 1979).

'deflecting' custom or supplies from the employer in dispute. The 'policing' of picket lines by responsible union officials, who might ensure that numbers were no larger than necessary, was also advised. The Government also issued a consultation paper on the law of picketing. This reviewed all the main proposals for reform of the law which had been canvassed in previous years. It was sceptical about the utility of any of these, but seemed to view with most promise the possibility that a statutory code of practice might be introduced.[60]

The concerns to which these events gave rise can be seen as focusing on four types of activity, often, but by no means automatically, related to one another. First, there was the use of secondary, and more widespread forms of picketing, notably in the 1972 miners' strike and in the winter of discontent. In so far as this affected employers, customers, and suppliers, this can be viewed as simply a facet of the more general concern with secondary action which has already been discussed. But there was a second aspect of picketing in the winter of discontent which gave rise to particular concern, namely the use of pickets to induce *employees* not yet participating in the strike to join it, or at least not to cross picket lines mounted at their places of work. Conservatives identified the practice as being closely related to one of the iniquities of the closed shop. As Prior later put it: 'Much of the sting of the closed shop and the picket line lay in the fear that a torn up union card could mean a torn up right to work' (1986: p. 160). But to threaten to expel a member in accordance with union rules, for failure to obey an instruction to take industrial action, could not be regarded as *per se* unlawful. This seemed to some to amount to 'lawful intimidation'.[61]

Thirdly, there was the concern, again raised during the winter of discontent, over the disruption of essential public services. Finally, there were the public-order problems of mass picketing, sustained by flying pickets and 'outsiders', and the attendant confrontations with police. Here the concern was not so much with violence as such. Notwithstanding certain specific incidents of violence, for example during the construction workers' dispute of 1972 and at Grunwick,[62] the disputes of the 1970s, even when there were mass gatherings, were predominantly peaceful. One study characterizes the usual activity on picket lines as consisting of 'pushing and shoving', contrasting it with the 'stoning and shooting' of the turn of the century, and with subsequent developments in the 1980s (Geary 1985: chs. 2, 5, 6, and 7).

---

[60]  The full text of the document is reproduced in 130 *IRLIB* p. 5 (7 Feb. 1979).

[61]  The notion of lawful intimidation emerged in exchanges following the statement on the law of picketing by the then Attorney-General, Mr Sam Silkin, on 25 Jan. 1979: OR HC vol. 961 cols. 706 ff. Contrast the prohibition on intimidatory picketing contained in s. 3 of the Trade Disputes and Trade Unions Act 1927, which embraced threatening otherwise lawful economic harms; and see ch. 8 below on the wider provisions now contained in ss. 3–5, Employment Act 1988.

[62]  See *R. v. Jones* [1974] ICR 310; Clutterbuck (1978: pp.75–6).

The concern with public order was in Conservative minds more about the fact that at episodes like Saltley, large numbers of individuals appeared to have been allowed to 'get away' with breaking the criminal law. The problem was therefore not the state of the law, but its (lack of) enforcement—the perceived 'negative' side of police discretion in these matters. One recent study suggests a simple and compelling explanation for such events. It arises from the fact that if a mass picket or demonstration does escalate, the police will usually be faced with a conflict, and therefore choice, between the exercise of their two main functions: to preserve the peace and to enforce the law. It is perhaps not hard to understand why they may choose to opt for the former (Kahn et al. 1983: ch. 5).[63] Nevertheless, it was surely this aspect of the events at Saltley which caused the deepest and most persistent concern in Conservative ranks.[64]

How did Conservative proposals for tackling these different problems develop? As for the public-order problem, the fact that this was one of enforcement and not of the substantive criminal law, raised a difficulty. The courts, however willing prospectively or retrospectively to endorse broad police discretions, hold back from dictating how these should be exercised.[65] Police forces up and down the country are technically independent of Government, save that the Metropolitan Police in London answer to the Home Secretary, an independence often depicted as an essential feature of the Rule of Law of which the Conservative Party is the self-proclaimed guardian. A simple instruction to the police to adopt a tougher line on enforcement was neither a practicable nor a politically attractive option.

A far more constructive, and indeed proven, solution seemed to lie in the use of a code of practice such as that issued by the NUM in 1974. It was this on which Mr Prior first seized. The October 1974 manifesto promised that the Conservatives would 'seek ways of regulating the conduct of picketing based on the strict arrangements adopted by the National Union of Mineworkers in February 1974'.[66] An Opposition amendment moved in the debates on the TULR Bill earlier that year suggested that this might be achieved by giving the Secretary of State power to draw up statutory regulations for approval by both Houses of Parliament.[67] Ironically, the Labour Government had itself drawn attention to the virtues of the code, and in particular of its advice on restricting numbers, when announcing its own proposals for legislation in March of that year.[68] Labour having dropped

[63] Such reasoning appealed to the Home Secretary of the day, see Maudling (1978: pp. 160–1). The Labour Government's January 1979 consultation paper para. 14 observed that to compel police to reduce numbers at an otherwise peaceful mass picket might itself give rise to disorder.

[64] On the symbolic status of Saltley in Conservative mythology on picketing, see Clutterbuck (1978: pp. 73–4); Kahn et al. (1983: p. 75).

[65] See cases at nn. 48–9 above, and esp. R. v. Chief Constable of Devon and Cornwall ex. p. CEGB [1982] 1 QB 458 (CA).

[66] See Craig (1975: p. 425).

[67] OR St. Cttee. E TULR Bill 1974 11th sitting (20 June 1974) cols. 595 ff.

[68] OR HC vol. 870 col. 1479 (22 Mar. 1974).

the proposal, the Conservatives duly picked it up. The Conservatives also argued that a code might ease concerns about secondary picketing, revived by the 1976 Act, barring the general solution for which they pressed, of a narrowing of the TULRA section 13 immunities.[69]

The escalation of the Grunwick dispute in 1977 revived the debate, and in particular highlighted two other proposals. Lord Robens, the former Donovan Commissioner and Coal Board chairman, suggested that the 1974 Act be amended to provide that:

picketing may only be performed by persons at their place of employment or their former prior employment, to enable dismissed strikers to also picket.

This, he argued,

would have very obvious advantages. It would enable peaceful picketing to actually take place, it would assist the police to perform their function, and prevent the 'rent-a-picket' and others from turning peaceful picketing into mass intimidation.[70]

As described by Robens, such an amendment might therefore help to solve the problem of mass picketing, for 'outsiders' of all kinds—flying pickets and non-workers alike—would lose the section 15 protection. Although the idea was not entirely new,[71] proponents like Robens did not, however, spell out how in practice the change would be enforced.

The other idea linked the proposal of a code of practice to the 'right to stop' debate. As *The Economist* put it, in a leading article in October 1977, the Conservatives had scope to offer the unions 'a deal on picketing: if the unions agree to drop mass pickets and settle for a small number in a dispute (say six), there is no reason why pickets should not be able to put their case to those crossing picket lines' (8 Oct. 1977: p. 11). Others, however, remained cautious. The CBI's national congress held in November 1977 recommended that the law on picketing should not be altered.[72] Mr Prior for his part emphasized that the law did not need changing: the problem remained one of enforcement. Regarding mass picketing, as well as exhorting the Government again to issue firm guidance, he thought a way forward might be for the CBI, TUC, and—notably—the police, to agree on a policy effectively to outlaw it: 'All that should be permitted is a small and specified number of pickets authenticated by their union.' He firmly rejected, however, a right to stop vehicles as a quid pro quo.[73].

The winter of discontent sharpened anxieties all round. Those concerned now included the Prime Minister, Mr Callaghan. He drew a distinction

[69]  See e.g. OR HC vol. 960 cols. 1622–3 (16 Jan. 1979).
[70]  Letter to *The Times* (2 July 1977).
[71]  The idea had been raised in 1972 (see e.g. OR HC vol. 845 col. 801 (7 Nov. 1972)), and was described by Kidner (1975: p. 256) as 'perhaps the only way in which the law could be made more stringent'.
[72]  See (1978) 16 *BJIR* p. 252.
[73]  See Prior (1977*c*); OR HC vol. 935 col. 208 (12 July 1977).

between 'ordinary' picketing designed to stop the blackleg from doing the job of the striker, and that which concerned him which was 'intended to stop another worker from doing the job that he usually does'.[74] The CBI, which as recently as September 1978 had still been talking cautiously about 'enforcement' and 'guidance', now demanded an immediate change in the law so that workers might only be allowed to picket if themselves in dispute, and only outside their own employers' premises.[75] Others, including the British Institute of Management (BIM) and even the Institute of Personnel Management (IPM), soon put forward similar proposals.[76]

Mr Prior now responded swiftly, arguing on 12 January that: 'Events of this week have shown that the issue of where pickets can operate and who can picket must be considered afresh.'[77] Sensing a new opening, the Conservatives now joined in pressing the Government to amend the law along these lines.[78] Tougher reform of the law had rapidly grown popular, even among trade unionists, and these events boosted afresh the Conservatives' chances of electoral victory in 1979.[79] There was an obvious political strategy open to Mr Prior: firstly to offer his support to Labour if it would introduce legislation, and secondly, if this 'great prize' (Prior 1986: p. 156) were not achieved, to make action an election promise. In the event, the Labour Government did not legislate before it fell. So now the Conservatives had to consider more precisely what to propose. The secondary action question was, as we have noted, to be held in abeyance. Logically, that could go for this aspect of picketing too. This fact was confirmed by the decision in *United Biscuits* v. *Fall*[80] in January 1979. The plaintiff was the victim of picketing in the road haulage dispute, which cut off supplies to its business, although neither it nor the suppliers were directly party to the dispute. In granting an interlocutory injunction, the High Court was able to draw directly on the earlier Court of Appeal cases, as well as suggesting a test of its own to supplement those which they had developed.[81] Following judgment, picketing ceased. The company later revealed that the litigation had been planned and executed with great care, and was clearly well pleased with the result, which also attracted wide media coverage.[82] The case showed that the Court of Appeal's approach could work as well for secondary picketing as it did for secondary action in general.

[74] See OR HC vol. 960 col. 1546 (16 Jan. 1979), and *Financial Times* (24 Jan. 1979) on his support for those who wished to cross picket lines.

[75] See CBI (1978: p. 47, paras. 25–7) and *Financial Times* (12 Jan. 1979) respectively.

[76] For IPM and BIM proposals, see *Personnel Management* (Mar. 1979: p. 5).

[77] See *Financial Times* (13 Jan. 1979).

[78] See e.g. OR HC vol. 962 cols. 1143 and 1154–5 (14 Feb. 1979).

[79] For recognition by writers sympathetic to Labour and the unions of the extent of the damage done, see e.g. Taylor (1982b: pp. 206–9); Crouch (1982a: p. 219).

[80] [1979] IRLR 110.

[81] Ibid. at 113–14. The new test suggested that action might be unprotected if inconsistent with or in disregard of union instructions.

[82] See the account given by the company's group personnel director published in *Personnel Management* (May 1979: pp. 9 and 15).

As for the public-order aspect, Mr Prior's continued preference was for tackling this mainly by the introduction of a code of practice, for which the union movement had now provided two fresh precedents.[83] Specific sections of the code might also address the problems of disruption of essential services and of so-called lawful intimidation. It was its possible further assistance with both these problems which particularly attracted Mr Prior to the idea of narrowing the section 15 immunity: 'By restricting pickets to their own place of work, much of the intimidation and wholesale disruption would be overcome' (1986: p. 159).[84] Narrowing section 15 clearly had the general attraction of offering a way out of the sterile debate over the criminal law; but it was yet to be spelled out precisely how the change would be given its civil law 'teeth'.[85] The 'intimidation' problem was, however, also to be further tackled by the reintroduction of a right to claim unreasonable exclusion or expulsion from a union where a closed shop operated (Prior 1986: p. 160).[86]

Thus it was that the 1979 manifesto promised that the 'right to picket' would be limited to 'those in dispute picketing at their own place of work'. In addition it expressed a general concern over secondary action—of the picketing and other kinds—and promised an immediate review of the law 'followed by such amendment as may be appropriate in the light of recent decisions in this field' (*Conservative Party Manifesto 1979*: p. 10). The changes proposed were no doubt thought likely to help loosen the potential union grip on essential services. In addition, the manifesto stated that the Conservatives would 'seek to conclude no-strike agreements in a few essential services', although making no proposals for legislation specifically on this aspect. The notorious Ridley report leaked a year earlier had recognized that the problem could not easily be tackled by direct legislation, and had concluded that where unions in certain industries 'have the nation by the jugular vein the only feasible option is to pay up'.[87]

### (c) The Activities of SLADE

There was one further type of industrial action which became of concern to Conservatives towards the end of the 1970s. This was related to the recruitment tactics employed by the art union SLADE, which sought to boost its membership by recruiting employees from non-union art studios. When such employees showed no desire to join or be represented by SLADE, the union then sought to bring pressure upon them to join, by

---

[83] This was also the CBI's preference: see *Financial Times* (19 Jan. 1979).

[84] As has been noted, this might also help to frustrate mass picketing.

[85] Prior above n. 77 hinted that it might be linked to a narrowing of the s. 13 immunities, as did the CBI: see *Financial Times* (19 Jan. 1979).

[86] See further Lewis and Simpson (1981: pp. 120–2). A similar right had also existed between 1974 and 1976.

[87] See *The Times* (18 Apr. 1978); *The Economist* (27 May 1978). At one point Mrs Thatcher had suggested that it might be necessary to ban strikes in some essential services. Mr Prior stressed that this was not yet party policy. See *Financial Times* (8–9 Jan. 1979).

organizing blacking, by SLADE members employed at the printers, of work emanating from the target studios. This activity attracted particularly widespread condemnation because of the way in which employees rather than employers were seen to be its target. We may recall the similar distinction which Mr Callaghan drew in another context. It provided an ideal case for the Conservatives to push their approach of tackling specific limited problems about which there was broad consensus. They condemned the tactics in a series of debates, characterizing them as an 'abuse' of the trade-disputes immunities.[88] This conception pointed to an obvious way of responding to the situation: if the immunities were privileges which were here being abused, then a solution might be for the privileges in this case to be withdrawn.[89] This, Mr Prior urged the Government to do.

An alternative or complementary solution was also suggested. One facet of the Opposition's criticism of the recognition procedures contained in the EPA 1975 was that they could not be invoked by the employer. If employers were enabled to invoke the procedure here, argued Mr Prior, then SLADE's claims might be adjudicated upon by ACAS rather than by industrial action, and trade-disputes immunities withdrawn if the union opposed the pro- cedure.[90] There are technical difficulties with both these ideas, which we will return to in the next chapter. For the moment we need only note Mr Prior's pledge that if Labour did not act, the Conservatives would upon their return to power set up an enquiry into the activities of SLADE and take such action as seemed appropriate in its light.[91]

## (4) CONCLUSIONS

We can conclude this chapter with a summary of the most important themes underlying the development of Conservative policy between 1974 and 1979. The period witnessed an intense debate within the party as to whether the experiences of the Heath Government indicated that a more conciliatory or a more uncompromising strategy was called for. While the tensions remained deep and unresolved beneath the surface, formal policy was rapidly established and developed firmly on the basis of the former approach. In particular, it was central to Mr Prior's strategy to cultivate the support of trade unions and their members. Although the events of the winter of discontent gave the Conservatives a political boost, they can hardly have helped allay continuing fears about the hazards and uncertainties of major confrontation with the unions. The participation of the unions would also be actively needed in the annual assessment approach to economic planning.

---

[88] See OR HC vol. 934 col. 463 (29 June 1977); vol. 950 col. 799 (18 May 1978); vol. 964 col. 984 (16 Mar. 1979).
[89] OR HC vol. 934 col. 469 (29 June 1977).
[90] Ibid. col. 475.
[91] OR HC vol. 963 col. 1543 (8 Mar. 1979).

The Prior approach further acknowledged some legitimacy in the unions' basic economic and social claims, while holding its own distinct view about how the balance between the powers of capital and labour should be struck.[92]

From this perspective we can see the specific measures formally proposed at this stage as not primarily concerned with the general economic effects of union activity—the tactics of the national forum were the preferred manner of tackling that problem. Rather, the proposals looked to the more direct harms and disruption which industrial action was perceived as sometimes causing: harm to public services, to 'innocent' employers and employees, and to the maintenance of public order. Even then, there appeared to be no general theory alone at work: the development of each proposal had its own peculiar history in the events of the 1970s. Finally, we can note again the fact of considerable support for the measures proposed, particularly in the wake of the winter of discontent. This was regarded as of critical importance to the success, and so would help determine the pace, of change: it was calculated that it would be extremely hard for opponents to accuse the Conservatives of being 'anti-union' or to mount effective opposition to their proposals, if the Government could argue that it was responding to pressures from among trade unionists themselves; and further political ammunition was to be provided by the outcome of the general election of May 1979.

[92] See further discussion in chs. 3 and 10 below.

# [3]
# The Employment Act 1980

## (1) INTRODUCTION

Mr Prior had repeatedly committed himself before the general election to full consultations on any proposed changes to labour law. We have noted his desire to bring about change if possible through dialogue with the trade-union movement, and his fears of the consequences of repeating the errors of 1971. Yet at the same time the manifesto had made clear the Government's commitment to take action on the 'specific abuses' which it identified, and this was confirmed in the Queen's speech and subsequent debate on the address.[1] Commentators therefore questioned how meaningful any consultations would actually be. Prior confirmed that consultation did not mean negotiation: 'This is not an arbitration at which you end up splitting the difference.'[2] Nevertheless, his strategy was to publish a series of consultation papers on each proposal in advance of any bill, and to meet with and judge carefully the mood and likely response of the unions even before publishing any proposals.

In the event these meetings rapidly established that trade-union opposition to any changes in labour law would be both comprehensive and implacable, but at the same time that the resolve, coherence, and strength of any anti-legislative campaign might be considerably less than might at first have been anticipated.[3] The Government therefore pressed ahead with the publication of three working papers on 9 July 1979, on picketing, the closed shop, and funding for ballots.[4] Meantime on 7 June the then Mr Andrew Leggatt QC had been appointed to investigate the alleged activities of SLADE. By August, discussions with the unions had reached deadlock.[5]

## (2) THE EARLY WORKING PAPERS

### (a) The Working Paper on Picketing and Responses

This document summarized the nature of Government concerns on picketing, particularly arising from events of the previous winter. It stressed

---

[1] See OR HC vol. 967 cols. 47 ff. (15 May 1979).
[2] See Prior (1979c).
[3] See Dorfman (1983: pp. 112–23); Prior (1985).
[4] Discussion of the balloting issue is deferred to chs. 6 and 7. For the text of the picketing working paper, see DE Press Release of 9 July 1979.
[5] See (1980) 18 *BJIR* p. 122.

the value of voluntary guidance, and that police powers were already quite adequate. However, it went on to propose the narrowing of section 15 of TULRA. It suggested that the application of section 15 be limited:

(i) to those who are party to the trade dispute which occasions the picketing, and
(ii) to the picketing which they carry out at their own place of work (Working Paper on Picketing: para. 8).

The document spelled out firmly for the first time, that to make the restriction effective, a corresponding removal of section 13 protection would also be necessary. One suggested way to achieve this would be to remove section 13 protection where picketing was no longer protected under section 15 (para. 10). However, an alternative also discussed would be to restrict section 13 protection in respect of secondary action in general. The suggested manner of achieving this was the restriction of TULRA section 13(1) immunity to contracts of employment, as in 1974 (para. 11). Government thinking was therefore at this stage no further advanced than this previously tried solution. The document made clear that if wider changes to section 13 were to be made, this would need to be in the context of its wider review of the law on immunities. Nevertheless, it wished to explore how amendments to sections 15 and 13 might work together in relation to picketing (para. 12). This demonstrates an important consequence of the Government's commitment to act generally in the field of secondary action, should the court decisions not go its way: to introduce an effective and coherent regime on picketing in the mean time required careful consideration now of how the law in the two areas would eventually fit together.

Finally, the document canvassed the possibility of giving the Secretary of State power to draw up a code of practice 'in the absence of comprehensive and effective voluntary guidance', possibly with the assistance of ACAS:

The Code would have status in law in that it could be taken into account in court proceedings. As a document approved by Parliament it could be expected to have considerable moral force, as well as helping to bring about a more consistent interpretation of the law by police and magistrates (paras. 13 and 14).

This quotation hints at the potential for assisting in the law enforcement problem which it was thought that a code might offer. Although later the subject of much controversy, every one of these ideas—involvement of ACAS, relevance in court proceedings, addressing the code to the police as well as others, and encouraging 'consistency' in enforcement—had been canvassed in Labour's January 1979 consultation paper.[6]

The working paper elicited a diverse range of responses from within the ranks of employers and their organizations.[7] The CBI broadly endorsed the Government's proposed approach, whilst stressing the need for 'proper and

[6] See paras. 20–1 of that document reproduced in 130 *IRLIB* p. 5.
[7] For a list of respondents as at 14 Nov. 1979, see OR HC vol. 973 Written Answers cols. 612–14.

uniform enforcement of the criminal law'. It suggested that restriction of section 13 ought to be limited to the picketing context for the time being (CBI 1979a: paras. 6–11).[8] Others, however, called for more stringent restrictions, and in particular, an expansion of the role of the criminal law.[9] Many respondents were clearly troubled by the shortcomings of existing remedies. This related both to the procedural difficulties of bringing civil actions, and to the perceived inadequacy of having to rely solely on civil law in any event. It was suggested that the latter problem might be corrected by the extended criminalization of picketing, or, in some not very clearly defined way, by the state playing a greater role in the initiation of proceedings.[10] The former might be tackled by procedural reforms. In particular, both the CBI and IPM urged the introduction of a procedure for obtaining an injunction against the 'act of picketing', avoiding the difficulties which might be encountered in identifying individual pickets, and subsequent 'avoidance' tactics.[11]

The responses revealed no single clear agreed perception of the nature of the 'picketing problem', and no great coincidence with the Government's own perceptions. This is perhaps not so surprising, given, as has been noted, that 'picketing' is in fact used to refer to a variety of different activities with different aims. Recent research supports the view that the decision to further a dispute by picketing, and the choice of particular tactics, will be closely dictated by a whole series of logistical factors peculiar to the industry or organization of the workers involved.[12] Furthermore, however comprehensively employers' organizations may have canvassed their members, actual experience of industrial action is likely to have formed only one source of input generating the overall response.[13] So too, the Government's own views, as we have seen, were not borne out of simple research, but out of a complex of wider pressures and influences. Criticisms which focused on the lack of hard evidence showing any new, widespread, or ongoing problems of the type described in the working paper[14] therefore failed to undermine the relevance of the wider policy influences on the Government, although they may have helped to point them up. In reality, there was clearly no possibility of the Government responding positively to any major new suggestions on policy. It was already clear, for example, that there was no question of any

[8] A letter from the Director-General suggested that great care and consideration were needed before making any wider alteration to the immunities. See 147 *IRLIB* p. 6 (24 Oct. 1979).

[9] See e.g.: I.o.D. (1979a: para. 36h); AIB (1979); CBI (1979b) comments of Dunlop; AIMS (1979: para. i).

[10] See I.o.D. (1979a: para. 32).

[11] The procedure in RSC O. 113 for obtaining vacant possession of property as against unnamed occupiers—aimed chiefly at squatters—was urged as a precedent. See CBI (1979a: para. 9); 158 *IRLIB* p. 10 on the IPM proposals and IPM (1979: para. 2); the IPM also wrote to Mr Mayhew expressing its concerns that the substance of the proposed restriction might be too narrow: see *Personnel Management* (Nov. 1979: p. 15).

[12] See Kahn *et al.* (1983: ch. 4) where five main factors are identified.

[13] See the remarks of researchers such as Joyce *et al.* (1984: pp. 66–71) and Daniel and Millward (1983: pp. 214–15).

[14] See e.g. Lewis *et al.* (1979: ch. 4).

express changes in criminal law being introduced. However, the responses did perhaps provide some food for thought on the *mechanisms* by which the Government's favoured approach might be implemented. This was particularly so with regard to the matter of remedies. Here, the calls for the repeal of TULRA section 14 and for the introduction of a procedure to obtain an injunction against the act of picketing raised important issues to which the Government was later obliged to turn, as shall we.

### (b) The 'SLADE' Working Paper

The Leggatt report on *Trade Union Recruitment Activities* was published on 17 October. It fulfilled its main function, which was to provide authoritative documentation of the alleged activities of SLADE, for to suggest appropriate legislative action was not within its terms of reference. Nevertheless, it confirmed that the activities in question would be protected by existing TULRA immunities, except for a possible argument that freelance target members might not be 'workers' as legally defined, and therefore not the subject of a lawful trade dispute (Leggatt 1979: paras. 170–1).

The Government responded with a six-paragraph working paper[15] arguing that the tactics in question were 'an abuse of industrial power' which it believed would be deplored by reponsible trade unionists, and that it was in the interests of the union movement to ensure that such tactics could not lawfully be used. It suggested that they might be rendered unlawful either by removing them from the protection of TULRA section 13, or by narrowing the definition of a trade dispute in TULRA section 29. The characterization of this activity as an 'abuse of privilege' had, as has been noted, a valuable rhetorical ring, and points easily to the logic of removing the privilege. The alternative approach of narrowing section 29 was perhaps inspired by the comments in the report on its relevance to the issue of immunity in some cases. Either proposal would of course have the same effect of removing section 13 protection. The earlier proposal to link a remedy to the recognition procedure had disappeared—the Government having already decided to abolish the procedure.[16] In any event, to characterize these as recognition disputes did not quite hit the mark, for they were, at least in the first instance, about union *membership*, which is of course a very different thing. The working paper confirmed that the Government wished to be extremely precise in targeting just this one type of activity, and intended to ensure that a legislative provision would not cover 'disputes over recognition and demarcation and does not restrict primary action in disputes over union membership'.

A reply to a Parliamentary question shortly after the Leggatt report had been published, stated that TUC pressure for reform would not be enough:

[15] The text is reproduced in 149 *IRLIB* 21 Nov. 1979.
[16] See DE Press release of 25 Sept. 1979.

the Government would press ahead with measures to ensure that individuals harmed by these activities would have a legal remedy.[17] However, the proposals, as has been noted, suggested the solution of exposure to the economic torts. Whilst this might give remedies to the 'target' employer and to the employer of those taking action, it could not be certain to provide one to the 'target' employees. To ensure that would require the introduction of a new statutory remedy. It became beyond doubt, however, when the Bill was published, that it would give a remedy to employers only.[18] We can return to this point in a moment.

## (3) THE EMPLOYMENT BILL

The Employment Bill was published on 6 December 1979.[19] In a speech to the Institute of Directors (I.o.D.) the day before, Prior reiterated his themes, warning that a modest measure was coming which could only be seen as of very limited relevance to the wider problems of industrial relations, a speech largely repeated when he opened the second reading debate.[20] Not surprisingly, the industrial-action clauses closely followed the working papers.

### (a) The 'SLADE' Clause

This was clause 15 of the Bill, which reached the statute-book entirely unaltered as section 18 of the Act.[21] It provided that section 13 protection would not be available where action had the object of compelling membership of one or more particular unions. In order to avoid affecting disputes within a firm or at one site, it was necessary to distinguish the employees taking action from the 'target' employees. The clause concentrated on the torts mentioned in TULRA section 13(1), opening up a remedy for the employer of those taking action, for interference with contracts of employment, and for the 'target' employer whose commercial contracts were thereby interfered with, provided that target employees had a different employer and place of work from those taking the action. The operation of, and thinking behind, the clause was explained at some length to the Standing Committee by the then Solicitor-General, Sir Ian Percival.[22] He made a number of noteworthy points. First, great stress was laid on the fact that the clause created no new remedy—that it merely 'restored' existing common-law rights of action. Secondly, the causes of action restored were deliberately

---

[17] OR HC vol. 973 col. 216 (6 Nov. 1979) Mr Mayhew.
[18] See OR HC vol. 976 col. 68 (17 Dec. 1979) Mr Prior.
[19] 1979 Bill no. 97.
[20] See I.o.D. (1979b: p. 78); OR HC vol. 976. col. 58 (17 Dec. 1979).
[21] But now repealed by EA 1982 s. 21(3), Sch. 4. See the discussion in ch. 5 below.
[22] OR St. Cttee. A 28th sitting (25 Mar. 1980) cols. 1515 ff.

only those mentioned in section 13(1) of TULRA, all of which revolved around a particular *contract* of the plaintiff. Thirdly, the clause was intended to provide a 'checklist' of conditions which had to be satisfied for the cause of action to be restored, so that both legal advisers and, if necessary, courts, could easily and with certainty ascertain whether the clause applied or not, simply by applying the checklist to the facts. Here, focusing on a particular contract was crucial: there would be no room for uncertainty, for the contract concerned would actually have to be identified in the pleadings, and the clause thereafter referred to 'the contract concerned' for this reason.

The approach of relying on the existing torts had obvious advantages. It allowed the clause to be as simple and low-key as possible, while conveying the symbolic message about 'abuse of privilege'. It avoided introducing a new remedy, which might give the Opposition the opportunity to raise a host of issues and objections, as well, surely, as smacking rather too much of the unfair industrial practices of the IRA. But the approach had other consequences. First, it could not be guaranteed to give a remedy to 'target' employees. However, this did not appear to concern the Government. The working paper had attracted little interest or response and Mr Prior acknowledged that the activities of SLADE itself were largely a thing of the past.[23] He therefore hoped and expected that the clause might not actually be used at all: that its mere presence might be a deterrent to any incidental revival of the practices.[24] The clause was therefore in large measure symbolic—of the 'specific abuse' approach, and of the Government's special concern at how unions could on occasion pressurize employees as well as employers. Secondly, and more importantly, the approach of removal of immunity, combined with the desire for precision and certainty, generated a very particular approach to the removal of section 13 protection. This clause therefore set important drafting precedents for punishing 'abuses of privilege' by the withdrawal of immunity, and for identifying the scope of withdrawal by reference only to the primary torts referred to in section 13(1), thereby focusing the action on a particular contract of the plaintiff. These proved to be of some significance when the problem of secondary action later came to be addressed, as we shall see.

### (b) The Picketing Clause

The Bill contained clauses enabling the introduction of a code of practice (clause 2), and altering the applicability of TULRA sections 13 and 15 to picketing (clause 14). The latter can be considered first. Clause 14(1) substituted a new section 15 altogether, retaining its 'peaceful attendance lawful' formula but limited to attendance at a person's own place of work.

[23] Ibid. 29th sitting (25 Mar. 1980) col. 1571. SLADE was in fact shortly to disappear in a merger with the NGA.
[24] Ibid. cols. 1573–4.

Although a number of respondents to the consultations had suggested a need for it, no definition of 'place of work' was offered. However, other problems raised during the consultative process were addressed. Thus, provision was made, for the attendance of trade-union officials, and to cater for those who did not have a fixed place of work, for whom it would be impractical to picket their own place of work, or who had been dismissed in connection with the trade dispute in question.[25] The first of these flows naturally from Prior's support, which has been noted, for the 'policing' of picket lines by union officials. It would also provide a clear defendant if legal proceedings became necessary, for as we shall note, the Government advocated suing organizers as a way of overcoming some of the procedural difficulties alleged to exist. The other provisions amounted to special definitions of place of work for difficult categories. The Government secured that the numbers who might be able to swell picket lines by taking advantage of these provisions were kept to a minimum, by ensuring in the final Act that union officials could only picket in the company of members whom they represented, and former employees only if they had not subsequently taken a new job.[26]

Sub-clause 2 forged the promised link with TULRA section 13 by providing that 'nothing done in the course of picketing' would attract the protection of section 13 unless also within the new section 15. The Government viewed this change as vital, for it gave the clause its teeth: the principal cause of action which it saw as involved was again for inducing breach of contract.[27] This will be important when we come to the matter of remedies.

The Government had drawn back at this stage from tampering with section 13 in any more general way, as well as from further restricting the narrowed section 15 protection to only those who were parties to the trade dispute in question. Consideration of these matters was deferred to the stage of the introduction of any subsequent secondary action clause. Nevertheless, Mr Prior acknowledged that the new section 15 protection would be extremely restrictive, but argued that this was justified because of the special public-order connotations which picketing had.[28] This sits uneasily with the Government's repeated claims that the narrowing of section 15 would not affect the criminal law and would be of no interest to the police,[29] and is further evidence of Mr Prior's perception that a measure chiefly designed to give employers relief against flying and outsider pickets would also help to alleviate the public-order problem of mass picketing. In fact, Government

[25] Union officials and former employees had been mentioned by e.g. the EEF (1979b: para. 4); mobile workers by e.g. the BIM (1979).

[26] For amendments on these points which were resisted, see OR HL vol. 410 cols. 620 and 632 (12 June 1980).

[27] See e.g. Mr Mayhew in OR St. Cttee. A 26th sitting (20 Mar. 1980) col. 1407.

[28] See the later working paper on secondary action (n. 82 below) paras. 9 and 12; Prior (1986: p. 159).

[29] See e.g. OR HC vol. 976 cols. 67 and 75–6 Mr Prior (17 Dec. 1979).

speakers regularly put forward three reasons why the picketing restriction should be especially tight—tighter than that later introduced on secondary action. These were, first its use to 'intimidate' workers, secondly the public-order connotations, and thirdly its particular effectiveness at spreading damage to 'innocent' parties.[30]

In the debates, much attention was given to the problem of remedies. Mr Prior faced attacks from not only the Labour Party, but also many Conservatives who thought his proposals too weak.[31] In committee, Mr John Gorst tabled amendments proposing the removal of TULRA section 14 in the context of picketing[32] and the banning of 'demonstrators' from the vicinity of picket lines by the criminal law.[33] We are already aware of the Government's commitment to leave the criminal law untouched, but it is worth devoting some attention to the debate over the former amendment, in view of the subsequent change of heart on section 14 in the EA 1982.[34]

### (c) The Trade Union Immunity

The 'blanket' immunity in tort for trade unions embodied in section 14 was the focus of and symbol for attacks on the immunities in general, almost from the moment it was introduced.[35] Even the most faithful defenders of the immunities thought it wider than strictly necessary.[36] Yet Kahn-Freund thought that the storm which it caused was 'a storm in a teacup' being of the view that the whole issue 'looks much more important than it is' (1977: pp. 274–5). To understand Kahn-Freund's remarks we need to appreciate one key fact about the immunities as a whole contained in the 1906 and 1974 Acts. This is that the 'individual' immunities which those Acts contained, themselves also protected trade unions, because they related to 'acts done', by whomever they were done.[37] It followed that were section 14 to be repealed, a union would only be exposed to action where section 13 already did not apply, and in this case individuals would already be exposed to action as well. Kahn-Freund therefore reasoned that the key and only practical question regarding section 14 was whether repealing it and therefore making available an *additional* defendant in the shape of the trade union would in fact alter or improve the plaintiff's situation. He concluded that the answer was no (1977: p. 275).

---

[30] See e.g. Mr Mayhew OR St. Cttee. A 28th sitting (25 Mar. 1980) col. 1496.

[31] Prior (1986: ch. 9) and Wigham (1982: pp. 213 ff.) chronicle Mr Prior's battle with right-wing Conservatives throughout this period.

[32] OR St. Cttee. A 27th sitting (20 Mar. 1980) col. 1466.

[33] Ibid. 28th sitting (25 Mar. 1980) col. 1502.

[34] EA 1982 s. 15(1). See the discussion in ch. 5 below.

[35] See e.g. Dicey (1914: pp. xliv-xlviii) and Pollock (1908: pp. v and 96-7).

[36] See e.g. Wedderburn (1965: p. 221).

[37] This assumes that a trade union is for these purposes a 'person'. Cf. *EETPU* v. *Times Newspapers* [1980] QB 585; Interpretation Act 1978 Sch. 1.

This reasoning rested on two assumptions. The first was that the immunity was only of any real significance in the context of damages claims. A damages award against an individual might in practice be worthless, not so against a union. However, an injunction awarded against the organizers of industrial action would have the same practical effect as one against the union. Even in respect of damages claims, however, there would be no difference in practice. This conclusion arose from the second assumption: that the 'individual' immunities would in any case be broad, covering the general field of industrial conflict. Even if a blanket immunity for unions existed, the commission of unprotected torts by individuals would only occur either in a context other than industrial action—and trade unions would acknowledge the right to compensation for this or it would occur as the result of an eccentric or perverse legal decision—and trade unions would be happy to indemnify their unfortunate members on such occasions, as in *Rookes* v. *Barnard*.[38]

In the context of a more restrictive general system of industrial-conflict law, Kahn-Freund's conclusions would have to be reconsidered, as the third edition of *Labour and the Law* suggests (Davies and Freedland 1983: pp. 363–6). A union exposed to the size of damages claim made in a case such as *GAS* v. *TGWU*[39] might welcome the opportunity to avoid it, and decline to indemnify individual defendants. In general, however, employers showed little interest in damages claims even when between 1971 and 1974 no protection for unions was in force. The chief concern must therefore be with injunctions. Here, the reasoning must also be revised in the context of a more restrictive climate. Kahn-Freund's argument involved an implicit assumption that an injunction when granted would be obeyed; but he himself had earlier suggested that the atmosphere which engendered such a consistent respect for the law, and obedience to injunctions, was itself a product of the wide berth which the law normally granted to unions' activities—so that this attitude might not persist were the law to become more interventionist (1959: p. 10). The experience of the IRA both confirmed this prediction and illustrated that in these circumstances critical differences between the position of an individual and that of a union might arise, for the ultimate form of punishment of an individual contemnor is committal to prison, whereas the availability of a union's funds opens up the possibility of a sequestration order or heavy fine.

Thus Mr Gorst's argument was simple: enjoining individuals might no longer be an adequate remedy against picketing unprotected by the new TULRA section 15, for the simple reason that such an injunction might well not be obeyed. However, both Mr Prior and the Attorney-General who supported him, were optimistic. Prior cited the *United Biscuits* case where picketing had ceased following the injunction.[40] The Attorney-General relied

---

[38] [1964] AC 1129.
[39] [1976] IRLR 224 HL.
[40] OR St. Cttee. A 25th sitting (18 Mar. 1980) col. 1344.

on the *Duport Steels* case[41], where action declared unlawful by the Court of Appeal had ceased, pending appeal to the House of Lords.[42] Mr Gorst thought them too optimistic. If a swarm of bees descends, he argued, one must not just swat one or two, but go for the hive: 'If the bees are deprived of their honey, they will take notice. They will not come back.'[43] In other words, repeal of section 14 would not merely provide a *remedy*, it would also provide a *deterrent* against unlawful action. Mr Gorst pointed out that this would equally apply to disobedience of injunctions, which would also carry the threat of pecuniary loss.[44] Others supported him, emphasizing that the move towards a narrower immunity required a reconsideration of the remedies necessary to support it.[45] Mr Mayhew for the Government repeated the view that the new law would be effectively enforceable as it stood, and argued that, to the extent that there were difficulties, repeal of section 14 would create as many problems as it solved.[46] As for going for the 'hive', he perhaps tellingly remarked, 'I can think of no better way of getting stung.'[47] Government speakers therefore sought to play down and deflect this issue chiefly by arguing that the problem would not arise, or that it was not relevant to the 'primary' remedy of injunction.[48] Indeed, evaluation of the section 14 protection as relevant only to damages claims was very common at the time.[49] Knowing of Mr Prior's attitude to the experience of the IRA, however, it is hard to believe that he placed much weight on these two arguments alone. Two further arguments, however, seem to have resolved him against tampering with section 14.[50]

First, the enforcement of injunctions against unions, rather than individuals, was evidently thought to involve political problems of its own. The main argument for enforcement against the union was that it had a proven effectiveness as a deterrent, when compared with the 'martyrdom' of individuals. This was stressed at the time by, for example, Sir Leonard Neal, drawing on his own experience of the IRA period.[51] But no one argued that

---

[41] [1980] ICR 161.

[42] OR St. Cttee. A 25th sitting (18 Mar. 1980) col. 1356. In fact compliance amounted to replacing ISTC pickets with those from other unions: see Hartley *et al.* (1983: pp. 34, 72, and 74).

[43] OR St. Cttee. A 27th sitting (20 Mar. 1980) col. 1468.

[44] Ibid.

[45] Ibid. col. 1475 Mr Wolfson.

[46] Ibid. 28th sitting (25 Mar. 1980) col. 1485–6.

[47] Ibid. col. 1487.

[48] See e.g. Mr Mayhew ibid. col. 1490: the question of exposure of union funds was 'quite irrelevant' when the plaintiff seeks an injunction.

[49] See e.g. Lewis and Simpson's (1981: p. 196) comment that 'Given the efficacy of the labour injunction against union officials, it seems probable that employers would gain a significant advantage from being able to sue trade unions in tort only if they wished to pursue claims for damages.'

[50] A later amendment similarly removing s. 14 in relation to the secondary-action clause was also resisted. See OR HC vol. 982 col. 1504 (17 Apr. 1980).

[51] See his article in the *Daily Telegraph* (17 Apr. 1980) and letter to *The Times* (31 Mar. 1980); see too the article by Sir W. Goldsmith of the I.o.D. in the *Guardian* (30 June 1980).

to sequestrate a union's assets would not be *politically* controversial. Mr Prior appeared to conclude that 'martyrdom' of individuals—if it came to that[52]—was in this respect the lesser of the two evils:

I had fought to prevent [making the union liable], as once again it would have risked taking us back to the 1971 Act in which unions were made liable for their members' actions: I feared that it could become the cement of union solidarity. In my legislation I was seeking new ways to avoid bringing the unions into the courts, which would quickly bring to the fore emotive questions of solidarity and loyalty (1986: p. 159).

To add force to this position, Prior recognized the enormous symbolic importance of the immunity, for to tamper with it would in the union movement's eyes be seen as a return to the law of *Taff Vale*, a case of perhaps greater symbolic significance to the movement than any other.[53] Thus, the very act of changing the law in this respect would itself be a highly controversial and provocative step, which would hardly fit well into Mr Prior's overall strategy. The Government also indicated in these debates its proposed solution to the procedural problems raised in the consultations. The consistent advice was to sue the *organizers* of picketing, rather than individual pickets, whereby it was argued that such problems as there might be regarding identification and rotation of pickets could be overcome.[54] Prior successfully resisted all attempts to toughen up the picketing clause, but there was a further ground on which another battle in the war with the right wing of his party was to be waged: the code of practice.

### (d) The Code of Practice

As has been seen, Prior had long been persuaded of the virtues of the code of practice approach to picketing problems, the example by which he was most taken being that of the NUM in 1974. Initially he sought to persuade the TUC to issue a code, taking the line that while their 1979 code was inadequate, particularly as it did not proscribe flying pickets outright, nevertheless the Government would only issue its own code 'if no other authoritative, comprehensive and effective guidance is available'. In the mean time it would introduce the necessary enabling powers.[55]

In drawing up his proposals, Prior was able to draw on an ample body of precedent in relation both to the code's legal status and to its content. Precedents for statutory codes started with the broad-ranging code issued in

[52] For the IPM's proposal for avoiding 'martyrdom' by making attachment of earnings the primary mode of enforcement, see *Personnel Management* (April 1980: p. 5).

[53] See OR St. Cttee. A 28th sitting (25 Mar. 1980) col. 1491 Mr Mayhew, and Mr Prior's subsequent Green Paper (DE 1981a: para. 53).

[54] See e.g. OR St. Cttee. A 25th sitting (18 Mar. 1980) cols. 1329 and 1344 Mr Prior. Once again the *United Biscuits* case provided a handy example.

[55] See e.g. OR HC vol. 976 cols. 61 and 66 (17 Dec. 1979). The powers created in 1980 were of course also used to introduce a code on the closed shop, to which the Government appeared committed from the outset. On the new code on industrial action ballots, see ch. 9 below.

conjunction with the IRA 1971.[56] This was to be drafted by the Secretary of State, but required an affirmative resolution of both Houses of Parliament to become operational. Although it did not itself have the force of law, its provisions were admissible in evidence, and had to be taken account of, in any relevant court or tribunal proceedings.[57] These provisions were to be operated in the light of section 1 of the Act which set out the 'guiding principles' to which all those involved in its operation were to have regard. Section 2(2) elaborated further on matters to which the Secretary of State was to have regard when drawing up the code itself. The 1971 code was therefore closely integrated into the operation of the IRA and the implementation of its underlying policies. With this may be contrasted the codes issued by ACAS under section 6 EPA 1975. The mode of origination and legal status of these are similar to those of the 1972 code, but they are to be taken into account only in proceedings of tribunals or the Central Arbitration Committee (CAC). More importantly, ACAS itself was deliberately established as an independent institution, not merely of each side of industry, but especially of Government.[58] It was subject to no guiding principles beyond the broad injunction to promote the improvement of industrial relations and development of collective bargaining.[59]

Mr Prior opted for something in between the two. Codes were to be issued by the Secretary of State with approval of both Houses of Parliament. We noted that the working paper discussed the value which a code might have in promoting uniformity of enforcement, and the clause predictably provided that the code would be relevant in court as well as in other types of proceeding, as had also been mooted in Labour's own consultative paper.[60] Others doubted whether the code would have the 'considerable moral force' which the working paper claimed. The I.o.D., for example, urged that:

there is no virtue in any code of practice . . . without the authority of the law behind it, and . . . the status in law the Government believes such a code would have . . . would in practice be negligible (1979a: para. 34).

A similar view was expressed by the Centre for Policy Studies (CPS) which rushed out a publication while the codes were being finalized entitled *Give the Picketing Code the Sanction of Law* (CPS 1980a).[61]

A further objection from this lobby attached to the possible involvement of ACAS. We have noted Mr Prior's hope that ACAS might participate in the drafting of codes, no doubt adding to their 'considerable moral force'.[62] The

---

[56] IRA 1971 s. 2. Parts of the code remain in force.

[57] Ibid. s.4.

[58] EPA 1975 s. 1 and sch. 1, pt. 1.

[59] Ibid. s. 1(2). Cf. text to n. 63 below.

[60] See n. 6 above.

[61] The arguments re-emerged in CPS (1980b: pp. 7–14).

[62] He argued that the Government wished to 'restore' ACAS's reputation for impartiality. See OR HC vol. 976 cols. 69–70 (17 Dec. 1979).

I.o.D. was hostile to the suggestion, arguing that the inclusion of the promotion of collective bargaining in its terms of reference meant that ACAS was not an impartial body (1979a: paras. 9 and 35). ACAS, however, saw things differently, and declined to assist in the drafting of a code as it did not wish to risk its highly valued reputation for impartiality.[63] On this point Prior was hamstrung: his own terms of reference in preparing the code referred to the promotion of good industrial relations, but not to collective bargaining. In the context of a Bill which also repealed the recognition procedure and schedule 11 of EPA 1975, the Government rejected amendments to insert a mention of collective bargaining into the clause, although unwilling to remove the mention from ACAS's terms of reference.[64]

Turning to the content of the code, there were a number of available sources to plunder including not least the codes of the NUM, TGWU, and TUC. We have seen the attractions for the Government of recommendations of small numbers, sections dealing with the policing of picket lines by union officials, and the preservation of essential services and supplies, as well as the virtues seen in a simple statement of the limits of the—particularly criminal—law. All these matters gained a mention in Prior's code. In drawing up the content, however, he faced pressures exerted from two important lobbies. As we have seen, many politically to the right of Prior urged tougher laws on picketing and that any code itself be given the force of law. Although unwilling to respond directly to these demands, he was nevertheless able to show more sympathy towards this lobby in devising the content of the code itself. In a publication following the code's introduction, the CPS acknowledged its satisfaction on this point (1980b: p. 2).

Many chiefs of police, however, lobbied strongly the other way. Members of the ACPO made clear in evidence to the Select Committee on Employment that they were not about to yield up their discretionary powers in these matters, and resented the idea that the Code might be addressed to the police as well as others.[65] Their role had once again come under scrutiny as a result of the steel dispute in early 1980. As steel unions sought to increase pressure on the Government by extending the dispute to the private sector, flying and mass pickets re-emerged onto the scene. The culmination was a mass picket at the Hadfields steel company on St Valentine's Day. Events were all too reminiscent both of Saltley and the winter of discontent.[66] Once again the police opted for a strategy of restraint, one which was subsequently articulately and convincingly defended by the local Chief Constable.[67] Not all police opinion was the same. The Police Federation, representing more junior ranking officers, thought that express criminal controls on numbers on picket lines might be introduced, but nevertheless re-emphasized and

---

[63] See ACAS (1981: p. 9).

[64] See OR St. Cttee. A 5th sitting (7 Feb. 1980) col. 219.

[65] See Select Committee on Employment (1980a).

[66] A resemblance not lost on Prior (1986: p. 161).

[67] See Brownlow (1980) and his evidence to the Select Committee on Employment (1980a).

defended the importance of police discretion in enforcing any law.[68] Among senior police officers only Sir David McNee appeared to seek greater police powers in relation to mass and secondary picketing.[69]

Mr Prior for his part held fast to the commitment to leave the police to do their own job, and to steer clear of changes in the criminal law; but it was a close run thing. Mrs Thatcher was dissuaded from rushing through legislation on picketing, in favour of repeating the winter of discontent strategy of having the Attorney-General make a statement reminding one and all of the comprehensiveness of existing laws.[70] Government speakers acknowledged that the text of the speech would form the subject of a Home Office circular to Chief Constables.[71] Prior meantime urged the TUC to reissue a code of practice. The TUC, however, declined[72] and it seems to be at this point that the Government resolved firmly to issue its own code, for references to it cease thereafter to be 'conditional'. When it came to the publication of the code, this whole debate seemed to focus around one issue in particular: the inclusion in the draft code of the notorious edict that numbers on a picket should not exceed what is reasonably needed for peaceful persuasion—which would rarely be more than six.[73] Chief police officers giving evidence to the select committee took particular exception to this threat to police discretion. Prior, however, set much store by this feature—which appeared to have been crucial to the success of the NUM code in 1974—and retained the express figure in the final code, although toning down its status.[74] Other alterations stressed police discretion, and that the code did not in any way affect this.[75] The steel dispute already mentioned revived and stoked the fires of the picketing debate—and it drew it even closer together with that on the other key issue to which we may now turn: that of secondary action.

*(e) Secondary Action*

As in 1976, Mr Prior's hopes that he would not have to propose measures on secondary action were to be frustrated. Although the Court of Appeal added

---

[68] See *Police* (May 1980: pp. 14 and 16). A clause suggested by the Federation was tabled in the Commons but rejected by the Government. See OR HC vol. 983 col. 1463 (13 Apr. 1980).

[69] See McNee (1980: pp. 41 ff.), submissions made in the context of the public-order law debate then getting under way.

[70] See OR HC vol. 979 col. 238 (19 Feb. 1980).

[71] Ibid. col. 244; further on the Government's strategy, see *Guardian* (19 Feb. 1980).

[72] See OR HC vol. 979 col. 225 (19 Feb.1980). On the TUC's reasons for declining the request, see TUC (1981c: p. 21).

[73] See para. 30 of the draft code reproduced in 167 *IRLIB* p. 3 26 Aug. 1980. Six was the number mentioned in the NUM Code of 1974, that of the official APEX picket at Grunwick, and that of the average picket in 1979–80 at single entrance sites surveyed by Daniel and Millward (1983: p. 247).

[74] The code became operative on 17 Dec. 1980—see SI 1980/1757.

[75] See code of practice: Picketing (1980), esp. para. 28, also paras. 27 and 33. Prior responded specifically to pressure from the ACPO on this point. See Prior (1980: paras. 6–8).

more strings to its bow in April 1979 in *ANG* v. *Wade*[76], the House of Lords held in the *MacShane*[77] case that the test of whether an act was in contemplation or furtherance of a trade dispute was a purely subjective one. The decision effectively overruled the key Court of Appeal cases on this point, although certain of their Lordships clearly had considerable sympathy with Lord Denning's approach.[78] The decision was handed down just after publication of the Employment Bill. At the second reading debate Mr Prior told the Commons that the Government would consider the case and if necessary bring forward further proposals.[79]

Less than a month later the steel strike was under way, the action soon spreading to steel firms in the private sector. A number of private firms swiftly applied for injunctions, but failed in the High Court. However, the Court of Appeal, led by Lord Denning, granted the injunctions the next day, notwithstanding the decision in *MacShane*. The House of Lords reversed this on 7 February, rebuking Lord Denning and affirming *MacShane* in even stronger terms. Once again, however, some of their Lordships expressed great regret at the present state of the law and hinted that Parliament might now see fit to intervene.[80] Mr Prior has related how the events of this dispute, rekindling concerns over both secondary action and mass picketing, placed him under intense pressure to rush through special legislation, or at the very least to introduce proposals to ban all secondary action outright. In the event he was able to avoid both courses, in part by suggesting that the much talked of 'review' of the law on immunities should be elevated to the status of a Green Paper to follow the Bill (Prior 1986: p. 169). His immediate proposals were published five days after the incidents at Hadfields, on 19 February.[81] Mr Prior was not shy about the source of his inspiration: 'Actually, what we are trying to do in this proposal is to frame the law very much along the judgements of Lord Denning in the Court of Appeal' (Select Committee on Employment 1980*b*: para. 17). In fact, the proposals followed Lord Denning precisely, in the suggestion that action be permitted in so far as it affected 'first customers and suppliers' but no further.[82] Mr Prior believed 'that anything more restrictive at that stage simply would not stick. How could one realistically expect the law to prevent people on strike from trying to black or disrupt supplies to or from their company?' (1986: pp. 161–2).

[76] [1979] ICR 664.

[77] [1980] ICR 42—decision handed down on 13 Dec. 1979.

[78] See Lord Wilberforce, who alone thought that there was an objective element in furtherance, although agreeing with the other Law Lords on the outcome [1980] ICR 56A–C; Lord Diplock 57F–G; Lord Keith 62H–63B.

[79] OR HC vol. 976 col. 68 (17 Dec. 1979).

[80] *Duport Steels Ltd.* v. *Sirs* [1980] ICR 161. Lord Diplock at 184G; Lord Edmund-Davies at 186E; Lord Keith at 188F–189C.

[81] Coverage in the press of 20 Feb. 1980 demonstrates how these proposals were perceived as a further response to the 'picketing problem'.

[82] See the text of the proposals in *The Times* (20 Feb. 1980: paras. 18 and 19).

How might such a restriction be given legal effect? The Court of Appeal had proceeded by narrowly interpreting the 'golden formula', but their decisions showed the difficulty of establishing a single or clear legal test. Furthermore, Prior's concern to get the degree of restriction just right dictated that the appropriate measure be more precise. The working paper emphasized that '[p]eople need to know with greater certainty than that when and in what circumstances they are to be deprived of their rights to protect themselves.'[83] Amendment of the golden formula did not look like the most promising approach. Nor, however, would a simple return to 1974 be satisfactory: to restrict immunity to interference only with contracts of employment would strike at some, if not all, first customer or supplier action.

The 'SLADE' clause however set a more promising precedent. The sanction for the action to be proscribed could still be withdrawal of immunity. Here it seemed quite clear that the common law could be relied upon to provide a remedy.[84] The action in question would be defined specifically by reference to the *contracts*, interference with which is contemplated by TULRA section 13(1): protection would extend to employment contracts, and the commercial contracts made with first customers and suppliers, but not beyond.[85] Finally an 'objective element' would be introduced, requiring that action be reasonably capable of furthering the trade dispute in question and taken predominantly for that reason. This would ensure that first customers and suppliers could not simply be gratuitously attacked. In addition it was suggested that immunity should only extend to first customers and suppliers 'who regularly conduct a substantial part of their business with' the primary employer. Such parties, argued the paper, 'may be said to be commercially affected by the outcome of the dispute'.[86] The implied reasoning was that such parties could not be regarded as wholly 'extraneous' and hence 'innocent'.[87] The addition of this test narrowed even further the circumstances in which first customers or suppliers could be regarded as legitimate targets of action, making the working paper's approach perhaps narrower than that of the Court of Appeal. Finally, the working paper announced the Government's intention to publish a Green Paper 'later this year'.[88]

---

[83] Proposals on Secondary Action (para. 13).

[84] The Government appeared to contemplate an action for breach of or interference with commercial contract, brought by either party to the contract: para. 19. In fact, for secondary employers to sue, this assumed a point not confirmed until *Dimbleby* v. *NUJ* [1984] IRLR 161.

[85] Proposals on Secondary Action (paras. 17–19). The perceived mischief of 1976 had been that it was the extension of protection to action which disrupted *commercial* contracts, which had facilitated a spreading of frictional disruption. Thus, under the 1980 proposals, action which attacked commercial contracts was again the target, and even secondary employers would not thereby be permitted to sue, if *only* their employment contracts were interfered with. This was to change in 1990, as is described in ch. 9 below.

[86] Ibid. para. 18.

[87] Cf. the test of 'extraneous' parties in IRA 1971 s. 98.

[88] Proposals on Secondary Action (para. 21).

The overall picture is of a now well-defined conception of secondary action, fashioned out of a more general concern by immediate political factors. It embodied both an anxiety over disruption, and a view about the legitimate goals of industrial action. It took up the arguments in documents such as the TUC guide annexed to the concordat, that pressure directed at the primary employer was legitimate and necessary; but it turned those arguments to its own advantage by then putting beyond the pale any action which did not have such aims.[89] In particular, sympathy action aimed 'outwardly' at putting pressure on the Government would be unprotected.[90] Politically, the TUC and Labour Party had been reluctant to focus their case on such action, yet it was particularly action of this type which had aroused Conservative concerns in 1979 and 1980. To be able to strike at that, the first customer and supplier concession might seem to the Government to be an acceptable price to pay. Nevertheless, the fact that the proposal tried to define both proper objectives and acceptable disruption created formidable problems.

General reaction to the working paper was along the lines of the picketing responses, with broad support coming from the main employers' organizations and some, notably small employers, also urging that secondary action be outlawed altogether—an argument led by the I.o.D. (1980: para. 4). This said, their response went on to make a series of detailed points on the mechanics of the proposals. First, if a secondary employer could sue for breach of his commercial contracts but not for breach of his employment contracts, the union might be tempted to initiate a primary dispute at the secondary employer's premises. Thus it was argued that unions would have an incentive to start fresh full-scale strikes where previously they had no dispute. The I.o.D. therefore urged the Government 'to state unequivocally . . . that interference with a commercial contract should not be immune simply on the grounds that the interference took the form of interference with a contract of employment' (para. 9).

Secondly, any commercial contracts, interference with which was to be protected, should be clearly stated to be contracts to which the employer engaged in the dispute was a party, or the protection might still go wider than first customers and suppliers, notwithstanding the objective tests (para. 10). Thirdly, the requirement that the secondary employer conduct a substantial part of its business with the primary employer was too lax, as a dispute at a large firm could lead to a whole range of small firms with which the large firm did only a tiny part of *its* business experiencing industrial action. Nor, however, would the reverse test do, because then disputes at small firms might generate industrial action at much larger firms 'out of all

---

[89] Cf. the TUC code in DE (1979: para. 9). Prior described the clause later added to the Bill as 'related directly to the recognised purposes of secondary action': OR HC vol. 982 col. 1490 (17 Apr. 1980).
[90] Cf. the analysis in Davies and Freedland (1984a: pp. 830–42).

proportion to the seriousness of the dispute'. The I.o.D. concluded that both tests must be used, each of the employers regularly conducting a substantial part of their business with the other (para. 11). Other organizations also criticized this aspect of the proposal, and suggested how it might be improved.[91]

The responses in general illustrated the immense difficulties which the Government faced in translating its objectives into a clear and precise measure.[92] The new clause to the bill, tabled on 17 April 1980,[93] followed the lines anticipated by the working paper, but took up a number of the suggestions made in the consultations. It made clear that if interference with commercial contracts was to be protected, then the primary employer must be a party to those contracts. It also abandoned the 'substantial part of business' test altogether in favour of a requirement that action be specifically aimed at a subsisting contract between primary and secondary employers. Other provisions not foreshadowed in the working paper dealt with associated employers, and with picketing, and repealed TULRA section 13(3). The clause did not, however, pursue the idea, put forward in the working paper, that objective tests should apply to *all* forms of industrial action. This is understandable as the chief aim of such tests had always been to restrict secondary action. To require *primary* action to fulfil an objective test was superfluous to the Government's aims. The policy was to be that *MacShane* was to remain good law, and primary action entirely unaffected by the clause.

In its general mechanics, the clause followed closely on the precedent of the SLADE clause. In reply to an amendment, Lord Mackay explained in very similar terms how the operation of the clause revolved around identifying a particular commercial contract of the plaintiff, and making available a claim relating to it on one of the grounds mentioned in section 13(1). In addition, it thus formed the method in sub-section (6) of narrowing the test of the business relation necessary for secondary action to be justified.[94] There are a number of specific issues concerning the operation of what became section 17 which we can consider. In order to apply the section it is necessary to identify both the primary employer and the nature of the commercial relations between those affected by a piece of action. These features create scope for much capriciousness in the operation of the section, and for avoidance tactics by either employers or workers. How far did the

---

[91] See e.g. the EEF's letter to Mr Prior of 20 Mar. 1980 commenting that the test proposed had been 'almost universally and strongly criticised'.

[92] *The Times* (19 Feb. 1980) suggested that, before even the working paper was out, the draftsman had gone through more than fifteen different versions of the clause.

[93] See OR HC vol. 982 col. 1483 (17 Apr. 1980). On the proposed revision of the law in this area in 1990, see ch. 9 below.

[94] OR HL vol. 110 col. 728 (12 June 1980). As was implicit in the working paper, even the secondary employer would have to rely on disruption to a commercial contract. Honeyball (1989: at pp. 107–8) points out that the use of contract in s. 17 was not essentially integral to its objectives, but fails to identify the main reason for its use, namely the *certainty* which it was believed it would provide.

Government anticipate, and how far seek to deal with, some of these problems? We can ask a number of questions in turn.

Can workers avoid the section by declaring a new primary dispute with what would otherwise have been a secondary employer? This was the issue raised by the I.o.D. The Government felt that this tactic could not in any general way be guarded against. It argued that it was therefore particularly important to allow realistic exemptions in the clause, for were it too stringent, unions might pursue a wholesale strategy of avoidance in this way.[95] The key case for which provision was made was that in which custom or supplies are deliberately transferred to an associated company of the primary employer. The clause would allow for the associated company then to be treated as though it were the primary employer itself. Mr Prior argued that without such a provision a group of companies could act deliberately so as to 'nullify the effect of the action at one company' and avoid secondary action. He warned that in the absence of such a protection, the associated employer would surely 'attract' a primary dispute.[96]

The grant of this specific protection prompts the question as to whether associated employers ought generally to have been treated as one for the purposes of this provision. Under the unamended TULRA regime the Court of Appeal had been prepared sometimes to look at the substance rather than the form of such situations;[97] but such an approach to section 17 was firmly rejected by the House of Lords in *Dimbleby* v. *NUJ*,[98] where action against a plaintiff whose only commercial contract was with an associated company of the primary employer was held not to comply with section 17. As a matter of interpretation on this specific point, the case appears to have been rightly decided. Prior had himself stressed that the associated employer exemption was to be strictly limited.

The subsection does not . . . provide, as some have mistakenly believed, for the automatic extension of secondary action to any employer who is associated with the employer in dispute.[99]

The debates also considered the position of the sort of action typically involved in the ITF's campaign against 'flags of convenience'. Prior relates that some cabinet members wanted the campaign outlawed,[100] fearing that otherwise foreign ships might be deterred from entering British ports. He states that for his part he was more concerned about the effect on British seafarers of the availability of cheap foreign crews (1986: p. 162). He argued

[95]   OR HL vol. 410 col. 718 (12 June 1980) Lord Gowrie. The effectiveness of this technique to 'manufacture' a trade dispute has since been doubted in *Universe Tankships* v. *ITF* [1983] 1 AC 366.

[96]   OR HC vol. 982 cols. 1491–4 (17 Apr. 1980).

[97]   See *Examite* v. *Whittaker* [1977] IRLR 312 and *Porr* v. *Shaw* [1979] 2 Lloyds Reps 331.

[98]   [1984] IRLR 161.

[99]   OR HC vol. 989 col. 1207 (28 July 1980). The context makes clear that this covered secondary action both aimed at and taken against an associated employer.

[100]   Its legality having been confirmed in *NWL* v. *Woods* [1979] ICR 867 HL.

that dockers or tugboat employees who blacked ships operating flags of convenience would be employed by the ships' first customers or suppliers, and their action would therefore remain lawful under section 17.[101] Such action was however held outwith section 17 and unlawful in the *Marina* and *Merkur Island Shipping* cases.[102] Contrary to Prior's prediction, intermediate contracts existed, rendering the action too remote from the target dispute. These cases may therefore have been rightly decided as a matter of law, although they reveal that section 17 failed to reflect the expressed intentions of its proponent with regard to this particular type of action.

These cases illustrate the more general problem which was created by the possible existence of intermediate contracts between the primary employer and the main customer/supplier. In *Marina*, for example, the legality of the action turned on whether agents had hired port authority services on their own or on the shipowners' behalf—a point on which there was no explicit evidence. The debates show that the Government did not wish to protect action which struck at an intermediate contractor, where this simply happened to be the nature of the commercial arrangements between primary employer and immediate target. To this extent it was prepared to accept some risk of capriciousness in operation, although given its stated views on the position of the ITF campaign, it seems not to have appreciated the extent of the risk in that particular type of case.

The question then arises as to whether *deliberate* avoidance of the clause by creation of intermediate contracting arrangements was anticipated. This might in theory be achieved by the deliberate organization of commercial relations between either associated or unassociated companies. Thus, in the *News International* dispute of 1986–7 it was suggested that 'buffer companies' were deliberately established so as to avoid section 17, demonstrating the ease with which a 'chain' may be set up between associated companies,[103] while in *Shipping Uniform Inc.* v. *ITF*,[104] the charterers were specifically instructed to hire port authority services on their own and not on the shipowners' behalf.

As for associated companies, the attention given to other problems which they raised, suggests that this one may have also been recognized in 1980. When this issue arose again in 1982, the Government argued that it was not 'a serious possibility' that corporate structures would be altered deliberately in order to meet the possibility of future secondary action, and that it would be

[101] OR St. Cttee. A 25th sitting (18 Mar. 1980) col. 1317.

[102] *Marina Shipping* v. *Laughton* [1982] ICR 215 CA; *Merkur Island Shipping Corp.* v. *Laughton* [1983] 2 AC 570.

[103] See Ewing and Napier (1986: p. 300). In the seafarers' dispute of 1988, an existing corporate structure whereby a separate company within the P & O group operated at each affected port, resulted in the spreading of action from one port to another falling foul of s. 17; but this was arguably a case in which what might at an early stage have been 'secondary' employers, had, as matters developed, become parties to an entirely genuine primary dispute: see Auerbach (1988: pp. 234–5).

[104] [1985] ICR 245 QBD.

'not an easy business' to do so.[105] With post-Wapping hindsight we may be tempted to judge that statement more cynically than we ought. In all events, it seems less likely that the manipulation of commercial relations between *unassociated* employers, specifically to avoid industrial action, even if anticipated as a theoretical possibility, would have been regarded as a serious threat to the operation of the legislation. This is particularly as the later cases, which raise a suggestion that it was easily achieved, are of a kind in which the Government specifically argued that action would remain lawful. No doubt the political and practical constraints upon extending an already complex provision intended to effect clear and limited legislative change also played a part here. We have already noted one possible method of avoidance by *employees* which the Government recognized but felt that it could not completely legislate against. This factor is also important when considering the repeal of section 13(3) of TULRA 1974, which must be examined both within and beyond the context of section 17.

### (f) The Repeal of Section (13)3

Section 17(8) of EA 1980 simply repealed TULRA section 13(3). There was no disagreement between Government and Opposition speakers regarding the central goal behind this step, but the potential 'side-effects' were the subject of much dispute. The legal technicalities involved in that debate are of great theoretical complexity, and might with some justice be thought by non-lawyers to typify how the legal issues can become far abstracted from the social realities with which they are supposed to grapple. Nevertheless, the genesis of the provision is worth considering in some detail, both because it has been the subject of much controversy among labour lawyers, and because it in many respects typifies how the many different relevant considerations— legal, political, tactical, drafting, and so on—can interact to influence the final form of a particular provision in a technical and controversial area of the law. We need to start by considering the debate concerning both the principal and the side-effects of the provision. To do that we need first to go back to TULRA 1974.

We have seen how the key protection in section 13(1), covering interference with contracts, was in 1974 limited by Conservative amendments to apply only to contracts of employment. The aim was to ensure that secondary and more widespread forms of action remained unlawful. However, as Lord Wedderburn later showed, the actual result was rather more complex.[106] Direct interference with commercial contracts, such as by persuading a secondary employer to cease supplying to a primary employer, remained actionable. But if *indirect* interference were alleged, such as by persuading secondary employees to black a primary employer's goods, use of

---

[105] OR HL vol. 434 col. 602 (2 Aug. 1982) Lord Glenarthur.
[106] See Wedderburn (1974: pp. 541–3).

some unlawful means had to be shown.[107] But the most obvious source of unlawful means—the interference with the contracts of secondary employees—would not in fact be available. Such interference would, because of section 13(1), not of itself be actionable, and section 13(3)(*a*) stated that actions protected by section 13(1) could not be used as unlawful means in order to establish a liability in tort. Without any unlawful means, indirect interference of this type with commercial contracts therefore remained lawful, albeit that section 13(1) did not apply to such contracts. As we saw, in 1976 section 13(1) was amended to cover all contracts.[108] So both direct and indirect interference with commercial contracts became protected, the latter now enjoying dual protection, for section 13(3)(*a*) remained in force.

Section 17 aimed once again to attack certain types of secondary and more widespread industrial action, by relying principally on exposing it to liability for indirect interference with a commercial contract by use of the unlawful means of interference with secondary employment contracts. It was therefore necessary to ensure that the earlier error was not repeated, and that section 13(3) should not prevent the interference with employment contracts from providing the unlawful means in such a case.[109] Such was the line of reasoning which Government and Opposition agreed lay behind section 17(8). However, one element implicit in this reasoning needs to be spelled out at this point. The main premiss is that something needed to be done about section 13(3) in order to ensure that interference with employment contracts could now form unlawful means for the purpose of establishing another tort. It follows that it might not be sufficient to ensure that section 13(3) did not prevent this from being the case. One had also to be sure, or to make sure, that *nothing else prevented it as well*.

In fact there *was* another potential obstacle: section 13(1) itself. For it was arguable that the wording of section 13(1) *of itself* prevented actions which it protected from being available as unlawful means. However, conflicting judicial *dicta* left the status of this argument in law uncertain by 1974. The view that actions rendered legally non-actionable might nevertheless still form unlawful means for other purposes was chiefly associated with a *dictum* of Lord Pearce in *Stratford* v. *Lindley*,[110] and this view can conveniently be referred to hereafter as the Pearce doctrine. It was in case the Pearce doctrine was good law that section 13(3)(*a*) had originally been enacted 'for the avoidance of doubt'. The point here is that if it was assumed that removal of section 13(3) alone would ensure that the unlawful means became available, it must have been assumed that nothing else would obstruct its availability. In

---

[107] *Thomson* v. *Deakin* [1952] Ch. 646; the line between direct and indirect interference may not be clear. See e.g. *Stratford* v. *Lindley* [1965] AC 269.

[108] TULR(Am)A 1976 s. 3(2).

[109] The problem was noted in the working paper on secondary action (para. 5) and in DE (1980: paras. 18–22).

[110] [1965] AC 269, 336. There is also an issue as to whether 'not actionable' is limited to the primary employer, which need not be pursued here.

particular, it cannot have been thought that section 13(1) would do so. Whether or not the draftsman actually considered the relevance of the Pearce doctrine, it therefore follows that, given the agreed view of the purpose behind the repeal of section 13(3), *integral to the reasoning behind that view is an assumption that the Pearce doctrine is indeed good law*. The significance of this point will be explained shortly.

So far, the reasoning behind the need for section 17(8) which Government and Opposition seemed to share, has been taken as sound. But that reasoning must now be attacked, for section 17(8) was arguably not needed to achieve its agreed purpose at all. This argument turns on the opening words of section 17:

(1) Nothing in section 13 of the 1974 Act shall prevent an act from being actionable in tort on a ground specified in subsection (1)(a) or (b) of that section in any case where . . .

Although the only *torts* exposed by the section are those referred to in section 13(1), *nothing* in section 13 *as a whole* can prevent the elements of such a tort from being established.[111] So where section 17 applies to action, section 13(3) cannot be relied upon to prevent an interference with contract from being treated as unlawful means. In effect, section 13(3) is treated as if repealed for the purposes of actions permitted by section 17. It may be argued that this reasoning overlooks the words of section 17(1)(a) which stipulate that 'the contract concerned is not a contract of employment.' The argument would be that where the contract *is* a contract of employment, section 17 will not remove any protection relating to it. However, the words quoted refer to the contract, interference with which is alleged to constitute a tort on one of the grounds mentioned in section 13(1). This is indeed a commercial contract. The words cannot refer to the contract breach of which is said to amount to unlawful means. The reference is to 'the contract', and the commercial contract is the only one to which the words can be applied.[112]

So section 17(8) was not needed for the purpose for which it was apparently intended, for that purpose was already achieved by section 17(1). Indeed, section 17(1) achieves it rather better, because, unlike section 17(8), the effectiveness of section 17(1) in this regard is not affected by the legal status of the Pearce doctrine. This can be seen if we assume for a moment that the Pearce doctrine is bad law, that is, that something which is protected by section 13(1) cannot be treated as unlawful means. But if interference with secondary employment contracts is for some reason *not to be treated as protected by section 13(1) at all*, then it remains available as unlawful means. That is precisely the effect which is once again achieved by the opening words of section 17(1). For just as they ensure that section 13(3) cannot prevent the establishment of a section 13(1) tort in a case to which section 17 applies, so

---

[111] Accordingly it is submitted that Wedderburn (1982a: pp. 789, 793, and 798) is misleading in suggesting that ss. 17 and 18 do not affect the whole of s. 13.

[112] Cf. Sir Ian Percival's account of the operation of s. 18, discussed above.

do they equally ensure that section 13(1) itself cannot do so in such a case. It follows that even if the Pearce doctrine is bad law, section 13(1) still cannot be used to prevent interference with secondary employment contracts from being available as unlawful means. The debates give the impression that this point was entirely overlooked at the time, given the apparent common ground that some express treatment of section 13(3) *was* necessary to the general objectives of section 17.[113] We will return to this point in a moment. First we may turn to consider the debate over the alleged side-effects of the repeal.

Given the common (but apparently erroneous) view that it was necessary to do something about section 13(3) in order to achieve the Government's objectives in section 17, the Government argued for a simple repeal. It reasoned that when in 1976 section 13(1) protection was extended to all contracts, section 13(3) had become redundant. Section 13(1) was now alone sufficient to ensure that primary action which had the consequential effect of interfering with commmercial contracts, would be protected. However, the Opposition urged that repeal should be effected, if at all, only 'for the purposes of' section 17, or some similar suitable wording—ironically the very effect which it is suggested was already achieved by the wording of section 17(1). The Opposition feared that some primary action would otherwise become unlawful, something which the Government stated it had no wish to achieve. This fear was explained by Lord Wedderburn in House of Lords committee debates.[114] The argument, in essence, was as follows.

Expansion of section 13(1) had not rendered section 13(3) redundant. Indeed, section 13(3) was first introduced *alongside* a section 13(1) which covered all contracts. This was because section 13(3) had a wider aim than simply blocking a contract-based action which required unlawful means of the type to which it referred. It was there to block *any* liability in tort which required such means. In particular, the tort of interference with business by unlawful means gave a further potential cause of action to those who had business relations with a primary employer, which were interfered with as the result of a primary dispute. Even if such a person could not because of section 13(1) rely on interference with *contracts*, interference with business could still be pleaded. The only thing clearly frustrating this was section 13(3), which precluded use of the most obvious source of unlawful means: interference with primary employment contracts. If section 13(3) were repealed, defendants would have to trust to section 13(1) having that effect; but as we have seen, the Pearce doctrine suggested that section 13(1) could not safely be relied upon in this respect. So primary action would be put at risk.

The Government's short response to this was simple: there was no tort of interference with business by unlawful means, so the problem would not

---

[113] See Prior OR HC vol. 982 col. 1495 (17 Apr. 1980); Mayhew ibid. col. 1603.

[114] See OR HL vol. 410 cols. 671–8 (12 June 1980).

arise.[115] But like the status of the Pearce doctrine, this too was a controversial issue. The textbooks offered evidence, and Lord Wedderburn was able to cite case-law, demonstrating the existence of the tort.[116] In the Government's favour it might be argued that the textbook writers had done no more than identify certain common features of the existing, recognized torts and that *dicta*—mostly of Lord Denning MR—suggesting that there was an entirely separate general tort, were unsound. However finely balanced the arguments might or might not have been, the Opposition were bound to regard the Government's response as inadequate. Maybe it was right that no general tort existed, but the legality of primary action was at stake if it did. Given the cross-party consensus with regard to primary action, this was surely too big, and a quite unnecessary risk to take. Lord McCarthy pressed the Government with further amendments on this point but to no avail.[117]

To summarize so far. There were two questions regarding the existing law, the answers to which were uncertain or disputed, namely:

1.  Is the Pearce doctrine good law?; and
2.  Is there a general tort of interference with business by use of unlawful means?

The Government's position rested on the answer to (1) being 'yes' and that to (2) being 'no'. The Opposition argued that the answer to both questions was likely to be 'yes'. We should also note that the Government's answer to the first question was bound up with its view of how section 17 affected *both primary and secondary action*, a point to which we shall return.

Why did the Government decline to effect only a partial repeal of section 13(3) given the possibility, however remote, of the consequence to which the Opposition had drawn attention? Lord Hailsham, the Lord Chancellor, put the linked arguments for the Government's position. First, the tort alleged by the Opposition did not exist. Given this, and given that section 13(1) now protected contracts of all kinds, section 13(3) had become otiose. If this was wrong (which it was not) the problem would not in any case be solved simply by retaining section 13(3), for such a tort would pose a general threat to the whole structure of immunities of section 13, and really require a new immunity all of its own. Finally, if section 13(3) was left on the statute-book, the judges might be encouraged to experiment with the development of such a tort. 'Satan will find some mischief still for idle courts to do.'[118]

To make sense of these arguments it may be that one needs to step back from the process of pure legal analysis, and to take account of the Government's broad strategy in this area, and the political and practical constraints upon the options open to it. For it is ultimately a political decision which we are seeking to explain, and that decision would have been

[115] See OR HL vol. 410 cols. 678 ff.
[116] See e.g. Davies and Freedland (1979: pp. 608–10); *Carlin Music* v. *Collins* [1979] FSR 548.
[117] See OR HL vol. 411 cols. 1140 ff. (8 July 1980).
[118] Ibid. col. 1141.

influenced by a consideration of the political as well as the legal implications which different approaches entailed. From this perspective one can envisage how the problem may have been viewed. The reasoning might be as follows:

Sections 17 and 18 both aim to impose partial restrictions in a very clear and precise way. The basic technique is to define the action to be restricted by reference to the contractual relations between the various parties involved, in the belief that such relations are usually well defined and easily identifiable, and that they are the focus of operation of the major economic torts which industrial action usually involves, and which are covered by TULRA section 13(1). That approach will, however, be undermined if other torts which do not turn on contractual relations, and which are not covered by section 13 protections, become recognized and are pleaded by plaintiffs. That is, sections 17 and 18 can only operate in the precise manner intended, if the grounds referred to in section 13(1) are the only ones on which plaintiffs can and do rely. As Lord Hailsham put it 'If it [the alleged tort] is not validated by subsections (1) and (2) [of section 13] it cannot have anything to do *with contract or with this clause.*'[119]

Theoretically, one could introduce new immunities guarding against the development of new torts, such as a general tort of interference with business by unlawful means. Indeed, as has been noted, Lord Hailsham suggested that this would be the most proper response if such a tort already existed. But one can imagine that such a course would be a political impossibility for a Government elected on a promise to reduce what it regarded as the excessive privileges enjoyed by trade unions. Having ruled out this possibility, one must then weigh up the possible effects of a partial or alternatively a complete repeal of section 13(3) alone. If development of new torts was a general risk which could not wholly be guarded against, then in addition to ensuring that amendments operated correctly with respect to the torts already dealt with by section 13, the best course might be to stress that the most important torts associated with industrial action, and those on which attention should concentrate, were those mentioned in section 13(1). Mr Mayhew, for example, observed that: 'Section 13 will continue to protect the acts specified therein, which are the acts that workers and their trade union officials are likely to commit in pursuit of a trade dispute with their own employer.'[120] If this was indeed the view taken of the risks involved in a full repeal, what were seen as the alternative risks of a partial repeal? It is here that Lord Hailsham's final argument comes in, namely that a partial repeal might be seen as legislative support for the view that the business means tort existed and was legitimate. This could only fortify plaintiffs' counsel, and in turn the judiciary, in pursuing the development of the tort in ways which might undermine the delicate structures of sections 17 and 18 altogether. The uncertainty regarding possible judicial reaction to a partial repeal was

[119] Ibid. col. 1142 (emphasis supplied).
[120] OR HC vol. 982 col. 1603 (17 Apr. 1980).

compounded by the fact that the provision was expressed to be 'for the avoidance of doubt'.[121]

Given these uncertainties, and the political impossibility of granting fresh immunities, one might be able to make some sense of (even if one did not agree with) the view that on balance less risk would be involved if the provocative provision were simply repealed altogether, and attention focused on the more conventional torts. It was such a view which it is suggested must have lain behind Mr Mayhew's comment to the Commons that the Government had itself considered a 'for the purposes' repeal, but rejected it: 'we decided not only that that was unnecessary, but that it would involve a complex provision which might remove the immunity for some primary action.'[122] Indeed, the Government seemed also to have another concern about how a partial repeal would be treated by the courts, namely that they might go the other way, and develop its effect as an immunity.[123] Before dismissing such fears as too fanciful, one should consider the examples of the courts arguing in both kinds of way in cases decided since 1980.

An example of the court developing the torts by reference to the immunities occurred in *Merkur Island Shipping* v. *Laughton*.[124] In *Torquay Hotel* v. *Cousins*[125] the suggestion was made that 'interference' with contract short of any actionable breach may be tortious. This was widely criticized as bad law and policy, but to guard against the doctrine, section 13(1) of TULRA covered interference with contracts as well as breaches.[126] In the *Merkur* case Lord Diplock cited section 13(1) as proof of the existence of the cause of action and approved the decision in *Torquay Hotel* on this point.[127] So a provision designed to guard against a particular development helped to encourage it. An example of the courts expanding an immunity in an unpredicted way may be found in the story of the repeal of section 13(2), which is told in chapter five.

In judging the intent behind section 17(8), we should not therefore automatically reject possible explanations of it simply because some of the legal assumptions involved are open to challenge. Rather, we should consider the range of plausible political explanations of the chosen approach. From that point of view one cannot conclude that the Government was insincere in its expressed view at this time that it was right that primary action should continue to be protected.

So far it has been argued that section 17(8) seemed to serve not one but two purposes. The first is the agreed purpose of ensuring that section 17 'worked'

---

[121] Cf. the comment of Henry J in *Barretts & Baird* v. *IPCS* [1987] IRLR 3, para. 63 that 'Philosophers may delight at the implications of the repeal of a provision passed "for the avoidance of doubt", but there is no pleasure for those who must grapple with doubt reborn.'

[122] OR HC vol. 982 col. 1603 (17 Apr. 1980).

[123] OR HL vol. 410 col. 680 (12 June 1980).

[124] [1983] 2 AC 570.

[125] [1969] 2 Ch. 106 (CA).

[126] Although this was also a change only made in TULR(Am)A 1976 s. 3(2).

[127] [1983] 2 AC 570, 608E.

properly by exposing, where it was thought appropriate, an effective action for indirect interference with commercial contracts. The second is the wider purpose of removing a provision which, if only amended, might encourage the courts to undermine the carefully devised framework of section 17 and indeed section 18. It has also been argued that section 17(8) was in fact not needed to achieve the first purpose. Should we go on to conclude that the only real aim of section 17(8) was the second one? Two arguments might favour this view. First, it may seem hard to believe that the effect of the opening words of section 17(1) was overlooked, especially as those words appear to have been carefully chosen in preference to a simple removal of section 13(1) protection. Secondly, section 13(3) was also a potential obstacle to the operation of section 18, if the 'target' employer wished to sue, for he would wish to rely on interference with his commercial contracts by the unlawful means of interference with the primary employer's employment contracts. In fact the opening words of section 18 again solve the problem in the same way as they do with section 17. The argument would therefore be that the Government must have realized this, or it would have thought it necessary to deal expressly with section 13(3) in drafting what became section 18. If it realized that the opening words rendered this unnecessary in relation to section 18, it must have realized the same thing when using the same words in section 17.

There are a number of points to be made in response to such arguments. First, no one on Government or Opposition sides ever alluded to this effect of the opening words of sections 17 and 18. If the Government indeed recognized it, one might have expected it to point it out, rather than arguing as it did that specific treatment of section 13(3) was needed to make section 17 work. Secondly, it is suggested that the choice of opening words was indeed deliberate, but has a more general explanation, the approach being that, once the cause of action had been defined, there was no reason why the action proscribed should enjoy any immunity at all, and that in a general sense it was advisable for all possible obstacles to be removed. But this need not imply a specific and well-developed concern with section 13(3). Indeed, the wording was also used in the picketing clause (section 16) and later in section 10 of the Trade Union Act 1984, which made immunity conditional upon balloting, a section which also applies only to specified causes of action.[128]

Turning to section 18, it is suggested that the threat which section 13(3) posed to its operation may itself easily have been overlooked. We may recall that historically the section 13(3) problem had been identified and explored in the context of secondary action, and even there had not been understood by the Conservative Opposition in 1974. The clause which became section 18 was introduced at a point when the 1979 Government believed that it might yet escape having to legislate on the matter of secondary action. As we have seen, its working paper on picketing revealed that its thoughts on how it

[128] See the discussion in ch. 7 below.

might tackle that task if it had to were then still at an early stage of development. Sir Ian Percival's account of the operation of what became section 18 is also consistent with the view that the Government overlooked both section 13(3)'s relevance to section 18, and the effect of the opening words upon it.

Even if when it came to section 17, the relevance of the opening words in this context was recognized, the Government may have been unwilling to rely on this argument alone. What was crucial after all was how the clause would be applied by a court. It might have been thought too hazardous to rely on a court to spot the relevance of the words, and correctly follow through their effect, on top of having to apply the rest of the section. The Opposition did not appear to notice the point. If the Government noticed it but were unhappy about relying upon it, this would give it a reason not to draw attention to it, for it would then find it very hard to resist an Opposition claim that section 17(8) was completely unnecessary. In conclusion, whether or not the technical effect of the opening words was indeed spotted by the Government, it is still probably fair to say that section 17(8) did indeed have two purposes, although it was unnecessary to achieve the single purpose normally attributed to it.

This saga has an important coda. Two contentious questions of law have been identified which were both pertinent to the operation of section 17. In *Hadmor Productions* v. *Hamilton*[129] both were considered. Hadmor sued union organizers when Thames Television employees blacked programmes which Hadmor had produced for transmission by Thames. However, because Hadmor appeared to have no clear contractual right to have the programmes transmitted—only a 'business expectation'—it relied on the tort of interference with business by unlawful means. The Court of Appeal accepted both the existence of the tort[130] and that interference with the Thames employees' contracts could be treated as unlawful means. Lord Denning achieved the latter result not by ruling that the Pearce doctrine was good law in its own right, but by arguing that the repeal of section 13(3) must be taken as a signal that the previous doubt was now to be resolved on the basis that *henceforth* the doctrine was to be treated as sound.[131] This reasoning may be wrong as a matter of statutory interpretation, but it does lead to the same result—on this point alone—which, it has been argued, the Government assumed would be achieved. But the Court of Appeal's view on the existence of the tort, meant that its decision parted company with the Government's views, and produced the very combination of two 'yes' answers which the Opposition had feared.

The House of Lords, speaking through Lord Diplock, also answered 'yes' on the question of the existence of the tort,[132] but held that the Pearce

---

[129] [1983] 1 AC 191.
[130] Lord Denning at 202G–203A; Watkins LJ at 207D–E; O'Connor LJ at 209D.
[131] At 203A–C and 204C–D; Watkins LJ appeared to concur.
[132] At 224H–225C, 228H–229C.

doctrine was bad law. It is important to note that Lord Diplock took this view of the doctrine in its own right, that is, before considering how if at all section 13(3) and then section 17(8) had affected it.[133] He then went on to hold that the position was unaffected by section 17(8). Certainly it could not be so affected for the reasons given by Lord Denning—that was simply wrong as a matter of statutory interpretation.[134] However, Lord Diplock did feel that consideration of section 17 fortified him in his conclusion that the Pearce doctrine was still bad law, for if it was now good law, primary action would be unlawful, and section 17 as a whole demonstrated that this could not have been Parliament's intention. Nevertheless, Lord Diplock stressed that he would have reached the same conclusion about the effect of section 17(8) had it stood alone as a separate section.[135]

The position after *Hadmor* was therefore as follows. The Government had worked on the basis that the answers to the questions: (1) is the Pearce doctrine sound?; and (2) does the alleged tort exist?, were: (1) 'yes'; (2) 'no'. Lord Diplock answered in reverse: (1) 'no'; (2) 'yes'. However, in respect of primary action the same result was achieved, namely that it was still protected, for only two 'yes' answers would undermine that. Thus it was that, although Lord Diplock answered both questions in the opposite way than did the Government, he was fortified by the fact that the result with regard to primary action was the result which Parliament had so clearly intended. The conclusion with respect to primary action appears satisfactory. But what of secondary action? For we may recall the earlier argument that the Government's approach to regulating secondary action necessarily assumed that the Pearce doctrine was good law. Lord Diplock firmly stated that it was bad law, a conclusion which thenceforth applied as much in a case of secondary action as in one of primary action. It is perhaps significant that Lord Diplock did not consider in any detail *how* section 17(8) was intended to operate in respect of secondary action, and how his decision would affect that matter. It might seem, then, that the decision in *Hadmor*, whilst in its roundabout way fulfilling the Government's aims with regard to primary action, undermined them with regard to secondary action, returning the law to something like the position it had reached in 1974. Once again, however, this view overlooks the effect of the opening words of section 17(1). For, as has been argued, these ensure section 17's effectiveness whatever the status of the Pearce doctrine. This was, however, not an argument upon which Lord Diplock relied.[136]

The conclusions are as follows. Section 17(8) was unnecessary to fulfil the principal purpose which is generally taken to have lain behind its introduction. In addition, Parliament's wishes with regard to its impact on

---

[133] At 231C–F.
[134] At 232D–E.
[135] Ibid.
[136] Although Lord Diplock did make the point in the *Merkur* case at [1983] 2 AC 610C, without relying upon it.

the legality of both primary and secondary action were fulfilled by a decision which took a contrary view to the Government on the two key issues of law relevant to its effect, and in spite of the fact that this result was only fully achieved by a line of reasoning on which neither Parliament nor the courts sought to rely. The important thing, it might be thought, is that the tale has in this sense at least a happy ending. Regrettably, however, this is not so, for Parliament failed altogether to take account of the effect on primary action of the repeal of the *other* limb of section 13(3), an effect which has now too been illustrated in the *Barretts & Baird* case,[137] but which cannot be dealt with here.

## (4) THE EMPLOYMENT ACT 1980: INITIAL ASSESSMENT

We can conclude this chapter by drawing out a number of important themes from the discussion of the measures affecting industrial conflict introduced by the 1980 Act.

### (a) Striking a Balance

A constant theme of Mr Prior's was that he sought legislation which would command a consensus among the majority on both sides of industry and gradually gain acceptance as a backcloth for industrial relations, which would survive changes in Government. However misguided or even naïve we may think this aim, there is no reason to doubt its sincerity. Mr Prior's claim when introducing the Bill was that all parties, employers, employees, and others affected by industrial action, had legitimate claims, and that his measures were designed to strike a balance between them. The story of section 17 demonstrates the extent of his concern not only to ensure that those parties whom he believed should have a right to legal redress were able to enjoy that right, but equally that the rights of workers to take what had in his view to be recognized as legitimate forms of industrial action were preserved as well.

The problem with all this, of course, is that these measures only reflected one particular subjective perception of where the balance lay. It was open to others—not least the leaders of the trade-union movement—to take a different view.[138] But even in terms of the Government's own expressed standards and objectives at the time, the 1980 Act is open to criticism. Mr Prior himself conceded that the picketing provisions were indeed very restrictive. The same can be argued for those on secondary action. Their objective of containing only 'excessive' disruption was unlikely to be achieved given that large-scale primary disputes are capable of being far more disruptive than much secondary action; and the justifying claim that only

---

[137] *Barretts & Baird* v. *IPCS and Duckworth* [1987] IRLR 3.
[138] For such a perspective, see e.g. Lewis and Simpson (1981: chs. 8 and 9).

'excessive' union power would be restrained by these provisions overlooked the fact that, as Lord McCarthy argued forcefully in the debates, the need to take secondary or sympathetic action is almost by definition the hallmark of a union which is weak.[139] So, while not necessarily doubting the sincerity of Mr Prior's wish to strike a balance, one may question *on his standards alone* how effective the measures contained in the 1980 Act were likely to prove in realizing it.[140] Ironically, the real severity of the absolute ban on sympathy action, and the case-law emasculation of the gateways to legitimate secondary action, mean that the position will in reality be little worsened when the gateways are at last abolished in 1990.[141]

### (b) The 'softly-softly' Approach

A key aspect of Mr Prior's approach when contrasted with that of the IRA, was the commitment to proceed in a piecemeal way, allowing the pace and extent of change to be dictated by public opinion, and the level and degree of both hostile and favourable reaction from within the union movement. This was the 'softly-softly' or 'step-by-step' approach. Mr Prior's perspective was indeed long-term:

While I could not expect the legislation to be fully accepted or be properly effective during the first period of Conservative Government, if we won a second time the trade unions would have to come to terms with it. It was therefore all the more important not to push our reforms too far in our first period of Government, for fear that one might undo everything by re-kindling Labour's and the unions' fighting spirit (1986: p. 159).

A direct consequence of the approach was therefore that not everything which might ideally have been thought desirable could be achieved in the first measure.[142] The arguments, for example, regarding whether a repeal or partial repeal of TULRA section 14 was needed to make the new measures work effectively were extremely finely balanced; but however that was, it was regarded as simply too soon to take such a provocative step.

The softly-softly approach did, however, provide room to draw on the reception given to earlier measures, in the development of later ones. The perceived failure of the IRA, a wholesale change in labour law, had forced the entire project to be abandoned; but if more limited changes were tried and proved unsuccessful, that might have the reverse effect and encourage support for wider reforms to be implemented. The virtues of such a strategy were argued by bodies such as the Engineering Employers' Federation (EEF) in its response to the consultations on picketing (1979*b*: para. 3); the

---

[139] OR HL vol. 411 cols. 1097–8 (8 July 1980).
[140] See further discussion in ch. 10 below.
[141] See further discussion in ch. 9 below.
[142] Prior (1985) and (1986: pp. 170–1) suggests that he would have liked to introduce a few further measures, at a sufficiently slow pace.

subtleties of the EEF's approach were also displayed in its lobbying of members of the House of Lords in July 1980, when there was a move organized by a group of Conservative peers, to push through amendments to toughen up the secondary-action clause. An EEF memorandum urged

that the Bill should now be enacted without delay, and without incorporating more radical changes which would make it in practice a less effective measure. . . . It is important that the debate on the Green Paper should be reasoned and not vitiated by bitterness stimulated by the enactment of an Employment Bill containing stronger remedies and powers than are generally seen to be reasonable and necessary to fulfil the immediate need.[143]

The way in which the softly-softly strategy permitted account to be taken of changes in public opinion, events of recent disputes, and wider electoral considerations, was, as we will see, something which commended it to every Employment Secretary to succeed Prior, and made it a key underlying determinant of the shape of the whole corpus of legislation with which this book is concerned.

### (c) The Mechanics of the Legislation

We have seen how practical and political considerations suggested the simplest and most elegant mode of introducing the 1980 changes, by providing that 'Nothing in section 13 of the 1974 Act shall prevent' proscribed activity from being actionable. The very same wording introduces sections 17 and 18, and even section 16(2). There was little resemblance here to the approach of the IRA with all its baggage of a special court, unfair industrial practices, and the creation of new remedies and powers in the hands of the Secretary of State. 'In short, nothing firm, focussed and predictable for union activists to get their teeth into . . .'[144] Yet we have also seen that this approach still left considerable difficulties when it came to defining the action to be excluded, pushing the draftsman in the direction of using the imperfect proxy of a web of contractual relations to describe patterns of industrial action, and inevitably resting on assumptions about the operation of the economic torts themselves which could not be relied upon to hold true.

Such problems helped spark off discussion of the idea that these matters might be altogether better dealt with under a system of 'positive rights' rather than immunities. This is a discussion to which we shall return at various points. At this juncture we may note the more general attraction which positive rights held for Mr Prior in terms of his desire to be seen to be even-handed as between the claims of trade unionists and those of employers and others. Prior observed that an immunities system was bad not only because it

---

[143] Memorandum from EEF D-G to certain members of the HL, dated 4 July 1980.

[144] The description of the new Act in the *Guardian* (14 Aug. 1980).

encouraged unions' hostility to the law, but also because it encouraged the hostility of others to the unions.[145]

Other effects of the political and strategic constraints affecting the Government have been noted. The need to keep the legislation as simple and low-key as possible meant that not every potential problem could be catered for—on some matters the Government simply accepted an element of risk. In addition, the legislation was not developed purely on the basis of what was the best legal view of what the effect of any particular provision was or might be. The concern, particularly with regard to section 17, that in any litigation the Act should in fact operate as intended, necessitated the rather different operation of trying to second-guess how the courts were likely to react to the provisions. Subsequent case-law suggests that by this test the legislation has not been wholly successful, although its authors would no doubt wish to argue that they have overall achieved a good success rate. It is tempting with hindsight to criticize some of their judgments as poor or eccentric, but labour lawyers ought surely to be among the last to argue that the task of anticipating judicial thought processes is anything less than an exceptionally difficult one.

### (d) The 'Ideology' of the Restrictions

The industrial-conflict measures contained in the 1980 Act cannot be seen as reflecting a simple commitment to an economic or political ideology which is implacably hostile to trade unions and trade-disputes immunities, and looks with unqualified favour upon the regulation of an atomistic market by common law. These measures were no doubt not *incompatible* with such a view—in a way in which it would be hard to argue of, say, much of the IRA, but that is a different matter. The influence has been seen of much more complex and specific concerns with the harms which the Government believed that certain types of industrial action could involve. Yet it has also been argued that the Act was much influenced by the balance of political calculations of different wings of the Conservative Government concerning the most appropriate posture to strike towards the union movement. The Government's approach was not developed simply on the basis of empirical research into patterns of industrial action any more than the expressed views of employers' organizations necessarily or exclusively were.

It was therefore no surprise to find the Government's views often differing sharply from those of employers. This was particularly notable in the case of the typically small employers' organizations which resisted strongly the idea that enforcement of the new law should be exclusively a matter for the parties and the civil process.[146] It is as well to recall the simple fact that the

---

[145]  OR HC vol. 982 col. 1501 (17 Apr. 1980).
[146]  Cf. Joyce *et al.* (1984: pp. 66–71).

Government had its own particular concerns and priorities in industrial relations, and it would surely be surprising if it did not count itself among the many parties to whose interests it had regard in shaping legislation. This is a factor which will be of recurring importance as our story unfolds.

# [4]
# Trade-Union Immunities:
# The Debate 1980–1981

## (1) INTRODUCTION

As we have seen, the Conservatives' 1979 manifesto contained only a short and specific agenda for action on industrial-conflict law. Although it did refer to an 'immediate review' of trade-union immunities, the main import of this appeared to relate to the possibility that the Government might wish to amend the law on secondary action in the light of the then awaited decision of the House of Lords in the *MacShane* case. The indications are that Mr Prior for his part would have been happy to leave the 1980 Act to settle in, at least for the foreseeable future. Although there were areas where, given enough time, he would have liked to have gone further, notably in respect of 'union labour only' arrangements, another Bill might not have emerged under his auspices until the other side of a second Conservative election victory (Prior 1986: pp. 170–1). However, in the face of extreme pressure to take some action during the steel dispute of early 1980, Mr Prior advanced the idea of a Green Paper on 'trade union immunities' to be issued after the Employment Bill had become law (p. 169).

Thereafter, the promise of the Green Paper was a frequent element of the response to those who urged tougher amendments to the Bill. It has been seen that there was no shortage of such amendments or responses to the Government's consultative papers, suggesting further provisions which might be introduced. More generally too, the return of a Conservative Government pledged to break with the past policies of both Conservative and Labour administrations had stimulated a wider reappraisal by a number of other bodies of future policies and prospects.

In the field with which we are concerned two important policy documents were issued: the CBI's *Trade Unions in a Changing World: The Challenge for Management* (CBI 1980) in February 1980, and the Centre for Policy Studies' *Liberties and Liabilities: The Case for Trade Union Reform* (CPS 1980b) in November of that year. Although ostensibly put forward as the initiator of a debate, the Green Paper which duly appeared in January 1981 (DE 1981a) must therefore at least at first and in part be viewed as a further salvo in a cross-fire of opinion which had already been live for some time. The CBI and CPS documents articulated the two main lines of approach within the ranks of those who were essentially sympathetic to the Government's outlook.

The CBI adopted the consensus-building approach, arguing that trade unions were to be viewed as 'partners' in the market economy which could help bring benefits to both employers and employees. It concentrated on trade-union and collective-bargaining structures and how they might be reformed, rather than on legal controls and restrictions on union activity (CBI 1980: ch. 1). Legislation might be of some assistance, it suggested, but only in assisting over a long period the necessary changes in deeply rooted perceptions and attitudes (p. 16). Nevertheless, the document did devote some attention to strike tactics—but those which might be used by employers. In particular it encouraged employers to co-ordinate and co-operate with each other in fighting strike action. In this context the 'mutual strike-fund' proposals which had been discussed at the CBI's 1979 conference were mentioned, and employers were discouraged from using tactics against each other which specifically took advantage of a strike situation, such as the poaching of custom from a struck employer (pp. 22–3).[1]

These proposals are of particular interest for two reasons. Firstly, they show an inventiveness in devising tactics which aim to reduce the economic harm which industrial action causes to a particular firm, without the need for any legal restraint upon those taking action. Secondly, they suggest the legitimacy of a doctrine of 'employer solidarity' in both an economic and an ethical sense which might have implications for the view taken of solidaristic action by employees of a very similar kind. Indeed, the connection may be closer than that, for it is the use of co-operative tactics of this kind by employers which often necessitates the use of secondary blacking and picketing by employees, an argument which EA 1980 section 17 to a small extent recognized. These are themes to which we shall return in later chapters.

Set against the consensus ethos of the CBI were the views of the CPS. The CPS was established in 1975 by Sir Keith Joseph and Mrs Thatcher, to promote policies associated with the philosophies of the 'social market economy'.[2] With the advent of a Government more sympathetic to its ideas, the CPS saw an opportunity to push concertedly for implementation of its preferred policies. *Liberties and Liabilities* restated the case which had been put from various sources to the right of Mr Prior, for a number of legal measures going beyond the 1980 Act. Concern was expressed that 'an important opportunity was lost to implement more substantial reforms in the areas covered by the Act.' Without follow-up measures, the result would be 'profoundly unsatisfactory' (CPS 1980b: p. 2). Specific proposals included a

---

[1]  Cf. EEF (1979a: para. 5e).
[2]  See its inaugural publication CPS (1975).

series of new criminal restrictions on picketing and demonstration, measures to curb strikes in essential services, and the repeal of TULRA section 14. Although endorsing the wisdom of a step-by-step approach, the document proceeded on the basis that the voluntarist system had broken down (foreword by Sir L. Neal). The preferred strategy was not to enact a single large piece of legislation; nevertheless a string of Bills was proposed, with several coming on stream within the next year (p. 55).

## (2) THE GREEN PAPER

It was against this background that the Green Paper was published in January 1981. Mr Prior himself later explained how it had been written:

the part of the Department which is responsible for industrial relations put a number of submissions and drafts to me which we went through in considerable detail to try to see whether we had all the eventualities examined. Then we tried to put as fairly as we could the pros and cons. It is true that we consulted a few outside individuals to make certain that we had got as good a description and fair list of proposals as we could find, and from that we gradually reached a consensus of what we thought should be in the Green Paper.[3]

Prior explained that he and his colleagues had sought to cover all the major points which had arisen during the passage of the various legislation since the IRA 1971.[4] The form of the Green Paper very much reflected the background to its conception. Although entitled *Trade Union Immunities*, it dealt also with matters such as the closed shop and union membership issues, and the legal enforceability of collective agreements. A closing chapter considered the idea of switching from a system of trade-union immunities to one of positive rights.

As revealing as any part of the specific discussion was the introductory chapter. This set out a perception of the 'trade union problem' which was largely based on the Donovan Commission's analysis, by then over a decade old. The very high level of unofficial strikes and the disorderliness of much day to day industrial relations remained the focus of concern (DE 1981a: pp. 5–6). This had been the view of the CBI (1980: ch. 1) and was consistent with the approach of the 'Prior administration' during the passage of the 1980 Act. For example, one of its arguments against repeal of TULRA section 14 had been that it would be irrelevant to the vast majority of strikes, which were unofficial, a view which the Green Paper repeated (DE 1981a: pp. 33–4).[5] The Paper was also prepared to see a share of the blame for existing industrial relations problems as lying with employers as well as employees, and it suggested a number of initiatives to which they might turn their

---

[3] In evidence to the Select Committee on Employment (1981: p. 192, para. 965).

[4] Ibid. para. 966.

[5] Nevertheless, the 1990 Employment Bill will now extend union responsibility to 'unofficial' action: see ch. 9 below.

attention (pp. 7–8). In this respect it again echoed the CBI's policy document, both in giving attention to industrial relations and collective bargaining issues, and in perceiving these as shared problems. Nevertheless, the detail of the Green Paper was confined to considering specific legal proposals.

The CBI's document had focused chiefly on industrial relations in the private sector (1980: p. 3). The Green Paper, appropriately enough for a Government document, touched on broader issues. It questioned whether it was in the nation's best interests that the relations between trade unions, employers' organizations, and Government continued to operate on such an ill-defined footing. When the interrelated activities of the three were so important to the national economy, it seemed sensible to have the operational basis of their relationship more clearly defined and understood. The National Economic Development Council (NEDC) pointed the way, although it was not sufficient in itself (DE 1981a: pp. 8–9). Here we may detect—in the most veiled and oblique language—the voice of Mr Prior still pleading the case for some form of 'national economic forum', as he had been doing since the mid-1970s. The muted tones of the plea are understandable, for he held out little hope by 1981 that this concept might yet be realized (Prior 1986: p. 170).

In the area of industrial-conflict law, the Green Paper discussed the immunity of trade unions as such, secondary action, picketing, the definition of a trade dispute, the use of secret ballots, and the problem of national emergencies and disruption of essential services. In addition, the section concerned with 'union labour only' practices considered changes to the immunities, the legal enforceability of collective agreements was discussed, and the closing chapter looked at positive rights. The choice of subject-matter indeed reflects those major issues which had been raised during debates and consultation on the 1980 Act. Many of the preoccupations can, as we shall see, be traced back to 1971 or further, giving the overall agenda a rather conservative look. In relation to each proposal discussed, a series of 'pro' and then 'con' arguments were set out. Although the document avoided any clear statement of preferred policy on any point, the 'pro' and 'con' arguments in many cases followed precisely the lines of the debates which had taken place between Mr Prior and his more right-wing opponents during the passage of the 1980 Bill.

Thus, while at one level the Green Paper fulfilled Mr Prior's stated aim of presenting a fair-minded and balanced view of opposing arguments, the criticism was also levelled that the dialogue which it set out was a narrow one between two select protagonists.[6] It was argued that the 'con' arguments tended to concentrate on practical problems and adverse side-effects which might be involved in the implementation of each proposal, rather than on broader arguments of principle. This viewpoint concluded that many of the arguments which might have been put forward by, say, the TUC, were

[6] See e.g. Benedictus and Newell (1981); Wedderburn (1981: p. 12, para. 2).

therefore neglected altogether.[7] In support of this assessment, it could be observed that the Green Paper's discussion rested throughout on the assumption that the only issue at stake was whether there should now be further legislation, no question arising of there being any further discussion of the measures enacted in 1980.[8] Nor indeed would one realistically have expected anything else. Ultimately the 'pro'/'con' style of discussion tended to push towards one simple conclusion: that whilst further measures in some areas might be desirable, they were at least for the time being either impractical or impolitic or both. The 1980 Act had gone far enough for the moment, and it would be unwise to push any further.

In short, the Green Paper appeared as not merely the latest salvo, but also the self-proclaimed last word, in the debate between Mr Prior and those who pressed for further legislation. Although Mr Prior never ruled out the prospect of further legislation before a general election, as politically he obviously could not, there seemed in reality to be little or no prospect that he would introduce this.[9] In any event, he made it clear that if there was to be further legislation, he would adopt the same approach as with the 1980 Act, with full consultations around a series of working papers, rather than a single White Paper.[10]

## (3) RESPONSES TO THE GREEN PAPER

More than three-hundred written responses to the Green Paper were submitted by employers' organizations, trade unions, practising lawyers, academics, and others. The House of Lords debated the issues in April. The House of Commons Select Committee on Employment was active, taking extensive oral and written evidence over the summer. It published a report and recommendations on 21 July which included the text of a number of further submissions it had received, being in many cases copies of those sent to the DE itself.

The major responses to the Green Paper might be divided broadly into three camps. In the first were those who essentially argued that the Green Paper's approach was simply too narrow and legalistic. On this view, a broader grasp of the contemporary industrial relations scene would reveal that the state of the current law, and hence possible changes to it, were of little or no relevance. Even the Green Paper had overestimated the power of legal changes to have any effect on industrial relations, beyond antagonizing and exacerbating them, a respect in which the 1980 Act might already have gone too far. This view was advanced chiefly by practising and academic

---

[7] See TUC (1981b) for their assessment.
[8] The possibility of further considering s. 17 of the 1980 Act was ruled out at para. 146.
[9] Cf. the measured analysis offered in 178 *IRLIB* 10 Feb. 1981.
[10] In evidence to the Select Committee on Employment (1981: p. 187, para. 943).

lawyers and by industrial relations experts[11] although not all such respondents were in this camp.[12] Two related strands of thought can be seen in these responses. First, there was of course the voluntarist or abstentionist approach to industrial-conflict law which, as well as largely descriptive of the framework of our industrial-conflict law before 1980, also argued prescriptively that absence of legal intervention in industrial conflict was the most preferable and 'mature' state that a system could attain.[13] Secondly, and more importantly for immediate purposes, these documents emphasized the *practical* constraints—whatever one's view of the ideal state of the law—on introducing beneficial or effective legal restrictions. This, we might term the 'limits of law' argument.

The two other camps of opinion drew supporters from the ranks of the many employers' organizations which responded to the Green Paper. In the second camp were those who put forward a shopping list of proposals for legislation, mostly, but not all, drawn from those which the Paper had discussed. Most in this group supported the continuance of the softly-softly approach and were therefore prepared to relegate some items on their lists to a lower level of priority; generally it was felt that the *timing* of the next round of legislation was a delicate matter of political judgement, for the Government. All, however, agreed that the 1980 Act had not gone far enough, that there were certain serious anomalies which still existed, and that these priority matters therefore required prompt action. The majority of the Select Committee were in this camp.[14] Those who took this approach put forward a familiar mixed bag of proposals. As was noted in connection with the 1980 Act, smaller, and typically less heavily or non-unionized employers felt themselves to be less capable of 'self-help' and in greater need of direct Government or state support when turning to law.[15] The 1980 Act was criticized for relying too heavily on the willingness of aggrieved parties to initiate litigation.[16] Among the larger employers' organizations, there was some significant closing of ranks when compared with the 1979 position. Central to the CBI's approach were the three themes of predictability, stability, and accountability. Significantly, the CBI identified the last of these less with any balloting issue, and more with the need to remove the immunity in tort of trade unions as such, a proposal which formed the lynchpin of its approach (1981: paras. 18–24). As for predictability, this might be achieved not by making collective agreements directly legally binding, but by making trade-disputes immunities contingent upon disputes procedures having been

---

[11] See e.g the submissions of Undy, Martin, Davies and Freedland, Sykes, Hendy, Wedderburn, and Williams, all of which appear in Select Committee on Employment (1981).

[12] Notable exceptions were Dr C. Hanson and Mr L. Bloch, Solicitor, a co-author of *Liberties and Liabilities*.

[13] See the discussion in chs. 2 above and 10 below.

[14] Select Committee on Employment (1981: Report, pp. viii ff).

[15] See e.g. the call by the Union of Independent Companies for the state funding of legal costs: ibid. pp. 228 and 230.

[16] Ibid. pp. 231–2.

followed and exhausted at the moment when industrial action is called (para. 42). The I.o.D. put forward the same idea and developed it, pointing out that the restriction would be inappropriate in cases of secondary and sympathetic action. This might however have its immunity rendered conditional upon procedures having been followed in relation to the dispute which it purported to support. That could be achieved by amending the definition of a trade dispute itself (I.o.D. 1981: para. 40). Both organizations put forward schemes for requiring initial resort to arbitration where a disputes procedure did not exist.

In the third and final camp were those of the employers' representatives who were extremely cautious about the idea of any further legislation so soon after the 1980 Act. Supporters of this view could see the theoretical attractions of one or two of the proposals being put forward, but strongly questioned whether in fact the net benefit of further measures would be very great. This position also saw much force in the limits of law argument, and was typified by a particular concern about the damaging effects on industrial relations which further legislation might have. Thus, while the CBI and I.o.D. appeared to be drawing closer together, a countervailing development in employers' views was the apparently wider and more well-defined gap between these latter two groups. In particular, the more cautious camp drew its support largely from those organizations which were particularly concerned with matters of personnel and industrial relations management, such as the IPM.[17] As the British Journal of Industrial Relations concluded:

the evidence from employers uncovered an unexpected amount of conflict within their ranks. There was a difference between the views of the industrial relations practitioners and the company directors who were influenced by the need to maintain good relations with the unions, and senior managers who believed that it was necessary to take a firmer stand to deal with bargaining points.[18]

Nineteen eighty-one therefore saw some important shifts in attitude among employers' organizations. The CBI moved from an attitude of considerable scepticism, if not hostility, towards the Government's policies, towards robust and concerted support for its legislative proposals at the end of the year.[19] The reason appears to have been its shifting attitude to Government economic policies[20] and in particular its changing perception of the threat

[17] See the views of the IPM in Select Committee on Employment (1981: pp. 258 ff.), and the verdict of the IPM vice-president of Employee Relations in Personnel Management (Aug. 1981: p. 3). See too the replies of ACAS in ACAS (1982: p. 64) and of the Managerial Professional and Staff Liaison Group in Select Committee on Employment (1981: p. 218).

[18] See 19 BJIR (1981) p. 389. For argument that personnel/i.r. management had reached a peak of autonomous development at around this time, see Evans (1983: pp. 133–4); Brown (1981: chs. 3 and 6); Purcell and Sisson (1983); Clegg (1979: pp. 99–101). This view appeared to be shared by e.g. Sir W. Goldsmith of the I.o.D.: see Select Committee on Employment (1981: pp. 143–4, para. 818).

[19] See e.g. CBI memorandum on Employment Bill 1982.

[20] Cf. the legendary call of Sir Terence Becket for a 'bare-knuckle fight' over economic policy at the Nov. 1980 CBI conference. The CBI still supported the idea of a national forum in its Green Paper response (1981: para. 7).

which the Government's resolute pursuit of these might or might not pose to its chances of re-election.[21] As the CBI's fears about the adverse electoral impact of economic policies faded, so it found the idea of further labour law measures progressively more attractive. However, other bodies, notably the EEF, remained sceptical on this issue throughout the period, a view which strongly influenced the proposals and strategy which it advanced.

In terms of the issues covered, the debate of this period was wide-ranging. But that said, the views of those who had opposed the 1980 Act were simply ignored, and in truth, as against both his left and his right, Mr Prior's own position remained both clear and firm throughout. Predictably enough, following the expiry of the consultation period at the end of June 1981, Prior showed no signs of any intention of pressing ahead with legislation. When the House of Lords debated the Green Paper in April, Lord Gowrie for the Government warned that it should not 'raise expectations'.[22] It now appeared that if a further round of legislation was to be sure of reaching the statute-book before a general election, firm proposals would have to be tabled by the end of 1981. The I.o.D. claimed that Mrs Thatcher had assured them that the necessary Parliamentary time would be made available (1981: para. 81). Nineteen eighty-one had also seen further cabinet splits on economic policy, centring around a highly deflationary budget in the spring. Mr Prior's strong opposition to the Government's line had become apparent.[23] In September he was replaced in a cabinet reshuffle by Mr Norman Tebbit, someone who was more in tune with the Government's economic policies, and would be willing to press ahead with a further round of legislation. We turn in the next chapter to consider what he did.

[21]  See Taylor (1982b: p. 184); Soskice (1984: pp. 316–18).
[22]  OR HL vol. 419 col. 222 (1 Apr. 1981).
[23]  See Prior (1986: ch. 7).

# [5]

# The Employment Act 1982

## (1) INTRODUCTION

Mr Tebbit became Employment Secretary on 14 September 1981. On 15 October he informed the Conservative Party Conference that proposals had been prepared for consideration by ministers with a view to publication of a bill in the forthcoming Parliamentary session. He explained that: 'It will seek to improve the working of the labour market, which can only be to the advantage of workers and consumers, who are the same people in different roles.'[1] On 9 November he told Parliament that the forthcoming proposals would be divided up into 'those concerned with improving the operation of the labour market' and 'those concerned with personal liberty, particularly the closed shop'.[2] The proposals appeared, in a single consultation paper, on 23 November. Mr Tebbit now expanded on his earlier themes, explaining that the operation of the labour market would be improved 'by providing a balanced framework of industrial relations law'. The proposals would help those who had lost their jobs 'as a result of the inefficiencies in British industry that have been fostered by restrictive practices, buttressed by trade union immunities'.[3] When the subsequent Bill reached the House of Lords, Earl Ferrers for the Government explained that while its first objective was to protect the liberty of the individual, its second was 'to improve our economic performance as a nation'.[4]

It is evident enough, then, that the accession of Mr Tebbit signalled a clear and deliberate shift in the Government's rhetoric with regard to trade-union immunities. The regulation of industrial conflict was not to be seen as simply a matter of striking an equitable balance between the strength of employers and employees, and of tackling the worst and most destructive abuses of trade-union power. It was also to be presented as an important arm of the Government's economic, and in particular, labour market, policy at a much wider level. Such an approach had indeed been urged by bodies such as the I.o.D., which stressed that 'industrial peace' was not an adequate goal by

[1] See *Conservative News* (Nov. 1981).
[2] OR HC vol. 12 col. 316.
[3] OR HC vol. 13 col. 631.
[4] OR HL vol. 431 col. 620 (15 June 1982).

itself: possible measures should be specifically judged according to their propensity to contribute to improved economic performance (1981: Introduction).[5] When the House of Lords debated the Green Paper in April, Lord Harris of High Cross, of the IEA, had criticized that document for its lack of any economic analysis and failure to attack the monopoly power of trade unions.[6] The rhetoric now used by the Government was no doubt more appealing to such critics; but what of the actual measures proposed? Mr Tebbit's proposals were followed by a Bill introduced on 28 January 1982.

## (2) MR TEBBIT'S PROPOSALS AND THE 1982 BILL

Mr Tebbit stressed from the outset that he too was following the 'step-by-step' approach, but that the time for the next step had now come. The Government would proceed now in those areas 'where there is the clearest support for change and where it is necessary to propose practical and workable remedies', whilst giving consideration to what other measures might be adopted in the longer term.[7] When presenting the Bill to Parliament, Mr Tebbit was cautious in his description of the proposed changes to industrial-conflict law, in notable contrast to his tone in relation to those in respect of the closed shop.[8] In turning to the detail, it may be useful to proceed by taking the 1980–1 debate as our starting-point, and considering in turn some of the more important measures canvassed in that debate, and the treatment which they received.

### (a) Positive Rights

The Green Paper had discussed the idea of replacing trade-union immunities with a system of 'positive rights'. There was indeed a fairly extensive debate on this topic in the early 1980s, one which is not entirely dead today.[9] There is no need here to present a full survey of the many arguments for and against a positive rights system which have been put forward; but some aspects of the debate have a particular relevance to our present concerns. As has been noted, the idea attracted Mr Prior for two reasons. First, the language of positive rights might lend itself to a more felicitous expression of the sort of partial restrictions on industrial action which he favoured. No doubt the experience of the drafting of section 17 of the 1980 Act helped to encourage this view (DE 1981a: pp. 90–1). Secondly, the establishment of positive rights, together with corresponding obligations, might be politically preferable

---

[5] See in a similar vein e.g. Gardiner (1981).
[6] OR HL vol. 419 cols. 242 ff. (1 Apr. 1981).
[7] See Tebbit (1981).
[8] OR HC vol. 17 cols. 737 ff. (8 Feb. 1982).
[9] See e.g. Kahn-Freund and Hepple (1972: pp. 5–6); O'Higgins (1976); Macfarlane (1981: esp. pp. 169–70); Elias and Ewing (1982: pp. 356–8); Wedderburn (1985b); Ewing (1986); Wedderburn (1987).

to the present system of immunities, which was thought to encourage unions to be especially hostile to legal regulation, and employers to be especially hostile to the privilege which immunities appeared to represent.[10]

It is then perhaps not without significance that critics of the idea included both Lord Wedderburn, who insisted that no restrictions on peaceful industrial action were acceptable,[11] and bodies such as the I.o.D., which feared that to grant positive rights would signal endorsement of the validity of some strike action, and suggested that the present system encouraged the attitude that industrial action should be the exception rather than the rule (I.o.D. 1981: paras. 68–70). The debate over positive rights therefore had a significant political dimension, the proposal seeming most attractive to those ranged in the centre ground.[12] But all sides seemed to be agreed that a change-over would be a major undertaking,[13] giving rise to a host of legal and policy issues, and that the introduction of a positive rights system would not obviate the need to face the substantive questions regarding how far such rights ought to extend. Almost every respondent to the Green Paper was lukewarm about or rejected the idea, a position which the Select Committee, with one dissentient, endorsed.[14] It was hardly surprising that Mr Tebbit did not adopt the proposal.

### (b) Secondary Action

The Green Paper considered whether the constraints on secondary action contained in the 1980 Act needed to be built upon (DE 1981a: ch. 3, sect. B). Its discussion mirrored the debates between Mr Prior and those who had urged that all secondary action should be outlawed, and reflected Mr Prior's earlier conclusion that section 17 represented the narrowest restriction which it was reasonable, or for the time being prudent, to impose. Nevertheless, this remained a highly contentious issue, particularly as section 17 seemed to some, by its mechanics of first outlawing secondary action and then providing 'gateways' to legality in certain cases, actually to lend an air of approval and legitimacy to some action of this kind. A number of employers' organizations continued to urge further restrictions, including members of the CBI and I.o.D. as well as the small business lobby.[15] Mr Tebbit nevertheless chose not to introduce any proposals directly dealing with secondary action. A number of factors may be thought to have contributed to this decision.

---

[10] See ch. 3, text to n. 145 above.

[11] See Wedderburn (1981: pp. 40 ff.), and generally on positive rights (1985b: pp. 509 ff.).

[12] The SDP was from its foundation an enthusiastic supporter.

[13] Lord Hailsham LC thought it would take several years and require a Royal Commission. See Select Committee on Employment (1981: p. 4, para. 678).

[14] Ibid. Report, pp. v–vi, paras. 2–10.

[15] See the proposals of the CBI (1981: p. 155, sect. B); I.o.D. (1981: p. 284, paras. 49–51), and others mentioned below. The eventual removal of the main 'gateways' in 1990 is discussed in ch. 9 below.

First, although support for a further restriction was widespread, it was most intensely and consistently voiced by those representing the typically small, non-, or little unionized businesses, which nevertheless saw themselves as heavily dependent upon their commercial links with larger, unionized, enterprises.[16] These businesses saw themselves as particularly vulnerable to the effects of secondary action taken in support of disputes at larger organizations. But their actual proposals were addressed less to the substantive law, and more to the idea that what was needed was a procedure which did not require a secondary employer to initiate a civil action unaided. Small businesses argued that they simply lacked the necessary resources to mount litigation—one group, for example, calling for a state fund to provide indemnities against legal costs[17]—and that those which dared to litigate against trade unions with which they differed would face reprisals in the shape of further industrial action, contractual sanctions, or blacking.[18]

In effect this was a call for state intervention or support in such disputes, whether through some form of executive control, or by extension of the criminal law. As such it was most unlikely to find favour. The arguments, drawn particularly from the experience of the IRA, persuading against this type of measure, were likely to have been no more lost on Mr Tebbit than they were on Mr Prior. Furthermore, it was implausible that a Government which espoused the rhetoric of allowing employers and employees to settle their own disputes, would take legal powers to facilitate its own intervention.

Secondly, where wider support for some further measure in relation to secondary action *was* expressed, the frequent suggestion was that existing protections ought to be made subject to secondary employees having demonstrated their desire to lend support in a ballot.[19] However, Mr Tebbit, as we shall see, wished to take a more long-term view of the possibilities of legislating in the area of secret ballots, where he recognized that formidable legal and practical problems existed,[20] and any such action was therefore for the moment to be deferred.

Finally, there was a matter of legal technique. As we have seen, section 17 of the 1980 Act was a response to judicial decisions in relation to the first limb of the 'golden formula'—the meaning of 'in contemplation or furtherance'. This was a matter where direct legislative amendment of the formula was thought to be too difficult to enact with the desired degree of precision, and the less elegant approach of section 17 was adopted instead. In 1982, however, the Tebbit administration turned its attention to the golden formula itself, and in particular to its second limb, the definition of a 'trade dispute'. Here as we shall see, simple and effective direct amendments *could*

[16] See the evidence of the AIB, UIC, and NCT, reprinted in Select Committee on Employment (1981: at pp. 224, 228, and 231).
[17] See ch. 4 text to n. 15 above.
[18] See e.g. AIB (1979: p. 23, para. 4); submission of Lionel Bloch, Solicitor, in Select Committee on Employment (1981: p. 214).
[19] See e.g. CBI (1981: paras. 25–9).
[20] See Tebbit (1981: p. iii).

be introduced, considerably overlapping with and tightening up the 1980 restrictions. It is to a consideration of the formula and the changes made to it in 1982 that we can therefore now turn.

### (c) The Golden Formula

Professor Wedderburn, who coined the expression 'golden formula' to refer to the words 'in contemplation or furtherance of a trade dispute', described it as the 'bedrock of British workers' rights to organise and take effective industrial action' (1965: p. 214). The reason is not hard to grasp: the formula determines the scope of the immunities from common law without which, as the Green Paper of 1981 correctly stated, 'most industrial action would be illegal' (DE 1981a: para. 34). This much is, to labour lawyers at least, platitudinous. The golden formula is rightly regarded as of enormous importance today because of the way in which it distinguishes those forms of industrial action which are to be regarded as legitimate from those which are not. Some have argued that the formula therefore *itself* reflects a more general theory about the proper limits of the right to strike, which may appropriately be dubbed the 'golden formula theory' (Simpson 1983: p. 463).

However, the formula appears to have been invented with a less substantial object in mind. It was first used in the Conspiracy and Protection of Property Act (CPPA) 1875, which sought to set out clearly the relevance of criminal law to industrial action. The need for such a measure had arisen primarily out of the decision in *R. v. Bunn*[21] in which gas stokers threatening industrial action were found guilty of a criminal conspiracy. Section 3 of the 1875 Act reversed that decision by providing that—within the golden formula—action which was not of itself a crime, would not become a criminal conspiracy simply because it was done by more than one person. But to understand the scheme of the 1875 Act, it is important not to focus alone on section 3: sections 4–7 must be considered as well. These demonstrate that the Act was intended as a more comprehensive measure, for they declared that some specified forms of industrial action were indeed to be treated as criminal. In fact the 1875 Act attempted to lay down a complete criminal code in respect of industrial conflict, to replace the existing common law founded on conspiracy, which had made no distinction between industrial action and other forms of activity. The Lord Chancellor of the day explained that:

He should have been very glad, if it had been possible, to reduce to a code the whole law of conspiracy, and not merely the law of conspiracy as affecting trade disputes or disputes between masters and workmen . . . [but] . . . while he believed it would be hopeless to reduce to a code the whole law of conspiracy, it was quite possible, taking a particular area of acts, to say what should be a crime . . . [22]

[21] (1872) 12 Cox 316.

[22] OR vol. CCXXVI col. 37 (26 July 1875). When the wider task of reform was eventually undertaken just over a hundred years later, s. 3 was replaced by a wider provision covering almost all conspiracies—so that the golden formula could be all but discarded. See Criminal Law Act 1977 ss. 1 and 5(11).

In this light the scheme of the Act appears clear. First, in section 3, it removed the application of the general law of conspiracy to the field of industrial conflict. Then, in the sections following, it set out more precisely the new criminal code which would apply in this field. In this scheme of things the golden formula was simply the form of words used to *describe* industrial conflict, so as to distinguish it from other types of social activity. What it was not at this stage intended to do was to distinguish different types of industrial action *within* the field of industrial conflict. This view is further supported by three features of the 1875 Act.

First, the formula itself was nowhere defined. Indeed, in the speech of the Lord Chancellor quoted from above, the expressions 'trade strikes', 'trade disputes', 'disputes between masters and workmen', and 'trade disputes between employers and workmen' were used quite interchangeably. So it appears that little significance can be attached to the particular formulation— 'trade dispute between employers and workmen'—actually used in section 3. Indeed the marginal note refers simply to 'trade disputes'. Secondly, the draftsman expressly provided that section 3 was not to affect the law relating to other situations such as 'riot, unlawful assembly, breach of the peace or sedition', suggesting that if there was any concern, it was that the wording might extend beyond industrial conflict. No types of industrial dispute were singled out for exclusion. Finally, in sections 4–7 the Act made no use of the golden formula, presumably because the sections themselves described sufficiently clearly the actions which they proscribed, actions which were to be unlawful in whatever kind of dispute they occurred.

In the TDA 1906 the formula was used again when providing protection against common-law torts, which again might be committed in contexts other than the taking of industrial action. When the 1906 Bill was introduced it too contained no definition of what amounted to a trade dispute. However, the experience of certain cases decided under the 1875 Act alerted some to the possibility that the formula might be subject to misinterpretation. On the one hand it might be held to apply to certain kinds of commercial dispute other than industrial conflict; on the other, it might be held that not all industrial action was covered.[23] The Government at first saw no need to introduce a definition clause, the Attorney-General of the day arguing that:

the whole policy of this Bill was founded on the established right of workmen for any reason which they in their judgment thought sufficient to abstain from work.[24]

and that he had thought that

it was pretty clear and perfectly understood that the term 'trade dispute' related mainly if not solely to disputes arising from the exercise by trade unions of their functions.[25]

---

[23] See OR vol. CLXII cols. 137 ff. (27 July 1906).
[24] Ibid. col. 141 Sir John Walton.
[25] Ibid. col. 142.

However, the Government was eventually persuaded that a definition clause would be necessary, and what became section 5(3) was therefore introduced 'at the last minute'.[26] So even the definition clause was not intended to distinguish legitimate from illegitimate strikes. Rather it was intended in part to forestall just such a development in the case-law.

At this stage it may be remarked that even if this account of the original purpose of the golden formula as used in 1875 and 1906 is correct, it nevertheless remains the case that it has in modern times assumed the second, more contentious purpose which is commonly attributed to it. Indeed this is so, but a knowledge of this history can arguably assist a better understanding of more than one of the changes enacted in 1982. With this in mind, we can turn to consider the first.

*Section 29(1) and 'Political Strikes'.*   Few discussions of the policy issues surrounding industrial-conflict law can avoid a mention of 'political strikes'. Yet there is clearly no consensus regarding what this expression means. One possible meaning can for the moment be put on one side. Sometimes the 'right to strike' is itself viewed as a 'political' right in the sense of a human or fundamental right which intrinsically deserves protection regardless of the ends for which it is exercised. More commonly, however, debate focuses on an alleged distinction between strikes which pursue 'industrial' and those which pursue 'political' objects. Some writers argue that the latter are illegitimate, others that they should be pursued more actively, and many that the distinction is simply illusory.[27] Once again we need only consider those aspects of the debate which are of immediate concern to us here.[28] Our present interest arises from the introduction in 1982 of an amendment to TULRA section 29 which Mr Tebbit argued would 'bear directly on the position of political strikes'.[29] This was the amendment of section 29(1) to require that henceforth a trade dispute must 'relate wholly or mainly to' rather than be merely 'connected with' one of the matters listed therein.[30] This was the form of words that had been used in the IRA's definition of an 'industrial dispute'.[31]

There was however considerable confusion, not least among respondents to the Green Paper, as to the legal status of 'political' disputes even prior to 1982.[32] The Government argued as follows (DE 1981b: para. 37).[33] The matters listed in section 29(1) were clearly only industrial matters. Therefore

[26]   Kidner (1982: p. 51) and generally on the history of the 1906 Act.
[27]   For recent contributions to the debate, see Crouch (1982a: ch. 6); Hain (1986); Coates and Topham (1986); Fox (1985a: ch. 7).
[28]   This debate is considered further in ch. 10.
[29]   See Tebbit (1981).
[30]   EA 1982 s. 18(2)(c).
[31]   IRA 1971 ss. 167(1) and (5).
[32]   See the Select Committee's request in its report (1981: p. vii, para. 12) for a clarifying statement from the Government.
[33]   See also OR St. Cttee. G 29th sitting (29 Apr. 1982) cols. 1304–5.

a 'purely' political dispute would have no connection with such matters and so be unprotected even under existing law. In this sense, disputes which were purely and clearly political never had enjoyed protection. An example was the TUC's Day of Action against the 1980 Bill, which the High Court had declared unlawful.[34] The Government's concern lay with disputes which did have some connection with terms and conditions of employment, but which were largely or predominantly inspired by a political motive. Under existing legislation such disputes would be protected, having the necessary connection. Following the proposed amendment they would not. We need to consider each of these arguments in turn.

That the requirement for a 'connection' with the matters listed in section 29(1) would easily be fulfilled was forcefully confirmed by the trilogy of House of Lords cases in 1979–80, especially *NWL Ltd.* v. *Woods*,[35] the case which the Government acknowledged had specifically led to renewed concern.[36] However, the proposition that 'purely' political disputes were always unlawful appeared, on a reading of section 29(1) and the relevant case-law, also to be sound. This was so whether or not one accepted that a purely political dispute could in fact ever be found. In other words, one might argue in a particular case about the court's application of section 29 to the facts, but *if* a purely political dispute could be found, *then* it would not be protected. As long ago as 1954 Kahn-Freund had said as much, arguing that political disputes were unprotected, although the theory which identified a clear distinction between political and industrial disputes reflected in the 1906 Act was 'untenable' (1954*a*: pp. 125–7).

Reflection on the history of the 1906 Act may suggest how this bizarre combination could come about, for as has been argued, the legislature had no intention of restricting the protections which it enacted in 1906 to exclude any type of peaceful industrial action, and did not appear to address itself to a well-formulated issue regarding political strikes. Indeed, critics have argued that the 1906 Government was precisely in this respect at fault, for failing to take note of the fact that such action had already emerged on the scene.[37] It is arguably therefore misleading to suggest that English law deliberately excluded a right to take political industrial action, although the 1906 Act was soon interpreted to that effect. Kahn-Freund and Hepple suggest that a political rather than an economic right may be more commonly associated with a 'positive' right to strike rather than an immunities-based system (1972: pp. 5–6). It is suggested that whilst this may have come to be so, it should not be taken to have arisen as the result of any calculated decision on the part of the legislature in 1906. It may, however, be less easy to neglect the issue

---

[34]  *Express Newspapers* v. *Keys* [1980] IRLR 247. Cf. *ANG* v. *Flynn* (1970) 10 KIR 17.

[35]  [1979] ICR 867. The ability of workers to turn *any* dispute into one legally 'about' terms and conditions of employment, by an appropriate demand or strike notice, was strongly doubted in *Universe Tankships* v. *ITF* [1983] 1 AC 366.

[36]  See e.g. DE (1981*b*: para. 37); OR HL vol. 433 col. 283 (13 July 1982).

[37]  e.g. Phelps Brown (1986: pp. 47–8).

when establishing a system which explicitly defines the perimeters of a positive right.[38]

The form of action cited most commonly as exemplifying a political strike is of course action which is thought to pursue a quarrel with the Government rather than one with the immediate employer of those involved. It was in this sense that the 1980 Day of Action could be regarded as political. The problem of course, repeatedly pointed out ever since Kahn-Freund made his observations, is that Government involvement in most major disputes, whether by virtue of its role as paymaster in the public sector, or by virtue of the more general impact of some Government policy—usually an incomes policy—makes it hard not to see the Government as a relevant party, or the obvious target of action, in many major disputes (Kahn-Freund 1954a: pp. 125–7; Davies and Freedland 1984a: pp. 797 ff.).[39] Indeed, almost from the moment that the Donovan Commission had reported, large-scale, official, usually public-sector disputes had begun progressively to supplant unofficial action as the chief focus of Government concern with regard to the 'strike problem'.[40] This concern perhaps had three dimensions.[41]

First, as has been noted, such action may be a direct threat to the implementation of the Government's own policies. This would be enough to make it a cause of concern to a Government of any persuasion. Secondly, those on the right were particularly apt to characterize such action as political and hence illegitimate because it represented a challenge to the implementation of the policies of a democratically elected Government, and hence one which it was said ought properly to be mounted only through the ballot-box. On this view, political strikes were only a symptom of a more general constitutional problem which lay in the over-politicization of the trade-union movement during the 1970s.[42] Thirdly, disputes of this kind were said to represent a particularly serious and inexcusable example of the immediate harm and inconvenience which industrial action can cause. This was not simply a matter of the obviously large scale of the harm which disruption to a major public service might cause. More specifically, the 'public' or the 'consumer' was seen as being the major, if not the only, and an entirely innocent victim of such action, and workers and consumers were, as Mr Tebbit put it, 'the same people in different roles'.

---

[38] Cf. Ewing (1986: pp. 146–9).

[39] The problem was particularly acute in the docks dispute of 1989, precipitated by the Government's decision to procure the repeal of the statutory dock labour scheme. In a robust judgment this element of which was not challenged on appeal, Millett J held that the TGWU clearly had a trade dispute with employers over what terms and conditions would apply after abolition. This was against the backcloth of a determined policy by the union not to oppose abolition itself by industrial action. *ABP* v. *TGWU* [1989] IRLR 291 (Ch. D. and CA), and 399 (HL).

[40] See Durcan *et al.* (1983: pp. 378–81 and ch. 12); Edwards (1982); Hyman (1989b: pp. 179 ff.).

[41] Cf. the analysis in Beaumont (1982).

[42] For terse criticism of this view, see Fox (1985a: pp. 166–7).

Particular concern on the part of many Conservative politicians could be traced back to the period of the Heath Government, which saw several such disputes including two miners' strikes, a series of states of emergency, and at one point the imposition of a three-day week.[43] Mr Douglas Hurd, Mr Heath's PPS during this period, has described the problem thus:

in a public sector dispute the employee barely suffers. Any temporary loss of income is usually covered by the union, and is in any case quickly recouped out of the eventual settlement. The employer, the actual administrator of the public concern, does not suffer at all, for his salary is secure. It is the public, and only the public, which suffers, first as consumer, and later, when the bill comes in, as taxpayer. The public picks up the tab for both sides (1979: p. 107).

More recently, as has been discussed, the problem had resurfaced in a dramatic way during the winter of discontent, leading one writer, sympathetic to labour, to observe that this was 'no longer a classic struggle between organised labour and capital but part of an internecine war within the working class itself' (Taylor 1982b: p. 160). Even before this time, Kahn-Freund himself had articulated his concerns about the self-wounding and self-defeating nature of such disputes (1979: pp. 74 ff.).

This is a major issue to which we shall return at several points again. For the moment it suffices to note the background to the contemporary concern with 'political' disputes in a mixture of longstanding political principle and more recent industrial and legal history. The proposed amendment to section 29(1) would by no means provide a complete answer to this problem,[44] in part because, as the Government itself argued, cases in which the Government was indeed the paymaster, and the dispute was, for example, a straightforward pay or redundancy dispute, would continue to enjoy protection.[45] Nevertheless, in all the circumstances, it was an obvious alteration to make, albeit that an apparently clear theoretical test might prove hard to apply in fact. The Opposition not implausibly suggested that the 'wholly or mainly' test would allow the courts a dangerously wide discretion in their interpretation of the facts, particularly in cases where the Government's involvement, or the impact of its policies was less than clear cut.[46] Such cases were bound increasingly to arise, as the Government's privatization, contracting out, and local government reforms gathered pace.[47]

---

[43] On states of emergency in 1971–4, see Jeffery and Hennessy (1983: pp. 233 ff.); more generally on the period, see Clutterbuck (1978: chs. 2–9).

[44] See e.g. *Sherard* v. *AUEW* [1973] ICR 421 CA (dispute over Government legislation held within narrower wording under the 1971 Act); *ABP* v. *TGWU* (n. 39 above).

[45] See OR St. Cttee. G 29th sitting (29 Apr. 1982) cols. 1305–6 Mr Waddington.

[46] See ibid. 28th sitting (29 Apr. 1982) cols. 1265–7 Mr Radice, citing Roskill LJ in *Sherard* at 435E-H, also cited in the Green Paper paras. 192–200.

[47] Opposition fears were arguably confirmed in *Mercury Communications* v. *Scott-Garner* [1984] 1 Ch. 37 CA.

*Other Amendments to Section 29.*    This amendment to section 29(1) can also be seen as to some extent overlapping with section 17 of the 1980 Act, for action taken with a view to putting pressure on Government, or simply to showing sympathy for workers in dispute elsewhere, might, as well as being regarded as political, probably extend beyond the first customers and suppliers of the employer in dispute.[48] Other amendments to section 29 overlapped to some degree with the 1980 Act but were certainly more elegant and potentially more restrictive. Again, in some cases there was a direct precedent in earlier legislation. Disputes between 'workers and workers' were removed from protection,[49] although, inasmuch as it is ever possible to view an employer as neutral, and therefore not a party to such disputes, they would appear to be unprotected secondary action under EA 1980 section 17.[50] Section 17 would, however, only remove protection in respect of consequent breach of commercial contracts,[51] the 1982 amendment effectively extending to employment contracts as well.

The 1982 Act also required that a trade dispute be between workers and their own employer,[52] although workers might yet be *affected* by the actions of an employer other than their own,[53] or indeed, once again, by those of the Government. Here again there was obviously some potential overlap with EA 1980 section 17, the operation of which rested on the assumption that any trade dispute would only have one clearly identifiable employer party to it. Interestingly, the possibility that groups of companies might be restructured to take advantage of the provision was again raised, and the Government placed on record its view that this would be most unlikely to occur in practice.[54]

After 1982, the fact that a trade union was in dispute, would no longer be taken as an automatic indication that there was a dispute involving individual workers who were its members.[55] This amendment might be thought consistent with the view that unions ought to respond to the clear wishes of workers and not purport to issue demands on their behalf. As such, it paved the way for the notion that a ballot may provide the clearest indication of individual workers' views.[56] Certainly, this and the last mentioned change

[48] For an illustration of the relationship between political and sympathy action, see *Express Newspapers* v. *Mitchell* [1982] IRLR 465 QBD, and between political and secondary action *Duport Steels* v. *Sirs* [1980] ICR 161 HL.

[49] EA 1982 s. 18(2)(*b*); also excluded in 1971.

[50] Because secondary action as defined in s. 17(2) includes any case where the injured employer is 'not a party to the trade dispute'.

[51] s. 17(1)(*a*). Cf. Employment Bill 1990, cl. 4.

[52] EA 1982 s. 18(2)(*a*).

[53] As in *Crazy Prices* v. *Hewitt* [1980] IRLR 396 NICA.

[54] See OR HL vol. 434 cols. 601–2 (2 Aug. 1982). Cf. ch. 3 text to n. 105 above.

[55] EA 1982 s. 18(5).

[56] Cf. the suggested limitations on the authority of the union to give notices to terminate in *Boxfoldia* v. *NGA (1982)* [1988] IRLR 383, and the analysis offered by Millett J in *ABP* v. *TGWU* (n. 39 above) that the union normally enjoys authority even prior to the ballot, which is then put beyond question by a positive ballot result.

were bound to affect the legality of the ITF's campaign against flags of convenience as, most obviously of all, was the removal of protection in cases of 'matters occurring outside the United Kingdom' unless employees inside are likely to be affected.[57] As has been seen, Mr Prior had chosen not to attack the ITF directly, although his legislation had had this effect, albeit apparently unintended.[58] Under the 'Tebbit administration' this policy was reversed, the Government now giving greater consideration to the argument that foreign trade and British jobs might be seriously harmed by the ITF campaign.[59]

Although this account of the changes introduced by the 1982 Act is not yet complete, it will already be apparent that when added to the 1980 Act, its provisions would result in a significant catalogue of actions becoming unlawful, as compared with the situation before 1980. This point ought particularly to be borne in mind when considering the next change: the repeal of the trade-union immunity.

### (d) The Trade-Union Immunity

The immunity for trade unions as such has already received our attention in connection with the debates of 1980–1, during which some parties repeatedly and strenuously argued for its repeal. We have noted that, for those who favoured a narrowing of the substantive law, there were some powerful strategic or practical arguments in favour of a repeal, and to these we can return in a moment. But what of the arguments of principle? To some, the whole system of trade-disputes immunities is abhorrent. An early and powerful critic was Dicey, for the immunities appeared to offend a central principle of his theory of constitutional law, namely that all people should be ruled by one body of laws, applicable equally to all—the Rule of Law (1885: ch. 4; 1914: pp. xliv–xlviii). Theorists of the common law such as Sir Frederick Pollock were similarly outraged, for it had been their work to demonstrate that the common law was indeed built up of such generally applicable rules and principles (1908: pp. v and 96–7).[60] Writers such as Hayek have more recently combined this political argument with an economic attack, generating an insistent demand for a complete repeal of the immunities (1984: pp. 58 and 64).[61]

As the basis for an attack on the trade-disputes immunities in general, however, these views are open to obvious criticisms. First, few would seriously argue today either that all laws ought actually to apply to all sections

---

[57] EA 1982 s. 18(4); between 1974 and 1976 protection had been limited to disputes about matters having an impact within Great Britain.

[58] See discussion in ch. 3 above.

[59] See OR HL vol. 434 col. 608 (2 Aug. 1982) Lord Glenarthur; St. Cttee. G 29th sitting (29 Apr. 1982) cols. 1312–13 Mr Waddington.

[60] See Atiyah (1979: ch. 14, p. 402).

[61] See further, ch. 10 below.

of the community, or that this is even a remotely accurate description of the modern legal system. Even leaving aside the enormous wealth of 'social' legislation which has grown up since the war, the argument would be implausible with regard to the common law itself.[62] On top of this, it is in any case difficult to see how the trade-disputes immunities can as a whole be regarded as laws applicable to only one section of the community, for the specific immunities are not in fact restricted to 'trade unions', 'trade unionists', 'workers', or in any other way, but apply to any 'person' who fulfils their conditions. Although we have seen, and it is evident enough, that the immunities have in practice always been intended to apply in respect of a clear target—a target at which it has been argued that the golden formula itself was intended to aim—this would not appear to be enough to establish a violation of the 'universality' principle, unless that principle relates not only to formal or potential applicability, but also to coverage in practice; but not even Dicey appeared to require each law *in practice* to have an equal impact on every citizen.[63]

However, these critics may have had a more plausible case when attacking the immunity for trade unions itself. This did indeed apply expressly to 'a trade union', and was said to be particularly objectionable inasmuch as it appeared to apply to all torts, and regardless of whether or not the golden formula applied. It went too far to suggest, as did some, that it made a trade union an extra-parliamentary, or extra-legal body (Hanson 1984: p. 71), for the immunity could at any time be altered or entirely repealed by Parliament, as indeed occurred in 1982. Nevertheless it was argued that, as long as it remained on the statute-book, the immunity appeared arbitrarily and unnecessarily sweeping in its coverage. For this view there was a notably wider range of support.[64]

The earlier account of the origins of the golden formula should warn us that when attempting to understand the trade-union immunity, we should consider the scheme as a whole of the Act in which it first appeared—the TDA 1906. As we have already seen, the Government of the day perceived the activities of unions and the business of collective bargaining, and hence industrial conflict, to be for its purposes effectively synonymous. The specific immunities were intended to give complete protection against all the torts which were thought likely to be committed in the course of industrial action.[65] Even if those protections could be assumed to extend to trade unions as well as individuals, there was still a separate problem regarding the possibility that a trade union might be held liable for the unlawful acts of

---

[62] For argument that such legislation is not in fact incompatible with the Rule of Law, see Raz (1979: ch. 11); but Hayek (1976) appears in any case to be opposed to 'social legislation'.

[63] Although Hayek's position may now amount to this owing to his sweeping opposition to 'social legislation'. In the past, however, he stated the requirement more narrowly as for an absence of *reference* in legislation to particular persons or groups. See Hayek (1960: pp. 153–4).

[64] e.g. Wedderburn (1965: p. 221); Donovan (1968: paras. 902–11).

[65] See Kidner (1982) on the rather haphazard way in which this was achieved.

individual members, a risk which had emerged as a result of the decision in the *Taff Vale*[66] case. Thus a further clause was required in order to protect trade unions from the possibility that they might otherwise be held automatically liable for the unlawful acts of individual members. The Government's original draft of such a clause therefore attempted to set out the circumstances in which an individual would be deemed to be acting under the authority of a committee running a dispute. Given this context it is not surprising to find that this clause did not make use of the golden formula and did not deal with specified torts. The first was not needed, for the reference to disputes committees made its subject-matter obvious. The second was inappropriate, for the clause was designed to govern the liability of the union, whatever tort might be alleged.[67]

During the debate following *Taff Vale*, some advisers of the unions and the Government—notably including Sir Charles Dilke (Gwynn and Tuckwell 1917: p. 367)—had warned that a clause of this type would suffer the inevitable weakness that the protection which it afforded, could, and on past experience probably would, be substantially eroded by judicial creativity, and that nothing short of an absolute immunity in tort could provide an effective defence against this possibility. The Government of the day was eventually persuaded by this argument and abandoned the original clause in favour of a new clause providing complete immunity in tort—which became section 4(1) of the 1906 Act. The point which is particularly worthy of note in view of what follows, concerns how what today we would view as the two diametrically opposed options—complete immunity versus liability with an agency regime—were perceived by the Government of the day as being two different ways of achieving the same objective, namely to protect the unions against unwarranted legal action.[68]

With the abandonment of any reference to strike committees and so forth, the new clause was not on its face restricted to industrial conflict. However, what became section 4(2) expressly *preserved* the liability of the trustees of a trade union to be sued under section 9 of the TUA 1871. Section 8 of that Act had provided that the property of a registered trade union should vest in its trustees; section 9 gave them the power to bring or defend actions 'touching or concerning the property, right or claim to property of the trade union'. Politically, the Government was thus able to emphasize that all that it was doing was re-creating the position which had been believed to be the law under the 1871 Act and which certainly had in practice operated for thirty years, a situation which trade unions had not abused in all that time, and which had facilitated developments which had been conducive to the public good.[69]

---

[66] *Taff Vale Railway Co.* v. *ASRS* [1901] AC 426.
[67] For the text of the clause, see Kidner (1982: p. 46, n. 79).
[68] See Sir W. Robson OR vol. CLV col. 1490 (25 Apr. 1906).
[69] Sir John Walton OR vol. CLXII cols. 1731–2 (3 Aug. 1906).

More specifically—and crucially—the Government argued that the coverage of the section 9 liability coincided with the types of activity which unions might engage in *outside of industrial conflict*. The example usually given was that of a union newspaper containing libellous material. In *Linaker* v. *Pilcher*,[70] it was held that the trustees of a trade union could be sued for such a libel by virtue of sections 8 and 9 because the property in the newspaper business vested in them. Similarly, the Attorney-General opined that section 9 would cover the other stock case: that of the baby run over by the driver of a union vehicle.[71] If anything, *obiter dicta* in the *Linaker* case suggested that the problem might be the reverse: that section 9 liability might be so wide as to render nugatory the protection granted by section 4. The Government at first asserted confidently that the actual *ratio* of the case was 'entirely outside a trade dispute'.[72] However, doubts continued to be voiced, so to make double sure, an amendment was finally introduced providing that section 9 claims would only be available outside the golden formula.[73] Thus, section 4 as enacted read:

(1) An action against a trade union, whether of workmen or masters, or against any members or officials thereof on behalf of themselves and all other members of the trade union in respect of any tortious act alleged to have been committed by or on behalf of the trade union, shall not be entertained by any court.

(2) Nothing in this section shall affect the liability of the trustees of a trade union to be sued in the events provided for by the Trades Union Act 1871 section 9 except in respect of any tortious act committed by or on behalf of the union in contemplation or in furtherance of a trade dispute.

So, although like the rest of the 1906 Act, its development owed much to the vagaries of the political process, the basic aim behind section 4 seems clear, namely to solve by a different means the same problem which had been solved by applying the golden formula to the individual immunities. It looked like a particularly effective solution, for it would require *both* an expansion of the scope of section 9 *and* a contraction of that of the golden formula for the protection provided by the section seriously to be breached.[74] In that light it is perhaps not surprising that the Attorney-General resisted an amendment proposing that the golden formula be applied to section 4(1), stating that this point was dealt with by section 4(2).[75]

So the function intended for section 4 was in fact no more ambitious than that of other sections of the 1906 Act, namely to protect the business of industrial action from the civil law, and to do this so far as possible in a manner which would not easily be vulnerable to adverse judicial sentiment.

[70] (1901) 17 TLR 256.

[71] Sir John Walton OR vol. CLXIV col. 165 (5 Nov. 1906).

[72] OR vol. CLXII cols. 1783–4 (3 Aug. 1906).

[73] See OR vol. CLXIV col. 229 (5 Nov. 1906).

[74] The structure also proved to be impervious to developments in the tort liabilities themselves in a way which the individual immunities were not.

[75] OR vol. CLXIV cols. 213–15 (5 Nov. 1906).

When, following repeal of the IRA 1971, this objective once again motivated the legislature, the provision was re-enacted in a revised form.[76] As the 1871 Act had also been repealed in 1971, it was necessary to set things out rather more fully. So while section 14(1) of TULRA 1974 restated the general immunity in tort, section 14(2) provided comprehensive exceptions in relation to both real and personal property and personal injury. The effect was intended to be the same as that of section 4(2), or if anything to create a broader exception to the general immunity,[77] but once again bolstered by confining the exception to matters occurring outside the golden formula.

Of course, just as the Attorney-General of the day had suggested that 'the term "trade dispute" related mainly if not solely to disputes arising from the exercise by trade unions of their functions',[78] so—then as now—did the reverse perception and preoccupation apply, namely that in these matters the concern with trade unions was the concern with the business of collective bargaining and collective disputes. It is this very fact which may help to explain why section 4(2) was taken in theory, and indeed proved in practice, to be of little importance, and in discussion of the section was invariably confined to the obscurity of footnote status, glossed over as incomprehensible, or left out altogether.[79] In turn, however, concentration became focused on the 'blanket' nature of the section 4(1) immunity, even in the context of discussions which themselves reflected the main concern with industrial conflict.[80]

This tale suggests that criticism of the trade-union immunity which focused purely on its apparently arbitrary width was arguably pitched too high. In all events, what has remained consistently true is that the real focus of concern on all sides has been with the effect of the immunity in the context of industrial conflict. In this context, as we have seen, a very real practical debate among Conservatives began in 1980 regarding the effect of retaining the trade-union immunity while the individual immunities were being cut back. As was argued earlier, a persuasive case was made out in 1980 that a narrow system of general immunities required the deterrent and remedial support of the availability of the trade union as a defendant. It was suggested that the Prior administration, convinced that politically such a step was not at this stage to be contemplated, were obliged to argue the rather problematic case that the existing remedies against individuals would continue to be

---

[76] For example, doubts about the applicability of the old section to injunctions were resolved. The 1906 Act was intended to cover injunctions but the Government had rejected a clarifying amendment, believing it to be unnecessary: OR vol. CLXIV col. 209 (5 Nov. 1906).

[77] See Wedderburn (1974: pp. 537–8); and in Select Committee on Employment (1981: p. 24, para. 21).

[78] See text to n. 25 above.

[79] But for discussion of the case-law which did emerge, see Grunfeld (1966: pp. 173–5); Hickling (1967: pp. 590, 595–6, and 196–205).

[80] A more pertinent perception was perhaps ironically that of those judges who remarked *per incuriam* that the immunity was limited by the golden formula: per Lord Denning MR *Gouriet* v. *UPW* [1977] 1 AER 696, 703, 713; Lord Scarman *NWL* v. *Woods* [1979] ICR 867, 886H–887A.

effective as against unlawful industrial action. The Prior administration's stance in this debate was effectively reiterated in the Green Paper (DE 1981a: pp. 13–14 and 27 ff.).

Against this background, one can see three factors contributing to Mr Tebbit's decision to repeal the immunity, over and above an acceptance of the argument of principle that it was 'anomalous' (DE 1981b: para. 30). First, Mr Tebbit evidently took a different view of the likely political effect of a repeal. As to whether repeal itself might provide a focal point for union resistance, he had the advantage of some two-years' more experience than Mr Prior, including the rather ineffectual 'Day of Action' against the 1980 Act. In addition, as Mr Prior has himself suggested, Mr Tebbit's judgement of the state of the union movement in the 1980s was not so heavily coloured by a similarly close involvement in the experiences of the Heath Government (Prior 1985). Nevertheless, the charge of a return to *Taff Vale* was inevitably continually levelled by the Opposition, and Government speakers consistently resisted it, arguing that unions would continue to enjoy the same immunities as individuals, which had not existed at all in 1901.[81] Government speakers also cited Sidney Webb, who had supported the principle of *Taff Vale*,[82] although they failed to set this in the context of his advocacy of a system of arbitration as preferable altogether to the use of industrial action, which he regarded as a kind of private warfare.[83] Regarding the political risks of the prospect of enforcement measures being taken against unions, instead of individuals, Mr Tebbit may have preferred the view of Sir Leonard Neal to that of Mr Prior, and, as we shall see in a moment, the unions were also to be given some incentive and opportunity to avoid that process.

Secondly, if Mr Prior's claim that the repeal was not necessitated by the removal of some protections for industrial action in 1980 had looked debatable, the matter may have seemed beyond much argument in the light of the further restrictions which were being introduced in 1982. Employers' representatives argued that they must now at least have available the option of taking legal action against unions, particularly as the focus of the new laws was on those who are not in a position directly to negotiate a settlement— parties who might both feel a greater need of the law and be more willing to use it.[84]

This view might have drawn support from the evidence given in response to the Green Paper. For example, Mr J. Melville Williams QC stated that in his experience injunctions had virtually always been obeyed in the period up

[81] See e.g. OR HC vol. 17 col. 744 (8 Feb. 1982) Mr Tebbit, anticipating the charge when first presenting the Bill.

[82] See ibid. col. 745.

[83] See Webb (1906).

[84] See e.g. the chair of the I.o.D. Industrial Relations Cttee. in *Personnel Management* (Feb. 1982). This aspect had particularly alarmed the TUC at the time of introduction of the 1980 Act: see Murray (1980). Evidence of researchers such as Younson (1984) suggests that 'third-party' employers were indeed chiefly responsible for the pick-up in litigation immediately after 1982.

until 1971. Since the 1971 Act, however, the situation had never quite been the same, and the issue of whether or not to obey an injunction on any particular occasion was frequently the subject of hot debate within the union concerned (Select Committee on Employment 1981: pp. 254–5, para. 2(b)).[85] Mr John Hendy, another barrister specializing in labour law, felt that such a situation had specifically been re-created by section 17 of the 1980 Act (Select Committee on Employment 1981: p. 252, para. 6). The purpose of memoranda such as these was to argue that a further narrowing of the immunities would only exacerbate the situation and that the better course would therefore be to repeal section 17 and move back to a situation in which unions would feel able to comply with the law. But here was material which might equally be used to support the argument that if one nevertheless *did* intend further to restrict the immunities, the repeal of section 14 would undoubtedly be necessary in order to complete the job properly. Further material might have been found in the TUC's own advice to its members which, whilst not directly advocating law-breaking, emphasized that the general approach should be 'business as usual', and set out the hurdles to be overcome in obtaining an effective injunction, and the techniques of 'avoidance' which could be adopted (TUC 1981a: esp. pp. 14–17). As we saw in chapter four, the CBI regarded repeal of section 14 as the lynchpin of its proposals, and, given the decision to take a next step, the majority of the Select Committee's conclusion, that if it did nothing else, the Government had to do this, may have been politically accurate.[86]

Finally, we should reconsider an additional argument put by the Prior administration, namely that even if a repeal were wholly uncontroversial, it would still make little difference in practice, because the vast majority of industrial action was unofficial, and it was difficult to see how a union could in general be held liable for such action at all (DE 1981a: para. 128).[87] The Tebbit administration's approach appeared, however, to be rather different, as appears most evidently from the vicarious liability regime introduced in conjunction with the repeal, to which we can now turn.

## (e) The Vicarious Liability Regime

This discussion has suggested that the Green Paper's focus on unofficial action, whilst undoubtedly logical in terms of the statistics on *numbers* of strikes, might have been thought rather old-fashioned from the point of view of a broader concern with the actual impact of strike activity in the early

[85] This view of pre–1971 attitudes was also borne out by Davies and Anderman (1974: p. 34).

[86] See Select Committee on Employment (1981: Report, p. viii, para. 22). It is noteworthy that, given the Labour Party's current proposal to retain some of the post-1979 restrictions if returned to power, the extent of the 'trade union immunity' which it would permit has become the subject of close scrutiny and fierce debate. See the 'policy review' document Labour Party (1989: p. 25); *Guardian* (30 Sept. 1989).

[87] On developments in 1990, see ch. 9 below.

1980s. In addition, it was out of line with the sort of thinking which saw the trade-union movement as now characterized not by militant shop stewards and shop-floor workers but by highly politicized leaders who were out of tune with and unresponsive to their more moderate membership. If any general model of the contemporary trade-union movement appealed to Mr Tebbit, it seemed to be the latter.[88] Himself a one-time official of the airline pilots' union BALPA, he brought with him to his new post a firm and long-held belief that the unions' rank-and-file membership were predominantly moderate and 'realistic' and averse to taking industrial action, but often found themselves dragooned into it at the behest of their leaders.[89]

Such views found their most explicit expression in the TUA 1984 and EA 1988, to which we will turn in later chapters, but we should note at this point their well-established nature and strength. In debates over the vicarious liability regime, the Government made it plain that it was not seeking to exert any specific controls over unofficial action, a fact reflected in the structure of the regime itself.[90] It eschewed any broad doctrine that local organizers who are not union officials may represent and bind the union by virtue of their authority derived from the individual members themselves,[91] and it allowed the union through its rule-book itself to define, if it chose, which bodies or individuals were to be treated as part of the organization of the lower ranks.[92] This flexibility allowed to unions in determining liability for the acts of lower-ranking members was in sharp contrast to the position with regard to the President, General-Secretary, and executive committee. For their acts, unions were to be made responsible regardless of the provisions of the rule-book. The Government stated that this was because these were 'people who would normally be regarded by the general public as speaking for the union'.[93] If the relevance of the opinions of the general public to such an issue at first appears unclear, it may be thought less so, say, in the context of a high-profile war of words between union leaders and employers or Government over a particular dispute.

The imposition of vicarious liability along these lines was no doubt seen as a first and crucial step towards the imposition of greater 'accountability', which the CBI in particular had so closely identified with the repeal of the trade-union immunity. From an early stage Mr Tebbit intimated that if trade-union leaders were not made more responsive to the wishes of their members through the introduction of greater direct controls, he might have

---

[88] See too the strong attack by Sir W. Goldsmith of the I.o.D. on union leadership which 'disgracefully represents' its members, in *Personnel Management* (May 1982: p. 15). The analysis appears to have appealed to many in Government circles at the time.

[89] See e.g. his speech in *Conservative Party Conference Report* (1977: p. 39).

[90] Mr Tebbit OR HC vol. 24 cols. 286–7 (18 May 1982); Mr Waddington OR St. Cttee. G 28th sitting (29 Apr. 1982) col. 1249. The analysis in this chapter is of EA 1982 s. 15 prior to its amendment in 1990.

[91] The approach of Lord Wilberforce in *Heatons Transport* v. *TGWU* [1973] AC 15.

[92] ss. 15(3)(*b*) and (4)(*a*).

[93] Mr Waddington OR St. Cttee. G 28th sitting (29 Apr. 1982) col. 1242.

to move to legislation on the subject.[94] In Mr Tebbit's ideal world—whether it came about by voluntary or legislative change—members would have both the incentive and the opportunity to remove leaders who 'damaged' the union by leading or indeed supporting 'irresponsible' and illegal industrial action.

Further aspects of the regime may be noted. The need for it at all had been made evident by the enormous uncertainties and difficulties created by the absence of one in the IRA 1971. The framers of that legislation may have envisaged that most trade unions would 'register' to obtain what benefits it offered, a procedure which required that the union demonstrate that it had clear rules governing, *inter alia*, the conduct of industrial action.[95] Registration was, however, widely boycotted, and the well-known litigation, notably, in the *Heatons* and *GAS* cases[96] ensued. In 1982 the Government was therefore careful to ensure that a regime was introduced which would avoid any possibility of the legal position resting upon union rule-books which might be silent or ambiguous in this area. As we have seen, with the exception of the leadership, the regime introduced did not insist on a particular scheme of liability, leaving it to the rule-book—but *only* if the rule-book was itself clear. The Government was meticulous in its adherence to this approach, and resisted amendments which would upset it, for example, by allowing the union to escape liability where the rule-book was silent.[97]

The history also makes it evident that the main cause for concern related to the liability of unions in connection with industrial action. As the Government argued, it was here that the problems had arisen in the past, and here that the lines of authority, and union rule-books, were notoriously obscure. It was therefore its aim that the regime should cover the 'industrial torts', by which the Government meant those torts which were commonly committed in the context of industrial action.[98] In this area, however, we can witness the draftsman coming up against similar problems to those encountered in connection with some aspects of the 1980 Act. Once again the draftsman chose to proceed by reference to the torts mentioned in section 13 of TULRA 1974, but this raised the difficulty that other torts, such as interference with business, nuisance, and so forth, which might also be committed in the course of industrial action, would not be governed by the regime. The Government's stated view was that, as long as one of the torts mentioned in section 13 was alleged in the proceedings, the wording of the section would ensure that the regime applied in respect of those proceedings as a whole.[99]

---

[94]  See e.g. OR HC vol. 17 col. 744 (8 Feb. 1982).

[95]  See IRA 1971 Pt. IV, Sch. 4.

[96]  *Heatons Transport* v. *TGWU* [1973] AC 15; *General Aviation Services* v. *TGWU* [1976] IRLR 224 HL.

[97]  See DE (1981*b*: para. 34), and for resisted amendments, see e.g. OR HL vol. 433 cols. 214–18 (13 July 1982).

[98]  See ibid. col. 208 Lord Mackay.

[99]  Ibid. If such was indeed the intention—and there is no particular reason to doubt it—the drafting of s. 15(2)(*a*) might have been clearer had it referred to proceedings which 'include a

This solution may have had much to commend it. On the one hand, the main target was undoubtedly industrial action. On the other, the Government appeared to want not to tackle all liability in tort. As well as going far beyond its requirements, and perhaps beyond the scope of the long title of the Bill, this approach would give the Opposition a very wide area over which to raise amendments, debating points, and objections. The combination of restricting the regime to cases where a section 13 tort was pleaded, combined with the application of a 'mixed proceedings' rule, may have been the best solution which could be devised. In the Lords, Lord Mackay suggested the following approach to the problem, which it is worth setting out in his own words:

The torts not covered . . . fall into four broad categories. First, there are the torts specified in section 14(2) of the 1974 Act, for which unions are already liable if committed outside a trade dispute. . . . These cases are rare . . . and it would seem odd to start applying special rules of liability to them now. Certainly there has been no suggestion . . . of there being any particular difficulty in dealing with cases in that area . . .

Secondly, there are other torts which are of a nature which make it very difficult to imagine how a union could be considered liable in the type of cases in which they could arise, such as battery or assault. Thirdly, there is a further group of torts . . . where there seems no justification for treating trade unions differently from corporate bodies such as companies, charities or clubs. There seems, for example, no necessity to treat libel cases over an article in a union journal differently from similar cases arising from a newspaper article.

Finally, there are some torts other than those specified . . . which . . . could arise as a result of industrial action . . . However, if these were committed during industrial action they would almost certainly arise in cases which also involve the 'industrial torts', so that the 'mixed proceedings' rule . . . would apply.[100]

Underlying the whole approach adopted in this area there was, it would seem, one vital consideration. This is that, although often said to set out rules of 'vicarious liability', this regime was really designed to achieve objectives not normally associated with the idea of vicarious liability as commonly understood. Consider again the example which is perhaps paradigmatic in the general law of vicarious liability: that of the vehicle involved in an accident. Whatever rationale lies behind the search for some principle of vicarious liability in such a case, the search is in essence for a defendant to a claim in

ground', rather than the more ambiguous 'on a ground'. On the other hand, the actual drafting is more consistent with the general aim of focusing litigation on the torts mentioned in TULRA s. 13.

[100] Ibid. cols. 208–9; the Government here failed to anticipate the rise of litigation by *employees* to restrain industrial action. Thus in *Thomas* v. *NUM (S. Wales Area)* [1985] IRLR 136, the main arguments turned on torts such as nuisance and 'harassment', and the common-law rules of liability were applied. However, if the Government's 'mixed proceedings' rule is correct, arguably that rule should have applied, for the proceedings did include a *claim* for interference with contract, although that claim failed. The interim injunction in *Richard Read* v. *NUM (S. Wales Area)* [1985] IRLR 67 may be more like what the Government envisaged.

respect of a one-off incident, who will be held liable by virtue of facts and circumstances applying at the time of that incident.[101] The section 15 regime is, however, concerned with liability in respect of a continuous incident—a piece of industrial action—arising from a continuing and possibly changing relationship between principal and agent over a period which may extend through and continue after the duration of the incident itself. The point is that it is not merely that union liability for industrial action needed to be treated separately because of the practical difficulties which have been discussed. It is in addition that the *policy* considerations involved in determining a union's liability for industrial action are quite different from those involved in a more conventional problem of vicarious liability. So the legal tests devised to deal with industrial action would simply not be appropriate in a conventional case.

This perhaps becomes clearest when we consider the opportunity which the statutory regime gives to a trade union to 'repudiate' some industrial action, for which it might otherwise be held responsible. It would surely seem strange were it the law that, for example, a union should be responsible if a driver on union business causes an accident, but that it can *after the event* evade that responsibility by repudiating the driver's action. It would be hard to imagine what purpose could be served by such a provision, which would seem peculiarly capricious in its attitude to the accident victim. In the context of determining a union's liability for industrial action, however, the concept has a long pedigree. We may recall that the Government of 1906 had experimented with its own code determining when an individual would be deemed to have acted under the authority of a union strike committee. This original clause in the 1906 Bill also qualified its rules with the proviso that there would be no liability if 'the committee by resolution expressly repudiate the act as soon as it is brought to their knowledge'.[102] In the context of the 1906 Act, we may recall, the emphasis was on the union's perspective, and on protecting it from unfairly being held responsible for the acts of militant or unruly groups. Ironically, in the context of the 1982 Bill, the intended effect appears to have been the same, although the emphasis behind the provision was rather different.

Once again, the union was to be given the means to dissociate itself from groups engaging in unlawful action, but this time it seemed that the concern was with the alleged practice of union leaderships adopting no particular public stance with regard to such action, allowing it the benefit of some tacit support, and perhaps even retrospectively making the action official and endorsing the back-payment of strike pay after it was over.[103] Thus, Government speakers repeatedly issued the advice that union leaderships

---

[101] On the many bases and doctrinal underpinnings of vicarious liability, see Atiyah (1967: chs. 1 and 2).

[102] See n. 67 above.

[103] Cf. the Select Committee's majority suggestion (1981: Report, p. ix, para. 23) that a genuine effort to restrain unlawful action might be demonstrated by suspension of strike pay.

would have in future to give careful consideration before indicating support for unofficial action of doubtful legality. If in doubt, the responsible thing would be to have nothing to do with such action.[104] Wording such as 'endorsed' and 'behaved in a manner' was deliberately and openly chosen to catch informal support—the 'nod and the wink',[105] and section 15(5) set out strict requirements regarding how a repudiation was to be carried out in order to be legally effective. So, although making no claims to exert specific positive controls over unofficial action in general, the Government conceded under some pressure from the Opposition that it was nevertheless clear that action could not henceforth be made official without the union becoming liable for it, and that action which was not 'official' according to the union rule-book might still be caught if it received informal leadership support.[106] To avoid such a consequence, a strict and unequivocal procedure of repudiation had to be undertaken and then kept to by one of the senior officials—the people who were regarded as the public face of the union.

This doctrine of repudiation, so alien, it is suggested, to normal ideas of vicarious liability, seemed to Opposition critics to be more at home in the context of an action for contempt.[107] We have seen that the experience of the 1971 Act suggested that, whether damages were available or not, an effective injunction would remain the primary goal of those concerned by unlawful industrial action; but as we have also seen, both the Prior and Tebbit administrations preferred to paint the repeal of the trade-union immunity as being primarily concerned with damages claims, studiously avoiding mention of matters like contempt and sequestration. Yet we also saw that much of the underlying logic of the repeal rested on the deterrent effect which it was thought that the prospect of fines and sequestration might have.

The Tebbit administration must surely have contemplated the prospect of contempt actions returning to the scene. However, if deterrent effect was indeed intended, then it may have been hoped that unions would in fact take steps to *avoid* being held in contempt, rather than face the penalties.[108] At least the legislation may have in some sense proceeded on that assumption, for, as had been pointed out throughout the debate on this issue, if a defendant chooses steadfastly and in the face of all punishment to defy the court, there is little that anyone can do to stop that: the law must assume some basic persuasive or deterrent force.[109] The statutory regime did not, as

[104] e.g. OR St. Cttee. G 29th sitting (29 Apr. 1982) col. 1307 Mr Waddington.

[105] See OR St. Cttee. G 28th sitting (29 Apr. 1982) cols. 1255–8; HL vol. 433 col. 227 (13 July 1982).

[106] OR St. Cttee. G 29th sitting (29 Apr. 1982) col. 1308 Mr Waddington.

[107] See Wedderburn OR HL vol. 433 col. 206 (13 July 1982); in the *Heatons* case the doctrine was enunciated by Lord Wilberforce, but only in relation to contempt and not initial liability, a point he expressly stressed in the later *GAS* case at [1976] IRLR 224, 227 para. 11.

[108] Cf. the equivocation of the TUC (1982: pp. 20–1) on support for members faced by legal actions.

[109] After the *Stockport Messenger* dispute in 1983, in which the NGA suffered fines, sequestration, and a damages award, Mr Murray suggested publicly for the first time that the unions might have to learn to live with the new legislation. Kidner's (1986) review of subsequent developments argues that the new law has been 'successful' when deployed to its full effect.

introduced in 1982, apply to proceedings for contempt,[110] but the incorporation of the doctrine of repudiation to some extent anticipated the problem.
By offering up the carrot of repudiation at the earlier stage of establishing
liability, the Government gave trade unions the means, if they chose to accept
its advice, of avoiding the subsequent stick of contempt proceedings
altogether.[111]

In sum, the structure of section 15 revealed both a carefully and precisely
formulated policy, and some skilful drafting to carry it into effect. The policy
focused both on the actions of leadership, for which the union was to be made
absolutely liable, and on those of unofficial 'militant' groups, from which the
union was to be encouraged to distance itself with the means *not* to be held
liable. The approach therefore rested not on a two-fold distinction between
union leadership and grass roots, but on a three-fold one between leadership,
unofficial shop-floor activists, and rank-and-file members, a model in which
the last were seen as consistently moderate and responsible when compared
with the other two.[112] Thus the section was the result of the combination of
tactical and drafting sophistication with essentially crude and monotypic
political analysis.

The 1982 Act drew further on historical precedent in its approach to three
other aspects of trade-union liability. First, it took up an idea first put
forward by the 1906 Royal Commission, which advised that *Taff Vale* should
be left to stand, but that unions' provident and benefit funds should be
protected from suit (Dunedin 1906: para. 66). The 1982 Act adopted this
approach,[113] but picked up a lesson from the 1971 Act, avoiding its approach
of allowing *any* fund not available to support industrial action to be
protected, for that had invited widespread 'avoidance' by amendment of
union rules.[114] As the Government pointed out, what remained might
represent only a small proportion of unions' annual incomes, and bear little
relation to the losses suffered by plaintiffs.[115]

However, the Government did adopt another limitation which had been
applied in the 1971 Act, namely that on the size of damages awards in relation
to the size of the union involved. The Government explained that it had used
the 1971 limits as the starting-point for its calculations of the figures, and had
somewhat lowered the limits from those suggested in the earlier consultative
paper, notably as the result of pressures from the Conservative Trade
Unionists.[116] The Government was no doubt sensitive to the charge that it

---

[110] It is submitted that the section was correctly applied on this point by the CA in *Express &
Star* v. *NGA* [1986] ICR 589. This will change in 1990, as is noted in ch. 9 below.

[111] An early illustration of how effective this could be came in the Austin-Rover dispute of
1984. See Hutton (1985: pp. 260–2).

[112] Cf. the CBI's (1980: p. 11) lament at the decline of the full-time official and the rise of the
shop steward.

[113] s. 17.

[114] TULRA 1974 s. 20 testifies to the extent of the avoidance.

[115] See OR HL vol. 434 col. 597 Lord Mackay; Gennard (1977: pp. 47–8).

[116] Mr Tebbit OR HC vol. 17 col. 746 (8 Feb. 1982).

might otherwise be exposing some unions to financial destruction, a possibility which the Green Paper had also explored (DE 1981a: para. 131). However, it insisted that plaintiffs had a right to be compensated, and refused amendments which would apply the limits to each incident as opposed to each set of proceedings.[117] In addition, fines and sequestrations were not subject to any limits, and it was through these that the provision was to take its most devastating toll.[118]

Finally, we may note that section 9 of the TUA 1871 still lives on in the guise of section 16(2) of the 1982 Act. This provided in essence that action which was never previously protected by virtue of TULRA section 14(2) would not now enjoy the benefit of the new damages limits. The Government's case was that, as such action had never been protected, there was no need for it suddenly to receive special treatment. The Opposition pointed out that, the 're-enactment' of section 14(2) in section 16(2) was in fact wider in scope than the former, because it was no longer restricted to action occurring outside the golden formula. The Government replied that the earlier application of the golden formula was 'an anomaly' as there was no reason why torts of this kind should be treated any differently simply because they occurred in the context of industrial conflict.[119]

We can turn now to consider a further change to the trade-disputes immunities introduced in 1982, namely that relating to action associated with union membership and recognition issues.

### (f) Union Membership and Recognition Disputes

Chapters two and three discussed the steps taken in 1980 to outlaw recruitment tactics of the type alleged to have been used in the late 1970s by the union SLADE. This measure was perhaps the best example of the 'step-by-step' and the 'specific abuse' approach adopted by Mr Prior. For, as the later Green Paper suggested, SLADE's tactics were regarded as only the worst example of what was perceived as a general problem of the use of commercial and industrial pressure to 'impose' membership arrangements or requirements (DE 1981a: pp. 70–5). As the Green Paper's discussion reveals, there was here a combination of related Conservative concerns. In part, such action was viewed as a form of unfair 'discrimination' by a union or a contractor refusing to deal with a non-union firm or the products of non-union labour. In part, there was once again present the general hostility towards secondary action in the sense of pressures brought to bear upon a firm from 'outside'. But perhaps the deepest underlying concern related to

[117] OR St. Cttee. G 29th sitting (19 Apr. 1982) col. 1304 Mr Waddington; both alternatives had been canvassed in the Green Paper (DE 1981a: para. 131).

[118] In the seafarers' dispute of 1988, for example, the NUS, which began with overall assets of less than £3m, suffered fines totalling £365,000, and sequestration costs of £½m together with legal fees.

[119] For these debates, see OR HL vol. 433 cols. 253–60 (13 July 1982).

the Conservative hostility to the institution of the closed shop, and hence to related practices which aim to spread union membership by means of commercial and industrial pressures.[120]

Thus, we may note that the Green Paper set its discussion of these matters in the context of the section dealing with closed shop and union membership issues, rather than in the context of proposed changes to union immunities, and changes to immunities were in this connection seen as the adjunct to a wider set of proposals. These matters had become particularly topical at this time in view of the extensive use of these practices by a number of Labour-controlled local authorities, sometimes in conjunction with local trade-union organization.[121] These issues had always been particularly sensitive in industries such as construction, and while Mr Prior had been careful in 1980 to ensure that his provisions would not touch, for example, disputes over the use of 'lump labour' on building sites, construction employers subsequently lobbied intensively for changes in the law.[122] In general this appeared to be one of the areas where Mr Prior would himself have liked to push ahead, given enough time (1986: pp 170–1). Mr Tebbit for his part made no secret of his own principled opposition to the closed shop, and made no apology for devoting more than half of his Bill to it.[123] All in all it was no surprise that his proposals included some further action in this area.

Our concern here is not with sections 12 and 13 which, in brief, outlawed arrangements which preferred or required union membership or recognition, but with section 14, relating to industrial action.[124] This had two parts. The first removed TULRA section 13 immunities from action designed to further any of the activities rendered unlawful by sections 12 and 13. The Government confirmed that section 14 followed the 1980 Act in relying on the assumption that the existing common law rendered action thereby exposed unlawful, and speculation that the section relied upon the creation of a new statutory tort appeared unwarranted.[125] The second part of section 14 replaced EA 1980 section 18, which was accordingly repealed. It followed meticulously the precedents of 1980 in respect of removing TULRA section 13 protection from the action proscribed, focusing on contractual relations, and stipulating as simply as possible the proscribed purposes.[126] Its scope

[120] Some critics talked simply of the 'secondary closed shop'. See e.g. Gardiner (1981: pp. 2 and 5); and cf. the subsequent, perhaps rather too 'broadly stated' conclusion of Caulfield J in *Messenger Newspapers* v. *NGA* [1984] IRLR 397, 399 that after 1982 the closed shop itself was now unlawful.

[121] See e.g. OR HC vol. 17 col. 743 (8 Feb. 1982) Mr Tebbit.

[122] See the submission of the Federation of Civil Engineering Contractors reproduced in Select Committee on Employment (1981: pp. 320–5).

[123] OR HC vol. 17 cols. 737 ff. (8 Feb. 1982).

[124] s. 14 was rewritten in 1988 to bring it into line with the further changes made by the EA 1988, which are discussed in ch. 8 below.

[125] Cf. Lord Wedderburn OR HL vol. 433 cols. 154–7 (13 July 1982); Lewis and Simpson (1982: pp. 230–1).

[126] Although the need to range beyond existing contractual relations was reflected in the stipulation—in contrast to 1980 s. 17(6)—that the target need not be attacked through a contractual connection. It follows, however, that in such a case the cause of action would have to be interference with business, rather than contract, as in the *Hadmor* case.

was notably expanded to include *any* pressure exerted on an employer who uses or is likely to use non-union labour, or does not or is unlikely to consult with or recognize a trade union. This was an important extension, because EA 1980 section 18 was only concerned with action which aimed to cause employees to join a union, action widely regarded as objectionable because it pressurized employees who had no desire of the union's services. The new provision went much wider, for it would apply equally to a case where the 'target' employees, for example, were already members of the union and wanted to achieve recognition, as where they did not. The new provision reflected a more general opposition to secondary action or 'outside' pressure of any sort being used to further disputes with employers over union membership and recognition issues. The Government explained: 'what the Bill does not affect is the right of an employer and employee to make arrangements between them about the union matters in that firm. What it does strike at is pressure from outside on these matters.'[127] Having noted one extension of the old section which the new provision did make, we should also note one which it did not. The requirement that the 'target' employer be other than the employer of those taking the action, was retained, but the requirement that the employees be at different locations was dropped. Thus, recognition disputes within a single business would not be touched, but whether a dispute within a single building site about the use of non-union labour was affected, would depend on whether employees of a separate employer, brought on to site, were involved.[128]

We have now considered all the changes to trade-union immunities introduced when the Bill was presented, but we cannot move on without looking briefly at one other change affecting industrial action.

## (g) Amendment of Section 62 EP(C)A 1978

Section 62 EP(C)A 1978 provides in essence that workers dismissed during an industrial dispute cannot claim unfair dismissal unless it can be shown that the employer has 'discriminated' by not dismissing all those involved, or seeking later to re-hire only some. EA 1982 made three amendments to section 62, which had already been through more than one change since it was first introduced with unfair dismissal legislation itself in 1971.[129] The Government argued that all three amendments were in some sense technical or designed to correct 'anomalies' in the existing provision.[130] This seems most clearly to have been so in relation to the introduction of a requirement

[127] OR HL vol. 433 col. 150 (13 July 1982) Lord Mackay.

[128] Cf. the hesitation in the earlier proposals about the possibility of eradicating the 'deep-rooted' hostility of trade unionists in some industries to working *alongside* non-union employees (DE 1981*b*: para. 28); but refusal to work with non-union employees *brought on site* was now specifically among the Government's targets: see OR HL vol. 433 col. 174 (13 July 1982).

[129] EA 1982 s. 9; Wallington (1983) is a useful summary of the history.

[130] For the debates to which the text refers and from which it quotes, see OR St. Cttee. G 24th sitting (22 Apr. 1982) cols. 1108 ff.; HL vol. 433 cols. 116–18 (12 July 1982).

that to avoid a charge of discrimination the employer need only dismiss all those taking part in the industrial action at the time of the applicant's dismissal. In *Stock* v. *Frank Jones*[131] the House of Lords had held that the existing wording required the employer to dismiss everyone who had taken part in the action, even those who had returned to work by the time of the applicant's dismissal. This might indeed reasonably be regarded as an anomaly.

A similar, though perhaps not quite as strong a case, could be made in respect of the introduction of a three-month limit on the period during which selective re-engagement will be held to constitute discrimination. The Government pointed out that an earlier incarnation of the provision had also given a 'cut-off' point, namely the end of the dispute. That wording had, however, been regarded as dangerously vague and uncertain, and was later repealed.[132] The Government's simple argument was that it should have been replaced by some other provision, so that the employer's liability should not be open-ended. A fixed time limit would be unambiguous, and three months was argued to be not unreasonable as the vast majority of disputes were of much shorter duration.

It is when we turn to the third amendment that the claim to be dealing with anomalies and technical points looks weakest of all. After 1982 an employer need only avoid discrimination within the *establishment* at which the dismissed claimant was employed. Previously the relevant 'pool' was all participating employees of the same employer. The Government suggested that this too gave rise to an anomaly revealed by *Stock* v. *Frank Jones* because where there were several establishments in a large firm, perhaps in different parts of the country, an employer would presently have to treat all alike, even where the employees at some had returned to work, a fact of which the manager in charge of one particular establishment might not even be aware. Whilst it was correct for the Government to argue that problems of this type might indeed arise if *Stock* were left untouched, the amendment already being introduced in respect of that case would in fact have catered perfectly well to this problem as well. For that amendment would mean that all employees who had returned to work at the date of the applicant's dismissal would be excluded from the 'pool', whether employed at the same or at a different establishment. A further amendment specifically to restrict the pool itself in *all* cases to the applicant's own establishment was not therefore required to remedy this particular problem. What it *would* do would be to give the employer the opportunity to dismiss employees only at a particular establishment, without fear of a tribunal challenge.

Traditional wisdom had regarded section 62, like the usual lack of contractual protection for individual employees taking industrial action, as being of little practical importance in most disputes, because for an employer

---

[131] [1978] ICR 347.
[132] See Wallington (1983: p. 313).

either to want or to be able to dismiss an entire striking work-force was an extreme rarity. Such actions are rather more common today, a fact which has reinforced the case of those who argue that a positive individual right to strike should accompany one to organize a strike.[133] But the usefulness as a versatile tactical weapon of the ability formally to dismiss and then offer re-engagement to some or all of the work-force should also not be underestimated.[134] That the Government was in 1982 well aware of this appeared to be clear. At one point Mr Tebbit remarked that the changes intended to section 62 would allow employers to make a 'credible and legitimate response' when faced with industrial action.[135] The original draft of the clause would have provided for employers to issue an ultimatum to employees to return by a certain date or be dismissed.[136] Employers' organizations were, however, unhappy with this approach because of the difficulties in compliance which might arise and because of a principled objection to being required to give notice before exercising a right to dismiss.[137]

The Government certainly perceived some advantages of being able to deal with each establishment separately. It noted 'the different effects on profitability and continued viability of each establishment' which industrial action might have. Here it seems pertinent to remind ourselves that a combination of common law and statutory rules will usually bar any possible claim for a redundancy payment as well as for unfair dismissal,[138] and of the Government's view that '[s]trikes are bound to have an adverse effect on competitiveness which in many cases leads to losses of jobs and sometimes ultimately to closures.'[139] Also, the 'establishment' amendment would 'help to deter selective strike action in multi-plant undertakings, which has been a regrettable consequence of Section 62 as currently framed'. It was also noted in this connection that the originally proposed 'warning notice' clause had another disadvantage in that it applied only to strikes and not to other forms of industrial action, which might 'encourage action short of a strike which could be as damaging as a strike in its effects on the undertaking'. These comments will be of particular interest when we turn to look at the proposals of the EEF in section (1) below.

In conclusion it is surely a more realistic judgement of section 9 to take the view that the correction of the problem revealed in the *Stock* case provided

---

[133] The notorious examples are the Wapping dispute of 1986–7 and the seafarers' dispute of 1988. See Ewing and Napier (1986: pp. 291–2 and 301–4); *P & O European Ferries (Dover) Ltd.* v. *Byrne* [1989] IRLR 254; Ewing (1986: pp. 149–53); Napier (1987).

[134] For an example, see *Marsden* v. *Fairey Stainless* [1979] IRLR 103 EAT.

[135] OR HC vol. 17 col. 743 (8 Feb. 1982).

[136] 1982 Bill no. 56, Cl. 7.

[137] See OR St. Cttee. G 24th sitting (22 Apr. 1982) cols. 1110–11.

[138] A striker is normally in repudiatory breach of contract and forfeits redundancy protection: *Simmons* v. *Hoover* [1977] ICR 61 EAT; under the rule in s. 62 as presently worded, the *reason* for dismissal, both of the claimant and of other members of the pool is irrelevant: see the *Marsden* case n. 134 above; *McCormick* v. *Horsepower* [1981] ICR 535 CA.

[139] OR HC vol. 999 Written Answers col. 414 (26 Feb. 1981).

the opportunity for a reconsideration of the impact of the section upon industrial action in general, and the introduction of some more substantial changes.[140] Indeed we may note that amendment of the section had not been canvassed in the Green Paper at all—although it was mentioned in some of the responses—and that the Proposals preceding the Bill made no mention of the 'establishment' amendment (DE 1981*b*: paras. 38–9).

We can turn now to consider some of the more important proposals which Mr Tebbit chose *not* to take up in 1982.


## (h) Secret Ballots

As has been noted, Mr Tebbit was undoubtedly an enthusiast for the greater use of secret ballots in all aspects of trade unions' affairs. But as the debates of 1980 and 1981 had suggested, there were many difficult and substantial problems to be solved if ballots were in any sense to be legally imposed.[141] Mr Tebbit, continuing in the line of a 'step-by-step' approach, therefore chose to adopt a more long-term strategy, repeatedly warning the unions of the need to speed up 'voluntary reforms', and indicating that if progress were not sufficiently swift, legislative action might have to be considered.[142] In the mean time, the list of purposes for which state funds were available under the 1980 Act to defray the expenses of ballots, was enlarged.[143] In addition, the revised closed-shop code which came into effect in May 1983 included more stringent discouragement of disciplinary action, adding to a list which included cases where industrial action has not been affirmed in a secret ballot, cases where it is unlawful under the 1980 and 1982 Acts.[144]


## (i) Picketing

Mr Tebbit ignored calls for two further types of measure in relation to picketing. First, as we have seen, there was the call for tougher criminal controls, including conversion of parts of the code of practice into full legislation. However, following its resurgence during the steel strike of early 1980, picketing had somewhat drifted out of the public consciousness as a serious problem. In addition, Mr Tebbit would have had no particular cause to differ from Mr Prior's views that the substance of the criminal law was quite adequate and that the code came about as close as it was wise to get to

---

[140] Although the stream of subsequent case-law suggests that s. 9 has by no means eliminated all the hazards faced by employers who seek to rely on s. 62, especially those who initiate a lock-out.

[141] Some were set out by Earl Ferrers when rejecting a proposed amendment to the 1982 Bill to introduce strike ballots: OR HL vol. 434 cols. 568–71 (2 Aug. 1982).

[142] See e.g. Tebbit at n. 94 above; Tebbit (1981).

[143] See SIs 1982/953 and 1982/1108.

[144] Paras. 61–2; defended by Mr Tebbit: OR HC vol. 34 cols. 814–15 (21 Dec. 1982).

telling the police how to do their job.[145] The other type of measure, also canvassed in the Green Paper (paras. 172 ff.), was designed to combat the procedural problems of obtaining effective injunctive relief against picketing; but once again like Mr Prior, Mr Tebbit may have considered this to be in practice an insufficiently major problem to justify changes which would be difficult to implement and would again upset the sensitive position of the police. This view may have been especially reinforced in the light of Mr Tebbit's concurrent proposal to repeal the trade-union immunity, a step which would appear to open up a major alternative to the problems of enjoining individuals.[146]

### (j) Emergency Powers / Essential Supplies

The Green Paper considered the possibility of improving legal powers to maintain essential services and supplies. It has already been noted how this had returned as a central issue in the winter of discontent. However, although the early years of Conservative Government saw a steady stream of public-sector disputes involving steel, nurses, railway workers, pitmen, and Government employees, nothing approaching a repeat on the scale of the situation of 1979 had yet been threatened. Once again, Mr Tebbit may have had little reason to differ from Mr Prior's view that to increase Governmental powers in this area was likely to cause more problems than it solved. The lessons of the Heath administration, together with the Government's 'hands-off' rhetoric, even in relation to the public sector, precluded any suggestion of reintroducing statutory cooling-off periods or any similar provision.

The Government rejected an amendment to the Bill proposing to exclude from the golden formula industrial action which threatened 'life or limb' or 'urgent and requisite medical treatment', arguing that the responses to the Green Paper had confirmed the view that these types of industrial action would be very difficult to prevent by legislative means.[147] In reality, bearing in mind, no doubt, the advice of the Ridley report, the Conservative Government preferred at this stage to adopt a careful and *ad hoc* approach to major public-sector disputes, where necessary avoiding outright confrontation where this seemed particularly unwise. Although the policy was not always carried through with perfect precision, as perhaps in the steel dispute of 1980, it was broadly successful in avoiding a repeat of the winter of discontent.[148]

---

[145] See e.g. OR HC vol. 13 cols. 153–4 (17 Nov. 1981) Mr Waddington, arguing that the Code of Practice was largely being observed, and stressing again the breadth of the criminal law, which it was for the police to enforce.

[146] But on subsequent developments, see Auerbach (1987).

[147] OR HL vol. 434 col. 627 (2 Aug. 1982).

[148] For assessments of this policy, see Kahn *et al.* (1983: pp. 127–43; Holmes (1985*b*: ch. 6); Soskice (1984: esp. pp. 314–16).

### (k) Legal Enforceability of Collective Agreements

It was little surprise that no strong case was put in 1982 for directly reversing the statutory presumption that collective agreements are not intended to be legally enforceable contracts.[149] The Green Paper's discussion had rehearsed the notorious experience under the IRA that such a measure would achieve little or no practical effect (ch. 3B). Nevertheless, employers' organizations had suggested an alternative way of promoting the underlying main goal of greater compliance with collectively agreed procedures, proposing that immunities be made conditional upon such procedures having been observed.[150]

The Government did not adopt this idea either. In part it may not have seemed a high priority: the issue of unconstitutional strikes overlapped closely with that of union liability for unofficial action, the Tebbit administration's approach to that issue might be regarded as equally applicable to this.[151] In addition, there were still great practical problems with this approach. The chief problem, noted in a written answer, was that 'the majority of current procedure agreements are not sufficiently clear or comprehensive to bear the weight of legal interpretation.'[152] Mr Tebbit also pointed out that trade unions might simply race through, or avoid agreeing, complex procedures.[153] In general he concluded that this was not a problem which legal measures could help solve, at least not at this stage.[154]

### (l) The EEF Proposals

One final proposal rejected by the Government merits discussion. This was the EEF's call for a right for employers to lay off sections of their work-force without pay in the event of industrial action, whether internal to the enterprise or external, resulting in 'serious disruption' to the employer's business. The idea, which had been floating around during 1980 without receiving much sympathetic consideration,[155] was strenuously promoted by the EEF. It put the case in its reply to the Green Paper,[156] and subsequently lobbied hard during the passage of the 1982 Bill. It secured the tabling of amendments in the House of Lords, but these were rejected by the Government.[157] The proposal is of some theoretical interest and importance because it suggests an approach to the immediate damage and disruption

---

[149] TULRA 1974 s. 18.

[150] See e.g. CBI (1981: paras. 40–4); I.o.D. (1981: paras. 32–41).

[151] And cf. IRA 1971 s. 36(2) obliging a party to take reasonable steps to prevent its agent from breaching a binding agreement.

[152] OR HC vol. 17 Written Answers col. 103.

[153] See Select Committee on Employment (1982: para. 167).

[154] OR HC vol. 13 cols. 636–7 (23 Nov. 1981).

[155] See Prior (1986: pp. 167–8).

[156] Reproduced in Select Committee on Employment (1981: p. 233, para. 12).

[157] See EEF (1981–2); OR HL vol. 433 col. 177 (13 July 1982).

caused by industrial action, quite different from that entailed by making the action itself simply unlawful. In particular it is a solution which an employer may adopt not only regardless of whether he is in a position to negotiate, or influence negotiations, with those taking the industrial action, but also without any need to threaten or resort to litigation. This is not without significance, for as was noted earlier, the EEF was highly sceptical about the practical utility of further changes in the immunities and about whether such changes would in any case survive a general election.[158] Proposals which avoided litigation or direct confrontation with those taking the action therefore had an obvious attraction.

Yet *some* change in the law was still needed. In fact the proposal assumes that a number of conditions are fulfilled. Most of the direct harms which external or internal industrial action cause to a business can be avoided if three elements can be made to coincide. First, the employer must be reconciled to the loss of production while the disruption lasts. The actual loss of income involved may be quite small if order books are not completely full and it is possible still to fulfil most existing orders according to a revised schedule. Secondly, however, the employer must be sure that there is no significant contractual liability to customers for such delays as do occur. This may be achieved if it is the common practice in the industry for commercial contracts to contain 'force-majeure' clauses throwing onto the customer the risk of delays caused by events such as industrial action.[159] Finally, the employer must be relieved of liability in respect of the major overhead: the wages of employees. In an internal dispute, striking employees need not be paid. If, whether the dispute be internal or external, idle employees can also be sent home unpaid, then other overheads such as heat, light, and safety equipment can simply be switched off. It was for a legal provision giving this entitlement to lay off without pay that the EEF called.

The problem arose chiefly from the history of employment and collective bargaining practices in the industry. It was argued that while the right to lay off manual employees had been secured, there was no such right in respect of 'staff' employees, nor any prospect, given the current balance of bargaining power, that it might be collectively negotiated. The result was typically a co-ordinated bargaining strategy by manual and staff employees which employers could do little to combat.[160] The growth in employment protection laws was also cited as a further obstacle. At the same time, argued the EEF, internal action in which a few key staff employees were taken out to devastating effect, was becoming more prevalent, while the increased application of advanced technology to industrial processes had also increased

---

[158] See Frodsham (1981*a*); Soskice (1984: pp. 316–18).

[159] But see *B & S Contracts* v. *Victor Green Publications* [1984] ICR 419 CA on the duties which the employer may owe to the customer when seeking to rely on such a provision.

[160] See now *Bond and Neads* v. *CAV* [1983] IRLR 360 QBD on the general law, and also giving a very restrictive interpretation of existing collectively agreed lay-off provisions.

the propensity of external action of many kinds to affect businesses adversely.[161]

This proposal can be viewed in a number of lights. First, it sheds further light on the general problem of restricting the spread of the impact of industrial action beyond the primary employer. As we have seen, restrictions on secondary action represent a partial response to this problem, but these proposals demonstrate that the *consequential* effects of primary industrial action, through its impact on the primary employer's own commercial relations, were regarded by some as equally, if not more, serious. The proposal can be regarded as a plea for a statutory *force-majeure* clause to be implied into contracts of employment, shifting the major element of the risk of industrial action from 'innocent' employer to innocent employee, whilst, as we have seen, other elements might be similarly shifted out to the customer. In response to the argument that employers were asking to be relieved of legal liability for action which they had themselves taken, some supporters of the provision argued that such a situation would nevertheless have been 'caused' by the union taking the original industrial action.[162]

But a portrayal of the proposal as merely intended to facilitate a defensive response to events beyond an individual employer's control would be misleading. The EEF recognized tactical advantages as well. For example, one result might be that those planning industrial action might be to some degree deterred if they knew that it would adversely affect fellow employees or trade unionists.[163] Furthermore, in a case of selective internal industrial action, those laid off may be just as much involved in the underlying dispute as those actually taking the action, the action by key employees being simply the chosen means of furthering a dispute affecting a much larger group of employees within the firm. In such a case, lay-off is not simply an employer reaction to the *effects* of industrial action, but also a tactical response in the dispute itself.[164]

Although these issues are of great theoretical interest, we need not pursue them further here, for the proposals were not adopted by the Government. Lord Gowrie stated that while the Government was sympathetic to the proposals, it felt that there were nevertheless profound legal and practical problems involved. He suggested that, in line with the step-by-step approach, such measures might receive further consideration for possible incorporation in a future round of legislation.[165] Nevertheless, it was apparent that the Government had no great enthusiasm for these ideas. As has been suggested, they were in fact a good deal more controversial than the

[161]  See references given in nn. 156–7 above.
[162]  OR HL vol. 433 col. 178 (13 July 1982) Lord Harris.
[163]  See Frodsham (1981*b*).
[164]  Cf. EEF (1979*a*) advising members not to offer lay-off pay to those affected by internal industrial action; and cf. discussion in ch. 10 below.
[165]  OR HL vol. 433 col. 186 (13 July 1982).

EEF's presentation made them appear, and would have presented a major break from the strategy of opening up the availability of employers' existing common-law remedies. The Government may also have sympathized with the fervent opposition of bodies such as the I.o.D. which suggested that to adopt the proposals would be a dangerous encouragement of a 'strike mentality', because of the implied suggestion that strikes of this nature were to be accepted as a fact of industrial life.[166] Once again it may have been felt that the extent of the problem was open to question and that other measures in the 1980 and 1982 Acts would provide some relief.[167] But perhaps the main objection was to a claim for an employer 'immunity' of much the same kind as was so criticized when given to workers. Mr Tebbit stated that he was 'not persuaded' by the EEF's arguments for 'such a radical change in the law . . . to give employers the right to break their contracts at will'.[168]

### (m) The Repeal of TULRA Section 13(2)

One further alteration to the immunities has been left until last, namely the repeal of TULRA section 13(2) by EA 1982 section 19(1). The story has some similarities with that of the repeal of section 13(3) in 1980, although the history of section 13(2) is considerably easier to relate. The provision re-enacted part of TDA 1906 section 3. *Allen* v. *Flood*[169] is generally taken to stand for the principle that an act which interferes with a person's business or trade is not, of itself, unlawful. In 1906, however, the legal status of that authority seemed uncertain, in the light of the apparently irreconcilable decision in *Quinn* v. *Leathem*.[170] The 1906 Act therefore gave statutory effect to the principle of *Allen* v. *Flood*, a provision reintroduced in 1974 as section 13(2), 'for the avoidance of doubt'. In spite of the clarity of the legislative history, Lord Diplock remarked in the *Hadmor* case that section 13(2) must be taken to protect interferences with business which involved the use of unlawful means.[171] This *dictum* was then cited shortly after in the Scottish decision of *Plessey* v. *Wilson*[172] as the legal basis for holding that a factory sit-in could not be enjoined.

This decision, handed down on 23 March 1982, while the Employment Bill was yet to go before the Lords, presented the Government with a difficult problem. It could have ignored the decision on the basis that this was a Scottish case, where the law of trespass was arguably different,[173] that it was

---

[166] See Select Committee on Employment (1981: p. 149, para. 835, Mr Goldsmith).

[167] Cf. eg. the Government's comments—noted above—on the improvements which s. 9 would bring about in the employer's ability to respond effectively to selective industrial action short of a strike.

[168] See *EG* (May 1982: p. 190); *Personnel Management* (June 1982: p. 9).

[169] [1898] AC 1.

[170] [1901] AC 495.

[171] [1983] 1 AC 191, 229D–E.

[172] [1982] IRLR 198 CS.

[173] See Miller (1982).

based on a very poor piece of reasoning, deriving from an isolated and off-the-cuff dictum, and given only in an interim ruling. All in all it may have seemed unlikely that the heresy would be repeated or adopted in English law.[174] Set against this, there was legislation before Parliament to which new provision might easily be added. The Scottish TUC had reputedly hailed the decision as a 'charter for sit-ins', and employers north of the border were displaying some anxiety.[175] The Government could have offered them few excuses for simply doing nothing.

Amendment of section 13(2) was clearly an option, but the draftsman may once again have baulked at the thought of the likely judicial reception of an amendment to a provision expressed to be 'for the avoidance of doubt', as well as at the very mechanics by which such an amendment would in fact be achieved, without interfering, or providing a plank for further judicial interference with the remaining structure of immunities. By contrast a total repeal may have been considerably more attractive. In the years since 1906, *Allen* v. *Flood* seemed to have secured judicial acceptance, although on occasion with reluctance, and *Quinn* became conventionally, however unsatisfactorily, distinguished as a case of conspiracy.[176] *Repeal* of a provision originally enacted for the avoidance of doubt might indeed make sense in the light of that doubt having in subsequent years substantially faded. This was indeed the Government's preferred course. So far, at least, there appear to have been no adverse consequences.

## (3) THE EMPLOYMENT ACT 1982: INITIAL ASSESSMENT

The further restrictions on the immunities introduced in 1982 were undoubtedly substantial. Yet, Mr Tebbit's claim to be following in the 'step-by-step' approach appeared to be well founded. However, there need be no contradiction involved here, for the step-by-step approach at bottom dictates only the overall *timing* of changes, and of itself entails no restriction on their eventual extent. Mr Tebbit, as was noted, was already laying the ground for further possible measures, while the 1982 proposals were being put through. Although in outlook and rhetoric hardly conciliatory, he also displayed a strong pragmatist streak. Thus, his package caused anxiety to bodies like the IPM, but also fell well short of the agenda of documents like *Liberties and Liabilities*. Once again the CBI seemed to be the body most satisfied by the changes.[177]

[174] Cf. the subsequent Scottish case of *Phestos Shipping* v. *Kurmiawan* [1983] SLT 388 where the court argued around the *Plessey* decision in granting an interim interdict in respect of an occupation of a ship.

[175] See Miller (1982) on the prevalence of sit-ins north of the border; OR HL vol. 433 col. 295 (13 July 1982) for the Government's case.

[176] See Davies and Freedland (1984*a*: pp. 711–13).

[177] See *The Times* (15 Oct. 1981) for Mr Tebbit's own warning that his proposals might disappoint some Conservatives, and employers' views summarized in *Personnel Management* (Jan 1982: pp. 9–10) and (1982) 20 *BJIR* p. 118.

Nevertheless, the decision to press forward with key measures such as the repeal of TULRA section 14, effectively signalled the abandonment of any serious hopes of maintaining a consensus around a largely voluntarist framework of labour law, and a move towards a framework geared to cope, if need be, with the prospect of a less infrequent involvement of the law in industrial conflict. Yet even here there is a countervailing observation to be made, for that gearing was itself in part based on the footing that trade unions might be encouraged to behave in such a manner as to avoid actual litigation, and, by contrast with 1971, the 1982 Act carefully preserved the approach of 1980 of leaving remedies entirely to those aggrieved, who might choose whether or not to take them up. While comparisons between the TUC's campaigns of the 1980s and those of ten years before might have suggested that the unions would in general be in a more compliant mood this time around, uncertainty about outright confrontation with the union movement seems yet to have had some restraining effect. Perhaps, then, the words to emphasize at the start of this paragraph are 'if need be'.

As was mentioned at the start of this chapter, another apparent change was signalled by the early pronouncements that the 1982 measures were framed with regard to the economic and labour market effects of industrial action. Restrictions on industrial action would naturally be looked upon with favour by those concerned about the effect of union activity on inflation and competitiveness. Mr Tebbit was no doubt more eager than Mr Prior had been to commend his measures in such terms, being a more committed supporter of Government economic policies, and not inhibited by a preferred approach to economic problems which required the active co-operation of the union movement. The provisions contained in the 1982 Act certainly set up no tension with economic policy.

However, it seems harder to see a specific economic theory as the most important or key positive driving force behind the 1982 measures on industrial conflict. Looking at its package of provisions together, the 1982 Act seems similar to the 1980 Act in the way that each has its own particular history, sometimes going well back. The uncertainty preceding Mr Prior's departure meant that Mr Tebbit's proposals and subsequent Bill were produced with enormous speed. It seems clear that the 1981 Green Paper formed the main agenda from which they were drawn, increasing the traditionalist look of the changes introduced. Several measures revived provisions of the IRA 1971, which themselves reflected traditional Conservative preoccupations going back even further.[178] So there was evidently a healthy input of argument which dated well back before the ascendancy of the contemporary Conservative leadership. This was so, for example, with regard

[178] See e.g. CPC (1968: pp. 19, 27, and 30–1) on trade-union immunity, narrowing of the golden formula, pressure to impose a closed shop, and other measures; IOCCAUS (1958: p. 54) on political strikes, procedure agreements and worker–worker disputes.

to political action which Lord Hailsham called 'intrinsically immoral'[179] and in general with regard to action associated with the closed shop.[180] Some action appeared to fall into more than one category. The ITF were particularly unlucky, their activities falling foul of the legislation as unwarranted 'outside pressure', illegitimate concern with foreign affairs, and economically harmful interference with trade and employment.

Notwithstanding the shift in rhetorical tone, it would appear mistaken, then, to view the 1982 measures simply as an intended and coherently formulated instrument of labour market and economic policy involving a major departure from past practice. Mather's assessment that the 1982 Act 'succeeded because it recognised [the] connection between law and economics' (1987: p. 5) is altogether too simplistic. In common with the Prior administration, but again in its own way, the Tebbit administration pursued its own particular priorities and preoccupations in the choice of proposals which it adopted. Although many of the demands of employers' organizations were satisfied, some of their campaigns suffered notable defeats. As well as the EEF campaign, we may note again the failure of the small businesses lobbies to make any headway in their requests for greater support in tackling industrial conflict, and this notwithstanding the Government's frequent portrayal of itself as the friend of the small business.

Of course, there were still some consistent broad themes underlying these measures, and in particular a distinctive balance of general political and social attitudes. Like the 1980 Act, the 1982 Act rests on attitudes about the extent of both the 'social legitimacy' of union activity, and the acceptable degree of disruptive harms entailed by conflict. The attitudes to the latter were perhaps much the same in 1982 as in 1980, being broadly that it is unacceptable to spread industrial disruption or action beyond the confines of the unit which a dispute concerns, so as to involve 'innocent' or 'disinterested' parties. Mr Prior was limited in the degree to which he pursued the logic of this view, by the extent of his recognition of the argument that trade unions ought nevertheless to be allowed to wield sufficient power to match or balance that of capital. Mr Tebbit's legislation, particularly in its amendments to the golden formula, may be thought to reflect a rather narrower view of the nature and legitimate social functions of trade unions and of collective bargaining. When he presented the Bill to the Commons, Mr Tebbit stated that he accepted—and that the Bill would not affect—the three basic 'trade union rights' which the TUC had claimed in evidence before the Select Committee, namely the rights to combine, to be recognized for collective bargaining purposes, and to strike.[181]

---

[179] Oral evidence to Select Committee on Employment (1981: p. 9, para. 703).

[180] The link between attitudes to the closed shop and to industrial action was expressed in the decision in *Rookes* v. *Barnard* [1964] AC 1129. The Conservative Party subsequently argued that the Trade Disputes Act 1965 which reversed that decision should be repealed: see CPC (1968: p. 27).

[181] OR HC vol. 17 col. 742 (8 Feb. 1982).

The core of the argument in favour of trade-union immunities was to remain unchallenged in 1982; but, as Lord Wedderburn has pointed out (1985a: p. 43), the employment unit was now to mark the level at which workers' need for economic power balanced evenly with the disruptive harm caused by industrial action. Union functions, such as forming a medium for the expression of collective desires or points of view, for the purposes of bargaining and generally communicating with the employer, and of deciding whether or not to take industrial action, might then quite naturally be regarded as matters for decision entirely within the boundaries of that unit. Perhaps the strongest underlying thread here is the notion that, whatever internal problems or differences may arise, all workers share an overriding common interest with management in the fortunes of the enterprise, which therefore forms the appropriate crucible for union activity. Something of Mr Tebbit's philosophy here may have been revealed by a reminiscence (whether accurate or not one cannot say) which he offered to the Conservative Party Conference in 1981: 'Nothing in [the forthcoming proposals] would have impaired my work in the past as a trade unionist seeking to improve the lot of my fellows by improving our ability to create wealth and prosperity for our employers.'[182] The notion of a particular conception of the functions of trades unions seems to be an appropriate one on which to close, for it is a theme which will play an important part in the chapters which follow.

[182] See *The Times* (16 Oct. 1981). Cf. Tebbit (1982: paras. 157–8 and 162).

# [6]
# Democracy in Trade Unions: The Debate 1983

## (1) INTRODUCTION

In concluding chapter five, it was suggested that Mr Tebbit's claim to be following the step-by-step approach, pioneered by Mr Prior, was perfectly valid. Step-by-step is essentially a tactical or strategic doctrine, one of the wisdom of which Mr Tebbit was clearly persuaded. His difference with Mr Prior related rather to the *number* of steps which might be taken before pausing for breath. For Mr Prior, the limits of what could be achieved by the approach appeared for the time being to have been reached after only one bite at the cherry; Mr Tebbit was whetting appetites for a third bite even while the second was being taken. In retrospect it seems that, in respect of industrial conflict and perhaps also the closed shop, the passage of the Trade Union Act 1984 did, however, mark the end of an initial phase of legislation, the Government only returning to these issues early in 1987.[1] Nevertheless, at the time when the 1984 Act was taking shape, the prospect of more imminent further measures appeared as a distinct possibility. In September 1983 Mrs Thatcher indicated that the step-by-step process might go on indefinitely: 'I would think a Bill is needed in alternate years until we have got it right.'[2]

As we have seen, Mr Tebbit soon made it clear that the priority issue on his mind was that of 'democracy in trade unions', one which he considered eminently suitable for tackling in a single enactment of its own, should the unions fail to 'reform themselves'. However, we also saw that there were a number of other issues debated in 1981–2 which, although rejected then, might still have been thought to merit attention in future legislation. Of these, the issue which appeared to persist most strongly as a concern after 1982 was that of strikes in 'essential services'. In this chapter we must therefore look first briefly at the development of the debate over this issue in 1983–4, as the background to a consideration of the more central debate around the Green Paper, *Democracy in Trade Unions*, issued in January 1983 (DE 1983*a*). We will want to consider what relationship, if any, there was between these two issues, and the Government's approach to each. The

[1] See the discussion in ch. 8.
[2] Interview in the *Director* (Sept. 1983) quoted in *The Times* (12 Dec. 1983).

Conservative interest in the democracy issue certainly pre-dated the arrival of Mr Tebbit on the scene, and the discussion of his ideas on the subject will therefore be prefaced by an attempt to set them in some historical and theoretical context. In chapter seven we will turn to the detail of the 1984 Act's provisions on industrial conflict, concluding that chapter with an initial assessment of this Act.

## (2) STRIKES IN ESSENTIAL SERVICES: THE ARGUMENTS DEVELOP

During the period 1979–82, while the issue of strikes in essential services was ever present, the debate itself remained static. As earlier chapters have described, the issue was central to the controversy surrounding the winter of discontent, and gave the Conservatives a valuable political and rhetorical weapon, particularly in the subsequent general election. However, the Government's failure to act in this area up to this point appears to have been attributable to a number of factors. In practice, no dispute since 1979 had come near to re-creating the combination of circumstances of the winter of discontent. In addition, it was generally reckoned that there was no simple direct way of legislating to control strikes of this kind, while a number of other legal and non-legal measures, especially some of those adopted since 1979, might help to alleviate the problem. In general terms, to introduce direct restrictions would have run counter to the Government's rhetoric of staying out of even public-sector disputes, while yet retaining its influence over the way in which each was fought and settled.[3]

In 1982–3, however, the issue regained prominence, partly because of a bitter dispute over nurses' pay, but especially against the backcloth of the first ever national water strike. At the time, fears of major health hazards were raised, although in the event none of the vividly portrayed scenarios came to pass. The causes and course of the dispute are too complex to relate in full here, but certain features of interest may be mentioned.[4] First, if the immediate disruption caused by the dispute was not, as it turned out, very great, the terms upon which it was settled gave the Government greater cause for concern. The strike ended only after both sides agreed to accept the award of a second of two committees of inquiry. The settlement preceded imminent public-sector pay negotiations elsewhere, and was in clear breach of the Government's public-sector pay targets. Secondly, at an early stage the employers—the Water Council—had sought to settle the dispute in exchange for an agreement prohibiting a strike called without due notice, an attempt to mimic the restrictions contained in CPPA 1875 section 4, which had been repealed in 1971. Finally, complex arguments surrounded the applicability

---

[3] See discussion in ch. 5 above and Morris (1986: ch. 2 and *passim*), on which this discussion draws generally on all aspects of this topic.

[4] For a full account, see (1983) 21 *BJIR* pp. 124–5 and 271–3 on which this discussion draws.

and application of various possible dispute settlement procedures, each side at different stages accusing the other of unilaterally abandoning these.

The renewed political pressure in this area perhaps gained some cutting edge from the prospect of a general election in the coming year, and the appearance of proposals such as those of the SDP to take action in this area.[5] The Government was no doubt politically bound to put forward some ideas of its own. Although at the height of the dispute the Government openly toyed with the idea of introducing some form of statutory duty to maintain certain essential services,[6] the more realistic possible measures which now attracted renewed interest were the negotiation of some form of 'no-strike' agreement, or the rendering of the protection of trade-disputes immunities conditional upon the observance of procedure agreements. While the former had interested the Water Council, the latter had been widely canvassed during consultations in 1981–2.[7]

The aim of both proposals appears to be the same, namely to promote the use of procedures and mechanisms which make industrial action a 'weapon of last resort', but there is an important difference in legal terms. 'No-strike' agreements are much discussed at the moment, but their legal effect appears often to be misunderstood. Put shortly, the no-strike clause stipulating that no industrial action will be taken while the agreement's procedures (which may or may not exhaustively lead to a settlement) are on foot, usually has no legal effect at all. Indeed, the non-legally binding nature of these agreements may be seen as of some symbolic importance, reflecting the co-operative faith which the signatories place in the agreement's ability to operate as a mutually acceptable instrument of dispute resolution.[8] In this sense, the no-strike agreement is simply a procedure agreement which rests on a strong and explicit consensus rather than on legal sanctions. If such consensus is thought to be absent, sanctions are the alternative. As we saw in chapter five, the experience of the IRA suggested that the most effective type of sanction for unconstitutional action would be withdrawal of trade-disputes immunities, rather than a contract action for breach of the agreement itself. Although many thought it unrealistic to hope that a *general* rule, even of this kind, could be successfully implemented, perhaps it offered a solution in the case of a few select essential services.

It was indeed this solution upon which the Government alighted in its June 1983 manifesto, promising to consult about the possibility of introducing such a change, although not promising to act (*Conservative Party Manifesto* 1983: p. 12). Employers' and other organizations in turn issued fresh policy documents, exploring further the possibilities for introducing such a change

---

[5]  See SDP (1982: pp. 42–3).

[6]  See OR HC vol. 37 col. 1050 (24 Feb. 1983); *The Times* (17 Feb. 1983).

[7]  For more guarded Government statements, see e.g. OR HC vol. 35 Written Answers col. 330 (24 Jan. 1983); HL vol. 439 col. 830 (24 Feb. 1983).

[8]  See Bassett (1986: pp. 87–9 and ch. 6); Lewis (1988); *IRRR* 414 (19 Apr. 1988) p. 2. Cf. TULRA 1974 s. 18(4).

both in respect of essential services and more widely.[9] However, although giving occasional assurances after June that it was still considering the matter,[10] the Government never put forward any firm proposals, and the issue resumed its former dormant state. The water dispute can be seen in retrospect as illustrating, and perhaps reinforcing, a continued pattern in which, while the promise of legal action at the time of such a dispute may be of great rhetorical value, and perhaps a political necessity, particularly near the end of a Parliament, yet the balance of substantive arguments remains consistently tipped against taking any legal measures. The events of this dispute perhaps confirmed that essential-service disruption could be weathered with rather greater ease in the 1980s than in the 1970s. Perhaps most crucially, though, the 'conditional immunity' solution seemed still to suffer from a basic drawback which all proposals to restrict industrial action in essential services may share in common. This is that it seems hard, whether as a matter of principle or of sheer pragmatism, to envisage proposals of this kind which are not linked to arrangements which aim to guarantee the pay levels of the employees involved, whether by providing in the procedures themselves for some form of arbitration, or for some other mode of independent pay assessment.[11] The Government, for obvious enough reasons, had little enthusiasm for such solutions where they seemed politically anything short of inescapable.[12] Furthermore, as has been suggested, once simple banning of strikes (whether civil or criminal) is rejected as a solution, the essence of all the different proposals boils down to an effort to postpone and reduce the use of the weapon of industrial action, rendering it a 'last resort'. To this goal, the ultimately enacted proposals in relation to strike ballots arguably had much to contribute, a suggestion which will, it is hoped, find support in the account which follows.

## (3) BALLOTS AND CONSERVATIVE LABOUR LAW POLICY

### (a) Before 1979

It will be useful at the outset to suggest some basic distinctions which can be made when considering different approaches towards the issue of strike ballots.[13] Legislation dealing with ballots is always, at least in form, concerned

---

[9] See e.g. Neal and Bloch (1983); Neal, Bloch and Grunfeld (1984); I.o.D. (1984) and (1985); CBI News (6 Apr. 1984: pp. 8–9).

[10] See e.g. OR HC vol. 50 Written Answers col. 125 (6 Dec. 1983); The Times (12 Dec. 1983); OR HC vol. 61 Written Answers col. 160 (5 June 1984).

[11] See e.g. documents cited at n. 9 above and the proposals of the then newly formed SDP (1982).

[12] On Mr Tebbit's views on this point, see Guardian (30 July 1984).

[13] This discussion draws particularly on the very clear article by Chafee (1930), although it is primarily concerned with what is here called the 'internal' function; see too Kahn-Freund (1970).

with the regulation of a trade union's *internal* affairs: that is, it acts upon the relations between members or parts of the union, rather than those between the union as a whole and 'outsiders'. Nevertheless, it is obvious that the way that a union is run will affect its relations with, and the impact of its activities upon, the outside world. Clearly, where such *external* effects cause concern, the alternative option of attacking these by external controls and remedies is always available; but the view may be taken that the most direct way of influencing the external activities of an association is to tackle the *causes* of those activities by turning to *internal* regulation in an effort to pre-empt the undesired external effect. So, although the *form* of regulation is always internal, the concern lying behind it may relate to either internal or external issues, or possibly both. A further distinction can be drawn between two types of internal issue. Internal measures may aim to protect individual members either specifically in their capacities as union members, or simply in some individual sense independent of union membership.[14] This distinction will prove to be of some significance.

There are therefore three different functions which intervention may hope to achieve, which can be labelled 'external', 'internal membership', and 'internal individual'. It should be repeated, however, that whichever one or more of these is being pursued, the *form* of regulation is always by definition internal. This is an important point, for there is a widely shared presumption—certainly one which one might hope Conservatives would share—that the state in a liberal democracy ought not to interfere in the internal affairs of private voluntary organizations such as trade unions. This presumption is enshrined in many conventions and constitutions, including for example that of the ILO on freedom of association,[15] although it is invariably expressed to be rebuttable by other arguments of principle. However, there may in any case be strong practical arguments which continue to caution against intervention. A Government proposing to intervene must therefore present or take a view upon arguments of both these kinds.

In fact it is not unusual to encounter legislation giving effect to external and internal concerns in relation to a number of types of association, most notably companies.[16] Regulation of the affairs of unions has been on the

[14] Chafee argues that the interests of members *qua* members are wider than those which are protected by the law of contract operating through the contract of membership and the rule-book alone, as the real object of intervention should be to protect the integrity of the overall *relation* between the member and the association. This concept provides in Chafee's account the justification for controls, such as those of natural justice, which are wider than those imposed by mere contract law: see Chafee (1930: pp. 1007–10). But the notion is also significant because of the *restriction* which it may entail on the content of regulations, as regulations which may conform with freedom of contract or even with natural justice may nevertheless offend against the spirit of the relation between member and association, and therefore ought not to be upheld.

[15] ILO *Convention 87 concerning Freedom of Association and Protection of the Right to Organise* (ratified by British Government 1949) Art. 3.

[16] Cf. now, Companies Act 1985, containing numerous regulations, some directed at protecting company members, others outsiders, others both.

legislative agenda for well over a hundred years.[17] In the latter half of this century the Conservative Party's concern has been of both kinds.[18] It was concerned with the external activities of the unions because of a number of adverse effects which these were perceived as having, and with the position of individual members because of its ideological suspicion of the unions as possible vehicles for the suppression of individual liberties. The latter concern is expressed most overtly in conjunction with the familiar libertarian objection to the institution of the closed shop.

The use of ballots has been seen as having something to contribute with regard to both problems. It is easy enough to see why this might be thought with regard to enhancing the protection for the individual (although we will want to explore this in more detail presently). With regard to the protection of outside interests, ballots have sometimes been thought of as inimical to the progress of industrial action in so far as the individual members of a trade union have been perceived to be less 'militant' or inclined towards 'political' action than their leaders. Ballots would therefore curb the power of such leaders to organize industrial action against the members' will. However, this perception has been neither consistently nor exclusively enjoyed by Conservatives. In the 1950s a Conservative Employment Secretary rejected a conference motion urging the introduction of strike ballots, inclining to the view that the leadership were more to be trusted than the rank and file.[19] The first formal Governmental proposals to use balloting as a method of controlling industrial action were those of Labour's 1969 White Paper, *In Place of Strife* (DEP 1969). The measure proposed there was clearly aimed at the protection of outsiders: it would have given only the Secretary of State the right to call for a ballot and only in a case where he or she was of the opinion that industrial action 'would involve a serious threat to the economy or public interest, and there is doubt whether it commands the support of those concerned' (para. 98). Only in 1971 was a similar measure introduced by the Conservatives.[20] So the idea that ballots might assist the control of industrial action in major strikes or public services was much favoured at this time.[21]

Undy and Martin have traced how during the 1970s, the Conservatives' preoccupation with the balloting issue moved away from strike ballots towards union elections; but towards the end of the decade the pendulum swung back. Once again the Labour Government's interest revived, forcing the Conservatives in turn to firm up their own policy, in particular by placing on a firmer footing the commitment, which had first emerged in the October

[17] The idea of regulating unions by a system of 'registration' was first floated in the majority report of the Royal Commission of 1867–9. Such a system was established by the Trade Union Act 1871.

[18] This summary of the history of Conservative Party policy draws heavily on the more extensive account in Undy and Martin (1984: ch. 1).

[19] See Gamble (1974: pp. 151–2) (the then Employment Secretary was Macleod).

[20] IRA 1971 ss. 141–5.

[21] Although not by the Donovan Commission (1968: paras. 426–30).

1974 election manifesto, to offer state funding for ballots. This was accompanied by a renewed intensity of criticism of the 'politicization' of union leadership, and of the close ties between the trade-union movement and the Labour Party (Undy and Martin 1984: pp. 12–17). Undy and Martin conclude that:

By the 1979 general election, Conservative Policy involved encouraging postal ballots 'at all levels' in trade unions, both in industrial action and in union elections. The objectives in the two areas differed. In the former, the Conservatives' objectives were primarily short term: ballots might be a means of reducing the frequency of industrial action. In the latter case, the party was concerned to change the whole political complexion of the trade union movement, to permit the large numbers of 'moderate' trade unionists to influence the political tenor of union leaderships. Doing so would have a major impact on industrial relations and on politics by leading to a more limited, and more generally legitimated, role for trade unions (p. 17).

### (b) Mr Prior's Approach

Undy and Martin go on to relate the legislative history of the provisions which followed, contained in the EA 1980, and providing for state funding of ballots. For our purposes only two points need be noted. First, the scheme applied only to postal ballots.[22] However, the Government were eventually persuaded that workplace ballots were not entirely without merit and what became section 2 of the Act was introduced to provide for some obligation upon employers to facilitate these. Secondly, the Government's firm commitment at this stage was to voluntary support, in the sense that there was no obligation on the unions either to make application to the CO or to hold ballots in any circumstance at all. The views of Mr Prior on the latter point were made clear during the debates on the 1980 Act, when a series of amendments were proposed to provide for various forms of 'compulsory' ballot scheme.[23] Mr Prior rejected them all, explaining:

After long and anxious consideration, we decided some time ago—and we have been examining the issue for a number of years—that the most likely means of achieving our aims, which are so widely shared, is by encouragement and the provision of funds rather than by compulsion. The importance of that—and it is amply borne out by the TUC's attitude—is that no-one can reasonably accuse us of meddling in unions'

---

[22] s. 1 of the 1980 Act was not so confined but the relevant regulations were: SI 1980 no. 1252 Reg. 6(b).

[23] As we shall see, notions vary regarding what constitute 'compulsory' or 'voluntary' norms in this field, although which category particular measures are perceived as falling into may be an important factor in determining their impact. In this discussion, 'compulsory' denotes any measure, failure to comply with which is *capable* of resulting in the imposition of a legal sanction, regardless of whether the decision to seek or apply that sanction may lie at the discretion of some third party, whoever that may be. Prior appeared to use the term in this way. See e.g. his reference to triggered ballots, backed by the sanction of loss of immunity, as 'the compulsory route' which he thought 'would land us in a great deal of difficulty': OR HC vol. 983 col. 312 (22 Apr. 1980).

affairs. . . . Considerable pressure is being exerted within the TUC to dissuade unions from taking the cash. Some unions are resisting that; and where some lead others will follow. I do not believe that that would have happened if we had moved to compulsion.[24]

This was a reference to the move within the TUC to focus the unions' opposition to the 1980 Act as a whole around a concerted refusal to take up funds for secret ballots. The campaign of opposition to the IRA had been expressed in the policy of de-registration and refusal to appear before the NIRC. But the 1980 Act did not offer any such special arrangements from which the unions could wilfully 'opt out'. The ballot funding scheme came the closest to it. This policy was a conspicuously weak one as the only practical 'downside' of this strategy was on the side of those unions which could have made good use of the money on offer. Nevertheless, the boycott became TUC policy and was to remain so throughout the period under consideration. To this extent Mr Prior's prophecy was not immediately fulfilled, but the rhetorical case for compulsory measures was in the longer run correspondingly strengthened.

The purely pragmatic arguments against interfering in the internal affairs of trade unions need to be explored further. Chafee suggested three principles which might favour non-intervention, and all three may be thought to have contributed to the attitude of Mr Prior:

The *Dismal Swamp* principle suggests that the peculiar rules, customs, and practices of organizations such as trade unions are not easily susceptible of outside regulation by the legal process and through the application of conventional legal mechanisms and rules (Chafee 1930: p. 1023). In practical terms this translates into the observation that it may be extremely difficult to devise legislation seeking to mould trade-union practices into a uniform prescribed pattern, and it may be even harder to predict what the outcome of such an attempt will be.

The *Living Tree* principle suggests that legislative intervention is bound to frustrate the autonomous development of the organization (Chafee 1930: p. 1027). Taken with the dismal swamp principle, it suggests that the 'natural' processes of growth and development of the organization might stand a better chance, given the right encouragement, of leading to the successful adoption of the desired changes.

The *Hot Potato* principle suggests that legislative or court interference may of itself generate resentment and hostility amongst the membership of the organization, severely diminishing the likelihood of the original intervention achieving its desired effect. The very act of intervention renders the entire issue controversial in a manner which was not originally intended (Chafee 1930: p. 1026).[25]

---

[24] OR HC vol. 983 col. 304 (22 Apr. 1980).

[25] An argument which is particularly pertinent in view of the British unions' 'tradition of voluntarism': cf. Flanders (1974: at p. 352).

These arguments taken together make a strong practical case for avoiding compulsory measures—a case of which Mr Prior was apparently convinced. Further evidence was considered in the 1981 Green Paper. This looked in particular at the experience of compulsory balloting under the American Taft–Hartley legislation and on the one notorious occasion of the 1972 rail dispute under the IRA, which seemed to refute the suggestion that where a ballot was externally imposed, union members would be likely to prove less militant than their leaders. On the contrary, as the hot potato argument might predict, the ballot often became the focus of a rallying cry to support and defend the union against external attack—the result in 1972 being a clear majority in favour of industrial action. The 1981 Green Paper concluded that there were in practice only two options currently available: to continue with the current policy of providing support and encouragement for voluntary reforms such as by provision of public funds, or to supplement this by enacting a right for a certain number of members to be able to 'requisition' a ballot, an idea for which a precedent could be found in company law (DE 1981a: paras. 245–56).[26]

It is worth stressing the context in which the idea of requisitioned, or 'triggered', ballots was here put forward: that is, the proposal remained within the context of a discussion of possible solutions to the growing problem of the external damage which industrial action might inflict on the community. In other words, even the proposal to legislate for *membership triggered* ballots was not one put forward primarily to deal with an internal problem.[27] This is once again reflected in the concern expressed over the likely outcome which such ballots might produce: such a concern would surely be irrelevant if the only issue was whether the measure was necessary in order to protect internal membership interests. This is reflected too in the counter-arguments which the Green Paper offered to the proposal: it pointed not only to 'dismal swamp' type arguments about the practical difficulties of drafting such a piece of legislation, but also to the possibility that even a compulsory triggering measure might be considered an unwarranted influence in unions' affairs, producing a wave of hostility which might frustrate the ability of any unions to participate in the public-funding scheme (DE 1981a: para. 258).[28]

The 1981 Paper's final argument, relating to the effect which triggered ballots might have on unofficial action, should also be noted. If such action were not covered, it argued, then this would surely become the preferable form for action to take and 'a premium would be placed on irresponsible behaviour' (para. 260). This argument is parallel to the Prior administration's argument that to expose trade unions to vicarious liability in tort would, if it had any effect, only encourage unofficial action, which was the largely

[26] Cf. Companies Act 1985 ss. 368 and 376.

[27] In this respect the company law trigger provisions may be contrasted.

[28] Cf. Prior at n. 23 above.

predominant form.[29] On the other hand, the Paper argued, if unofficial action *were* to be covered by the legislation, then unofficial leaders might thereby gain the means to secure respectability and recognition (para. 258). Yet why should this consequence necessarily or automatically be considered undesirable? From an internal point of view, the ideal power structure might be a matter for debate and for much difference of view. It is only from an external point of view that the logic becomes more apparent, in so far as unofficial shop-floor leaders are assumed to be of a militant pro-strike disposition.

### (c) Mr Tebbit's Approach

So the debate during the period of the Prior administration concentrated on the extent to which balloting might help to tackle the external strike problem, and even proposals to enhance the balloting rights available to members were judged no less by this measure. There was, however, a marked shift in the tone of the debate after Mr Tebbit succeeded Mr Prior. As has been seen, he preferred to emphasize the need to protect moderate and responsible trade unionists, of which he claimed himself to be a former example. As was noted, he quickly began to issue warnings that legislation might be needed if the unions did not reform themselves. The degree of correspondence between the language of this rhetoric and the richness, variety, and ever-continuing development of democratic processes—including the use of ballots—within trade unions, was seriously open to question.[30] It is important however to have a picture of the strength of the battle which was being fought at the purely rhetorical and public relations level. If it had been doubted before, the general election result and opinion polls ever since 1979 had confirmed that the Conservatives had a significant trade unionist vote to attend to. The new Social Democratic Party published its own 'Green Paper' on trade-union reform in September 1982 which included proposals to provide for members' triggered ballots.[31] Meantime, contrary to Mr Prior's expectations, the TUC policy of boycotting the public-funding scheme was holding fast in the face of internal pressures; but as Undy and Martin conclude:

The trade union movement was not sufficiently popular to be able to expect that its reassurances on its own democratic procedures would be accepted at face value: trade union reform was popular precisely because of public disquiet, which was only likely to be reinforced by Labour MPs expressing union complacency. More specifically, union failure to take up public funds obviously paved the way for firmer measures. If unions reformed their procedures to be eligible for money under the scheme, the

---

[29] See discussion in ch. 3 above. On developments in 1989 and 1990, see ch. 9 below.

[30] See: Undy and Martin (1984: *passim* but esp. ch. 3); (1982) 276 *IRRR* p. 2; and on union government, Undy *et al.* (1981: ch. 4).

[31] See SDP (1982: pp. 22–3); the slogan of 'giving the unions back to their members' appears first to have been used by the SDP.

Conservative objective of increased use of ballots was achieved; if they did not do so, the case for mandatory ballots was immeasurably strengthened—voluntarism had failed (1984: p. 46).

Having set the scene, we can now turn to look more closely at the actual functions which the Tebbit administration thought that the introduction of strike ballots might serve. In particular we will want to assess how far the emphasis on protecting the interests of union members extended below the rhetorical and into the policy level. In turning to this task we should recall that the 'libertarian' strand of Conservative thought generates a commitment to a version of 'freedom of choice' expressed in the matter of trade-union membership as a powerful hostility to the closed shop, the subject of extensive treatment in the 1980 and 1982 Acts.[32] We will therefore need to consider to what extent Mr Tebbit's internal concerns were of the membership or the individual kind.

Notwithstanding the steady flow of rhetoric, it is evident that the Tebbit administration at first viewed the prospect of legislating on strike ballots with little more enthusiasm than did that of Mr Prior. Replies to amendments moved during the passage of the 1982 Bill are revealing. An amendment to give the Secretary of State a power, similar to that contained in the IRA, to order a strike ballot where he thought action was taking place which was likely to cause widespread economic or personal damage or distress to persons not involved in the dispute, was rejected, Lord Gowrie arguing that:

this particular Government have, in my view, been rather successful in keeping out of industrial disputes, in trying to restore the authority of managers to manage, and of unions to negotiate with their employers free from Government intervention. We are sometimes criticised and teased for this. It is said that there are not enough beer and sandwiches at No 10 Downing Street. I am far from persuaded that beer and sandwiches at No 10 Downing Street are the best way of settling disputes.[33]

In reply to another amendment to introduce a more general balloting requirement, Earl Ferrers listed the many difficult technical problems which would have to be overcome.[34] The Tebbit administration was persuaded, as well as by principled political objections to any state involvement in disputes, generally by arguments of the dismal swamp and hot potato varieties. It therefore proceeded with some caution. Its early pronouncements indicated that legislation was by no means a certainty, and placed the emphasis on elections, rather than strike ballots, hinting that action on the former might help to tackle some of the goals of the latter.[35] Following the precedent of 1981, and no doubt anticipating the possibility of a general election within

---

[32] EA 1980 ss. 3–5, 7, and 9–10; EA 1982 ss. 2–8 and 11–14. The EA 1988 returned to the topic in ss. 10 and 11, and the Employment Bill 1990 contains yet further measures.

[33] OR HL vol. 433 cols. 235 and 248–9 (13 July 1982).

[34] See OR HL vol. 434 col. 568 (2 Aug. 1982).

[35] See e.g. *Guardian* (15 July 1982); OR HL vol. 433 col. 308 (13 July 1982); *Personnel Management* (Feb. 1983: p. 7).

the coming year, the Government's first more detailed analysis of the various arguments came in the form of a Green Paper published in January 1983.

## (4) THE GREEN PAPER

The Green Paper, *Democracy in Trade Unions*, considered possible legislation on elections, strike ballots, and the political fund. In line with the earlier rhetoric, the introduction stressed the need for basic minimal protections for union members, and for the Government now to consider acting in view of the lack of voluntary reforms (DE 1983*a*: para. 2). A later chapter set out in more detail the Government's concerns, and the pragmatic and principled arguments affecting the case for intervention. We can look at a number of aspects in turn.

### (a) The Broad Statement of the Problem

The Green Paper's discussion mingled arguments about the nature of the perceived problem with those which sought to justify legislative action as the means of sorting it out. However, as has been suggested, these two types of argument can and ought to be distinguished, whether or not each in fact draws on the same aspect of the situation being considered. The general introduction to the Paper suggested two basic causes for concern which demanded an improvement in union procedures and practices. First, unions were not sufficiently responsive to the wishes of rank-and-file members. Secondly, unions possessed the power through industrial action to cause damage to the economic and commercial interests of outsiders (paras. 1 and 3). So it was clear that the Government was still relying on both internal and external arguments in favour of action. With regard to the nature of the possible contribution to the external problem, the Paper confined itself at this point to saying that the external harms which unions could cause made it 'essential for their internal affairs to be conducted in a manner which commands public confidence' (para. 3).

The document relied little if at all on primary evidence of unions' practices and the development of these over the years.[36] Rather, it stressed two 'indirect' forms of evidence. First, it argued that there was now 'widespread public concern' about these matters (para. 1). Secondly, the unions had demonstrated their apathy and indifference towards voluntary change by throwing away the opportunities given them in the 1980 Act (para. 2). As has been noted, these phenomena were to some extent in the first case self-generating and in the second self-fulfilling, and doubt may therefore be expressed as to their strength as evidence of the *prior* existence of deficient practices and procedures as such.[37] Nevertheless, the Government had

[36] See n. 30 above.
[37] Mr Tebbit continued to voice his own concern, for example, in relation to the results of the GMBATU ballot held during the water strike. See *The Times* (27 Jan. 1983).

clearly decided that the issue merited a high level of priority and political attention.[38] As we shall see, that sense of priorities was by no means shared by all the respondents to the Green Paper.


### (b) The Arguments for Intervention

The authors of the Paper seemed to be conscious that, whatever the case for expressing concern at the state of existing procedures and practices, this would not by itself justify intervention by Parliament. We have already noted Chafee's broad pragmatic arguments cautioning *against* intervention, and that considerations of this kind appeared to have influenced Mr Tebbit as well as Mr Prior. However, the Green Paper in its introduction put forward two arguments of principle which in the particular case of trade unions were said to make a case *for* intervention. First, it was said that the unions enjoyed 'important legal immunities and privileges not afforded to other organisations' which were the source of their unique powers over both their members and outsiders. If unions wished to retain their claim to these immunities, granted by the state, it was fair that the state should also demand a certain *quid pro quo* in terms of internal controls and safeguards (para. 1). Secondly, with regard to the protection of members, the closed shop was singled out as a particular cause for concern, in so far as a member who declined to participate in a strike might face disciplinary action or even expulsion from the union with the attendant threat to his job. As unions which operated closed shops could not be regarded as 'voluntary' organizations, the presumption against state intervention was overridden (para. 3).[39]

No doubt the argument from 'privilege' may have been thought to have some appeal to public opinion, but its persuasive force was surely compromised by the fact that it was asserted at the very time when two Acts of Parliament had just severely diminished the trade-disputes immunities. Furthermore, in terms of the wider influence wielded by the union movement, whatever view might have been taken of, say, arrangements prevailing under Labour's 'social contract', the Conservatives had directed strenuous and largely successful efforts after 1979 towards ensuring that any earlier 'corporatist' trend was firmly reversed.[40] The unions were in effect being told that they must reorder their affairs having greater regard to national as opposed to sectional interests, at the very time when their role in

[38] On the role of the Green Paper in electoral strategy, see *The Times* (17 Dec. 1982 and 12 Jan. 1983).

[39] Chafee (1930: pp. 1021–2) refers to the 'stranglehold policy' which favours intervention by the court where the consequences for the individual of expulsion or other adverse treatment by the association are likely to be extremely serious.

[40] See e.g. Crouch (1982b: ch. 5); Lewis and Wiles (1984).

national politics and affairs had been sharply diminished and marginalized.[41] Whatever its potential popular appeal, this argument therefore looked increasingly tenuous in 1983.

The second argument is rather more complex, for there are really two issues bound up together. One concern relates to the effect which disciplinary action in the form of expulsion may have in a closed-shop situation. The other relates to the effect which taking industrial action may itself have—in a closed shop or not. Where there is a closed shop, the two are obviously linked, in as much as a member's decision whether or not to take industrial action may be influenced by both considerations. But arguments about the effect of taking industrial action go to the more general statement of the problem. It is the alleged consequences of being disciplined in a closed shop which alone form the alleged special ground for intervention.

Focusing just on this issue of expulsion from a closed shop renders it apparent that this is an internal individual, rather than a membership issue. Indeed, the Government had put in place a very extensive set of protections for individual closed-shop dissentients by 1984, Mr Tebbit having promised that after 1982 there would exist 'the most comprehensive and the most effective statutory protection for non-union employees that we have ever had in this country'.[42] In these circumstances, the argument that closed-shop arrangements undermine the essentially voluntary nature of trade-union membership to an extent justifying legislative intervention looked, like that based on privilege, conspicuously weak in 1983, however it might have appeared in, say, 1976. This weakness in the argument, although not acknowledged in 1983, clearly troubled the Government when it returned to these issues in 1987, when it felt obliged to abandon attaching any serious weight to the link between expulsion from a closed shop and dismissal as such.[43] Again, once we see the closed-shop argument as turning on the effects of expulsion, rather than those of taking industrial action, it can be seen that the question of whether or not there has been a ballot has little relevance to the truly underlying concern.[44]

In short, these arguments justifying intervention both looked distinctly weak in 1983, ironically being in part undermined by the very policies and legislation which the Conservatives had themselves introduced. It is hard to believe that they provided the true reasons behind the Government's conviction that intervention would now be appropriate. In search of better explanations of the proposal to intervene, we can return to look in more detail at the Conservatives' perception of the internal and external problems of industrial action.

[41] Cf. Martin (1985: pp. 77–8).
[42] OR HC vol. 17 col. 742 (8 Feb. 1982).
[43] See DE (1987: para. 2.15).
[44] Cf. the discussion of EA 1988 s. 3 in ch. 8 below.

*(c) The Effects of Strikes: Internal and External*

As we have noted, the Government voiced both internal and external concerns when arguing for greater use of strike ballots. Internally, membership deserved to have greater control over a decision which was of such importance to the situation of an individual member. That such decisions are of great importance need not be disputed. However, the Green Paper set out its own very particular conception of why this is so. The essence of the view put forward was that participation in a strike can invariably only have detrimental consequences for the worker involved, because of the loss of pay, and possibly the loss of job which may result (DE 1983*a*: para. 56). Whilst this no doubt was the Government's own view, it could not have been assumed that every individual considering whether or not to take strike action would agree. After all, the very purpose of a strike is to put pressure on an employer in order to obtain some benefit or improvement for the workers involved. An individual worker would therefore want to weigh up the potential benefits as well as harms which strike action might entail.

One might therefore have expected that if the concern was purely to extend the *control* of the worker over decisions affecting his or her interests in this regard, a more balanced picture of the pros and cons of any strike issue might have been presented. Similarly, workers might equally want a right to ballot on a leadership recommendation to settle, where it was feared that the leadership were 'selling out' their interests too willingly to an employer. It may be said that it was surely quite legitimate for the Government to set out its perception of the effect of strike action upon members' interests, in describing why it considered the problem to be a serious one. But this misses the point that if the issue is purely confined to a concern with the internal democratic process, then the Government's views on the substantive issue are irrelevant: the very purpose of enhancing that process is to allow members to voice their own views, whatever they may be.

Turning to the external argument, here there is no objection of this kind (although there may be others) to the Government acting on its own particular view of the external harms which strikes cause, and this it set out in clear language:

As the industrial power of unions has grown, the effects of exercising that power have become increasingly serious, not only for the strikers themselves and those at whom the strike is directly aimed, but for the community as a whole. Strikes damage economic performance, reduce living standards and destroy jobs far beyond the ambit of the parties to the dispute (para. 56).

The Green Paper went on to suggest that in recent years it had become increasingly common in large-scale disputes for the union deliberately to seek to put pressure on vulnerable third parties in order to bring pressure to bear on the Government to intervene and procure a settlement (ibid.). The

Government's reassertion of its view of what its own response should be in such matters has already been noted. Once again, its preoccupation with one particular type of dispute was evident, and we may note that this was a type which would embrace the more specific category of essential-service disputes, however defined.

It is clear enough then that the Government's own views on the economic effects of strikes, and on the nature of the general 'strike problem' at the time, informed its arguments in favour of intervention on both the internal and external grounds. It remains to be demonstrated how the Government proposed that measures to increase the use of pre-strike ballots might lead to the inhibition of major strike action, or in the paper's own words how they might be conducive to strike action being used 'sparingly' and 'responsibly' as well as democratically (ibid.).

## (d) Sanctions

The Green Paper showed little enthusiasm for the idea of a general ballot requirement for all kinds of industrial action. It recognized the limitations upon the ability to control particularly much unofficial action, to which the 1981 Paper and its responses had drawn attention, as well as the problems of controlling certain forms of industrial action short of a strike which might not involve any breach of contract. Not surprisingly, it rejected Taft–Hartley/ 1971 Act style provisions for reasons which have already been noted. However, it was more optimistic in the light of recent experience about the likely result from 'non-mandatory' ballots organized by unions or even employers.[45]

Ultimately, the paper preferred the idea of member triggered ballots, but it set out a number of pros and cons and difficulties of both member and employer triggers. It was also uncertain as to whether it would be necessary to have a 'supervisory body' to administer or oversee the conduct of a ballot. What is particularly noteworthy for what follows is that overall the paper was distinctly lukewarm on the benefits to be gained from any of the strike ballot proposals. Certainly, no particular enthusiasm was expressed for the idea of simply linking a ballot requirement to loss of immunity (DE 1983a: paras. 60–70). Overall, the chapter on strike ballots gave the impression that the Government was still undecided as to whether compulsory measures should be adopted, by contrast with that on elections, which concluded with a much firmer commitment to some form of legislative action (compare paras. 55 and 70). The major employers' organizations were also rather sceptical, as their responses to the Green Paper reveal.

[45] The authors of the Green Paper may have had particularly in mind the miners' ballots rejecting strike calls in Jan. and Oct. 1982.

## (5) RESPONSES TO THE GREEN PAPER

The major responses are worth considering each in turn:

### (a) The Engineering Employers' Federation

The EEF's response concentrated on the issue of strike ballots, which it saw as the only one raised in the Green Paper having a direct bearing on industrial relations as such (EEF 1983a: para. 2). It endorsed the Government's view that society had a right to expect that the strike weapon be used 'sparingly responsibly and democratically', but thought that imposing general balloting requirements was neither practical nor necessarily desirable (para. 7). However, it felt that there was a strong case for providing that major strikes in national industry negotiations ought to be subject to a ballot. It proposed that a sufficiently significant number of members should be given the entitlement to requisition a ballot, such right to be enforceable at the instance of aggrieved members through the courts (paras. 8–10). The EEF also suggested that an 'emergency' power might be given to the Secretary of State, similar to that contained in the IRA. Its observations pointed up the tension between the Government's desire to keep out of such disputes on economic and political grounds, and the perceived need for its intervention on social and administrative grounds:

It seems unwise in a country so exposed to damage by the monopoly power of unions, particularly in the public sector, for the state not to have the residual power to order a mandatory ballot, together with a cooling-off period for such a ballot to be held (paras. 11–12).

Giving evidence to the Commons Select Committee in March 1983, the EEF stated that strike ballots were not at the top of its list of priorities for further labour law reforms. That place still went to its proposals for lay-off provisions (Select Committee on Employment 1983: para. 35). Furthermore, its restatement of this reflected its particular approach to the essential services issue: lay-off rights would help EEF members to limit the damage done to their businesses by disruption caused by a strike in an essential service (para. 43). The EEF also confirmed that its proposals regarding trigger ballots were aimed solely at the specific case of national-level bargaining, however many employees might be involved (paras. 46–9).

### (b) The Confederation of British Industry

The response of the CBI to the Green Paper was also both limited and low-key. Again, an expression of strong support for the Government's general position was followed by extensive cautions about the impracticalities and possible undesirable side-effects of imposing strike ballots to any significant extent. Once again, however, stronger concern was expressed about 'major strikes in both the public and private sectors, especially those in public utilities . . . in other words, strikes serious enough to endanger the public interest'. Once again, the preferred solution was to provide for employee triggered ballots (CBI 1983*a*: para. 14).

### (c) The Institute of Directors

Characteristically, the I.o.D. took the opportunity of another Government Green Paper to publish a policy document floating wider proposals for labour law reform. A separate section was devoted exclusively to the problem of 'strikes in monopolistic public sector organisations'. Whilst democracy in trade unions was no doubt an important issue, it was this area which gave rise to 'the crucial industrial relations problems' (I.o.D. 1983: para. (vi)). On the democracy issue itself the I.o.D. only saw a case for Government intervention where proposals were 'firmly related to the improvement of economic performance' (para. (i)). It recommended that trade-union members be given the right to trigger a ballot on any official strike. It is noteworthy that the I.o.D. recommended that the sanction for refusing a ballot should be loss of immunity, but simply for the reason that this was the way that all existing legislation sought to regulate the conduct of disputes. However, it acknowledged that the sanction might look inappropriate in so far as members might be reluctant to embark on a course which could result in their own union being exposed to substantial damages claims (p. 10).

### (d) The Institute of Personnel Management

Not surprisingly, the IPM's response to the Green Paper was yet more cautious than those so far discussed. On strike ballots it expressed 'strong reservations' about any mandatory measures, but suggested that there might be a code of practice on the issue, superintended by an official such as the CO. Members alleging breaches of the code might complain to him once they had exhausted any internal complaints procedure, and he might have power to impose penalties on a transgressing union. Once again, separate attention was devoted to the problem of public-sector and public-utility strikes, which the IPM suggested required separate treatment in a further Government paper.[46]

Three common factors are clear in all these responses. First, the limited scope seen for strike ballot provisions—confined to large-scale strikes of one sort or another. Secondly, the lukewarm response on the general importance to be attached to the democracy issue, coupled with an equal or greater concern expressed about essential-service/public utility disputes and other matters. Finally, where compulsory measures *were* recommended, the favour

---

[46] See *Personnel Management* (May 1983: p. 7).

expressed for member triggered ballots. All reflect aspects of the more general debates during this period.[47]

## (6) THE DEBATES OF 1983: SUMMARY

In this period the issues of strikes in essential services, and democracy in trade unions, both dominated the agenda for a possible next step in the Government's labour laws. As for the former, this was mainly the result of external political pressures which the Government could not ignore; promotion of the latter was assisted by a lengthy and skilful rhetorical campaign conducted by the Government itself. The disparity between the politics and rhetoric fuelling these debates, and the substance of the issues themselves, showed through in the discussion of specific proposals for change. Although Government and employers shared concerns about the external effects of large-scale and public-sector disputes, the Government remained unpersuaded of the attractiveness of direct legal controls on such disputes, and—while believing that they might in theory have much to contribute to the external problem—uncertain about how to proceed with regard to strike ballots. Employers, by contrast, were willing to contemplate limited membership ballots, but only as one possible approach to the external problem, which they were more anxious to see tackled directly.

As for the internal arguments for ballots, employers showed little or no interest. Whilst the Government now made the protection of union members the centre-piece of its rhetoric, its internal concerns seemed to be more of the individual than the membership kind, and its principled arguments justifying intervention in the conduct of unions' affairs looked weak. Nevertheless, legislation did ultimately proceed, and in the next chapter we can turn to look at the detail of the measures adopted.

---

[47] See e.g. the HL debate in Mar. 1983, officially on the Green Paper, but very much preoccupied with the essential services problem. The Government's stance was steadfastly non-committal: OR HL vol. 440 cols. 727 ff.; col. 789 (16 Mar. 1983) (Lord Gowrie).

# [7]
# The Trade Union Act 1984

## (1) THE PROPOSALS FOR LEGISLATION

The Government's firm intentions became apparent from a series of statements over the summer of 1983, during the course of a general election campaign, and culminating with the publication of its *Proposals for Legislation on Democracy in Trade Unions* in July, shortly after the election. The promise to bring democracy to the trade unions remained firmly at the centre of industrial relations policy and was no doubt perceived as an important potential winner of trade unionists' votes. Although, as has been seen, the developing policy had substantial external goals in mind, it is therefore not surprising to find that the accent of the broad rhetoric remained on the internal benefits of the proposal. However, the 1983 manifesto also appealed to the wider electorate, arguing the external benefits which legislation might bring:

[trade unions] can be powerful instruments for good or harm, to promote progress or hinder change, to create new jobs or to destroy existing ones. All of us have a vital interest in ensuring that this power is used democratically and responsibly . . . some trade union leaders still abuse their power against the wishes of their members and the interests of society (*Conservative Party Manifesto* 1983: pp. 11–12).

It was also apparent from the manifesto that the Government had decided on its preferred method of providing for strike ballots: 'We shall also curb the legal immunity of unions to call strikes without the prior approval of those concerned through a fair and secret ballot' (p. 12). On essential services, the manifesto gave no firm commitments, but promised that the Government would continue to consult further on the possibility of taking legislative action. Once again it was apparent that the options had already been narrowed down—to the proposal that certain essential services 'be governed by adequate procedure agreements, breach of which would deprive industrial action of immunity' (ibid.).

Following its election victory, the Government published its legislative proposals in July. These were confined to the areas covered by the Green Paper, although separate consultations on the public utilities were still promised by Mr Tebbit when presenting the Proposals to the Commons.[1] As

[1] OR HC vol. 45 col. 763 (12 July 1983).

this account has sought to convey, the Government seemed most of all determined to avoid taking any direct measures on essential services; but that very resistance, combined with the undoubted political popularity of the balloting proposals, had perhaps rendered some action on strike ballots following the election inevitable.

The Proposals suggested that, as envisaged by the manifesto, ballots be made a prerequisite for section 13 immunity to be retained in respect of industrial action authorized or endorsed by a trade union. A number of factors may have influenced this approach. Certainly, for familiar reasons, there would have been no question of Government itself being given powers to intervene. As for the remaining choice between a members' or an employers' trigger, some suggestions will be developed in what follows. In general it will be suggested that, while now committed to introducing *some* sort of measure, the Government remained acutely concerned about the risk of giving unions or their members a weapon to turn to their own uses. No doubt in the light of the fact that the approach suggested at this point had found least favour both in the Green Paper and with respondents to it, the Proposals sought to demonstrate that it had merits from both the internal and external points of view:

The Government believe that this approach is the best means of providing unions with a powerful and direct inducement to hold ballots before calling strikes and it is therefore the most effective means of extending union members' democratic rights in this area while at the same time reducing the likelihood of irresponsible industrial action (DE 1983*b*: para. 8).[2]

We may note again the assumption that a balloting requirement was likely to lead to a reduction of levels of industrial action. While maintaining the 1980 and 1982 approach of restoring common-law remedies, and avoiding any role for Government or its officials, the Proposals contemplated the involvement of ballots in a far wider range of situations than had the IRA 1971. Yet this very generality ironically also helped the Proposals to appear less interventionist. Under the 1971 provisions the requirement to hold the ballot would only arise if the Secretary of State first took the positive step of invoking the necessary procedures: under the new proposals the employer need take no provocative first step during the negotiations at all: the threat of the sanction for failure to hold a ballot would already be hovering over the union from the start. The 'voluntary' nature of the proposed requirement was pointed up, the Proposals suggesting that the union would have a *choice* between holding a ballot or risking the possibility of legal action if it did not (DE 1983*b*: para. 8).

---

[2] When introducing the subsequent Bill to Parliament, however, the new Secretary of State Mr Tom King nevertheless argued that it was as a result of the responses to the Green Paper that this approach had been adopted: OR HC vol. 48 col. 161 (8 Nov. 1983).

It is worth noting, then, how the Proposals made little play of the negotiating significance of placing this weapon in the hands of the employer. The Green Paper had however touched on the point when it pointed out that 'strike ballots can be—and often are—an important tactical weapon' and that giving the trigger power to the employer would help to avoid the possibility of a union 'stage-managing' the timing of the ballot to its best advantage (DE 1983a: para. 67). What it did not add was that the proposal would by the very same token place this weapon in the hands of the employer; however it will be demonstrated that this was an aspect to which the Government's thinking was very much alive.

The Proposals acknowledged that concern centred on the problems of national strikes and strikes in public services. As has been argued, it was disputes of this kind which also now preoccupied the Government rather more than the problem of unofficial action. Consistently with this, the ballot requirement was to be confined to action authorized or endorsed by the trade union as determined under EA 1982 section 15 (DE 1983b: para 7–8), the structure of which was, as has been argued, itself reflective of the Tebbit administration's priorities in this regard. Of course, one cannot suppose that the Government itself intended to make great use of the legislation, but while the Government had earlier expressed concern that common-law control of action in certain public services might not be viable in the absence of a clear 'consumer' cause of action, Mr Tebbit now commented that such litigation as the new proposals might generate could well come from consumers.[3]

Two further aspects of the Proposals can be noted. Retention of the immunity would not be dependent upon the actual result of the ballot. Such a requirement was considered superfluous in as much as '[t]he Government do not believe that any trade union would persist with a strike call if it had been shown not to have the support of a majority of those directly involved' (DE 1983b: para. 9). Finally, we can note that—notwithstanding the shorthand jargon of 'strike ballots'—the Proposals would apply to all forms of industrial action which constituted a breach of contract. Mr Tebbit told the House of Commons that he thought this would cover a wide range of types of action[4]— although as we shall see this was to be the subject of much subsequent debate. An important preview of debates to come was also Mr Tebbit's observation that there was to be no requirement of a ballot in order to *end* an official strike because: 'The question is whether a union should enjoy legal immunity for breach of contract. There is no breach of contract once the strike is over and so the question does not arise.'[5] The curious logic of statements such as this is another matter to which we shall have cause to return.

---

[3] See OR HL vol. 440 col. 792 (16 Mar. 1983) and *The Times* (13 Dec. 1983) respectively.

[4] OR HC vol. 45 col. 771 (12 July 1983).

[5] Ibid. col. 769.

## (2) RESPONSES TO THE PROPOSALS

These may be considered briefly. Three responses illustrate a number of important continuing concerns which were voiced. The I.o.D. made four particular points. First, it strongly supported the proposal that retention of the immunity would *not* be tied to the result of the ballot:

> since it avoids tying negotiators' hands to the holding of a further ballot in order to call an end to a strike. If trade unions were statutorily tied to observing the results of a pre-strike ballot, it is inconceivable that they would not regard themselves tied in practice to the holding of a further ballot—which could well delay the ending of a strike.[6]

The logic of this reasoning may be rather difficult to unravel, but the concern is an important one to note. Secondly, the I.o.D. was concerned that linking the ballot requirement to breach of employment contract opened up the possibility of the provisions being avoided by the union giving express notice to *terminate* contracts on behalf of all employees. The ingenious solution which it proposed to this problem was to make *collective* strike notices to terminate void: 'Thus although no ballot would be held, the support of each employee for a prospective strike would be tested, insofar as he had to tender his own notice.'[7] The I.o.D. considered how far the range of action deemed to be in breach of contract would extend. It thought that some forms of action such as go-slows would indeed be covered and felt that the Government's approach was basically correct.[8] Finally, it continued to voice concern that something be done about essential services, and urged the Government to bring forward firm legislative proposals urgently.[9]

The EEF, by contrast with the I.o.D., feared that the breach of contract requirement would not catch a sufficiently wide range of potentially damaging industrial action in its net. It suggested that the proposals ought to cover 'any action, aimed to put pressure on a company, which deviates from normal methods of operation and customary practice' (EEF 1983*b*: para. 4). The EEF also drew attention to the fact that confining the ballot only to those to be called out on strike might be unsatisfactory in cases of what it called 'rolling strikes' or 'guerilla action', for example, where only a few selected key workers were called out on strike whilst others in the group were called upon to work without enthusiasm. The EEF felt that the ballot should involve all those to be involved in any action 'potentially damaging to their income and jobs' (para. 5).

---

[6] Letter dated 29 Sept. 1983 from the Director-General Mr Walter Goldsmith to Mr Tebbit, p. 2.

[7] Ibid.; on the facts in *Met. Borough of Solihull* v. *NUT* [1985] IRLR 211, 214 para. 18 (QBD), a collective notice in respect of unballoted action was held ineffective to terminate individual contracts. Cf. now also, *Boxfoldia* v. *NGA (1982)* [1988] IRLR 383.

[8] Letter dated 29 Sept. 1983 from Goldsmith to Tebbit, p. 3.

[9] Ibid. p. 6.

The IPM continued to question the benefits to be obtained from compulsory strike ballots, but welcomed the promise of separate consultations on essential services as well as the acknowledgement of the possibility of allowing workplace ballots which the Proposals contained.[10] Many of these various concerns were to be extensively debated in Parliament; changes were also introduced when the Bill itself was published. It is to a consideration of the Bill that we can now turn.

## (3) THE TRADE UNION BILL: THE DEBATE IN PARLIAMENT

### (a) Presentation

The Trade Union Bill was presented to Parliament on 8 November 1983 by a new Secretary of State, Mr Tom King. For our purposes, however, no particular significance need be attached to the departure of Mr Tebbit from the Employment Department which was the result of a cabinet reshuffle necessitated by an unpredicted resignation. Part II of the Bill essentially followed the lines of the Proposals,[11] making section 13 immunity for action authorized or endorsed by trade unions conditional upon the holding (but not the result) of a ballot. The detailed circumstances in which immunity would require a ballot are considered below. For the moment we may note that the ambit of the Bill was wider than that of the original proposal, as it now hinged on action which was either in breach of or 'interfered with' the performance of a contract.[12]

Mr King's second reading speech was relatively low key, emphasizing that the Government was only engaging in the minimum interventions which had been proved now to be necessary. Thus, in relation to strike ballots the presentation was again in terms of the unions having a 'choice', and it was pointed out that the Bill would introduce no Government imposed ballots, new supervisory agency, or special courts, nor require any rewriting of union rule-books or complex new procedures.[13] A regular theme of the Government's presentation of the Bill was that it would enhance and restore the reputation and image of the trade-union movement.[14] However, although the speech opened with the theme of members' rights, the section dealing in

---

[10] See *Personnel Management* (Nov. 1983: p. 11).

[11] Mr King acknowledged that the Bill had been 'masterminded' by Mr Tebbit: OR HC vol. 48 col. 157 (8 Nov. 1983). The following discussion looks at the provisions of the 1984 Act, prior to its amendment in 1988, on which see ch. 8 below.

[12] Trade Union Bill (no. 43) (26 Oct. 1983) cl. 6; *quaere* whether the procuring of the giving of a lawful notice of termination constitutes an interference: cf. n. 50 below. In any event, this would not protect against the new member action now created by EA 1988 s. 1: see discusssion in ch. 8 below.

[13] OR HC vol. 48 col. 159 (8 Nov. 1983).

[14] See e.g. Mr Gummer OR HC vol. 48 col. 235 (8 Nov. 1983) (referring also to the Conservative trade unionists' vote); Mr King OR HC vol. 58 col. 831 (25 Apr. 1984); report of speech by Mr Gummer to the Industrial Society in *Personnel Management* (Jan. 1984: p. 7).

detail with Part II put much stress on the privileges which unions enjoyed and the need to place corresponding obligations upon them with regard to the potential harm to the public and outside interests which industrial action can cause.[15] With regard to the internal function, much emphasis was laid on the 'compulsion' to strike which might threaten members of a closed shop. [16]

Examples cited by Mr King included the NUR strike call in 1982 and the call by the NGA to its members the same year to come out in support of the 'Day of Action' over the nurses' pay dispute,[17] perhaps once again reflecting the Government's main area of concern. These examples were also given by the minister of state, Mr Gummer, at the start of the Standing Committee debates, who also referred to the POEU/UCW strike opposing the privatization of telecom services in October 1982.[18]

### (b) The Choice of Sanction

The decision not to provide for member triggered ballots was quickly made the subject of Opposition attack. Two arguments were initially put forward by Mr Gummer:

We thought that such a provision would make it difficult for trade unions to conduct perfectly proper strikes. A union could be under constant pressure from a small group—the minimum would have to be small if it was to be a democratic instrument—to hold a ballot even though that union was conducting a perfectly proper and necessary strike.[19]

The immunities in question are given to trade unionists, and they should decide whether those immunities should be brought into play.[20]

However, neither of these arguments seems very plausible. The first is in direct contradiction of the Government's argument that no strike can be either 'proper' or 'necessary' if it does not have the support of the members involved. Nor is there any reason why the extent of the balloting requirement under a triggering provision would necessarily be wider than under the Government's proposals. If one were to compare these with, for example, the EEF's proposals, the reverse would clearly be the case. As for the second argument, it makes the issue the retention of the immunities rather than the holding of the ballot—and it is hard to see why the members should ever positively desire that the immunities be not brought into play.[21] More interesting perhaps was Mr Gummer's later response to the suggestion that the ballot would still be seen as being imposed from outside. He suggested that as there would always be a basic requirement for a ballot to be held, it

---

[15] OR HC vol. 48 col. 160 (8 Nov. 1983).
[16] Ibid.
[17] Ibid. col. 158.
[18] Or St. Cttee. F 25th sitting (7 Feb. 1984) col. 966.
[19] Ibid. col. 971.
[20] Ibid.
[21] Cf. the point made by the I.o.D. in their reply to the Green Paper; see ch. 6, sect. 5(c) above.

would become normal practice and not be seen as a contentious issue and the focus for a rally of solidarity in any particular case.[22]

We have already begun to see how, once the Government had settled upon the sanction of removal of immunity, the arguments dwelt as often on when a union ought to be entitled to retain the privilege of immunity as on when it ought to be required to have a ballot. Indeed, when asked why the Government had rejected the membership trigger option, Mr Tebbit himself appeared to suggest that the former was the correct perspective from which to view Part II, and in this sense he contrasted it with Part I:

If the governing bodies of trade unions are democratically elected, that is the best way to ensure that the union is run in accordance with the members' wishes. . . . However, there is no reason why the privilege of immunity from the civil law should be extended to a trade union that pushes men and women out on strike without asking them first.[23]

The Government rejected amendments to confine the remedy only to the employer and not to allow it also to affected third parties, arguing that:

Many people are damaged by strikes, and all that is asked is that there should be a ballot. If there is no ballot, the immunities will not exist. That does not seem unreasonable. Nor does it seem unreasonable that the union should lose the immunity from action not only by employers but by others who would be affected.[24]

Although employers may not have welcomed the possibility of consumer claims, opening up liability to claims by an unrestricted class of plaintiffs might have generally been hoped to maximize the effectiveness of the legislation, and, as has been noted, the Government appears specifically to have contemplated the possible role of consumer actions.

### (c) Mechanisms of Control: Legislation and the Rule-book

The use of withdrawal of the immunities was therefore far more than simply the most effective or simple sanction to apply to the strike ballot requirement; it followed very much as an essential aspect of the logic which justified internal legislation, namely the external harm which disputes caused, and which the immunities would otherwise sanction. Here, we may draw a comparison with the IRA. That statute provided for a mixture of benefits, detriments, and controls to be potentially applicable to trade unions. It was a central plank of this approach that the best 'package' would

---

[22] OR St. Cttee, F 25th sitting (7 Feb. 1984) col. 978; see too col. 1060 where Mr Gummer developed the idea that balloting should be 'an automatic regular activity' for which standing arrangements would exist.

[23] OR HC vol. 45 col. 772 (12 July 1983); Mr King, too, thought that while TULRA immunity was certainly 'a necessary privilege if trade unions are to function effectively' nevertheless 'that is not to say that it should be an unconditional privilege and free of any corresponding obligations': OR HC vol. 48 col. 160 (8 Nov. 1983).

[24] OR HC vol. 57 col. 112 (26 Mar. 1984) Mr Gummer; for a case of unballoted action where an outsider successfully sued, see *Falconer* v. *Aslef and NUR* [1986] IRLR 331 Co. Ct.

be on offer to those unions which submitted themselves to the controls involved in the process of registration. The justification for this was again the simple *quid pro quo* argument: it was fair that if unions were to enjoy privileges and benefits, the public should demand that they assume obligations to maintain certain basic standards. This was to be achieved by requiring unions seeking to register to reflect the Act's 'guiding principles' in the contents of their rule-books.

The essence of the argument in 1984 was much the same. The unions were told that the privilege of section 13 immunity was henceforth to be subject to certain minimum standards of conduct regarding its use. Once again they were also told 'the choice is yours'. But the mechanism of regulation was in 1984 a good deal simpler: the necessary stipulations were simply built into the legislation itself, without the need for the use of such a controversial figure as the Registrar of Trade Unions.[25] Nor was it necessary for the legislation to compel changes in the rule-book: provided that its requirements were met, it mattered not whether this was in fact in compliance with the rule-book as well.[26]

In comparing alternative mechanisms of control we can thus distinguish substantive issues from those essentially relating to style or tactics. Whether control is imposed by requiring a union to rewrite its rules along prescribed lines, or by direct legislative stipulations, is a matter of style or tactics rather than one of substance. Both approaches entail a close degree of rigid regulation, and may be more usefully contrasted with one which requires a union to adopt clear rules on a certain point, but allows it then to choose what the content of those rules shall be. Section 15 of the 1982 Act provides an example of both 'rigid' and 'open' controls being used at different points within a single legislative regime. The 1984 Act demonstrates that it may also be possible to avoid altogether appointing any special body or person to administer the regulations. Questions which require *ad hoc* adjudication, such as whether minor breaches of the regulations should be overlooked, can be simply delegated to the courts by use of tests such as 'so far as is reasonably practicable' in the regulations themselves.[27]

So, notwithstanding the great differences in style and technique, one can also see some important similarities between the approaches of the 1984 and

[25] Although the less controversial—and already existing—personage of the CO was chosen to superintend the 1980 Act's ballot funding scheme, nevertheless the fact that to accept money under the scheme would require a union to submit its practices and procedures to outside scrutiny gave it the same corporatist smack as the 1971 Act provisions and was the main argument of substance in favour of the TUC boycott.

[26] Although it might matter to the *union* to change its rules, as experience since 1984 has shown.

[27] See TUA 1984 ss. 11(1)(*a*), (5)(*b*), (6), (7)(*a*) and (*b*), and (8); the question of sanctions is also important here, loss of immunity being the consequence of any breach of the s. 11 requirements, whatever its gravity. This feature is well illustrated in *British Railway Board* v. *NUR* [1989] IRLR 345 (Ch.D.) and 349 (CA), and in *The Post Office* v. *UCW* [1990] IRLR 143. The Opposition moved an amendment to provide for the CO to adjudicate on complaints of breach of s. 11 instead, but this was rejected by the Government: OR St. Cttee. F 30th sitting (16 Feb. 1984) cols. 1147–50.

1971 Acts towards the internal regulation of industrial conflict. Nevertheless this does not mean that the actual model of the ideal trade union or of proper trade-union conduct which the 1984 Act sought to impose by these means is therefore the same as that aimed for by the 1971 Act. In fact this is far from the case. The broad area of concern of the 1984 and indeed the 1982 Act has already been outlined, and this differed demonstrably from the 1971 Act's avowed aims of achieving the kind of wholesale reforms and improvements of the system of collective bargaining which Donovan had recommended, albeit by a rather different means. In addition, Part II of the 1984 Act was obviously a very much more limited measure, concerned as it was only with ballots before strikes. Nevertheless, it would be a mistake to overlook its significance for collective bargaining, not, clearly enough, in terms of ambitious reforms of collective bargaining structures as such, but in terms of its impact upon the course or conduct of individual negotiations or disputes. It is to a closer consideration of this aspect that we can therefore now turn.

## (d) The Impact of the Ballot on the Conduct of Negotiations

During the debates, a good deal of the discussion was devoted to the various 'side-effects' which the imposition of the balloting requirement might have. As has been seen, many such issues had already been raised during the course of the earlier consultations. Would unofficial action increase? Would negotiations become drawn out and settlements delayed? Would hostile 'yes' votes be encouraged? How would the union or the employer be able to make tactical use of the ballot as a negotiating weapon? How would the answers to all these questions vary according to the nature of the sanctions employed? Notwithstanding that there was extensive discussion of such issues, to the outside observer much of it might have seemed unsatisfactory and inconsequential. Typically, the debate consisted of opposing assertions, an Opposition speaker asserting, for example, that strikes would get longer, the Government confidently responding that in practice it thought they would not. Such assertions were of course often backed up by argument, but characteristically this took the form of a theoretical scenario being postulated of how a particular dispute or negotiation might develop as a result of the legislation.

For example, the Opposition suggested that it was commonplace where some small dispute or incident of disruption broke out on the shop-floor for the employer to ring up the local union official to come and help sort things out. Under the new proposals, it warned, this would no longer happen: the official would stay well away in case by getting involved he were to fix the union with liability for the effects of the action. The employer would be left to solve the problem on his own.[28] The Government had another scenario:

[28] OR St. Cttee. F 25th sitting (7 Feb. 1984) cols. 974–5; on the concerns of some managers about a possible growth in unofficial action, see *Management Today* (Sept. 1983: p. 103).

unofficial groupings would find that they received no support from the official union organization if they embarked on campaigns of disruptive industrial action: in future they might want to think twice when they discovered that they would henceforth be on their own.[29] The difficulty with this type of argument, on both sides, is that it is very hard to draw any kind of general conclusion from such hypothetical illustrations, however plausible they may be in themselves. Clearly no one could predict or ensure that in broad general terms the legislation would have a characteristic and uniform impact.

Nevertheless, conscious as it must have been of the volatile new ingredient which it was now introducing to collective bargaining, the Government appears to have very carefully applied its collective mind to the question of what impact particular aspects of the new balloting procedure might have, having regard in particular to the types of dispute about which the Government itself was most concerned. As has been noted already, although many employers in the private sector continued to be concerned mainly about the disruptive effects of unofficial action, and therefore about how legislation exacting a price for official trade-union involvement might exacerbate that problem,[30] the Government now had a rather different perspective on matters.

This perspective is well illustrated by the response of Lord Gowrie in the House of Lords Committee debates to Lord Rochester, who yet again raised the spectre of an increase in unofficial disputes and fragmentation of union organization at local level:

I should not wish to underestimate the damage that unofficial strikes can cause, but I would venture to suggest that the noble Lord, Lord Rochester, may be living a little too much in the past. Unofficial strikes are no longer the predominant form of industrial action which they were considered to be at the time of the Donovan report . . . One does not have to be a very astute political analyst to be able to make a distinction between the general industrial landscape at the moment—its relative calm its increased productivity and its real and well founded anxieties about international competitiveness and the degree to which one now has to be competitive at home and abroad to maintain employment—and the 'battle' (though I would prefer if this 'battle' were not happening) between the public sector industries and ultimately the Government as paymasters *and as representatives of a somewhat different, from their point of view, political set of priorities*.[31]

With this view of priorities in mind, we may turn to consider three specific related aspects of the model of control which the Government introduced.

First, the ballot must *precede* the act of authorization or endorsement which generates the union's liability.[32] This requirement fits uneasily with

[29] OR HC vol. 48 col. 161 (Mr King) (8 Nov. 1983).
[30] Taylor (1984) suggests that private-sector employers and personnel managers were far more concerned about the possible impact of the new measures than the official stance of their own organizations suggested.
[31] OR HL vol. 453 cols. 707–8 (25 June 1984) (emphasis supplied).
[32] s. 10(3)(c).

the notion of endorsement, which involves approbation of action which is already taking place. The implication is that the union should not give its support to *unofficial* action which has been started, without a ballot having taken place. Yet characteristically unofficial action is action which is taken by those members who support the grievance voting with their feet by simply joining in. Those who do not support the action will only feel compelled to do so *if* the union endorses the action and therefore seeks to call out a wider section of the membership in support. As Mr Evans put it rather bluntly in debate: 'I think that most people will laugh at [the minister's] suggestion about telling groups of workers who are on strike that a ballot has to be held asking them whether they want to go on strike before the union can make the strike official.'[33] The requirement fits more comfortably with the authorization or calling of industrial action by the union organization itself. This we may take to be the key area of concern at this time: that, for example, during national negotiations, the union cannot call the members out first and then ballot them afterwards. Yet even in this situation it is difficult to see why the requirement is necessary: if the employer is unhappy about the lack of a ballot he could presumably obtain an injunction anyhow. The balance of convenience would surely weigh in favour of granting an injunction, as all the union would have to do is hold the ballot if it wanted the injunction lifted.[34] However, there is one crucial difference which the requirement does make: it means that the union cannot wait and see if the employer really intends to take legal action before deciding what to do, because by that time it may be too late. Again this was a consideration which the Government appeared to have had in mind, as the official DE Guide to the 1984 Act would seem to suggest:

It will not be possible for trade unions to provide themselves with immunity for industrial action for which they have previously given their authority by holding a ballot at some later stage—for example, on hearing that legal proceedings are being considered (DE 1984: p. 15).

In effect this considerably raises the power of the threat of the employer to take legal action if a ballot is not held: the union cannot call the employer's bluff without running the risk of litigation.[35]

Secondly, the ballot must have been held not more than four weeks prior to the first act which gives rise to the liability of the union.[36] The Government stuck steadfastly to this requirement although it acknowledged that four weeks was about the very minimum period which could safely be allowed for

---

[33] OR St. Cttee. F 29th sitting (14 Feb. 1984) col. 1103.

[34] Cf. the reasoning in *Solihull* [1985] IRLR 211, 215 para. 28 and in *Monsanto plc* v. *TGWU* [1987] ICR 269 CA per Dillon LJ at 275 E–G.

[35] Although it is always possible to hold a ballot and then call fresh action, the union must accept the risk that this may only be after incurring the costs of litigation based upon the original unballoted action, as occurred in some of the cases mentioned by Hutton (1985: p. 256).

[36] ss. 10(3)(c).

a major national ballot result to be processed and a decision upon it taken.[37] Two reasons were advanced. At first it was said that the union ought not to be able to wrest control from the members by seeking a 'yes' vote from them which might cover a wide range of eventual outcomes: the members were entitled to know that they were voting on the immediate situation only.[38] However, the Opposition responded to this by proferring amendments which would give the control of the time period to the members themselves, subject to an outside limit.[39] The Government, however, stuck to the requirement as drafted and now relied more heavily on its second argument: that the union should not be able to obtain a 'blank cheque' to call industrial action at the very start of the negotiations, so that a positive ballot would mean that the possibility of industrial action being called formed a backdrop to the entire negotiation.[40] This fact was very closely linked to the third aspect of the provisions.

Thirdly, the ballot requirement does not in fact apply in respect of all the acts protected by section 13 (although removal of protection if the requirement is broken does). As well as not applying to conspiracy, it does not apply to the acts mentioned in section 13(1) if they are only threatened but not committed.[41] Lord Gray of Contin expressed very clearly the link between this feature and the four-week rule:

The object of the Bill is not to provide guns to be aimed at employers' heads. The Government are aware that threats of industrial action are part of the ritual negotiations. That is why threats to induce breaches of contract have been consciously excluded from the grounds on which unions would be liable to actions in tort in the absence of a ballot. But the Government are not going to hand things to the unions on a plate by allowing them to hold ballots to back up those threats, and then to use those ballots to give them immunity for strike calls up to four months later.[42]

These three aspects of the balloting requirement all therefore carefully combined towards the same goal: to ensure that, in the Government's words: 'A strike should be a weapon of last resort—something to which a union turns only when negotiations have broken down.'[43] The affinity with the idea

---

[37] Time runs from the date on which the last vote may be cast: ss. 10(3)(c) and (5). In the docks dispute of 1989 the four-week period expired during the course of interlocutory litigation in which the employers sought injunctions and ultimately lost, but pending the outcome of which the union undertook not to support a strike. Subsequently Vinelott J in *BRB* v. *NUR* [1989] IRLR 345 at 348 para. 33 suggested that this problem for the union should weigh in the balance of convenience when considering a possible injunction. A Bill sponsored by Lord Campbell in 1990 (HL Bill 15) aims to remedy the problem by giving the court a discretion to extend the four-week period.

[38] OR St. Cttee. F 26th sitting (7 Feb. 1984) cols. 1013–14 Mr Gummer.

[39] OR HL vol. 453 col. 721 (25 June 1984). The Opposition chose sixteen weeks as the outside limit, but this was clearly merely an 'opening offer' in an attempt to persuade the Government to table a compromise amendment.

[40] Ibid. col 724.

[41] ss. 10(1) and (2).

[42] See n. 40 above.

[43] Ibid.

that immunity should be withdrawn from industrial action taken in breach of procedure agreement is obvious enough, and it will be recalled that this was the preferred solution with which the Government had toyed in relation to the problem of strikes in essential services. The Government itself on several occasions expressed the view that strike ballot provisions could help with the essential services problem.[44] However, the effect of the approach has a greater significance even than this because, as has been shown, it aims also to dampen the potency of the strike *threat* as a continuing factor affecting the course of the negotiations themselves. While a union can always prime its members for the prospect of industrial action should talks fail, it can only put the threat into actual and imminent operation by setting in train the calling of a ballot. To refine the metaphor used by Lord Gray, the Government allowed the union to keep its 'gun', but ensured that it needed a ballot for the gun to be fully loaded.

Of course, none of these ramifications would have followed had the Government followed the recommendations of the major employers' organizations and given union members the power to requisition the holding of a ballot, instead of providing the employer with the remedy. Nevertheless the employers' organizations were quick to pick up on the implications of the regime which was adopted. The EEF's guide to the Trade Union Act for example included a section entitled 'Industrial Relations Implications' dealing with the strategic possibilities which the legislation opened up and the pros and cons of different tactics (EEF 1984: paras. 19–25).

This discussed a number of different aims which might lie behind the threat or taking of legal action, such as terminating or preventing industrial action; giving the employees a chance to have a ballot; accelerating a drift back to work; pressurizing union officials to remove their support for action; obtaining financial compensation via a damages award; and asserting employer authority in an 'untidy' climate (para. 20). It then considered some of the possible consequences, including the risks of a 'yes' vote increasing the pressure on the employer, of seriously damaging employee relations and of attracting adverse publicity. Against this were set the possibilities that carefully used legal action could halt action while buying time for a settlement, strengthen the employer's long-term position, or draw in senior union officials to promoting a settlement (para. 21). To this may be added the perspective of documents such as the CBI guide to the Act which based its analysis not on the question: 'When must a union ballot its members?', but on the question: 'When can the trade union be sued?' As the document pointed out, a number of defaults can lead to this situation, of which failing to hold a ballot at all is only one (CBI 1984: pp. 19–20).

These documents arguably provide a striking illustration of the extent and potential of the strategic weapon of legal action which the legislation placed

---

[44] See e.g. the 1983 manifesto (p. 12); *The Times* (12 Dec. 1983); Lord Gowrie OR HL vol. 440 cols. 789–90 (16 Mar. 1983).

into the hands of employers, particularly when contrasted with the lengths to which the Government was concerned to go to ensure that the least strategic advantage should be given to the unions.[45] A similar picture can be seen to develop when one turns to consider the scope of the balloting requirement in terms of the types of action which it was intended to cover.

## (e) The Range of Action Covered

The poorness of fit between the distinctions generated by legal concepts and those considered to be of social importance, and the challenge of adapting the former to the demands of the latter, provide one of the many fascinations of the study of law as a social science. Labour law abounds with such problems. In particular, the inadequacy of the raw concept of breach of contract as a proxy for that of industrial action has been the subject of three different types of solution in three different kinds of situation. This was to prove a cause of considerable confusion during the debates on both the 1984 and 1988 Acts,[46] and it may be as well to set out in advance of the discussion here, the three types of issue involved.

*The Contractual Issue.*   The courts have on occasion sought to extend the range of types of industrial action which constitute a breach of the contract of employment, by widening the range of the terms which are to be implied into the contract in the first place. The leading case is *Secretary of State for Employment* v. *Aslef (no. 2)*,[47] where the Court of Appeal held that a work to rule could be a breach of contract because, if designed deliberately to obstruct the running of the employer's business, it constituted a breach of an implied term that the employee would not act in such a manner as to frustrate the very purpose of the contract of employment. This has a knock on effect in terms of tortious actionability of industrial action, because the wider the scope of breach of contract, the wider that of the tort of inducing breach of contract.

*The Tortious Issue.*   Where industrial action upsets an employer's business relations with third parties, they may nevertheless be unable to obtain a remedy for inducement of breach of contract, if his business contracts

---

[45] Although the Government rejected the description of the Part II mechanism as an 'employer trigger' because 'there is no intention in the Bill to change the balance of power between employer and employee': OR St Cttee. F 25th sitting (7 Feb. 1984) col. 964 Mr Gummer.

[46] Failure to distinguish between the three issues which are discussed in the text led to statements such as the following by Mr Gummer: 'People will not be covered by this part of the Bill unless it is explicit—or clearly implicit—in their contract that they are required to work voluntary overtime': OR St. Cttee. F 26th sitting (7 Feb. 1984) col. 1002. Nevertheless, as is argued below, the basic strategy behind the drafting was really quite clear.

[47] [1972] 2 QB 455; more recently see the *Solihull* case [1985] IRLR 211.

contain a *force-majeure* clause providing protection in the event of just such an interruption. The courts have sought to restore the tort-based remedy in these circumstances by holding that if an 'interference' with contract is caused, a tort will have been committed. The leading cases are *Torquay Hotel* v. *Cousins*[48] and *Merkur Island Shipping* v. *Laughton*.[49] Although the principle was in each case applied only to *commercial* contracts, it would appear potentially equally capable of applying to contracts of employment. That is, it might be held tortious to call on employees to take action which was not an actionable breach of their contracts, because it disrupted their contractual relations with their employer.[50]

Thus industrial action may be held actionable as a tort although involving no actionable breach of the express terms of the contract, as a result of either, or conceivably both, of these doctrines being applied. Nevertheless the scope of both doctrines remains considerably uncertain and the second in particular has been the subject of much criticism. We have seen that some employers' organizations were more concerned than others about the range of serious forms of industrial action which might not be actionable in tort. However to the legislator a simple solution to all these problems is always theoretically available:

*The Descriptive Approach.*    The legislator can choose simply to describe as directly as possible in common parlance the types of action to which the particular enactment is to extend, without tying himself to concepts such as tort or breach of contract. This, it will be recalled, was the thrust of the EEF's request that the balloting requirements should cover 'any action, aimed to put pressure on a company, which deviates from normal methods of operation and customary practice'.[51] The fact that such a legislative approach could succeed had been proved by the decision in *Power Packing Casemakers Ltd.* v. *Faust*[52] that as section 62 of the EP(C)A 1978 was expressly stated to apply to a strike or 'other industrial action', it was unnecessary in considering whether one of those descriptions applied to a piece of action, to enquire as to its contractual status.

The Government made it clear on several occasions that it was indeed its wish that the balloting requirements should apply to as wide a range of types

---

[48] [1969] 2 Ch. 106 CA.                                                              [49] [1983] 2 AC 570.

[50] The Government believed this to be the case: it gave the example of a lorry driver who refuses to cross picket lines but whose contract permits this as an exemption from normal duties under a '*force-majeure*' clause. The pickets would not have induced a breach of contract, but, opined Mr Gummer, 'it is reasonable to suppose that the courts might hold that they acted unlawfully in inducing the lorry drivers to interfere with the performance of their employment contracts': OR St Cttee, F 26th sitting (7 Feb. 1984) col. 1004. It remains unclear after the *Merkur* decision whether at least a technical breach of contract is still required to found this head of liability. The relaxed approach typified by the decision in *Union Traffic Ltd.* v. *TGWU* [1989] IRLR 127 suggests that in practice it may not be.

[51] See sect. 2 of this chapter.

[52] [1983] ICR 292 CA; see now *Express & Star* v. *Bunday* [1987] IRLR 422.

of industrial action as possible, yet it declined to adopt any purely 'descriptive' solution to the problem. There are a number of ways in which this might have been done. A rather elegant solution was that set out in an amendment proposed by Lords Orr-Ewing and Mottistone, both supported by the CBI.[53] This would have made failure to hold a ballot in respect of any strike or other industrial action, of itself a breach of statutory duty, actionable at the suit of anyone adversely affected.[54] Lord Gowrie indicated that the Government sympathized with the amendment but rejected it because it would involve a major change in the way that industrial action was regulated. He also sought to reassure the proposers by arguing that:

It would be quite wrong to underestimate the extent of contractual obligations or the circumstances in which an employee can be held to be in breach of his contract. There is no doubt that in many cases action such as working to rule, go slows and overtime bans would be held to be in total breach of contract.[55]

This was followed by a crucial practical observation:

The Government do of course share the view . . . that the holding of ballots should be the normal prerequisite of any industrial action of whatever kind—that is integral to the Bill. I believe that the effect of the Bill will be that any prudent trade union will organise a ballot rather than risk the possibility that the industrial action which it proposes to organise could make it liable to legal proceedings.[56]

Here the tactical significance of the requirement that the ballot must precede the first authorization or endorsement can once again be seen.

The essence of the Government's approach was then to stick to the existing and well-tried method of simply enlarging the range of circumstances in which industrial action would be unprotected from the strictures of the economic torts. In other words: 'This is not an extension of the restrictions on the trade union, but merely a replacement of the protection given by the last Labour Government. Our protection is based upon a ballot having been held; their protection was given whether a ballot was held or not.'[57] This is indeed the nub of the Act's basic approach. It follows that the extensive debate over such matters as whether *Torquay Hotel* was good law or would be 'legitimized' by the Act was largely irrelevant: the 1984 Act no more confirmed the existence of this form of tort than had section 13(1) of the Act of 1974.[58] Once again some comparison may be drawn with the IRA. That

[53] The CBI's basic goal was the same as that of the EEF: see *CBI News* (25 Nov. 1983: p. 5).

[54] OR HL vol. 453 cols. 731–2 (25 June 1984).

[55] Ibid. cols. 737–8.

[56] Ibid. col. 738; but the interplay between ss. (1) and (2) of s. 11 may cause even the prudent union difficulties, esp. where the proposed action may not have the same contractual status for all intended participants.

[57] OR St. Cttee. F 26th sitting (7 Feb. 1984) col. 1003 and 27th sitting (9 Feb. 1984) col. 1051 Mr Gummer.

[58] Contrast the view of Hutton (1984: pp. 215–18). Arguably the real damage had already been done in the *Merkur* case, wherein Lord Diplock committed the very fallacy of suggesting that the 1974 Act had proved the existence of the *Torquay Hotel* tort: [1983] 2 AC 570, 608E.

statute introduced a new definition of 'industrial disputes' which would qualify for protection, which was narrower than the range in common experience of possible trade disputes. So too might the 1984 Act have proceeded, by redefining a trade dispute as a dispute over matters listed in section 29 of TULRA, which had been the subject of a prior ballot. More simply still, it might have been provided that an act done in the course of a strike or other industrial action would not receive the protection of TULRA section 13 if not preceded by a ballot.

The 1984 Act does seem to set out in this sort of way, requiring the ballot to relate to a particular 'strike or other industrial action', where 'strike' is broadly defined as 'any concerted stoppage of work'.[59] But the need to exclude any application to mere threats or conspiracy led the draftsman to go further and home in on the torts adumbrated in sections 10(1) and (2). The alternative might have been to expose general liability in tort, *save* for threats and conspiracy. However, the chosen approach harmonizes more with that first developed in 1980 of working specifically around a contract-based tort, and with the general focus in 1984 (which is considered further in a moment) on the interference with an employer's contracts which industrial action invariably involves. As has been seen, the Government argued that in practice the Bill would achieve almost as broad a coverage as the descriptive approach, in any event; and as with the earlier legislation, once the trigger is sprung, *all* section 13 protection is removed.

One other consequence of the rejection of a purely descriptive approach can be mentioned. As was noted, the approach is most useful where it is desired to regulate all that would be considered to be industrial action in common parlance, regardless of its legal status for other purposes. At one time this could readily be done by employing the golden formula, as was done in social-security legislation. Thus, when the formula became narrowed for the purposes of industrial-conflict law in 1982, social-security law nevertheless continued to use the old definition.[60] By hinging the balloting requirement on the sanction of industrial-conflict law, the 1984 legislation as it were adopted the new narrow definition by default, without giving the matter any direct consideration. From the point of view of the employer or third party this would not matter: the important thing would be to have a legal remedy, and it would be a matter of indifference whether this was as a result of the lack of a ballot or of the action falling outside the golden formula. From the point of view of the members however, the distinction would appear illogical, if the object is to ensure that they have the right to be balloted as the 'normal prerequisite of industrial action of whatever kind'. Members might indeed particularly wish to be consulted if proposed action

[59] ss. 10(3)(*a*). (11)(1)(*a*), (4), (11). Cf. now the *Monsanto* case [1987] ICR 269 (CA) and *The Post Office* v. *UCW* [1990] I RLR 143 (CA).
[60] Social Security Act 1975 s. 19(2)(*b*).

ran the risk of being unlawful—but the issue disappears from view when control of both unlawful and unballoted action is put into the same hands.[61]

### (f) The Constituency of the Ballot

Entitlement to vote must be given to all those employees who are expected to be requested to participate in action interfering with or breaking their employment contracts, and to no others. The ballot will be invalidated if anyone excluded from participating is subsequently called upon to take such action.[62] Once again these requirements are difficult to justify purely from the members' perspective. Where for example selective strike action is taken, the constituency on whose behalf this is done is much wider than those who take the most direct action; this wider constituency might understandably feel that they have some genuine interest in being involved in the decision-making process. Once again, comparisons both with social-security law and the section 62 regime may be made, both for similar reasons finding it necessary to employ a concept of persons interested in the dispute which is wider than the concept of those who directly participate in or are the immediate victims of industrial action.[63] Concern on this point was not confined to trade unionists anxious to emphasize the collectivist perspective: one may recall the EEF's view in its response to the Proposals, that the ballot requirement ought to cover all those likely to be involved in action 'potentially damaging to their income and jobs'.[64]

Concern that the Bill would not deal adequately with 'selective action'—a particularly common strategy in 'essential service' disputes—was also expressed by Sir Ian Percival, the former Solicitor-General, when the Bill was introduced to the Commons:

In my view, there is something almost indecent when about half a dozen people halt an operation and then everyone on whose behalf they are taking that action turns up with no work to do and expects to be paid. I hope that during the lifetime of this Parliament we shall consider the question of 'lay-off' in those circumstances. However, all the union would have to do is . . . to ballot the six people involved.[65]

The individualistic emphasis of the Government's approach was also conveyed by the requirement that the ballot paper contain a question asking the member whether he is prepared to take action in breach of contract.[66]

---

[61] Cf. the increasingly important but highly complex issue as to whether it is *ultra vires* a trade union to call upon its members to take industrial action which is or might be unlawful under civil or criminal law, on which see Elias and Ewing (1987: pp. 119–32 and 237–40).

[62] Trade Union Act 1984 ss. 11(1) and (2).

[63] Social Security Act 1975 s. 19(1)(*a*); EP(C)A 1978 s. 62(4)(*b*)(i).

[64] See sect. 2 of this chapter.

[65] OR HC vol. 48 col. 183 (8 Nov. 1983). Cf. ch. 5 text to n. 161 above.

[66] Trade Union Act 1984 s. 11(4). The Government eventually deleted from the Bill the alternate question referring to interference with contract, as this was thought to be too technical and complex. See OR HC vol. 57 col. 683 (2 Apr. 1984). Further changes were made in 1988, which are discussed in ch. 8 below.

The Opposition heavily criticized this as 'intimidation' but could not technically fault the Government's reply that striking was indeed normally a breach of contract which might have important consequences.[67] Of course, to put the contract question alone suggests a highly limited view of the factors affecting the employee's decision. On the one hand, a major risk involved flows not from the law of contract, but from the possible loss of a right to claim unfair dismissal. On the other, as has been pointed out, an employee might want to consider the benefits which industrial action hoped to secure, in order to make a balanced judgement. Nevertheless, as the Opposition clearly feared, the simple contract question might convey a clear and potent message to the ordinary union member, and reflected the aspect of the matter which perhaps most interested the Government, namely that from the point of view of the *employer*, seeing that contracts were duly performed was of key importance. Just as Mr Tebbit had commented about the provisions as a whole that '[t]he question is whether a union should enjoy legal immunity for breach of contract',[68] so Mr Gummer now commented that '[o]ne cannot sue someone for breaking his employment contract' but that employees should be reminded of their contractual duties 'to ensure that a contract between employer and employee has seriousness and validity'.[69]

### (g) *The Impact of the Miners' Strike*

The Bill's later progress through Parliament took place against the backcloth of the early months of the 1984–5 miners' strike. This dispute provided large daily reserves of ammunition to all parties on issues ranging across the economic, political, and industrial relations debates. Inevitably, the extensive discussion of it in Parliament extended on occasion to the continuing debates on the Bill. For present purposes we need only consider the specific effect which the dispute had on the shape of Part II, namely in relation to the relevance of the ballot result. As has been seen, the Bill as originally drafted provided that the retention of section 13 immunity would be unaffected by the actual result of the ballot. In the House of Lords, however, the Government introduced an amendment to provide for the further require-ment that a majority vote in favour of the proposed action be also obtained. The Government made it clear that this was prompted by events of the miners' strike.[70] But what more precisely was the connection?

[67] See e.g. OR HL vol. 453 cols. 743–6 (25 June 1984) (Lord McCarthy; Lord Gray of Contin); cf. *Simmons* v. *Hoover* [1977] ICR 61.

[68] See n. 5 above.

[69] OR St. Cttee. F 29th sitting (14 Feb. 1984) cols. 1108–9; presumably Mr Gummer had in mind the rule against ordering specific performance of an employment contract (cf. TULRA 1974 s. 16).

[70] OR HL vol. 453 col. 706 (25 June 1984). The Government quickly dropped the original idea of requiring a majority of those eligible as opposed to those actually voting: see *Guardian* (4–5 and 14 June 1984).

Some commentators[71] have pointed to the fact that the NUM leadership had persistently declined to hold a national ballot in respect of the strike, suggesting that, if not in clear breach of the national rule-book, this appeared at the very least to constitute a wilful bending of the rules. But however that may be, this would not in itself explain the amendment, which directed itself not to a failure to hold a ballot, but to a failure to obtain a majority. The Bill as it already stood would tackle the former issue, and in any event it was certainly arguable that at this stage in the dispute a majority of the *national* membership in favour of industrial action would have been obtained.[72] However, as between different areas of the union, support varied. Some of these areas, acting as trade unions in their own right, balloted their memberships in accordance with their own rule-books. Some of these ballots failed to show majority support.[73] It was to these results that the Government alluded in explaining the amendment.[74]

No doubt the political purpose of focusing on these selected area results was to throw weight behind the suggestion that a national ballot, if held, would not have obtained a majority, and the accompanying suggestion that the union leadership was therefore defying the majority of its members. But in reality, whatever the arguments about whether a national ballot should have been held, and about whether it would have shown majority support, at no point was it ever suggested that the union's leadership would have readily ignored a majority vote against action, had that emerged from a ballot. Nor was it ever suggested that this was something which the leaderships of other unions were in the habit of doing. The amendment therefore appears to have been little more than another political device in the battle against the miners, and its practical significance was surely minimal. Notwithstanding the controversial circumstances of its birth, it can best be viewed as 'the cherry on the top'[75] of Part II.

However, as will be discussed in chapter eight, a number of the developments of the miners' strike were to have a much more significant impact upon legislative policy, which was ultimately manifested in provisions contained in the Employment Act 1988. As matters were to develop, the 1984 Act and the events of this dispute, together provided a springboard for a considerable strengthening of the Government's use of internal regulation, in particular in relation to ballots before industrial action. In concluding this chapter with an initial assessment of the provisions contained in the 1984 Act, it is therefore worth opening with a further discussion of some aspects of the model of internal regulation underlying the provisions which it introduced.

[71]  e.g. Drake (1985: pp. 156 and 180).
[72]  See Lloyd and Adeney (1986: pp. 87–90); Lloyd (1985: p. 24).
[73]  Or in some cases the 55% support required by the rules; for a summary, see Ewing (1985: p. 162).
[74]  See n. 70 above.
[75]  Lord McCarthy's description: OR HL vol. 453 col. 701 (25 June 1984).

## (4) THE TRADE UNION ACT 1984: INITIAL ASSESSMENT

A central issue running through our analysis of the provisions contained in the 1984 Act, has been the question of the nature of the mix of external, internal individual, and internal membership concerns underpinning them. The Government in its pronouncements did not seek to disguise its view that significant external benefits would flow from the new controls, but its rhetoric at all times above all stressed the great importance of its internal objectives. Whether or not it devised the slogan of 'giving the unions back to their members', the Government rapidly proclaimed that crusade as its own, clearly believing that to do so would give it a valuable political asset at a time when all political parties were engaged in an open fight for the votes of trade unionists. The Government therefore explicitly claimed that its measures would secure important internal membership protections, while at the same time also putting into place a valuable safeguard with regard to the external effects of industrial action. But our analysis has suggested that in reality the underlying balance of objectives was rather different. The 1984 Act represented not a major substantive shift away from exclusively external preoccupations in favour of a new-found enthusiasm for burning issues of trade-union democracy, but the culmination of a number of political developments against the background of longstanding Conservative pre-occupations, resulting in a key shift of legislative *technique* from restriction to regulation. The Government's external preoccupations remained as strong as ever; but its basic commitment to the progressive introduction of further legislation in this field on an almost indefinite basis, combined with its growing political conviction—immeasurably strengthened by the arrival of Mr Tebbit at the DE—that new measures might, indeed must, yet be combined with a concerted pitch for the votes of union members, together rendered the plunge into regulation perhaps inevitable.[76]

In the field of industrial action, as we saw, the plunge was taken only after considerable hesitancy on the Government's part. The weapon of the ballot—with its inherent volatility by virtue of the very fact that its precise impact is always beset with risk and uncertainty until the result of any particular vote is known—is not one to which a legislator determined to pursue external goals will turn lightly. The Government was perhaps somewhat reassured by its own widely proclaimed conviction that union leaderships had become over-politicized, and that moderate memberships could be relied upon to act as a restraining force—a view which clearly also inspired its confidence in the prospects of success—in its terms—of the new balloting requirements in relation to elections and political funds also contained in the 1984 Act.

[76] Simitis has identified the logical place of such developments in the context of his analysis of the progressive processes of 'juridification' of industrial relations: see Clark (1985: pp. 81–2).

However, beneath the brashness of this rhetoric, the Government was clearly acutely aware that ballots before industrial action was a particularly problematic and uncertain area into which to venture.

Faced with that realization, the Government took what steps it could to ensure that the structures and requirements of the legislation would encourage the promotion of its external objectives, and minimize the opportunities for statutory ballots to be used by trade unions as a means to prosecute more effective industrial action, or to enhance their bargaining positions in negotiations. The decision to make loss of immunity the sole sanction, together with the linking of the balloting requirement to the concept of union liability contained in section 15 of the EA 1982, were two key elements, which, by dovetailing the new provisions into the earlier legislation, aimed to ensure a continuity with the strategies and priorities already developed.[77] Further details and mechanics of the new requirements sought to deny such strategic opportunities for the unions as might otherwise be created.

In wider terms, the Government aimed also to encourage union members to adopt an individualistic rather than a collective or membership approach to voting in ballots, which it was believed would in turn enhance the likelihood of predominantly negative ballot results being achieved, thereby leading to a direct inhibition of large-scale and official industrial action. Government speakers talked little of any alleged intrinsic value in the balloting process, preferring to concentrate on the damage caused by industrial action, and the risks incurred by individuals who participated in it.[78] As we saw, the belief that ballots offered considerable scope as a tool with which to 'depoliticize' the overall complexion of the union movement in this way, was a constant spur over a number of years to the development of Conservative policy ideas. We may consider, for example, the debates on section 6 of the Social Security (no. 2) Act 1980, the provision which 'deemed' union members in dispute to be in receipt of a certain amount of strike pay. The Government then suggested that:

the combination of financial responsibility being transferred back to trade unions and the proper balloting procedures that we hope many unions will adopt . . . will mean that the average chap who is involved and is called upon to strike will have the opportunity to think carefully both of the financial consequences and of the overall

[77] Cf. also the removal by s. 18(5) of EA 1982 of a trade union as a potential party to a trade dispute, a move which, as was suggested in ch. 5, may in itself have strengthened the argument that industrial action initiated by a trade union without the explicit support of the members concerned (demonstrated e.g. by a ballot) may not be protected by the immunities. Cf. now the analysis of Millet J in *ABP* v. *TGWU* [1989] IRLR 291.

[78] Cf. Macfarlane (1981: ch. 5), and McKendrick's conclusion (1986: p. 52) that the historical pattern has been that 'when industrial action is viewed as undesirable or a result of excessive union power, there is a greater readiness to protect the member who refuses to participate in industrial action.'

consequences of his action. By balloting, we should see a different trend in the 1980s from that which we have seen in the 1970s. That is our earnest hope . . . [79]

Even if members could be encouraged to exercise an individualistic perspective, and be given the opportunity to exercise their votes accordingly, it was by no means an automatic conclusion that this would result in a moderating influence coming to bear. Certainly, as we saw, that assumption could not be based on the experiences of the period of the IRA. Clearly, however, the Government believed that the lack of any preoccupation with actively reforming collective bargaining, the considerably simpler regulatory structures, and the other structural features of the 1984 provisions which have been mentioned, would together help to minimize the likelihood of many of the adverse effects associated with the 1971 Act coming to pass, in particular that attributed to the nature of the legislation of itself encouraging a sense of collective threat and hostility. In addition, the limitation of the scope of the 1984 regulation to rendering a ballot the price of immunity, ensured not merely that ballots were only required to begin but not to end strikes, but more specifically that members were therefore to be afforded a new control only over executives which might be inclined to support industrial action, and not one over those which might be inclined simply to settle.

The Government appears also to have been reassured by the view that the wider political and economic climate of the time could also be relied upon to have an impact on the thinking of individual union members in relation to industrial action, the crucial feature here, of course, being the soaring levels of unemployment. In times of recession, when unions are weakened, individual members can be relied upon to be generally more ready to resist participation in collective action, for fear of jeopardizing their own individual labour market position, notwithstanding that strongly supported collective action might yet hold out the prospect of some gain for the group involved.[80] Mr Tebbit regularly encouraged employers to communicate directly to employees the economic and industrial 'facts of life' in a recession.[81]

The provisions contained in the 1984 Act therefore reveal the influence of a number of critical judgements exercised with a wide range of degrees of sensitivity and sophistication. On the one hand, the Government showed itself well aware of the minefield which it was entering, and showed a considerable grasp of the lessons of both more and less recent experience.

[79] OR HC vol. 985 cols. 636–7 (21 May 1980) Mr Lester.

[80] Cf. the analysis offered by Crouch (1983: p. 130), and Kahn-Freund's (1979: pp. 23–4) distinction between 'reasonable' and 'rational' decision-making and the relation of direct and representative democracy to each. Undy and Martin (1984: p. 167) suggested that it is such wider environmental factors rather than the choice of method of consultation which is likely to determine the typical response to strike calls, so that the effect of increased use of ballots might be quite different in times of prosperity.

[81] See e.g. Tebbit (1983); *Employment Gazette* (June 1982: p. 228).

This meant that, after careful consideration, it was able to conclude that the powerful pragmatic arguments of the kind raised by Chafee, did not preclude action in the field of strike ballots altogether, as appeared at first to have been supposed. Rather, the implications of such arguments could be absorbed and then incorporated into the development of the legislation itself.

On the other hand, what has surely been confirmed from the vantage point of 1990, is that this area of the law is indeed a dismal swamp in which the project of anticipating and addressing 'loopholes' and problem areas may be a potentially never-ending undertaking. More striking still is the fact that the legislation was fashioned so dependently upon the basis of political and economic circumstances and assumptions, which, even when founded in current fact, were inevitably precarious in anything beyond the short term. This is the picture which was to emerge in the period immediately following the introduction of the 1984 Act, and leading up to the introduction of the Employment Act 1988.

# [8]

# The Employment Act 1988

## (1) INTRODUCTION

Part II of the Trade Union Act 1984 came into force in September of that year. It was to be almost four years before the next legislative changes in industrial-conflict law took effect in July 1988; and it was not until February 1987 that the Green Paper which formally initiated those changes was published. Why this lull in the step-by-step progress of industrial-conflict legislation? At least two factors can be seen as influential.

First, the lull is testimony to the *ad hoc* nature of the reforms of the 1980s. In the field of industrial conflict, the introduction of the Trade Union Act 1984 fulfilled the main manifesto commitment of 1983, on 'democracy in trade unions'; as we have seen, the other main topic of the manifesto—strikes in essential services—was one on which it was in fact most unlikely that the Government would introduce legislation. Whilst the step-by-step rhetoric had proved useful in justifying the further measures of 1982 and 1984, the reality immediately after 1984 was that, while there were a number of possible emerging subjects for further measures in this field, there was none which the Government considered it an essential priority to introduce. Industrial relations, for many years persistently at or near the top of every Government's agenda, had given way in terms of priority to the increasingly radical proposals brought forward in other fields during the Conservatives' second term.

Secondly, Mr King was succeeded at the Department of Employment in September 1985, by Lord Young as Secretary of State, and, in the Commons, by Mr Kenneth Clarke as Minister for Employment. Lord Young showed little enthusiasm for immediate further legislation in the field of industrial relations and trade-union activities.[1] Instead, the activities of the DE during the period of Lord Young's stewardship reflected his own background at the MSC, and his concern to take further steps to free up businesses from what were regarded as the bureaucratic and job-destroying effects of employment protection laws and other regulatory legislation. Thus, the principal piece of legislation to emerge during this period was the Wages Act 1986, which abolished the Truck Acts and curtailed the activities of Wages Councils; and

[1] See e.g. *The Times* (22 Jan. 1986).

the characteristic White Paper *Building Business . . . Not Barriers*, published in May 1986, proclaimed that '[t]he prime aim of the Department of Employment is to encourage the development of an enterprise economy' (DE 1986: Introduction).

Not surprisingly, however, the possibility of further trade-union legislation at some point was never ruled out by the Government,[2] and the familiar range of employers' organizations and other commentators continued to urge their own preferred preoccupations and agendas. The Institute of Directors and the Centre for Policy Studies issued further policy documents in 1984 and 1985, continuing to press for action on strikes in essential services, and measures to require greater observance of procedures as a prerequisite for the protection of statutory immunities.[3] These bodies clearly regarded the 1984 Act as an unsatisfactory and inadequate solution to such problems. The occasional Government contributions to the debate tended, however, to suggest a rather different agenda. Undoubtedly by far the greatest influence on Government thinking during this period were the legal developments of the miners' strike of 1984–5, and most particularly the string of actions brought by individual members of the NUM against the national and area unions. While before 1984, the idea of a members' trigger for balloting legislation had, among other things against it, the fact that it was considered unlikely ever to have any significant take-up, developments in the miners' strike now suggested to the Government a new potential for legislation empowering individual union members with legal rights to control and restrain industrial action. Government pronouncements in the months during and following the strike hinted most strongly at the possibilities for further incursions into regulatory trade-union law, where more could be done 'particularly in guaranteeing proper and effective rights to trade union members'.[4]

Possible measures mentioned during this period included extensions of the provisions of the 1984 Act, and greater controls for members over the use of union funds. Undoubtedly, though, the single most important and most seriously discussed idea was that of a right for members not to be disciplined for declining to take part in industrial action, or for crossing picket lines. This was certainly not a new topic; we can recall, for example, the heated debates during the winter of discontent over the concept of 'lawful intimidation'—involving the alleged threat of loss of a union card, and hence in a closed shop, employment, as a means to coerce support for industrial action—and the subsequent measures in the 1980 Act which aimed in part to address that issue. While the matter periodically resurfaced in the years following,[5] it was developments in the miners' strike which particularly

---

[2] See e.g. OR HC vol. 96 col. 103 (Written Answers) (22 Apr. 1986), in which the Government stated that it had no plans at present, but was keeping matters under review.

[3] See Neal *et al.* (1984); I.o.D. (1984), (1985).

[4] e.g. OR HC vol. 82 col. 142 (Written Answers) (2 July 1985). See too, *Financial Times* (20 June 1985).

[5] See e.g. Howard (1983).

refuelled Conservative concerns and—crucially—helped to open up the issue beyond its previous traditional setting of the closed shop. The debate now contemplated a number of other situations where such a right might be argued for, such as where there had been no ballot, or industrial action would for some other reason be illegal.[6]

The development of the debate along these lines was reflected in a policy document published by the I.o.D. in May 1986, *Law Reform and the Mining Dispute 1984–85*. In this, two names familiar from the debates of the early 1980s, Professor Grunfeld and Mr Lionel Bloch, set out their personal analysis of the legal events of the dispute, and the developments which might be built upon. Their proposals included new member-rights to inspect union accounts, controls over usage of union funds, restrictions on union rules permitting indemnification of members, the extension of the 1984 Act to allow members to restrain unballoted action, and fresh controls on union trustees (Grunfeld and Bloch 1986). This amounted in effect to a call for statutory codification—in clarified and extended form—of the various common-law principles articulated in this litigation. It proved to be remarkably close to the Government's own agenda eventually set forth in the Green Paper of 1987 and enacted in the Employment Act 1988.

Nowithstanding the customary zeal of such documents, Lord Young's persistent lack of enthusiasm for the topic meant that the Government's pronouncements on labour law during this period came almost exclusively from Mr Clarke, who for many months confined himself to issuing periodic reassurances that the whole matter was under review. Essentially political considerations seem to have been most responsible for the eventual timing of the next step, for it was only during the course of 1986 that the Government as a whole concluded that, with the prospect of a general election the following year, the time might be ripe for the publication of a further Green Paper.[7] This at last emerged in February 1987 under the title *Trade Unions and Their Members* (DE 1987). It is to a consideration of this document that we can turn next.

## (2) THE GREEN PAPER 1987 AND RESPONSES

It is illuminating to reflect on the progressive development in style and tone of the Green Papers of the 1980s. The 1981 Paper, *Trade Union Immunities*, perhaps came closest (although by no means as close as it purported) to the ideal of a genuinely open-minded consultative document, with its style of dialogue between at least two of the participants in the debate, and its pragmatic and cautious tone. The 1983 Paper, *Democracy in Trade Unions*, considerably stepped up the rhetoric and polemic, whilst still betraying some

---

[6] See e.g. (1986) 24 *BJIR* 122 (speech by Mr Clarke). For early opposition to this idea from the CBI, see (1985) 23 *BJIR* 450; *The Times* (15 July 1985).

[7] See e.g. *The Times* (3 Nov. 1986).

genuine signs of uncertainty as to how if at all some of its proposals might be implemented. By 1987, the tone of the document is unashamedly and aggressively polemical, and shows few signs of hesitation about the road ahead. The change perhaps reflects the growing confidence of the Conservatives through the mid-1980s that the union 'problem' was one which they finally had firmly under control.

The 1987 Green Paper opened with a review of the principal elements of the legislation of the previous eight years, and then swiftly moved on to the question of the rights of trade-union members, focusing particularly on the context of industrial action. Continuing the key assumptions underlying the 1984 Act, of militant pro-strike trade-union leaders and moderate anti-strike trade-union members, it argued that in recent years members had shown themselves increasingly unwilling 'to be precipitated into industrial action contrary to their best interests and to their own better judgment' (DE 1987: para. 1.2). The following paragraph went on to speak of 'high-handed', 'unfair', and 'unjust' treatment of union members, and of members now less willing 'to be intimidated by threats from union leaders' (para. 1.3). It was on the 'progress' made by members that the Green Paper set out to build, by suggesting new membership-rights.

After this brief and almost entirely rhetorical introduction, the document then turned to the question of a new right for members in relation to ballots before industrial action. In a passage which entailed an implied admission of the illogicality of its absence in the 1984 Act, such a right was described as 'a natural complement' (para. 2.5) to the existing rights of employers, customers, and suppliers. Crucially, however, the document specifically cited the events of the miners' strike as indicating that the right was one which might now have a significant take-up (ibid.). The proposed right would be given to any single member due to take part in action, but, critically, it would be limited to a right to *restrain* the conduct of industrial action without a ballot. The absence of a proposal to allow members (whether individually or in groups) to demand that a ballot be held, was explained by the proposition that the limited proposal 'should minimise the chances of court action interfering with the resolution of a particular dispute' (para. 2.8).

However, the earlier discussion of the development of the provisions of the 1984 Act suggests that perhaps a more prominent Government aim achieved by this approach was to ensure that provisions would not be introduced providing the opportunity for members to exert pressure in favour of industrial action being pursued. A right to restrain the union from supporting action, rather than, for example, one to compel it to hold a ballot, could be expected only to diminish the incidence of industrial action itself.[8] In this connection, it is worth noting the way in which the new right was envisaged as meshing closely with the structure of the 1984 provisions, in particular in the suggestions that, as in 1984, the right would operate where

[8] Cf. *Taylor* v. *NUM (Yorkshire Area)* [1984] IRLR 445.

action might be authorized or endorsed according to the tests of the 1982 Act, and would apply where the action contemplated might involve breaches of contracts of employment (DE 1987: para. 2.9).

The Green Paper then turned to the proposal which was to lead to perhaps the most controversial provision of the legislation which ultimately followed, namely the 'right to go to work despite a strike call'. Indeed it was in these passages that the document confronted most explicitly the deepest ideological issues concerning the collective conduct of industrial action. At stake, it argued, was the conflict between what it called the 'hard line view of the traditional philosophy of the trade union movement based on the concept of collective strength through solidarity' versus 'the individual's right to make his own choice', and in particular to 'choose to go to work rather than strike' (para. 2.10).[9]

The language chosen in which to portray this particular ideological conflict left little doubt, if any remained, as to which side of the issue attracted the Government's support; and the document proceeded to a depiction of the choice faced by individuals considering industrial action which we will also recognize as familiar from the discussion of the provisions of the 1984 Act. Once again it emphasized the dangers of participation in industrial action, in terms in particular of loss of wages and the threat of dismissal, at the expense of all other considerations (DE 1987: para. 2.11). As with the discussion of the 1984 provisions, one might point once again to the absence of any consideration of the other factors which might influence the union member considering whether or not to participate in industrial action. In addition, the discussion conspicuously accepted without criticism (or any suggestion that the law might need changing) the severe sanctions which can be visited by employers upon those who take industrial action, by contrast with its castigation of the sanctions which may be imposed by the union against those who do not. Once again, stress was placed on the sanctity of the contract of employment, and the position of the individual who has 'merely decided' that he does not wish to break it (paras. 2.12–2.13).

When turning to an assessment of the current legal position, the Green Paper was forced even further to render explicit the logic of its ideological impetus. Whilst other recent assessments have found an impressive and daunting array of common law and statutory controls,[10] the Green Paper felt that with the decline of the closed shop, in which area protection was most comprehensive, attention should focus on the (it argued) inadequate protections outside the closed-shop context. In shifting its attention away from the closed-shop context in this way, the Green Paper was more squarely confronted with the argument that those who are not prepared to abide by a

[9] Contrast the view of Lloyd LJ in *Iwanuszezak* v. *GMBATU* [1988] IRLR 219, para. 8, that 'where the collective interests of the union conflict with the interests of an individual member it only makes sense . . . that the collective interests of the members as a whole should prevail.'

[10] See e.g. McKendrick (1986); Elias and Ewing (1987: ch. 7).

union's rules and practices do not properly belong in the union. Here, it offered an alternative ethic, namely that 'those who disagree with the policies and actions of their leaders nonetheless value their membership and do not see why dissent should lead to expulsion' (DE 1987: para. 2.15).

Whilst stopping short of finding wisdom in the idea of a right to compel a union to maintain a contract of membership, the document nevertheless followed through this approach with the idea of 'compensation at a deterrent level, perhaps with a statutory minimum' where a union refuses to readmit (para. 2.19), an approach similar to that taken by EA 1980, sections 4 and 5 in the closed-shop context. Another suggestion then briefly considered but discarded, was that the protection might be limited to cases where action is unlawful (paras. 2.20–2.21). But the discussion concluded firmly with a reassertion of the wider 'issues of principle', namely that

Every union member should be free to decide for himself whether or not he wishes to break his contract of employment and run the risk of dismissal without compensation. No union member should be penalised by his trade union for exercising his right to cross a picket line and go to work (para. 2.22).[12]

Chapter three of the Green Paper turned to the question of 'safeguard and control of union funds'. The discussion and rhetoric of the chapter sporadically reflected the preoccupation suggested by this title, namely with the right of members to have proper control of union funds; but the bulk of the discussion focused on a rather different, albeit overlapping, preoccupation—with the effective enforcement of court orders in the context of industrial action.

Enforcement, as we have seen throughout this book, was a central concern from the earliest days of the 1980s legislation, emerging first in the debate over the immunity for trade unions as such, upon which the Prior and Tebbit administrations had differed so sharply. Although the repeal of this immunity in 1982 was in some quarters thought to have provided a cure for all enforcement ills, it did not prove to be so. Two broad areas of difficulty soon became apparent. First, the extent of the statutory restrictions on industrial and other forms of protest action was extended at precisely the same time as the progressive implementation of Government policies in other areas provided an increasing impetus to just such activities. With picketing and demonstration increasingly readily held unlawful in substantive terms, the courts found themselves more and more engaged in the process of developing the procedural laws which underpin the efficacy of the enforcement process.[13]

---

[11] The paper suggested that a member's right ought not to turn on principles of law which were 'sometimes unclear', and would require evidence of contracts which the member might not be able to adduce. The contrast with the lack of concern where similar problems face unions contesting actions is illuminating.

[12] The paper thereby perpetuated the blurring between the positions of the striker in unfair-dismissal law and in contract law, which we saw was a feature of the debate over the 1984 Act.

[13] See Auerbach (1987).

Here, the courts concluded more than once that an invaluable technique lay in the co-option of other parties to the task of enforcement, most notably in the encouragement or requirement of unions to discipline their own members who persisted in industrial action which had been declared unlawful.[14] The second 'problem', however, was that of the continuing capacity of the unions themselves—notwithstanding the formidable obstacles—to sustain major industrial struggles, the decade seeing a series of prolonged and bitter disputes. Out of the miners' strike emerged the perhaps curiously complementary idea that union *members* could be used to restrain the *union* itself, and its officers, who continued to sponsor industrial action in the face of court orders. The unprecedented orders issued in that dispute, for the removal of a union's trustees and the placing of its assets into the hands of a receiver, aimed to strike at the heart of a union's control of its funds, by subverting the *legal* control vested in the trustees.[15]

The 1987 Green Paper's account was forthright in its analysis of this issue. By contrast with the coyness of a document such as the 1981 Green Paper, it discussed openly the implications of a situation in which a union deliberately defies an injunction, placing itself in contempt of court, and exposing itself to the risks of fines and sequestration. If the 1982 Act had addressed the problem of individual martyrdom, it was the problem of martyrdom of the whole union—which that Act had perhaps helped to generate—which the 1987 Green Paper now confronted.[16] Drawing in detail on the example of the miners' strike, it concluded that controls on trustees, particularly through the weapon of receivership, might provide a particularly effective way of thwarting a union's leadership. A statutory provision might remove any suggested restriction on the power exercised in the miners' strike, which may have rested on the court's view that the union's trustees were acting in breach of its rules (DE 1987: para. 3.14).

This chapter also considered two further possible new controls in this area, namely restrictions on the ability of a union to indemnify its members in respect of criminal penalties, and new rights to inspect union accounts. Both can be seen as building on existing common-law controls and in particular on developments in the miners' strike.[17] Once again, while both can be described in terms of a need to protect and control union funds, both can

---

[14] See: ibid. at pp. 237–9; Auerbach (1988: pp. 236–8); *Rayware* v. *TGWU* as reported in the *Guardian* (23 Nov. 1988). The contrast with the then proposed ban on discipline for *non-participation* is noteworthy.

[15] TULRA 1974 s. 2(1)(*b*); *Clarke* v. *Heathfield* [1985] ICR 203, 606 (CA). 'Martyrdom' of officials was narrowly averted by the court in *Taylor* v. *NUM* (*Derbyshire Area*) (No. 3) [1985] IRLR 99.

[16] It will be recalled that the degree of political risk involved in the martyrdom of unions, as opposed to individuals, was a matter on which Mr Tebbit and Mr Prior had differed, but also that the structure of EA 1982 s. 15 still aimed to give unions the opportunity and incentive to avoid this consequence.

[17] On indemnities, see *Drake* v. *Morgan* [1978] ICR 56; *Thomas* v. *NUM* (*South Wales Area*) [1985] IRLR 136. On inspection of accounts, see *Taylor* v. *NUM* (*Derbyshire Area*) (*No. 2*) [1985] IRLR 65.

equally be seen as additional weapons in restraining unions from conducting industrial action in the face of orders of the court, a view which, as we shall see, was to be expressed by the Government in debates on the subsequent Employment Bill. Once again, it was upon this aspect that the substance of the Green Paper's discussion in fact concentrated most (DE 1987: paras. 3.15–3.26).

A chapter on the closed shop reviewed developments in the 1980s both in the law on the closed shop, and in relation to the institution itself. Once again, the chapter embodied perhaps the most explicit and pure statement yet of the logic of the Government's ideological approach in the field, in its conclusion that the time was now ripe to remove all remaining legal protections for the closed shop, both in terms of protections for the conduct of primary industrial action, and in terms of the very narrow remaining protections for employers who dismiss non-members of unions. The discussion thereby impliedly conceded the pragmatic expediency of earlier measures such as the balloting requirements of the 1980 and 1982 Acts, but argued that the step-by-step approach had itself helped to change attitudes on the closed shop, paving the way for more radical measures (DE 1987: ch. 4).

The central preoccupation with the matter of enforcement was most clearly expressed by the inclusion of a chapter devoted solely to the topic. The Green Paper suggested that members had at present to be 'exceptionally determined and sometimes courageous' in order to claim and enforce rights against their trade unions (ch. 6, para. 6.3). In the miners' strike, it may be observed, the working miners suffered from no lack of financial and other forms of support from a variety of sources, but no doubt it could not be assumed that such a pattern would always be repeated in less dramatic and extraordinary circumstances. The Green Paper therefore proposed a more enduring and official institution, a new 'Commissioner', empowered to fund and provide other forms of support for member actions (paras. 6.14–6–19).

In concluding this analysis of the Green Paper of 1987, perhaps two points deserve particular emphasis. First, it is worth referring once again to the bold openness of the ideological position taken by the document, in particular in terms of its unequivocal commitment to the rights of the individual as opposed to trade-union and collective rights. The commitment to the right not to be disciplined for failure to participate in industrial action—regardless of the existence of a closed shop, a ballot, or of the lawfulness of the action— above all displayed the firm primacy given to the protection of individual rather than union-membership rights. While this was a stance which it has been argued in this book ultimately underlay many aspects of the 1984 legislation, the 1987 Green Paper marked its first clear and unequivocal expression as the central conception behind the Government's pursuit of rights for trade-union members in this area.

Secondly, we should note a vital feature of the approach of the Government to one aspect of the logic of where the emerging clarity of its position on the rights of union members might otherwise have led it. With the demise of the allegedly compulsory nature of membership in a closed shop as a credible debating point, and in the context of a comprehensive assault upon the virtues of collective bargaining and the utility of industrial action, the Government might have simply concluded that those who do not support or subscribe to the tenets and values for which trade unions stand, are better off as non-members—and then confined its continuing attack to those values and tenets themselves.

Such an approach would, however, have undermined any attempt to exploit the central insight upon which the entire Green Paper rested, and which the Government believed it had hit upon in the events of the miners' strike, namely that dissenting and aggrieved members can be a powerfully effective instrument in restraining the pursuit by trade unions of industrial action: for such a force can only be harnessed if the members in question stay *inside* the union. Economists have for many years recognized the importance of the fact that dissentient partakers of any institution may choose between two different methods of exercising their grievance, namely 'exiting' the institution by leaving and seeking a better situation elsewhere, or remaining and exercising the 'voice' in order to exert pressure for change from within.[18] In pursuit of the Government's wider goals of altering the external behaviour of unions themselves, the Green Paper proposals aimed to provide a range of new techniques designed to encourage dissentient members of unions to opt for the strategy of 'voice' rather than 'exit'. Arguably, it was once again this desire to alter the external effects of union activity which predominated even over internal individual goals.

This analysis remains pertinent when we turn to consider the responses to the Green Paper. In particular, employers' organizations, whilst welcoming or expressing indifference towards many of the other proposals, were predominantly and strongly opposed to the suggested right to opt out of industrial action, even where there had been a ballot.[19] This was essentially because employers' organizations had come to value the stability and predictability brought to collective bargaining by the balloting requirement introduced in 1984, something which had lead to ballots becoming, in ACAS's words, 'a permanent part of the negotiating scene'. (ACAS 1987: p. 14). The introduction of such a sweeping right of dissent would, it was feared, undermine the authority, and indeed the point, of a ballot, and encourage the abandonment of the practice.

Moreover, employers strongly questioned the need for such provisions, referring to an argument which has already been discussed. The EEF, for example, urged that the ending of legal protection for the closed shop 'makes much less convincing the case for giving the dissenter legal protection against union discipline' as 'a union member who does not wish to comply with the

[18] See Hirschman (1970).
[19] For a summary of the CBI and EEF responses, see *Personnel Management* (June 1987: p. 7); see too, CBI, *Employment Affairs Report* (May/June 1987: p. 2).

decision of a strike ballot would be able to resign from the union' (EEF 1987*a*: para. 9). Similarly opposed were the Conservative Trade Unionists who again put the point simply and clearly: 'Where fair and proper ballots have been conducted amongst those concerned it is considered that the majority view should be accepted by all concerned and breach of this principle is inconsistent with continued membership of the union' (CTU 1987: para. 7). The importance attached by these organizations to the balloting process itself, and their iteration of the principle that members who do not wish to be bound by a union's practices can and should stay outside the union, contrast illuminatingly with the Government's approach to ballots before industrial action as merely one means of attempting to influence the behaviour of trade unions, and with the Government policy of persuading dissentient members to remain inside their unions in order to exert their influence through the medium of voice.

The other main proposal about which employers' organizations expressed strong reservations was that of a Commissioner for the Rights of Trade Union Members. Once again, the fear appeared to be that such a figure could only operate as a disruptive and destabilizing influence on industrial relations, and it was clearly felt that the need for a Commissioner was far from proved.[20] Notwithstanding these objections, and in particular the force of the arguments on the right not to strike, the Government persisted in its adherence to these proposals, and in its manifesto published for the general election of June 1987 announced its intention to bring forward legislation on the lines set out in the Green Paper (*Conservative Party Manifesto* 1987: pp. 23–4). In a move symptomatic of the Government's increasing confidence in its ability to push through its views on such issues, there was no further consultation document following the election, before the publication of an Employment Bill in October 1987.

## (3) THE EMPLOYMENT BILL

The Employment Bill contained measures which aimed to implement all the main ideas set out in the Green Paper and the 1987 manifesto. In the area of industrial conflict, however, it also contained three new provisions. First, a highly complex clause contained new controls on the union's ability to select the constituency for a ballot before industrial action where more than one workplace is involved. Secondly, provision was made for the introduction of one or more codes of practice governing the conduct of ballots and elections. Finally, a clause dealt with the specific position of those who organize industrial action taken by Crown employees.[21]

As with the previous legislation of the decade, the Employment Bill 1987 survived its transformation into the Employment Act 1988 with its principal

[20] See e.g. EEF (1987*a*: para. 17).
[21] 1987 Bill 17, cls. 16, 17, and 29 respectively.

elements essentially intact, and the major alterations were the product of Government rather than Opposition amendments. With such a frank Green Paper preceding it, there were perhaps few surprises to be found in the Government's broad statements during debates on the Bill. Nevertheless, a number of more specific exchanges are illuminating, and particularly in relation to some of the more complex provisions, the changes which were made, and the surrounding debates, do provide some useful insights into how it was envisaged by the Government that those provisions should operate. We can therefore turn now to look in turn at each of the provisions affecting industrial conflict.

### (a) Ballots before Industrial Action

*A New Right for Members.*   Clause 1 of the Bill contained the promised new right for members to restrain their union from authorizing or endorsing industrial action which lacks the support of a ballot complying with the various requirements of the Trade Union Act 1984. As promised, the provision was limited to this right to *restrain* support for industrial action, and did not create any right to procure that a ballot be held, either to initiate or indeed to call off industrial action. The right was to be given to a single member of the union without the support of any required number of colleagues, but, if desired, with the support of the new Commissioner, as subsequent provisions of the Bill made clear.[22] This combination was no doubt considered to be most likely to maximize the chances of the provision actually being used, although the Government, continuing to pursue its non-interventionist rhetoric, nevertheless stressed that only a member who was actually involved or likely to be involved in the industrial action would be able to exercise the new right.[23]

In its mechanics, the provision was broadly designed to follow the lines of the existing provisions in the 1984 Act, in terms, for example, of the various procedural requirements with which a ballot would have to comply, and of the scope of the section only extending to industrial action for which the union could be held legally responsible under the provisions of section 15 of the 1982 Act. An express provision made it clear that it was not intended that unions should have to hold separate ballots in order to comply with the 1984 Act and with the new provisions. Nevertheless, the Government clearly envisaged that the new provision: might enhance the effectiveness and enforceability of existing requirements, as members might be better placed than the employer to detect invalidating irregularities in the conduct of the ballot.[24]

---

[22]  Ibid. cl. 19(7).
[23]  See OR HC St. Cttee. F 1st sitting (12 Nov. 1987) col. 18. Mr Cope.
[24]  See OR HL vol. 496 col. 16 (25 Apr. 1988) Lord Trefgarne.

In fact, the drafting even went so far as to follow the 1984 Act in terms of applying only to cases of industrial action which might involve members in the breaking of or 'interference' with their contracts of employment. As was suggested in the discussion in chapters six and seven, there was in fact no necessity for this cumbersome and inelegantly couched drafting in 1984, but it appeared to have been settled upon at that time as a result of a combination of factors, including a belief that this was the best way of ensuring that the provision followed the contours of the common law, and a preoccupation with the symbolic importance of the contract of employment and its observance, regardless of the extent or nature of its legal significance for the individual participant in industrial action.

At the time of presentation of the 1987 Bill, the Government's thinking appeared to be barely further developed or clarified than it had been in 1984. Once again, Government speakers stressed that the clause was intended to cover all instances of industrial action, and urged the view that it was very likely that in practice it would.[25] Once again it was suggested that, although never yet applied in that way, the tort of interference with contracts might logically extend to employment as well as commercial contracts.[26] Yet the clause itself made it clear that a member's right of action under the provision was not to be dependent on whether or not a tort was likely to be committed by the organizers of the industrial action, a logical enough approach given the Government's aims;[27] and the Government itself correctly cited the *Faust* case in support of the proposition that a reference in legislation to 'industrial action' pure and simple should not be interpreted as being restricted to industrial action in breach of contract.[28] The Government also seemed clearly to recognize the consequent irrelevance of the contract issue to the vulnerability of the employee to loss of unfair dismissal protection.[29]

The commitment despite all this to wedding the provision to a requirement of interference with or breach of contract appeared to be the result both of the belief that this was as a matter of drafting essential to the dovetailing of the new provision into the 1984 Act requirements, and, once again, of the preoccupation with the sanctity of employment contracts and the importance of their observance. Mr Cope, the new junior employment minister, simply commented that '[o]ne cannot get away from the contract of employment.'[30] Once again, the concern with observance of the contract of employment seemed mainly to be inspired by a consideration of the perspective of the employer anxious to ensure the conduct of business as usual, rather than that of the employee.

---

[25] OR HC St. Cttee. F 1st sitting (12 Nov. 1987) col. 9 Mr Cope.
[26] Ibid. 2nd sitting (17 Nov. 1987) cols. 38–9 Mr Cope.
[27] 1987 Bill 17, cl. 1(7).
[28] OR HC St. Cttee. F 1st sitting (12 Nov. 1987) col. 5 Mr Cope.
[29] OR HL vol. 494 col. 432 (7 Mar. 1988) Lord Trefgarne.
[30] OR HC St. Cttee. F 1st sitting (12 Nov. 1987) col. 8.

This approach led to further drafting complications in 1987. The notion of inducement, original finding a mention in 1984 because of its role as a component in establishing the principal tortious liability of organizers, now served as the trigger for the new individual member's right which, as the Bill itself testified, was not intended to be restricted to cases where a tort was involved. Although this was a vital and precisely formulated requirement set out by Jenkins LJ in *Thomson* v. *Deakin*, the concept had been watered down progressively over the years to the point where almost the mere presence of entirely peaceful pickets on a picket line can now be held to constitute an inducement.[31] Nevertheless, a case under this new provision would almost by definition be brought by a person who was determined not to take part in industrial action notwithstanding any inducement, and the same Bill would also introduce a right to adopt that stance free from fear of any union discipline.

The possibility therefore existed that a court application made pursuant to this provision might be defeated by the simple assertion that the stance of the member in question, of itself demonstrated that there had been no inducement sufficient to trigger the right which the provision conferred. The solution adopted to this unusual problem was to retain the inducement trigger but to provide that

references to an inducement . . . include references to an inducement which is or would be ineffective, whether because of that member's unwillingness to be influenced by it or for any other reason . . .[32]

The inconsistencies, confusion, and bizarre implications of the drafting of this clause were made much of by the Opposition during the Commons debates, and appeared to some extent at last to sink in with the Government. When the Bill went into committee in the Lords, the Government proposed and ushered through amendments to the clause, to delete the requirement, which was indeed entirely superfluous to its aims, that the industrial action in question be in breach of or an interference with the contract of employment. The Government itself, in the shape of Lord Trefgarne, now repeated the simple argument that the member's job may be at risk whatever the status of the industrial action contemplated.[33]

Nevertheless, even at this point, the hinging of the provision upon the concept of *inducement* was still left intact, making it, and the subsequent special definition of inducement along the lines indicated above, look even more peculiar in the final Act. The concept could readily at this stage have been replaced with the notion that a member must be likely to be 'called upon' or 'requested' to take part in industrial action. Such terms would have

[31] *Union Traffic Ltd.* v. *TGWU* [1989] IRLR 127 (CA).
[32] 1987 Bill 17, cl. 1(5).
[33] See n. 29 above.

required no special definition, in as much as a call or request does not—unlike an inducement—change its character simply by virtue of being rejected or ignored. The failure of the Government to put forward any further amendment along these lines may be attributable to simple oversight of the existence of such a possible approach; but it may also be that the Government actually preferred the concept of an inducement to that of a call or request, on the footing that, for example in a picketing context, it may not always be possible to characterize the act of inducement as involving a clearly defined *type* of action or behaviour on the part of the organizer.

However that may be, the result was a provision which was more consistent with the logic of the Government's objectives in the 1988 and indeed 1984 Act provisions, than was the original draft in the Bill, while still being a good deal more complex than it need have been. The Government also took the opportunity of the 1987 Bill to amend the provisions on ballots before industrial action in the 1984 Act, henceforth also to apply to the new member action, to take account of the weaknesses which were perceived as having emerged in these provisions during their initial period of practical operation. The new measures involved a tightening up of the procedural requirements for the conduct of ballots, and the introduction of much more stringent controls than in 1984 on the union's ability to determine the 'constituency' which any one ballot will cover. We can consider each aspect in turn.

*Ballot Question and 'Health Warning'.*   The 1984 Act's provisions establishing a positive ballot result as the price of all statutory protection, for almost all types of industrial action, had a more significant, widespread, and rapid impact on union behaviour in collective negotiations than perhaps any other measure discussed in this book. Research and survey evidence suggests, as has been noted, a rapid increase in the use of such ballots following the coming into force of the 1984 provisions, prompting the ACAS view that they had become an established and regular feature within two to three years, and a growing fondness on the part of employers for the practice as denoting predictability and stability. The evidence also indicates that the absence of a ballot (or one held in compliance with the legislation) accounted for a significant proportion of successful injunction applications in this early period.[34]

A person approaching this evidence with the outlook and assumptions which it was suggested underpinned the 1984 provisions, might have been tempted to conclude that it painted a dismal picture for trade unions, and one of remarkable success for Government policy. Where ballots had not been properly conducted, bullying leaders had been tamed and chastened by the injunction. Where ballots were now being conducted, it would be a safe bet

[34] See Evans (1987); ACAS (1987: pp. 13–14), (1988: p. 11); Wilkinson (1987); *IRRR* 417, 1 June 1988, pp. 2–7.

that members were by and large voting against industrial action and putting a stop to it in that way. In truth, however, the evidence indicated a phenomenon of rather greater complexity, with implications which were far less welcome from the Government's point of view. Upon a closer and more careful examination, three related features stand out.

First, the great majority of ballots held were producing votes in favour of rather than against industrial action.[35] Secondly, unions had learnt rapidly to use the ballots as a positive instrument in collective bargaining. Where a majority was obtained in a ballot, it was by no means automatic that industrial action would then follow, the result of the ballot itself often proving enough to encourage the employer to make a fresh input to the negotiating process (Wilkinson 1987: pp. 17–18 and 34–5). Finally, the tight framework established in the 1984 Act appeared in fact to leave unions with a good deal of room in a number of significant areas to make tactical choices in the use and conduct of the ballot (pp. 45–8). We have seen in the earlier discussion of the development of the 1984 Act provisions, that the Government was at that time only too well aware of the dangers of delivering to the unions 'on a plate', a tactical weapon to use against employers, and that a number of detailed aspects of the balloting requirements sought to minimize that risk. We saw too, however, how difficult it was to predict at the time what the effect of any particular requirement might be, and how much of the Parliamentary debate on the provisions was concerned with the contention between different scenarios which it was suggested would surely follow.

In retrospect, what perhaps emerges most strongly is the extent to which the intended operation of these various 'safeguards' which the Government incorporated into the provisions, was critically dependent upon the veracity of the central assumption that when faced with a ballot upon their own actual participation in imminent industrial action, members would on the whole be inclined to vote against. We saw this in particular in the combination of the exclusion of the application of the legislation to threats and conspiracy, the required 'health warning' in the ballot question, and the four-week rule. The object was to ensure that unions would not obtain broadly based mandates at the very start of bargaining—the gun to point at an employer's head throughout the period of negotiation; instead they would have to wait and call a ballot only when specific and imminent industrial action was contemplated.

But in a context where union negotiators know that they can command strong support from the membership at almost any stage in negotiations, the implications of a requirement such as the four-week rule can become reversed. A strong majority ballot early in the negotiations may have an especially powerful effect on the employer's position, if the union intimates

---

[35] See e.g. ACAS n. 34 above. A Government reply of 18 July 1989 indicated that ACAS was aware of 1,023 statutory ballots up to 31 May 1989 of which 115 produced votes against action: see *EG* (Sept. 1989: p. 508).

that if progress is not made within a period of four weeks, then it will be 'obliged' to call industrial action without further delay because of the requirements of Government legislation. This was but one example of the ways in which union negotiators became adept at manipulating the legislation to their advantage.[36]

The opportunity of the 1987 Bill was therefore taken in order to plug some of the perceived loopholes which had emerged. Amendments to the 1984 Act introduced by paragraph 5 of schedule 3 to the 1988 Act have the effect of requiring a ballot to stipulate specifically whether members are being invited to consider a strike, or some other form of industrial action, or if both, to ask separate questions—in effect to take a separate vote—regarding each. In addition, the required health warning is rewritten, and is to appear as a separate statement 'without being qualified or commented upon by anything else on the voting paper'.[37]

In fact, these provisions did not appear in the original Bill as published. The initial catalyst for their introduction appears to have been the changes to clause 1 which were introduced when the Bill reached the House of Lords. We may recall that in 1984, the Government's confusion on the finer points of the law extended to the area of the ballot question, the unsatisfactory result being that in all cases the union was required to ask whether the member was prepared to take action involving a breach of the contract of employment, even where the particular action contemplated might not entail any such breach. In clarifying its understanding of the law and its implications on clause 1, the Government also saw the need to revise the ballot-question provisions. Thus, the ballot-question and health warning were now to be separated out, with the health warning in every case now simply to state (precisely) that

If you take part in a strike or other industrial action, you may be in breach of your contract of employment.[38]

Taken literally and grammatically, this statement is unimpeachable as a proposition of law, given that 'you may' implies 'or may not', thereby covering all eventualities; but the desired impact of the statement upon the reader was obviously still intended to be achieved, by the arousal of a fear that the risk of a breach of contract would be involved. Once again, the crude impression or effect created by such a statement was the main objective, rather than a desire to encourage members to reflect upon and probe its logical meaning, or precise legal implications and relevance.

That assessment was reinforced beyond doubt by the introduction at an even later stage of the remarkable new requirement that the health warning may not be 'qualified or commented upon by anything else on the voting

---

[36] Cf. Elias and Ewing (1987: pp. 163–4). See also, generally, Wilkinson (1987: ch. 2).
[37] EA 1988, sched. 3, para. 5(8)(c).
[38] Ibid.

paper'.[39] This was a direct reaction to attempts by unions to place the health warning in a proper and informed perspective by the appearance of words on ballot papers such as 'This has no special significance as all strikes involve a breach of your contract of employment.' Such, apparently, was the Government's concern on this point that it felt it necessary to introduce this further amendment at the eleventh hour stage of third reading in the Lords, and at the expense of reneging on its explicit assurances in earlier debates that there would be nothing in the Bill or any subsequent code to prevent unions from commenting upon the legal significance of the health warning.[40] The rewriting of the ballot question also provided the opportunity to outlaw the practice of seeking approval for any, or a wide range of possible types of strike or industrial action. Once again, the Government was clearly concerned that it had emerged as a significant tactical weapon in the hands of the union to be able to keep the employer guessing and uncertain as to precisely what type of industrial action might be initiated within the four-week period.

The nature of these amendments, and the timing of their introduction, manifests their characteristic as *ad hoc* and piecemeal responses to perceived loopholes and problem areas which had emerged, so that no more in its 1988 version than in its 1984 version could the structure of the balloting regime be regarded as expressing any clear or definitive principled view about how ballots before industrial action ought to be conducted, or about the proper extent to which they ought to be regulated.[40a] Moreover, these changes suggest that the Government well understood the deeper implications of the research and survey evidence on the period since 1984, and was troubled by them. That impression is reinforced by the appearance in the Bill when published of controls on the choice of constituency for a ballot, which were entirely unheralded in the Green Paper or manifesto. It is to these that we may turn next.

*The Constituency of the Ballot.*   What became section 17 of the 1988 Act introduced detailed and complex controls on the union's choice of the constituency of any proposed ballot. In its complexity and tortuosity the section perhaps even surpasses its namesake, section 17 of the 1980 Act, and it would require more space than can be taken here to set out in full its precise mode of operation and effect, and the main areas of uncertainty and ambiguity; but, as with section 17 of the 1980 Act, the broad intended effect of the provision can be relatively easily grasped and stated, once we understand the nature of the Government concern which gave rise to its introduction.[41]

[39]  Ibid. See OR HL vol. 496 cols. 51 ff. (25 Apr. 1988).
[40]  See the earlier debates at OR HL vol. 494 cols. 1015–17 (14 Mar. 1988).
[40a]  Indeed, amendments added to the 1990 Bill will change the rules once again.
[41]  For a fuller analysis of section 17, see Bowers and Auerbach (1988: pp. 13–18).

Prior to 1988, and under the 1984 Act, a union enjoyed a significant discretion in choosing which of its members to ballot on industrial action. The only requirement was, in essence, that it should ballot all the members whom it contemplated might subsequently be called out, and then to abide by this by not in fact calling out anyone who had not been entitled to vote in the ballot.[42] Provided that this rule was observed, unions remained free to adopt whatever tactics they preferred when choosing which groups of members to call out and in what combinations, in order to bring the most effective pressure to bear upon the employer.

If the Government was concerned about this fact before 1987, it may simply have concluded that it could not be tackled by a specific provision, as the different tactics open to unions were simply too many and varied. However, between the publication of the Green Paper at the beginning of that year, and that of the Bill towards the end, a particular alleged tactic had been singled out for specific attention. The concern was that, where opinion was divided on the question of industrial action, a union might actively manipulate the make-up of the balloting constituency in order to generate the greatest and most effective 'yes' vote, by a form of gerrymandering, submerging an anti-strike section of the work-force in a constituency which was packed with votes from pro-strike sections.

What caused the Government to alight on this particular issue appears to have been the mention of it in some responses to the Green Paper, and in reports published over the summer of 1987, and in particular the IPM's report *A Guide on Workplace Balloting* (Wilkinson 1987).[43] This report presented a detailed survey of the experience of IPM members of how unions had responded to, and often turned to their advantage, the requirements of the 1984 Act, and it contained many illustrations of the sort of practices and tactics which have been discussed earlier in this chapter. When summarizing the various problems for employers which it had identified, it commented that '[t]he hidden factor in ballots on workplace issues is very often the constituency' (Wilkinson 1987: p. 45) which could be manipulated by inclusion or exclusion of particular groups in order to swing the ballot in favour of a particular result. The report commented that such manipulation 'is clearly an abuse of the system' (ibid.).

It was this sort of discussion which inspired the Government to introduce the new provisions contained in clause 16 of the Bill. In essence the clause aimed to require that where a union had 'arbitrarily' constructed the constituency for a ballot which went any wider than a single place of work, then it would have to hold separate ballots for each place of work involved. The test of arbitrariness would be determined by asking whether the choice of whom to include or exclude could be demonstrated to have been made on a particular acceptable basis. If an acceptable basis could not be shown, then

---

[42] TUA 1984 s. 11(1).
[43] See OR HC St. Cttee. F 13th sitting (14 Jan. 1988) col. 473 Mr Nicholls.

the requirement for separate workplace ballots would flush out the abuse, preventing the smothering of the views of moderate workplaces by aggregation of votes from elsewhere.

In order to realize this concept, however, it was necessary to go to considerable lengths. The new requirements were introduced by way of a series of amendments to sections 10 and 11 of the 1984 Act. The clause needed to spell out what was or was not an arbitrary basis of selection. Clearly, the broad intention was that the basis should be seen to be logical in terms of its relationship to bargaining arrangements; from this, the clause proceeded on the more specific assumption that in any properly drawn constituency there would be no discrimination as between members who shared the same occupational description or grade. The clause therefore proposed a basic rule requiring separate workplace ballots, but created an exception where those eligible could be grouped together by reference to occupational description or grade. To combat discriminatory inclusion as well as exclusion, a further provision restricted the exception to cases where *every* person who could be chosen because of their grade or occupation, had in fact been so chosen.

A new definition of place of work was also required, that concept performing two distinct functions in the clause. First, only when more than one place of work was involved would the clause operate at all. This fitted logically enough with suggestions in the IPM report that manipulation was not really a serious problem within small or single workplace operations (Wilkinson 1987: ch. 5); secondly, a series of separate workplace ballots was to be the requirement which would prevent the distortion which it was thought would otherwise be produced by an artificial constituency. It should be noted that this was not the most logical means of enforcing the principle. In theory, a more logical sanction would be simply to invalidate a ballot based on an artificial constituency altogether; but since manipulation of a ballot confined to a single workplace was thought to be of little concern, the requirement of separate workplace ballots would be an adequate penalty to achieve the objectives of the clause. Furthermore, for both its functions, the definition of place of work was extremely tightly drawn, to relate to a particular premises of the employer, tighter even than the restriction on picketing in the 1980 Act.[44]

The IPM reacted to the new clause with alarm. It suggested that the Government had failed to grasp the subtleties and complexities of the problems facing employers in this area, and as discussed in its earlier report. Most seriously, the clause 'appears to be a double edged weapon' as 'some corporate organizations . . . have always in the past managed to submerge the votes of a few notoriously militant sites in the overall results of a normally acquiescent workforce' (IPM 1988: p. 3). It concluded that 'it would be

---

[44] 1987 Bill 17 cl. 16(4); cf. on 'place of work' for picketing: *Rayware Ltd.* v. *TGWU* [1989] IRLR 134.

more helpful from an employer's point of view if clause 16 was omitted' (ibid.). In general, the IPM once again reaffirmed its traditional faith in voluntary rather than legislative initiatives, particularly where unions' internal constitutional processes were concerned.

The Opposition for its part pointed to the intense difficulties which the provision would cause for unions, given its many complexities and uncertainties of application, and the difficulty which even professional lawyers would have in threading their way through its provisions. In fact, with the Opposition's help, the clause was considerably redrafted during the course of its passage through Parliament. The occupational description or grade test was attacked as too narrow. The Government acknowledged that what it was looking to protect was a genuine 'bargaining unit', but thought that this expression itself could not be used.[45] Eventually it introduced amendments rewriting the clause to require a 'common factor' relating either to terms and conditions of employment or to occupational description.[46]

This, however, created a new problem relating to place of work: discrimination by reference to place of work was not to be allowed, yet this might often be a genuine distinguishing term in the contract of employment. So a further proviso excluded reliance upon a factor which individuals share 'as a consequence of having the same place of work'.[47] This proviso did not however take account of the fact that there may be other terms and conditions which differ on a geographical basis, so that in such cases selection on the basis of place of work would have an obvious bargaining logic. An example might be the balloting only of workplaces in London where only the level of a London weighting remains in dispute. The debates do not reveal whether the Government clearly recognized or took a view upon this point. It may have been assumed that the union would be protected where a factor (London weighting) would itself be acceptable, even if the place of work test (place of work: a workplace in London) could also have been applied to produce the same constituency. However, on the wording of the section this is technically unlikely to be so, as any factor shared *as a consequence* of having the same place of work is excluded (enjoying London weighting is a consequence of having a workplace in London).

Other Government amendments during the course of the Bill's passage clarified that no global ballot would be needed in addition to any separate workplace ballots, and that a majority in any workplace ballot would protect the calling of action at that workplace regardless of the position obtaining at other workplaces.[48] At the late stage of third reading in the House of Lords, the Government also accepted some Opposition amendments tabled by Lord Wedderburn which helped to clarify, for example, that the tests of the clause

[45] OR HC St. Cttee. F 14th sitting (19 Jan. 1988) cols. 508–10 Mr Cope.
[46] See OR HC vol. 127 col. 397 (8 Feb. 1988) Mr Cope.
[47] TUA 1984 s. 11(1B)(*b*)(iii) (as amended).
[48] OR HC St. Cttee. F 14th sitting (19 Jan. 1988) cols. 505 and 514.

would apply not only union by union, but also employer by employer, whilst yet permitting aggregate ballots to be held across different unions and different employers.[49]

The result is a section which is somewhat clearer on reaching the statute-book than the clause which first appeared in the Bill, but which still seems remarkably disproportionate in its complexity and severity to the extent and seriousness of the perceived problem which it set out to tackle. For students it perhaps provides an even more graphic and compelling illustration of the degree to which the conceptual machinery and methods of the law are ill-suited to be applied to the social realities of industrial relations and collective bargaining. For trade unions it means a section which requires considerable expertise to begin to fathom, and demands that a union planning a ballot at more than one workplace must go through a question and answer process of some twelve or more stages, in addition to all the existing questions about secondary action and so forth, in order to determine whether the ballot which it proposes to hold will be effective, and the action proposed, lawful.[50] The package of new provisions on ballots before industrial action contained in the 1988 Act testifies to the extent of the unease on the part of the Government which the experience of the 1984 Act's initial operation had created; but an even clearer and more explicit testimony of the Government's anxieties was to be found in a document published after the Act had become law, namely the code of practice on ballots on industrial action, introduced under the powers contained in section 3 of the 1980 Act, which were expanded to cover the field of ballots and elections by section 18 of the 1988 Act. It is to this that we may turn next.

*Code of Practice on Ballots on Industrial Action.* A frequent theme in this book has been the many problems generated for an interventionist strategy in industrial conflict, by the degree to which legal concepts and controls are poorly suited to the task of manipulating and controlling the social realities of collective bargaining and conflict. It is their potential for overcoming problems of this type which accounts for much of the appeal which codes of practice seem to offer in this field. A code of practice can be an attractive alternative to statutory controls. It need not be written in the technical and precise language of legislation, and can deal much more openly and directly with the currency, concepts, and realities of industrial relations. In the hands of a Government, it can go further than might be thought appropriate in legislation, setting out views on what the Government believes are to be regarded as good practices and principles, without necessarily imposing precise requirements about how or how stringently these should be

---

[49] OR HL vol. 496 cols. 42–3 (25 Apr. 1988).

[50] Cf. the concerns of ACAS (1989: p. 13), and the comment of Lord Donaldson MR in *BRB* v. *NUR* [1989] IRLR 349, 350 para. 9 that 'the balloting law is not simply expressed. It is not something that you can go to the average trade union member and say, "Well, that is the law. Now you know whether it has been complied with or not."'

implemented. If, in addition, the code is granted the curious legal status conferred by section 3 of the 1980 Act, while not being directly enforceable, it may be assured of being a strong influence upon the way in which the law is subsequently applied and developed.

All this we have seen in the context of our discussion of the code of practice on picketing issued under the 1980 Act, and a code was of course also issued under that Act in relation to the closed shop. In the earlier discussion of the 1984 Act, it was suggested that the practical problems can be particularly acute when the law turns to the task of regulating the internal affairs and procedures of organizations such as trade unions, and codes might have an obvious appeal to those concerned with the balloting issue. Indeed, as was noted in chapter six, when the Government in 1983 first canvassed the notion of ballots before industrial action, the IPM, an organization instinctively hostile to direct legislation, but nevertheless one which believed that a more systematic use of ballots might make a useful contribution to industrial relations, suggested a code of practice as a possible way forward. The IPM envisaged a code as a substitute for legal controls, and one which would be supervised solely by the CO.[51] In section 18 of the 1988 Act, the Government supplemented its battery of legal controls by amending and expanding the existing power of the Secretary of State under section 3 of the 1980 Act to issue codes of practice, to include codes to promote 'what appear to him to be desirable practices in relation to the conduct by trade unions of ballots and elections'.[52]

Once again, this was a provision not heralded in the Green Paper or the manifesto, and once again, its inclusion in the 1987 Bill appears to have been the result of the concerns expressed by employers in responses to the Green Paper and in other documents appearing during the course of the year, about the many tactics and strategies which unions were showing themselves able to adopt even within the tight framework of the 1984 Act. As has already been remarked, it would be quite impossible to address every such concern by way of direct amendment to the legislation, but a code of practice might be a forum in which a number of the key issues could be set out.

The Government seems in particular to have been persuaded to introduce a code on ballots before industrial action by the arguments and lobbying of the EEF, and almost as soon as the Bill containing the relevant provision had been published, the EEF issued a document thanking and applauding the Government, and setting out its own detailed suggestions as to what the code itself should contain (EEF 1987a: para. 16, and 1987b).[53] These included recommendations on ways of ensuring secrecy and fairness; a recommendation

---

[51]  See ch. 6. text to n. 46 above.

[52]  EA 1980 s. 3(1) as amended.

[53]  According to an EEF press release of 18 Jan. 1988, the DE had expressed interest in the Federation 'developing its thoughts on a code'. The Industrial Society had also issued a code at the end of 1986.

that a ballot should not be held until all collectively agreed disputes procedures have been exhausted; a suggestion that the voting paper be accompanied by statements from both the union and the employer, setting out the background and issues of the dispute as each side sees it; and a recommendation that where several ballots are held by different unions, all results be simultaneously announced and formally communicated to the employer.

The EEF's document ran to a mere nine pages, focusing on the problems thought to be of particular concern within the engineering industry. The Government's draft code published in November 1988, by contrast, ran to more than fifty pages and over one-hundred paragraphs, equalling in length the codes on picketing and the closed shop put together. Furthermore it went into exhaustive detail into every area and every stage of the balloting process, the TUC identifying some twenty-three new stages through which a union would have to pass when conducting a ballot and before in fact initiating industrial action. The document took up in one form or another most of the suggestions put forward by the EEF, and supplemented these with provisions designed to combat a number of other possible forms of perceived abuse.[54] Although the revised code eventually presented to Parliament in early 1990 either omitted or watered down a number of the most controversial passages contained in the original draft, the thrust and intent of the first version remained intact.[55] The draft thus remains an invaluable and illuminating guide to the thinking and concerns lying behind the final document.

There is no need here for a detailed commentary upon or critique of the many provisions in the draft code, a task which has more than adequately been undertaken elsewhere.[56] However, what is important for present purposes is to note the extent to which the draft and final codes gave further expression to Government concerns about the whole experience of the 1984 provisions since their introduction, and the ways in which certain provisions were designed to harmonize with and bolster the various elements of the legislative framework after 1988. In particular, two broad features which showed particularly clearly in the first draft should be firmly noted. First, the thrust of much of the draft code was aimed at further defusing the potency of the ballot as a positive weapon in the hands of the union, by suggesting a wide range of circumstances in which the union should not hold a ballot, delay the holding of a ballot, downgrade the significance of a majority vote, or refrain

---

[54] See DE (1988).

[55] See DE (1990) for the final code, and the illuminating comparison between it and the first draft, in 387 *IRLIB* 24 Oct. 1989 pp. 2–9.

[56] For comprehensive criticism and analysis of the first draft, see Hendy *et al.* (1989). For the concerns expressed in responses from the CBI, IPM, EEF, and ACAS, see *Personnel Management* (Mar. 1989: p. 15), and *IRLIB* 372, 7 Mar. 1989 pp. 14–16.

from following up a positive ballot with the actual calling of industrial action.[57]

This aspect was illustrated most starkly in the draft code by its suggestion that a union may 'feel it would not be justified' in calling action where a majority of less than 70% of those entitled to vote has been obtained (DE 1988: para. 98). This remarkable paragraph was reminiscent of the code of practice on picketing's 'requirement' that the number of pickets at any one place should not exceed six, but proved to be even more controversial, given the explicit provision in the substantive legislation that only a simple majority of those voting is required to enjoy statutory protection.[58] Had it remained a feature of the final code, this stipulation would, like the six pickets requirement, undoubtedly in due course have found its way into the substantive common law.[59] In the face of intense criticism, however, the Government deleted the mention of any specific figure from the final code, whilst retaining the recommendation that unions should take into account the sizes of the majority and the turnout (DE 1990: para. 54).

The second broad feature worthy of note is the way in which at frequent points the draft code urged trade unions to provide detailed information to the employer and to individual members concerning the conduct of the ballot, and even to provide such information to any potentially affected party who may request it (DE 1988: paras. 88–94). Here, thinly disguised, was surely an attempt to coerce unions into placing as much evidence and information as possible into the hands of those who may have a statutory right to have the conduct of any industrial action restrained by injunction. The code could therefore be regarded as another instrument designed to maximize the chances of the various statutory controls in fact being used, and of any irregularity in the conduct of a ballot being discovered, and action then restrained by injunction.[60] Again, although watered down in its specifics, the tone of the final code remained much the same.[61]

## (b) Discipline and Industrial Action.

Prior to the appearance of the draft code, perhaps the most controversial aspect of the 1988 Act was its enactment, in sections 3 to 5, of the Green Paper proposal to outlaw the disciplining of members who decline to take part in industrial action, regardless of its lawfulness or of the existence of any ballot. The Government pushed through these provisions in the face of

[57] Cf. the conclusions of Hendy et al. (1989: pp. 81–2). In the final code (DE 1990), see e.g. paras. 8–10, 46, 53–4. See too the comments of Mr Fowler on publication of the final code, reported in Personnel Management (Oct. 1989: p. 9).

[58] TUA 1984 s. 10(3)(b).

[59] Cf.: Thomas v. NUM (South Wales Area) [1985] IRLR 136; News Group Newspapers v. SOGAT '82 [1986] IRLR 337; P & O European Ferries (Dover) Ltd v. NUS 24 May 1988.

[60] Cf. Hendy et al. (1989: pp. 73–4).

[61] See e.g. DE (1990: paras. 33, 34, and 52).

intense and widespread opposition from organizations ranging across the political spectrum. Many of the arguments on both sides which were raised at the time of the Green Paper proposals were canvassed once again in the Parliamentary debates, and need not be restated here, but some further points which emerged can be noted.

First, the restrictions themselves were extremely broad, the categories of behaviour for which discipline would be 'unjustifiable' extending beyond non-participation in industrial action, to include arguing against industrial action, or seeking to assist or persuade others not to take part.[62] Thus, the provisions went well beyond the alleged need to protect those who wish to honour their contracts of employment, also to confer protection on those who seek to encourage the activities of others, once again, a provision which it is hard to explain other than in terms of a broader desire to maximize the chances of successful activity which will undermine the conduct of industrial action. Secondly, in cases of expulsion, whilst stopping short of allowing the union to be compelled by injunction not to expel strike-breaking members, the sections operate a two-stage process in which a refusal to readmit following an initial tribunal finding of unjustifiable discipline, will expose the union to the likelihood of a much higher award. This aims to provide an incentive on the union ultimately to retain dissenting members who will thereafter be able to continue to exercise their voice from within the union's ranks. Thirdly, the Government suggested at a number of points during the debates that the provisions would facilitate a 'drift back' to work during the course of a dispute, by members who had initially supported industrial action.[63] The example of events during the miners' strike, and the prolonged arguments over the extent of drift back during the later stages of that dispute, at once spring to mind. In addition, this approach once again highlights the imbalance of provisions which require a ballot in order to initiate industrial action, but not one in order to call the action off.

The lack of genuine commitment to the internal democratic function which a ballot might be argued to fulfil was perhaps even more clearly to be seen in relation to the final point which can be noted at this stage, namely the Government's response to the argument that the new right would undermine the significance attached to ballots, and lead to a deterioration in the commitment of unions to the balloting process. As Lord Trefgarne now put it: 'A strike ballot is of direct benefit only to the union. It must hold one to retain its privileged position of immunity from legal proceedings.'[64] Thus, what in 1984 had been implicit in the legislation but refuted in the rhetoric, had by 1988 become explicit in the Government's own pronouncements: that

[62] EA 1988 s. 3(3)(*a*) and (*d*). S. 3 was not the first example of a provision of this type, but previous provisions, such as TDTUA 1927 s. 2 and IRA 1971 s. 65, were considerably narrower in their range. For an uncertain common-law doctrine, see *Sherard* v. *AUEW* [1973] ICR 421.

[63] See e.g. OR HC St. Cttee. F 4th sitting (24 Nov. 1987) col. 118 Mr Cope.

[64] OR HL vol. 494 col. 485 (7 Mar. 1988).

the principal function of the balloting requirement was as an external control on the union's ability to conduct lawful industrial action. This was a function which the balloting requirement would indeed not be impaired in performing by the introduction of the new controls on discipline. From the internal perspective, however, the best that could now be said by the Government was that the ballot is 'a useful indicator of the opinion of other employees'.[65]

At many points in this discussion it has been suggested that the key development in the Government's thinking during the second half of the 1980s, was the expansion of faith in the potential of dissenting members within the union as a serious force capable of being mobilized as a restraining power on the conduct of industrial action. Events of the miners' strike in particular awakened the Government's thinking to the range of different techniques or controls which might be employed to this end. For this reason, after the 1988 Act, the traditional distinction between industrial-conflict law and trade-union law looks increasingly difficult to maintain, with a number of controls of trade-union law finding their genesis in their perceived usefulness in controlling industrial action. Thus, in addition to further controls on ballots before industrial action, and the new rights not to be disciplined in relation to industrial action, the 1988 Act introduced three new rights for members, each of which must be considered primarily as instruments in the field of industrial action. It is to these that we may turn next.

### (c) Control of Union Funds

The 1988 Act implemented three proposals put forward in the Green Paper for new membership rights in relation to the control and oversight of union funds. Section 6 introduced a membership right to inspect accounts; section 8 outlawed the indemnification by a union in respect of penalties for unlawful acts carried out by individuals, by creating a right to take action in the name of the union to claw back any sums paid; section 9 introduced new controls on trustees who may apply union funds in pursuit of unlawful activity, embracing powers to remove trustees, and to appoint a receiver of the union's assets. Each of these provisions owed its existence to developments in the miners' strike and each built on the case-law established in the strike, expanding upon, and removing ambiguities in, the common-law controls.[66] The events of that dispute had suggested that, in a major conflict of this type, formal controls and restrictions on the legality of industrial action might not be enough: if a union is prepared to defy the law even at the cost of sequestration, then further controls on its ability to fund and deploy its resources in the conduct of the dispute might be needed. Once again, the drafting of each provision, and the Parliamentary debates, revealed further

---

[65] OR HL vol. 494 col. 485–6 (7 Mar. 1988).
[66] See further Bowers and Auerbach (1988: ch. 4 and pp. 62–6).

aspects of the Government's thinking on how each of these provisions might further that aim.[67]

Most important, perhaps, were the new controls on trustees. Section 9 confirmed the legitimacy of the application of a receivership to a trade union, first carried out in the miners' strike, and also removed any suggestion that the technique might only be applicable where a union had acted in breach of its own rules.[68] The new controls were made expressly applicable in cases where a union acts contrary to a court order, and where the court is compelled to order the removal of trustees. Section 8 outlawed all indemnities whether prospective or retrospective, once again removing what the Government regarded as possibly unhelpful limits on the common-law principle. Here, the Government cited examples not only from the miners' strike but also from the more recent and equally bitter *News International* dispute.[69] Section 6 was tailored to supplement the other rights in the Act, by enabling a member to be armed with the necessary information to take advantage of those rights. For this reason the Government insisted that the right to inspect should go back six years, corresponding to any possible limitation period for further action, and that the member could be under no obligation of confidentiality in relation to the information discovered, for the member must be 'at liberty to make use of the information gained. Otherwise, there is little use in having it.'[70]

In relation to each of these provisions, the new Commissioner for the Rights of Trade Union Members is to be available to assist members proposing to bring actions.[71] In keeping with its increasingly hollow sounding rhetoric of leaving those directly affected to take action without the involvement of Government or its agencies, the Government stressed that the Commissioner would have no 'roving brief', but only be enabled to assist a union member who wished to take action.[72] Nevertheless, the Commissioner is obliged to consider the degree to which there may be a wider public interest in the outcome of the proposed action,[73] and—notably—*not* specifically required to have regard to the member's financial ability to fund the proposed action. In addition, the Government suggested that it had concentrated on making the Commissioner available where the proposed action is one of a type where the membership of the union as a whole, and not merely the specific member applying for assistance, might be concerned about the

[67] Once again, a precedent, but one more limited in its scope, can be found in TDTUA 1927 s. 7, which gave the Attorney-General the power to restrain the expenditure of a union's funds on purposes rendered unlawful by s. 1 of that Act. The objective in 1988 was not dissimilar, but the technique of implementation was novel.

[68] Cf. *Clarke* v. *Heathfield* [1985] ICR 203 and 606.

[69] See e.g. OR HC St. Cttee. F 4th sitting (24 Nov. 1987) col. 121. Cf. *Longley* v. *NUJ* [1987] IRLR 109.

[70] OR HC St. Cttee. F 7th sitting (3 Dec. 1987) col. 247 Mr Cope.

[71] EA 1988 s. 20(7)(*a*) and (*b*).

[72] OR HL vol. 493 col. 1005 (22 Feb. 1988) Lord Trefgarne.

[73] EA 1988 s. 20(4)(*c*).

outcome of the proposed action.[74] This testifies equally to a concern to ensure the availability of the assistance primarily in cases where there are implications for the activity of the *union* as a whole, and not merely for its relations with a particular member. In these ways, the creation of the Commissioner can be seen as a further attempt, through the guise of increasing membership rights, to create a framework in which the perceived power of dissenting members to act as a break on the pursuit and organization of industrial action by the union as a whole, is likely to be exploited to its full potential.[75]

So far, the discussion has concentrated on the core provisions of the 1988 Act which deepen and widen the use of trade-union law as a means of restricting and controlling the conduct by unions of industrial action. As has been noted, this was a trend initiated in the 1984 Act and fuelled by the events of the miners' strike. But the 1988 Act also contained two provisions of a more traditional style, each widening the general restrictions on industrial action introduced in the early 1980s. These concerned the lawfulness of industrial action by civil servants, and the traditional and seemingly inexhaustible preoccupation with the closed shop. We may consider each in turn.

### (d) Crown Servants

Section 30 of the 1988 Act is the enactment of another provision which appeared in the Bill unheralded, and owed its existence to developments following the publication of the 1987 Green Paper. The decision in *R.* v. *Civil Service Appeal Tribunal ex parte Bruce*, handed down in June 1987, added another twist to the confused and unsatisfactory state of the law on the question of whether Crown servants can be said to have employment contracts. The decision favoured the view that, at any rate, employees like Mr Bruce (who worked for the Inland Revenue) do not.[76] The immediate implication was that the elaborate structure of restrictions enacted since 1980, might have little relevance to the conduct of industrial action in the civil service. As those restrictions operated by way of a persistent removal of immunities, their operation was, as we have seen, consistently and entirely dependent upon the assumption that without immunity, organizers would be liable in tort, primarily for inducing breaches of employment contract by those taking part in action. If Crown servants had no employment contracts, liability in tort might therefore fail to be established, before the question of availability of immunity was even reached.[77]

[74] OR HC St. Cttee. F 15th sitting (19 Jan. 1988) col. 555.

[75] On the latest measures which will expand the role of the Commissioner, see ch. 9 below.

[76] See [1988] ICR 649 (DC); [1989] ICR 171 (CA); and now too *McClaren* v. *Home Office* [1989] ICR 550; *The Independent* (8 Mar. 1990) (CA). For background and analysis, see Fredman and Morris (1988).

[77] See further Bowers and Auerbach (1988: pp. 23–6).

Section 30 directly addressed the position, specifically only for the purposes of industrial action, by deeming Crown servants to have employment contracts in this context. Tellingly, the presumption was also applied for the purposes of a claim of unjustifiable discipline brought under section 3. At the same time, the section extended to the Crown the application of sections 12 and 13 of the 1982 Act (concerning union recruitment and recognition practices), thereby overcoming the equally anachronistic historical doctrine that legislation is presumed not to bind the Crown or its agencies, unless the contrary is expressly stated. The Government suggested that this point had been simply overlooked in 1982,[78] which is perfectly believable, but the section as a whole perhaps testified to a Government concern that there should be no doubt whatsoever as to the applicability of its legislation to civil servants, at a time when its policies in a number of areas could be expected to have an impact in this sector.

In general, section 30 is a typical minor provision of the legislation of the 1980s, a direct by-product of the step-by-step approach. The appearance of a new Bill allows the opportunity for inclusion of provisions addressing new problems which are thought to have emerged, and the inclusion of a particular provision operating in a particular area then provides the opportunity for a general review of how the existing law operates in that area, and the introduction of some further accompanying amendments.[79] Another by-product of the step-by-step approach, the opportunity which it offers to develop and extend restrictions at a pace conducive with the Government's perception of changing public opinion, is typified by the 1980s legislation's approach to the closed shop and union membership arrangements, including in relation to industrial action aimed at enforcing or supporting such arrangements; and it is to the 1988 Act's provisions in this area that we may now turn.

### (e) The Closed Shop and Union Membership Arrangements

In broad terms, the incidence of closed-shop and union membership agreements and arrangements declined steadily during the course of the 1980s. As with the pattern of industrial action, and the decline of union membership levels, this had probably less to do with any direct effects of Government legislation, and more to do with factors such as the growth of unemployment and its effect on unions' organizational abilities, and the shift in concentrations of employment away from the areas and industries which were the traditional preserves of closed-shop arrangements.[80] Nevertheless, the Government's ideological zeal against the closed shop, and its belief that

[78] OR HC St. Cttee. F 20th sitting (28 Jan. 1988) cols. 798–9 Mr Cope.

[79] As we saw, another good example of the phenomenon was EA 1982 s. 9.

[80] See e.g. Dunn and Gennard (1984). See too the arguments in the Green Paper, *Removing Barriers to Employment* (DE 1989a).

it constituted a major source of union power as against both employers and individual dissentient members, resulted in progressive provisions designed to tackle such arrangements in the Acts of 1980 and 1982. In the field of employer sanctions to preserve such arrangements, this meant broad protections against dismissal for non-union membership, save where high majorities in supporting ballots were achieved. In the field of industrial action, as has been seen, this meant first, the targeted provisions of section 18 of the 1980 Act, and then their expansion into the rather wider controls of section 14, buttressing sections 12 and 13, of the 1982 Act, and circumscribing the use of industrial pressure to further union membership or recognition at another workplace.

The 1988 Act took these processes to their logical conclusion. In a move which once again testified to the somewhat cynical expediency with which the Government regarded the use of ballots by unions, section 11 repealed the protection against an unfair dismissal claim, which sufficiently high ballots had previously afforded. In a complementary provision, section 10 removed protection from all forms of industrial action which aim to enforce union membership agreements or arrangements or to require an employer to 'discriminate' against non-members, regardless of whether the members taking action have the same workplace or employer. As with the earlier provisions, section 10 was widely drawn, so that if just one of the reasons behind a piece of industrial action is proscribed, it will be unprotected. With this further expansion of what was first section 18 of the 1980 Act and then the second 'limb' of section 14 of the 1982 Act, section 14 was accordingly rewritten to concentrate on its first limb function of bolstering sections 12 and 13 of that Act.[81]

## (4) THE EMPLOYMENT ACT 1988: INITIAL ASSESSMENT

In a survey of the development of industrial-conflict legislation in the 1980s, the Employment Act 1988 is illuminating not merely in view of its own significance, but also because of the bright retrospective light which it casts upon the Trade Union Act 1984. Looking back on the decade as a whole, it can be seen that the legal developments of the miners' strike denoted an emerging climate in which the 1984 Act came to represent not merely a novel variant on the early policy of the progressive restriction of industrial action, but a hinge between that and a more full-blown policy of the regulation of trade unions' internal affairs as a means to influencing external outcomes in the field of industrial conflict. Corresponding with the deepening and widening of the approach of internal regulation as an alternative to direct external restriction, we find too an increasing boldness and honesty in the Government's own rhetoric concerning the 1988 provisions. Whilst the claims to be handing rights to trade-union members, and strengthening the

[81] EA 1988 sch. 3. para. 4.

internal democracy of trade unions, still not suprisingly formed a central part of the broad 'selling' to union members and public opinion of the measures introduced in 1988, any more than cursory examination of the documents and debates reveals a striking candidness of the Government's commitment to the internal individual rather than the internal membership dimension, but above all to the external goal of inhibiting industrial action itself.

Where the rhetoric still purported to mask such priorities, the structure and detail of the 1988 provisions nevertheless rendered them unmistakable. The discussion in this chapter has repeatedly suggested the many ways in which the 1988 Act, and the accompanying code of practice, seek to maximize the possibilities and potential for dissentient members to act to inhibit and restrain the conduct of industrial action, and, for good measure, for employers and others affected to be armed with new weapons as well. The provisions preventing discipline of non-participants in industrial action express, in a manner which the Government did not seek to rebut in debates, a priority in favour of ensuring that employment contracts are honoured, far above any commitment to the democratic significance or any other benefit of the balloting process.

As with the earlier legislation, the provisions of the 1988 Act were mirrored and complemented by parallel developments in the coincident major industrial dispute—the seafarers' dispute of that year—and more generally in the common law. Developments in the seafarers' dispute in general, typified the increasing preoccupation in the late 1980s—an age in which any major industrial action is readily held prima facie unlawful—with problems of enforcement and procedural effectiveness of injunctive relief.[82] In particular, and in stark contrast to the controls on discipline of non-participators, 1988 saw the further growth of seeds planted in the earlier *News International* dispute, whereby the courts increasingly looked to unions to discipline and restrain members who engage in industrial action which is declared unlawful.[83] Thus the common law showed the way to complete the circle of the legislation, helping to solve the problem of 'martyrdom' of the individual as well as that of the union, and to provide a flexible means of tackling the pursuit of industrial action, by harnessing internal forces at whatever level within the union seems to be most appropriate.[84]

Yet these strategies remain fraught with difficulties for courts and Parliament alike. Notwithstanding the care with which the 1984 Act was drafted, the inherent problems of this type of legislative technique, so articulately identified and described by Chafee some fifty years before, seemed to be borne out by the experience of operation of that Act following its introduction. Much of the 1988 Act, and of the code, represented a response to the various loopholes and new problem areas which the

---

[82] See Auerbach (1988).
[83] See n. 14 above.
[84] For further discussion of the legislative fruit of these seeds borne in 1990, see ch. 10.

Government had alighted upon in the period since 1984. Furthermore, however impressed it may have been by developments in the miners' strike, the Government can hardly have imagined that to have been a typical dispute or a paradigm of the context in which the 1988 provisions would usually operate. Perhaps not so surprising then was the extent to which the 1988 Act concentrated upon encouraging the dissentient member to 'voice' rather than 'exit', and upon maximizing the chances of that voice being exercised and having its effect.[85]

In summary, the 1988 Act was a peculiar and unique amalgam of two distinct trends of the 1980s, both of which can be regarded as by-products of the step-by-step approach. On the one hand, both in the logic of its provisions and in the tone and content of the accompanying rhetoric, the 1988 Act reflected a clearer and less qualified statement than before of the Government's ideological approach to industrial action and the conduct of trade unions in general, an emboldening which the step-by-step approach facilitated over a period of some eight or nine years. On the other hand, in going further down the road of internal union regulation, and the use of ballots before industrial action in particular, the 1988 Act committed the Government even more firmly than had that of 1984 to a complex framework of industrial-conflict law which owed as much to the conjunction of a number of historical events over the course of the decade as to any purist ideology or blueprint which might have appealed to it. In chapter nine we can assess to what extent that mixture is reflected in the very latest series of measures which are destined to find their way to the statute-book, in the Employment Act 1990.

[85] This has of course been complemented by a wider non-legal Government strategy of dividing and so undermining union opposition by courting breakaway and right-wing unions such as the UDM and EETPU. The most recent example was the failed attempt in Dec. 1989 to negotiate a settlement in the ambulance workers' dispute with the non-TUC APAP, which might if agreed have then been 'imposed' on the TUC unions. Further on this topic see Gamble (1988b: p. 218).

# [9]

# Into the Nineties

## (1) THE DEBATES OF 1989 AND THE 'SUMMER OF DISCONTENT'

The passage into law of the Employment Act 1988 fulfilled the commitments of the 1987 manifesto in the areas of trade-union and industrial-conflict law, and, as we saw, did a good deal more besides. The Government accordingly now turned its attention back to a variety of initiatives designed to push forward its individual employment law and labour market policies, based on the well-established ideas of freeing up the labour market and attacking perceived restrictive practices and burdens on business. Thus, the Bill introduced for the 1988/9 session, which became the Employment Act 1989, removed a number of statutory controls regulating employment in certain industries, notably of young children, and of women in coal-mining, and further eased the requirements of other employment protection laws.[1]

The 1988 Act having, as has been noted, effectively 'outlawed' the post-entry closed shop, 1989 nevertheless also saw the Government return to this most hated of trade-union 'restrictive practices' with an undiminished ideological zeal. The target was now the 'pre-entry' closed shop, and the handful of occupations where it remained a relevant organizational feature. A Green Paper published in March, *Removing Barriers to Employment*, proposed a new right not to be refused employment on the grounds of non-membership of a trade union, arguing that as many as 1.3 million people were affected, a figure which surprised many commentators (DE 1989*a*: paras. 2.7 and 2.28). Scepticism about the gravity of alleged restrictive practices was encouraged the following April, when a Monopolies and Mergers Commission report on alleged practices in television and film-making—specifically commissioned by the DE in 1988—exonerated the unions concerned.[2]

However, the most pertinent feature of this period for present concerns was the fact that the occasion of a new Green Paper was used as the opportunity to review the operation of existing laws in other areas, to see once again if any major new 'loopholes' had emerged. Thus, a chapter on industrial action proposed at last the removal of the 'gateways' to lawful secondary action contained in section 17 of the 1980 Act, so as to render all

---

[1] See esp. EA 1989 ss. 9, 10, 13–16, and sch. 3.
[2] See MMC (1989).

forms of secondary action unprotected (DE 1989*a*: paras. 3.1–3.12).[3] Although, as we saw in chapters two and three, the gateways were the subject of widespread hostility on the right from the moment when they were introduced, their rapid emasculation by the courts had rendered them of little practical threat to employers in practice, whatever the theoretical objections.[4] Thus it was that the need formally to remove the gateways may not for many years have struck the Government as very pressing. In fact, their repeal was only advanced at this particular point because of a specific dispute which suggested to the Government that they might yet have some unwelcome significance. As the Green Paper confessed, the catalyst was the concern raised in the Ford Dundee dispute in 1988 that single-union greenfield sites might be lawfully and effectively blacked by excluded unions, organizing at suppliers, easing through the 'first supplier' gateway of section 17(3) (DE 1989*a*: para. 3.10).[5]

This new proposal to narrow the restrictive framework was complemented by one to extend the regulatory framework, by expanding the role of the new Commissioner, in order to enable her to assist directly not only in statutory actions, but also in the very type of common-law action—based directly on the provisions of the union rule-book—which had occurred in the miners' strike (DE 1989*a*: paras. 4.11–4.18).[6] Again, there was a specific impulse for the proposal, in this case the indications from the Commissioner that she had had exceedingly little to do in her first few months of office, but might have had somewhat more to take on if the handful of members with grievances concerning rule-book matters had not had to be turned away.[7] Government disappointment at the virtually non-existent impact of the appearance of the Commissioner was also indicated by the proposal that her involvement might in future be publicly signalled in the title of proceedings to which she gave her support (DE 1989*a*: paras. 4.7–4.10). Finally, the March 1989 Green Paper proposed that both restrictive and regulatory frameworks might be expanded to cover workers engaged under contracts for services (paras. 3.13–3.22), suggesting perhaps a concern at the increasing inadequacy of a framework built around the tort of inducing breach of *employment* contract, in a period during which other forms of engagement had become increasingly significant in the labour market. The limitation may have appeared to be an

---

[3] The picketing gateway was to remain.

[4] See in particular the decisions of the HL in *Merkur Island Shipping Corp.* v. *Laughton* [1983] 2 AC 570 and *Dimbleby & Sons Ltd.* v. *NUJ* [1984] IRLR 161. Thus, the IPM in its response to this paper saw no real need for the proposal. See *IRS Employment Trends* 443, 11 July 1989 p. 5. The CBI thought it would 'serve to underline what is predominantly the case in practice', while a minority of its members thought that 'it would be counterproductive to legislate further.' See CBI (1989*a*: para. 6).

[5] It is noteworthy that it was an inter-union dispute over a 'new realist' single union deal which spurred the Government to act. Mr Howard relied on the example of this episode when introducing the subsequent clause of the 1990 Bill. See OR HC vol. 166 col. 46 (29 Jan. 1990).

[6] The extension would apply to actions based on rules concerning specific listed topics.

[7] See the analysis of the Commissioner's first annual report in 386 *IRLIB* 10 Oct. 1989 p. 16.

arbitrary one on the pursuit of the policies behind the secondary action and balloting provisions.[8]

The March 1989 Green Paper therefore signified the Government's continuing commitment to both tracks of its now dual-track policy on industrial conflict—restriction and regulation—and to the belief that where apparent deficiencies in the system emerged, these could be best tackled by tightening up or extending the relevant legal provisions. This abiding faith in the basic ability of the legal framework to provide solutions to each new problem as it emerged, was put to its most dramatic test in recent years by the events which followed in the summer of 1989: the so-called 'summer of discontent'. As the tenth anniversary of the Thatcher era was passed, and supporters reasserted the solving of the 'strike problem' as among the greatest achievements of the decade, worker resistance resurged in a range of disputes—in public transport, the docks, at the BBC, in local government, and elsewhere.

The detailed implications of the litigation arising out of these disputes has been usefully analysed elsewhere.[9] For the purposes of this book, however, four broad related features of these disputes deserve notice. First, the resurgence of industrial militancy at this point tended to support the views of those who had long argued that political and economic conditions were likely to be a greater determinant of the willingness of union members to engage in industrial action than was the existence or absence of legal restraints. At the risk of over-simplification, it is surely to factors such as the rate of inflation, and patterns of unemployment and demand for labour, rather than to the legal position, that one must look in seeking to explain the renewal of industrial conflict at this time. Secondly, the action predominantly affected public services and employment, causing the Government considerable political difficulties.

Thirdly, the grave legal difficulties experienced even by unions committed to pursuing primary action, in conventional trade disputes, only with the support of the required ballot, generated a wider than ever sense in public and popular opinion that the Government's trade-union laws had surely gone too far. The most graphic illustration of this was the TGWU's legal battle for its right to conduct the docks dispute, which was only won in the House of Lords after the original ballot's four-week 'mandate' had expired, industrial action only then proceeding with the support of a reballot after the passage of the Dock Work Act 1989 had been completed. In addition, the Court of Appeal had along the way added two new nuances to the law and procedure which have the potential if not checked to ensure an injunction against almost any type of dispute in the future (Simpson 1989: pp. 237–41).[10]

[8] Cf. *Shipping Company Uniform Inc.* v. *ITF* [1985] ICR 245, where threatened blacking action by self-employed pilots was held not to amount to secondary action.

[9] See Simpson (1989).

[10] As Simpson explains, the HL did not address these aspects of the CA judgments, which, whatever their theoretical weight as precedent, have already been seized on by employers in

Finally, the combination of the renewed industrial militancy together with the effective use of the legal process to delay or frustrate official union support, resulted in significant unofficial action in the disputes concerned. Workers employed on the London Underground engaged in widespread and effective unofficial action while their unions underwent the complex and lengthy processes of balloting and fighting off litigation in order to establish a lawful official dispute; dock workers in many parts of the country similarly lost patience with their leaders' requests that they wait for the legal process to be completed. In these conditions, the warnings issued in 1982 and 1984 that restriction and regulation of official action was likely to boost *unofficial* action were thus vindicated, and the Government's crude monotype of militant leaders dragooning unwilling members out on strike looked more implausible than ever.

## (2) THE OCTOBER 1989 GREEN PAPER

In terms of the implications of all of this for its labour law policy, the Government apparently remained unshaken in its conviction that, at least as an element of its weaponry for fighting the disputes themselves, a legislative response was as much on the agenda as ever. Throughout the period of these disputes, repeated threats were made that new laws might be introduced on unofficial action and on strikes in essential services (British Rail here being characterized as providing an essential service), with, as in previous episodes which we have considered, the precise nature of the threat varying from occasion to occasion, and from Government speaker to speaker.[11]

In the case of possible restrictions on essential services, the pattern in 1989 was much the same as had been seen on previous occasions in the 1980s, the notable example being the occasion of the 1983 water dispute, discussed in chapter six. However valuable as a political weapon the threat may have been thought to be at the time of the dispute itself, closer investigation of the possibilities for legislation soon led to the conclusion that the many practical and political problems ruled the matter off the agenda. As in 1983, so in 1989.[12] However, the constraints evidently did not appear to the Government to be similarly decisive with regard to unofficial action, and a Green Paper

---

subsequent challenges. For an illustration of the wider reaction to the CA decision, see *Justinian* in the *Financial Times* (19 June 1989). Lord Campbell's 1990 Bill (HL Bill 15) would permit the court to extend the four-week period. The Employment Bill 1990 sch. 2 para. 2(2) preserves in this respect the position under the 1984 Act.

[11] See e.g. the short debate in the HL on 28 June 1989: OR HL vol. 509 cols. 731–4; *Financial Times* (3 July); *Guardian* (4 July); *Guardian* (12 Sept.); *Sunday Correspondent* (24 Sept.); and *Financial Times* (25 Sept. 1989).

[12] On the eventual abandonment of the proposal after a fresh review, see *Independent* (1 September 1989). The Government thereby reverted to its own more usually expressed position that it had 'no present intention of legislating on [essential services] because in practice it is extremely difficult to formulate proposals that would be effective and enforceable': OR HC vol. 111 cols. 157–8 (24 Feb. 1987) Mr Clarke.

*Unofficial Action and the Law* was published in October (DE 1989*b*). So strong were the threats and commitments given during the course of the previous summer, that it is arguable that the decision to go ahead with proposing restrictions on unofficial action was as much as anything the political legacy of the decision *not* to propose anything on the question of essential services. The Government having thus committed itself to the proposal, the Green Paper opened with a brief attempt to justify the decision, by depicting unofficial action as a serious industrial relations problem, meriting a legal solution, and one incidentally not entirely divorced from the 'essential services' problem (ch. 1, esp. para. 1.9). Here, the document was noticeably thin and unconvincing, particularly in the appeal by the Thatcher Government for the first time in ten years to the authority—of all things—of the Donovan Commission (para. 1.4).[13] This deeply implausible stance suggested some considerable anxiety on the part of the Government to be seen to be concerned with tackling a general and longstanding phenomenon of British industrial relations, rather than with the direct by-product of its own legislation and economic policies.[14]

Indeed, what emerges most strongly from an overall reading of chapter one of this Green Paper, is a sense of Government frustration at the new discovery that *unofficial action prior to the holding and outcome of a ballot* can undermine much of what the balloting requirement was intended to achieve. As we saw in chapters four and five, much of the original appeal of the balloting idea to the Government, and indeed to others such as the CBI, lay in the belief that the balloting requirement would 'defuse' much of the threat of industrial action, promoting greater observance of procedures for dispute resolution, and the general demotion of industrial action to the role of 'weapon of last resort'. The October Green Paper's linking of the unofficial action and essential service issues, its concern at the particularly disruptive potential of lightning strikes, and its broad equation of unofficial action with *unconstitutional* action, all denote an alarm at the possibility that unofficial action might sidestep altogether the safeguards which the balloting requirement was supposed to provide.[15]

---

[13] Needless to say, there was no reference made to Donovan's fundamental rejection of legal solutions.

[14] The lack of any deep longstanding concern on the part of the Government was demonstrated by its repeated and then characteristic statement only a few months earlier that there was no force in the warning that legal restrictions would encourage unofficial action, as this was 'not a significant problem at the moment': OR HL vol. 504 col. 844 (23 Feb. 1989) Lord Trefgarne. See too the text to ch. 7 n. 31 above.

[15] See DE (1989*b*: ch. 1 generally). Mr Howard's presentation of the provision which followed in the 1990 Bill focused on the 'anomaly' that unofficial action 'does not have to be put to the test of a secret ballot': OR HC vol. 166 col. 47 (29 Jan. 1990). Commentators on the right such as Hanson and Mather (1989: paras. 21–24) and the I.o.D. (1989) put forward more sophisticated analyses of the current unofficial-action phenomenon, neither of which saw legislation as an attractive approach. The EEF (1989: para. 2) commented that 'the proposed measures may well have a rather larger role to play . . . in certain public sector enterprises which have been particularly exposed to unofficial action.' A similar analysis was offered by Sir John Banham of the CBI: see *CBI News* (July 1989: p. 5).

What then was to be the legal solution to this phenomenon? Here, the Government faced difficulties of two kinds. First, the proposal raised once again, but in a more challenging form than ever before, the problems of effective enforcement. As we saw in earlier chapters, one of the most important lessons which all ministers of the Thatcher era understood from the period of the IRA, was the political importance of avoiding the 'martyrdom' of individual trade unionists who defied the law. The solution to that problem implemented by the Tebbit administration was to make available the union itself as an alternative and more attractive defendant to proceedings. In pursuing that strategy, Mr Tebbit, as we saw, had explicitly accepted that it would be beyond the scope of such an approach to tackle unofficial action, but had willingly made that concession, being little concerned with the phenomenon in any event. But in 1989 this was the very issue which the Government had chosen to address. Secondly, however, it is vital to note that the 'problem' now being addressed was of a critically different type from that previously faced when questions of enforcement had arisen. On previous occasions, the question had been how, and how far, was it possible to enforce a prohibition on action which was unlawful for some reason independent of its status as official or unofficial: for example, the issue of enforcement of a prohibition on secondary action in cases where the action was official, and in cases where it was unofficial. Now, however, the mere fact of being unofficial was to be the source of the prohibition itself, without the need for unlawfulness on any other ground. All unofficial action—whether primary, secondary, or of whatever other type—was itself to be the target. Or that is what the Green Paper appeared to be saying (DE 1989b: para. 1.15).

Were the Government's aims indeed as sweeping as that, the task would surely have been recognized as barely less achievable than the outlawing of all strikes in essential services. Furthermore, the most logical measure in theory would have been a removal of trade-disputes immunities from all action which did not have the official support of a union—but nothing could be calculated more quickly to lead to the imprisonment of individuals. In fact, as has been noted, the Government's main concern was not with unofficial action in all its forms, but more specifically, with unofficial action occurring in an essentially 'official' dispute, but prior to the outcome of a union ballot, or of a court challenge, being known. The Green Paper picked its way through that rather narrower, but hard enough, problem by a combination of developing the liability of the union, and exposing the individual participant in unofficial action to a sanction which could not itself lead to proceedings for contempt.

Government statements over the summer had suggested that the solution to the matter might be to follow the doctrines already being developed in the late 1980s by the courts, by co-opting the union into policing unofficial action, by requiring it to discipline or even expel unofficial organizers in order to avoid legal liability for their actions.[16] However, on further consideration the Government may have reflected that this might be of doubtful efficacy, being unlikely to lead to an immediate halt to unofficial action, and would be open to obvious criticism so soon after the enactment of section 3 of the 1988 Act in relation to the right to discipline for *non-participation* in industrial action. Instead, the Green Paper proposed a different approach.

So far as the role of the union itself was concerned, the Green Paper opted for an extension of the responsibility to *repudiate*, rather than the creation of a duty to discipline or expel, to apply to 'officials', whether paid or not, who support unofficial action. With this would be coupled an enhancement of the mechanics of repudiation, to require its written communication individually to all members who may be involved (DE 1989*b*: ch. 2). This proposal can be seen as addressed directly to the role of the union in the period prior to the outcome of a ballot or legal dispute. Consider the position of a union—such as the TGWU in the docks case—which supports the *claim* of its members, but will not support *industrial action* in pursuit of the claim until a ballot has been held and any litigation resolved. Under the law as it stood in 1989, provided no employed official authorized or endorsed industrial action in this interim period, officials up to General-Secretary could actively support the *claim*, and would have no need formally to repudiate unofficial action in support of it.[17] This apparently led to Government concerns that unofficial strikers could draw considerable comfort and encouragement from the stance being taken by their union, while the outcome of any ballot was not yet known, and the legal right of the union to support the action had not yet been determined. Given that the union would indeed fully support the claim in question and *ex hypothesi* be in the process of doing all it legally could to support the industrial action as well, it is perhaps impossible to envisage that this should not be so. Nevertheless, the Government appears to have taken the view that an effective extension of the duty to repudiate to this interim period might limit the official sustenance which unofficial action could draw. A preoccupation with tacit support by the union also appears from the Paper's discussion of the proposal for individual notification of repudiation, and the degree of the Government's obsession with this issue was also suggested by its choice, as an example to illustrate the problem, of a case in which the union was in fact punished for contempt (DE 1989*b*: paras. 1.13 and 2.7).[18]

[16] See *The Independent* (22 May and 10 June 1989). On common-law developments, see DE (1987: para. 2.9).

[17] Cf. the comment of Millett J in the docks case that '[Mr Todd] was not prepared to abandon the interests of his registered dock worker members, but he was not prepared to support them with official action unless such action was both lawful and industrially justified' [1989] IRLR, 291, 299 para. 61.

[18] *Express & Star Ltd.* v. *NGA (1982)* [1986] IRLR 222.

Whatever the possible contribution of attacks through the medium of the union's relationship to unofficial action, this is an area which by definition can only squarely be addressed by considering the position of those involved in the action itself. Here, instead of making such people subject to injunction by the court, or discipline or expulsion by the union, the Green Paper simply and dramatically proposed that employers should be free to dismiss them on an individual basis without fear of an industrial tribunal challenge (DE 1989*b*: para. 3.10). That approach was no doubt encouraged by events at Tilbury in the docks dispute, where dismissals were challenged in the industrial tribunal, it being alleged that shop stewards and activists involved in the unofficial action had been unlawfully selected for redundancy on the grounds of trade union membership or activities.[19] Significantly, too, the right to dismiss was apparently to be available as against not merely individual organizers, but in fact any participant in the action concerned, the Government perhaps fearing that any such distinction might be too difficult for the employer to draw when confronted with action of this type. Whilst thus providing an immediate 'self-help' alternative to legal proceedings against unofficial action, the Green Paper also offered the employer the belt and braces of a right to restrain any industrial action taken in support of those dismissed (DE 1989*b*: para. 3.11). Reliance on that provision would of course bring the matter back into the arena of enforcement of an injunction, but at least this was to be by way of a further step down the road of options open to employers, a powerful new weapon having been made available first along the way.

The Green Paper therefore went some way towards addressing the difficult questions of how the problems of enforcement raised by the new proposal might be overcome, but at the same time prompted a host of new questions and uncertainties. The Government was evidently itself troubled by the issue of effective enforcement, as was to become clear when the eventual Employment Bill was published just before Christmas of 1989. It is with a consideration of the provisions of this Bill that we may conclude the present chapter.

## (3) THE EMPLOYMENT BILL 1990

This was promised in the Queen's speech for the 1989/90 session and published on 21 December 1989.[20] How does the Bill compare with the Green Papers which preceded it? Notwithstanding some severe criticism of the proposals in the responses to those papers,[21] the Bill contains measures

---

[19] *Payne and ors.* v. *Port of London Authority* (continuing).

[20] 1989 Bill 15. The text comments on the Bill as first published.

[21] On e.g. the 'highly critical' response of the IPM to the unofficial action proposals, see *Financial Times* (1 Dec. 1989). See too the lukewarm and mixed response of CBI members in CBI (1989*b*).

covering each one of the proposals which had been put forward in those documents, namely in relation to industrial conflict, an extension of the role of the Commissioner to cover certain rule-based actions, as well as the option for her name to appear in the title of actions,[22] and new measures in relation to secondary and unofficial action. We can examine each of the latter two in turn.

## (a) Secondary Action

Clause 4 of the Bill sets out the proposed new restrictions on secondary action to replace those contained in section 17 of the 1980 Act, which is to be repealed.[23] In outline, this contains all the various elements promised in the March Green Paper. Section 17 is essentially rewritten with broadly the same structure, omitting the gateways for 'first customer or supplier' action and for action against 'substituted' associate employers, while retaining the gateway in relation to picketing.[24] The scope of the new clause is extended to cover those employed under contracts for services as well as employees.[25] Perhaps inevitably, the process of rewriting and tightening up of the law in this area has also given rise to certain other changes. First, as we saw in chapter three, section 17 permitted a legal cause of action against secondary action, only if it could be based around *commercial* contracts. This limitation was a by-product of the historical origins and aims of section 17, and of the mechanics of the first customer and supplier gateway.[26] It is now omitted from the simpler clause 4, thereby opening up the theoretically more straightforward alternative for the plaintiff secondary employer, of relying upon a cause of action built around employment contracts.[27] In theory that entails a marginal further tightening of policy, as, if it could in practice have been taken, secondary action which had no disruptive effects on any commercial contracts did not forfeit protection under section 17, even where the virtually inevitable disruption to secondary employment contracts occurred.[28]

As is well known, the main issue surrounding the operation of section 17 over the years had concerned the frequently absurd and harsh consequences in industrial relations terms, of categorizing industrial action as secondary and unlawful in legal terms, purely because two separate legal employers happened to be involved. The operation of the law was seen to be particularly

---

[22] 1989 Bill 15, cls. 8 and 9. These add nothing of significance to the Green Paper.

[23] 1898 Bill 15, sch. 3.

[24] Ibid. cl. 4(3). Protected picketing will continue to be confined under TULRA 1974 s. 15 as amended.

[25] 1989 Bill 15, cl. 4(6).

[26] EA 1980 s. 17(1)(a). See ch. 3, text to nn. 85 and 94 above.

[27] In practice this change is likely to make little difference. In *Union Traffic Ltd.* v. *TGWU* [1989] ICR 98, for example, the evidence for disruption affecting existing commercial contracts was scant indeed, but an injunction was nevertheless upheld.

[28] This was recognized and accepted by the Government at the time. See e.g. OR HC vol. 982 col. 1600 (17 Apr. 1980) Mr Mayhew.

harsh where 'separate' corporate employers were in fact all part of the same group.[29] Clause 4 does nothing to alleviate this problem. On the contrary, it specifically provides that a separate trade dispute must be established with each legal employer, and may not be inferred from the existence of a dispute with another employer.[30] Even the provision in section 17 permitting an inferred dispute where an employers' association bargains on behalf of an individual employer will now disappear. The latter change will prove particularly relevant where the survival of national bargaining through an employers' association is one of the very issues in the dispute. Once again, the example of the docks dispute, and of the jurisprudence developed by Millett J on the issue, may have inspired the tightening up of the law.[31]

The only consolation for workers to be found in clause 4 is an express provision to the effect that action which is primary in relation to one dispute, may not be relied upon as secondary in relation to another. This problem of dual or ambiguous status was raised by commentators when section 17 first appeared, and would undoubtedly have been exacerbated by the above-mentioned changes entailed by clause 4.[32] Without a provision along these lines, lawful primary action in any dispute involving more than one employer might have become simply impossible—and it would appear still to be the Government's professed policy in 1990, as in 1980, that the conduct of genuine primary action should not be impeded by restrictions aimed at secondary action.

### (b) Unofficial Action

Clauses 6 and 7 of the new Bill give effect to the proposals of the October 1989 Green Paper on unofficial action.[33] As promised, the law in relation to the positions both of the union and of the individual participant is to be changed. Clause 6 addresses the role of the union. It makes the key revision to section 15 of the 1982 Act by extending the deemed responsibility of unions down to the acts of officials whether employed or not, and by widening the definition of those 'committees' the behaviour of which may fix the union with legal liability. As the Department of Employment's own guide to the Bill makes clear, the effect will be that a union must repudiate or face liability for almost all unofficial action, even when it is itself in the course of organising a ballot.[34] The drafting of the clause reveals that considerable

[29] See ch. 3 text to nn. 98–9 and 103–4 above.

[30] 1989 Bill 15, cl. 4(4). On the problems of establishing a 'genuine' trade dispute with each employer see refs. at ch. 3, n. 95 above.

[31] See EA 1980 s. 17(7); [1989] IRLR 291, 300 paras. 72–7, 297–8, paras. 424. Developments in the EEF/CSEU 35-hr. week dispute in 1989 may also have provided encouragement here. The EEF indicated it might seek changes in the law once the dispute was over (EEF 1989: para. 6).

[32] 1989 Bill 15, cl. 4(5). See e.g. Lewis and Simpson (1981: pp. 203–4).

[33] Mr Fowler told journalists that the Bill would not halt all wildcat action: see *Independent* (22 Dec. 1989).

[34] See the notes to clause 6 accompanying the DE press release 21 Dec. 1989.

further thought has been given following publication of the Green Paper, to the problems of how to fix the union with liability for, and how to bring the influence of the union effectively to bear upon, what in industrial relations terms is not action by the union at all.

In theory, the most extreme approach would presumably be to fix the union with liability for any action in which one of its members had any role. But to go that far would be to abandon any attempt to suggest a rational basis upon which such action ought to be regarded as action of the union itself. Instead, clause 6 extends the reach of union responsibility under section 15 further 'downwards', by working from the premiss advanced in the October Green Paper, that:

Very often the fact that a union employee or officer (whether an employed official or not) is involved in organising industrial action will be seen by others as amounting to union 'endorsement' of the action—particularly in view of the fact that many union officials, including many non-employed officials such as shop stewards, are elected (DE 1989b: para. 2.9).

Thus, while the membership will not in future themselves in their actions personally bind the union, the shop-floor and other representatives whom they choose may under the new rules do so.[35] That consequence emerges from an analysis of a number of features of the drafting of clause 6 which together embody a far-reaching extension of union responsibility. The rewriting of section 15 is in three main areas, namely, the role of 'officials', the role of 'committees', and the control which the union enjoys over its own liability.

As for 'officials', these are in future to include non-employed as well as employed representatives, and the wide definition of 'official' contained in the 1974 Act will apparently apply directly.[36] This extends not only to an official of a branch or section, but even to any person elected or appointed in accordance with the rules of the union.[37] Where union rules are silent, almost any person chosen by more than one member is therefore capable of being covered. As for committees, these are again to include any group of persons constituted 'in accordance' with union rules[38]—again presuming in favour of liability where rules are silent or ambiguous, and the mere presence of an official on a strike committee will be enough to fix the union with liability for

---

[35] The penetration of the revised s. 15, by reaching down so far as potentially to cover 'officials' chosen informally by the members on the shop-floor, will come close in practical effect to the 'bottom-up' approach of *Heatons Transport (St. Helens) Ltd.* v. *TGWU* [1973] AC 15.

[36] The gloss on 'official' and definition of 'employed official' in s. 15(7) are to be repealed by clause 6(7) and sch. 3, but leaving intact EA 1982 s. 21's adoption for that Act, of the 1974 Act's definition of 'official'. As the official or committee member in question may at this level actually be the person calling the action, new s. 15(3) introduced by clause 6(3) will apply to acts 'done' as well as those authorized or endorsed by the relevant person or committee.

[37] TULRA 1974 s. 30.

[38] 1989 Bill 15, cl. 6(3) introducing new s. 15(3A)(a).

whatever any member of that committee does.[39] The drafting here has clearly been aimed to catch *ad hoc* strike committees and joint shop stewards, or activists' committees, which might typically involve representatives of several different unions. As for the position of the union itself, if the rules do not explicitly deny the status of such officials or committees altogether, the only avenue to divest itself of liability will be statutory repudiation.[40] Here, as foreshadowed in the Green Paper, the requirement is to be to notify every member involved, but also, in a clear bid to increase the chances of the repudiation in fact affecting the members' behaviour, there is now to be a new compulsory 'health warning' in the requirement that members be told that they may face dismissal with no right of a tribunal challenge in the event that they take industrial action.[41]

Further new provisions require that notice of repudiation be served on the employer, and on any potentially affected third party who so requests within six months.[42] Here, the Bill is apparently developing a notion which it was suggested underlay parts of the code of practice on industrial-action ballots, namely that such an obligation is likely to facilitate successful legal action to rectify any failure by the union fully to comply: an employer seeking an injunction against the union will in practice need to do little more than testify to the existence of unofficial action and of a failure to receive any notice of repudiation. Even at this stage, building on the approach developed in the 1988 Act, clause 6 then authorizes the court to supplement its injunction with an order that the union do whatever may be 'appropriate' to ensure that action does not continue,[43] and then goes on to apply the same stringent rules all over again to the union when judging its subsequent compliance.[44]

Taken together, these provisions amount to a massive imposition of legal responsibility upon trade unions, combined with a concerted attempt to maximize the chances that repudiation by the union of unofficial action is carried out in such a fashion as to have a real impact on the prospects of that action continuing. At the heart of that approach, as foreshadowed in the October 1989 Green Paper, is the direct threat to the position of the repudiated unofficial striker, set out in clause 7, of dismissal on an individual

---

[39] New s. 15(3A)(*b*). This is achieved by extending the concept of acts done, etc. by an official.

[40] New ss. 15(3B) will over-ride whatever the rules say concerning attribution of liability, but with a saving for repudiation under new ss. 15(4).

[41] Clause 6(5) introducing new ss. 15(5), (5A), and (5B).

[42] Ibid. and clause 6(6) introducing new ss. 15(6A). This tightening up of the rules on repudiation was advanced notwithstanding the 'severe reservations' about the practicability of even the Green Paper proposals, expressed by CBI members in CBI (1989*b*: paras. 4–5).

[43] Clause 6(8) introducing new ss. 15(9). Cf. EA 1988 ss. 1(2), 9(3), and 23. A requirement on the union to take disciplinary action might well enter the picture at this stage, although the scope of these provisions is not restricted to union members.

[44] Ibid. In *Express & Star Ltd.* v. *NGA (1982)* [1986] IRLR 222 it was held that s. 15 in its then form did not extend to liability for contempt, where common-law rules continued to apply. However, the *Heatons* case notwithstanding, it is doubtful that the common law would extend liability for contempt as deep as will the revised s. 15 after 1990.

basis, with no recourse to an industrial tribunal. Again, the concept is taken up to the very limits of theoretical credibility, applying in any case where any participant in the industrial action is a member of any trade union which has issued a repudiation.[45]

Fittingly enough, clauses 6 and 7, alongside the other provisions of the 1990 Bill, thus dramatically reflect and express the distilled accumulated experience, understanding, and conviction of the 1980s Governments in relation to industrial-conflict law: the lessons of the Industrial Relations Act period; the pragmatic and *ad hoc* nature and advantages of the step-by-step approach; development of regulation, particularly through the ever-extending mechanism of compulsory ballots, as a valued adjunct to restriction; but perhaps above all of these, the centrality, and sustained presence throughout the period, of the problems of effective enforcement and implementation, and of the interplay between the roles of union members, lay activists, and leadership, and the impact of sanctions upon each. The appearance of such draconian proposals by way of a response to the 'summer of discontent' of 1989 also suggests a deep-seated and continuing belief in Government circles in at the very least the political contribution which such legal measures have to make, if nothing else. Before coming to our final assessment of this legislation, however, we need to return to the backcloth against which it emerged, and to turn to the developing debates of the 1980s which marked the wider political and theoretical response to the breakdown of the voluntarist consensus.

[45] Clause 7(1) introducing new EP(C)A 1978 s. 62A(2). This may expose an individual to risk of dismissal dependent on the actions of a union of which s/he is not a member. Clause 7(2) also effects the promised removal of all s. 13 protection where action is taken in support of those sacked.

# [ 10 ]

# The Breakdown of the Voluntarist Consensus (II): The Challenge to Voluntarism

## (1) INTRODUCTION

In the opening chapters of this book, it was argued that the development of the legislation of the last decade needs to be understood against the backcloth of the gradual erosion and breakdown, over the preceding years, of the conditions which sustained a consensus around the voluntarist approach to industrial conflict. It was, however, also argued that there is nevertheless a tendency in much of the literature to regard that consensus as having persisted undiminished right through to 1979, a year which is said to mark a sudden and profound break, heralding in a new era. Chapter two discussed some of the features of the erosion of political consensus in the period prior to 1979, and suggested that, to the extent that academic work has tended to prefer the 'sharp break' analysis, this may in particular have been encouraged by the fact of almost unbroken continuity, and indeed strengthening, of the formal voluntarist statutory framework of industrial-conflict law, right through to the end of the 1970s. A discontinuity is of course accepted as having occurred during the two and a half years at the beginning of the 1970s when the Industrial Relations Act was in force, but the particularly dramatic fate of that legislation, and the no less comprehensive manner in which Parliament thereafter reasserted the traditional approach, have permitted commentators to characterize that period as an exceptional and aberrational episode, of limited lasting import.

Whatever may become of the legislation of the last decade under the auspices of future Governments, the same will surely not be able to be said of it. This is not merely because of the sheer longevity of the new laws and of the Governments which passed them, when compared with the IRA and the Heath administration. It is also because the decade has witnessed a considerable shift in the debate among those likely to contribute to the political programme and ideas of a successor administration, away from a simple reassertion of the voluntarist approach. Against this backcloth, the academic debate in the 1980s also detached itself from a consensus around the axioms of voluntarism, and returned to the melting pot. The process which

Kahn-Freund himself was among the first to engage with in response to the erosion of political consensus, has since his death in 1979 developed rapidly into a wide-ranging and trenchant debate about the continued tenability of the voluntarist approach, and about possible alternatives to it. In no field has the discussion been more searching and passionate than in that of industrial conflict.

Notwithstanding then that the legislation of the last ten years was developed both historically and structurally from an abstentionist starting-point, for all these reasons our analysis of it cannot adequately be developed solely within the context of the assumptions upon which voluntarism itself rested. Instead, by probing deeper the foundations of the voluntarist approach, and assessing some of the alternative policies most frequently and articulately canvassed in the contemporary literature, it is intended that a broader framework may be constructed, within which the new legislation may be appraised, and viewed in its broader relation to what went before.

It is important at the outset to be clear about the general purpose of such an exercise. In chapter two it was suggested that the changing preoccupations of Governments charged with managing the British capitalist economy in the post-war era, increasingly drew them away from the agenda and assumptions of the voluntarist consensus. In those circumstances, a range of alternative policies attracted increasingly serious attention from all major political parties. The aim in this chapter is then not to present a defence nor a critique of any particular approach towards industrial-conflict law as such, or for its own sake, but rather to develop an analysis of the major arguments and policies which seem likely to have some strong appeal to modern Governments, and thereby to enhance our understanding of the roots of the legislative changes of recent years.

Yet that being said, it might still be thought that, even within the context of a progressively more fragile and fragmented consensus, so long as the most basic human rights remained unquestioned in modern British society, the standing of the right to strike would not readily suffer under scrutiny. Whether or not any intrinsic value is attached to the experience of participation in industrial action itself, is not the foundation of the right to strike readily revealed by a consideration of the alternative to it, namely a legal proscription of industrial action? For such a prohibition would entail a legal compulsion to do work, 'and a legal compulsion to work is abhorrent to systems of law imbued with a liberal tradition, and compatible only with a totalitarian system of government' (Kahn-Freund and Hepple 1972: p. 7). Or to put it more succinctly, the right of the individual to withdraw labour 'is that which distinguishes the free man from the serf' (IOCCAUS 1958: p 17). Although indeed of compelling appeal across a wide political spectrum, this is 'no slavery' argument turns out not to settle the debate. In fact it settles disappointingly little, because the technical thrust of the no slavery argument can be met so long as the law does not allow an *individual* to be compelled to do work, a condition which might be fulfilled notwithstanding the presence of restrictions on the legality of organizing *collective* withdrawals of labour. Thus do we find that TULRA 1974, section 16, the statutory embodiment of the no slavery principle, has remained untouched since 1979.

So, approaching the matter from a governmental perspective, considerable political scope exists for taking a more pragmatic and utilitarian approach to the right to strike, and the perceived 'strike problem'.[1] In chapter two it was suggested that such an approach might take the form of asking with what *effects* are strikes associated? Are they good or bad? How do they weigh up against one another? Viewpoints will differ on the precise effects of industrial action, and on how heavily each one deserves to be weighted in the scales, but given the assumption that one is concerned with industrial conflict occurring in the context of a modern capitalist market economy, it may be possible relatively uncontentiously to suggest the nature of the basic *kinds* of effects involved. Chapter two went on to suggest that, approaching the matter in this way, the debate can be seen as revolving around four basic types of effect associated with industrial action, which were labelled 'social', 'frictional', 'structural', and 'political'. This fourfold distinction provides us with the basic tools with which to analyse more closely in this chapter the traditional voluntarist approach to the legal regulation of industrial conflict, and some of the alternative approaches which have been canvassed in the more recent debates. First, voluntarism, both as originally stated, and as re-argued in the 1980s, will be considered. This will lead to a discussion of the ideas for dealing with the allegedly more serious adverse effects of industrial conflict which have been put forward by those who, whilst sympathetic to the values underlying the voluntarist approach, consider it to be no longer tenable by itself. Finally we will come to the more radical approach of the so-called New Right, who seek no truck with voluntarist values, but build from a different set of principles altogether. But it is to voluntarism that we may turn first.

## (2) THE VOLUNTARIST APPROACH AND COLLECTIVE BARGAINING

In chapter two it was argued that the voluntarist approach to industrial-conflict law, as most fully articulated in the writings of Kahn-Freund, sprang in essence from the insight that '[t]he right of workmen to strike is an essential element in the principle of collective bargaining,'[2] the strike being the autonomous sanction available to labour in the bargaining process. Given this, any argument in favour of collective bargaining provides at least the starting-point for one in favour of the right to strike. Many virtues have been claimed for collective bargaining, but in the tradition with which we are presently concerned, the arguments in support of it can be regarded as falling

---

[1]  For wider discussion of the right to strike and its different justifications, see Kahn-Freund and Hepple (1972: p. 8); Hyman (1989*b*: esp. ch. 3); Macfarlane (1981).

[2]  Per Lord Wright *Crofter Hand Woven Harris Tweed* v. *Veitch* [1942] AC 435, 463

broadly into two groups. 'Matching power' arguments allege the ability of collective bargaining and collective action to redress the inequality of economic bargaining power which would otherwise exist as between employer and employee. 'Industrial democracy' arguments involve claims about the political significance of the very conduct of collective bargaining, ranging from the notion that it provides a means of worker participation in the enterprise and control of the working environment, to the claim that it is an essential political feature of a democratic pluralist society. With regard to the other types of effect of industrial conflict, it was suggested that the consensus underpinning the voluntarist settlement did not recognize any serious adverse political or structural implications of its approach. As for frictional effects, these were regarded as sufficiently limited to be an eminently worthwhile price to pay for the social benefits of collective bargaining.

In as much as the legality of industrial action was thus supported because of its link to the institution of collective bargaining, one might expect to find that the extent of protection accorded was determined by reference to the processes of that institution;[3] but the immunities created in 1906 were not tied to the practice of collective bargaining, nor even strictly to the activities of trade unions or trade unionists.[4] As was argued in chapter five, this historical fact may be better explained in terms of the absence rather than the presence of a theory of what amounted to legitimate industrial action, on the part of the 1906 Government itself, which was content to accept the more general case that '[f]or those whose thinking could get beyond the prevalent legal traditions, the issue hinged on whether or not the unions were to be allowed to survive, to grow and to develop their functions' (Fox 1985b: pp. 183–4).[5] But how was this legislation fitted into Kahn-Freund's subsequent rationalization and prescription? One can detect two contributing strands of thought.

First, although the need for an autonomous labour sanction derived specifically from the nature of collective bargaining, the general need for matching power was not so linked, deriving from the simple and universal economic fact of workers' subordination.[6] Secondly, the dynamic system of

[3] A notion reflected in one form or another in the laws of many foreign systems. See Kahn-Freund (1977: p. 240); Kahn-Freund and Hepple (1972: ch. 7).

[4] Cf. the analysis of Macfarlane (1981: pp. 174–7) of the right to strike as a class right, enjoyed only by workers; but for criticism, see Smart (1985).

[5] The list of topics which might form the subject of a trade dispute has in various contexts been used as a crude proxy for referring to industrial conflict, collective bargaining, or collective agreements, in provisions which have taken more or less notice of the actual scope of the formula itself at the time of their enactment. See TULRA 1974 s. 30; EPA 1975 s. 126 (and after 1982, s. 126A); Social Security Act 1975 s. 19(2)(b); Local Government Act 1988 ss. 17(5)(d) and (8); Employment Act 1989 s. 14. Yet it remains the case that under the voluntarist framework the golden formula did not form a well-defined or restrictive link to the process of collective bargaining.

[6] See Kahn-Freund and Hepple (1972: ch. 2) who distinguish the 'equilibrium' from the 'autonomy' argument, only the latter being explicitly associated with collective bargaining.

British bargaining—the nature of our collective agreements and of their pattern of negotiation—made it unreceptive to the sort of distinctions typically made by legal systems which tied the right to strike to the collective bargaining process.[7] So the British right to strike, secured by the protections contained in the 1906 Act, was on this view an economic right, perhaps most advantageously exercised through the processes of collective bargaining, but neither needing to be, nor particularly capable of being, tied to that process.[8] Thus it was distinct from the right to associate in trade unions or participate in their activity (Kahn-Freund 1977: p. 228),[9] but yet not so lofty as to be regarded as an inviolable and absolute human right (Kahn-Freund 1977: p. 239). Kahn-Freund and Hepple suggested that the human or political right view of the right to strike tends rather to be associated with legal systems which enshrine that right in explicit or positive language (Kahn-Freund and Hepple 1972: pp. 5–6). But this need not necessarily be so. As Lord Wedderburn has pointed out, adoption of the language of positive rights in our law would not of itself resolve the debate surrounding the appropriate content and coverage of such rights.[10] Furthermore, even protection at the level of a written constitution is most unlikely to be without limit.[11] Indeed, buying into the language of fundamental or constitutional rights may invite the hazards of arguments that laws merely of the style of 1906 are unconstitutional, either in a general way,[12] or because they conflict with other rights typically protected at a constitutional level,[13] conceivably in some circumstances even freedom of association.[14] All in all, there may be a lot to be said for the British approach having put little faith in the idea of a positive or constitutional right to strike, however broad it may be thought that it should be.

Indeed, as was noted in earlier chapters, the language of positive rights may be more attractive to those who wish to enact some *restrictions* on industrial action in as clear as possible a form, than to those who favour none at all.[15] Certainly, writers like Lord Wedderburn see little merit in a

---

[7] Particularly that between conflicts of right and of interest: see Kahn-Freund (1954*b*: pp. 52–9); Wedderburn (1969).

[8] It would seem to follow that were the collective bargaining system to be so reformed and expanded as to cope with the full range of workers' grievances, industrial action which persisted outside the system would on this view become unworthy of protection: the extent of the rights guaranteed by the equilibrium and the autonomy arguments would have become coterminous. Donovan (1968) appeared to reason this way in its treatment of the legal enforceability of collective agreements: see paras. 212 and 500–18.

[9] Cf. *Drew* v. *St. Edmundsbury BC* [1980] ICR 513

[10] See esp. Wedderburn (1985*b*: pp. 509 ff.).

[11] Cf. n. 17 below.

[12] See the discussion of the New Right later in this chapter.

[13] For a warning, see Forde (1984).

[14] As in the Irish case of *Educational Co. of Ireland* v. *Fitzpatrick* [1961] IR 323.

[15] Cf. Davies and Freedland (1984*a*: pp. 785–9) and Ewing (1986) on the possibilities for more 'judge-proof' approaches than that adopted in 1906; and for further cautions, see Wedderburn (1987).

positive or constitutional right, while still according the right to strike the highest moral status, which cannot be assailed even by majoritarian decree (1982*b*: p. 8). At any rate, Kahn-Freund preferred simply to place emphasis on the fact of economic imbalance between employer and employee, and on the notion that a democratic pluralist society ought not to enact *general* restrictions on strikes, although these might well be necessary in particular cases (Kahn-Freund 1977: pp. 226 and 233; Davies and Freedland 1984*a*: p. 697). On this view, it is the *general* legal position of strikers which is seen as indicative of the state of preservation of other democratic pluralist and liberal values in a society.[16]

This picture of the combination of broad industrial democracy arguments of this type, with a matching power argument rather more loosely coupled to the institution of collective bargaining than might at first be imagined, throws further light on how the voluntarist rationalization of the framework of the 1906 Act could be sustained. In particular, the linking of the broad framework, through matching power, to collective bargaining, and hence to the wider demands of industrial democracy, immeasurably increased the stakes in favour of social effects. The association of the industrial democracy argument with what were regarded as fundamental values and characteristics of a society as a whole, meant that the possible harms associated with industrial conflict would have to be of a similar order to outweigh these benefits. Or, to put it the other way around, this view entailed that the right to strike could be restricted in order to meet competing concerns, *only* so far as the maintenance of a democratic society would allow.[17] The crucial question would then become how far restrictions might go before this 'democratic condition' was no longer fulfilled; voluntarism as originally propounded never really had to face that difficult problem, because the balance of effects seemed so clearly to tip in favour of abstentionism in any case.

By the 1980s, however, the sharpening of the debate over frictional, structural, and even political effects had brought this issue to the very centre of the debate. Faced with this new and more challenging scenario, writers who have traditionally supported the voluntarist analysis have responded in a variety of ways Kahn-Freund, as has been suggested, did not flinch from recognizing the full implications of the problem, but could venture no more than that 'the law can make no contribution' (1979: p. 79) to the adjustments which he identified as necessary. Others have argued passionately that Kahn-Freund's very way of depicting the problem put into question the exercise of *any* right to strike (Lewis 1983: p. 121), or 'opens the way to the State control of trade unions that he still resisted' (Wedderburn 1986*b*: p. 847). If the

---

[16] Cf. Macfarlane (1981: pp. 192–6).

[17] These elements are characteristically present in international standard-setting instruments which refer to the right to strike. See e.g. *European Social Charter* (1961) Articles 6 and 31.

democratic condition were to be preserved, then the 'moral right' of workers to strike, whatever the circumstances, had to be upheld.[18]

A second group have attempted to construct a less purely principled defence, by simply pointing to the series of pragmatic arguments, well rehearsed at least since Donovan, and aimed at deterring would-be reformers, regardless of their political persuasion. First, legal restrictions on industrial action would provoke such a hostile reaction as to be unworkable— in Chafee's terms this is the 'hot potato' argument. However, an alternative solution might lie in changes to the way in which unions behaved and to the system of collective bargaining itself; but here too the law had no role to play, for legal mechanisms which attempted to mould the collective bargaining system would get bogged down in its dismal swamp, and frustrate its development and improvement as a living tree. These writers have then concentrated upon considering the types of non-legal change which may be required today—twenty years on from Donovan—and on the modes of persuasion and non-legal sanction which might help to secure such changes. In fact the proposals are many and various, and cannot be explored individually or in any detail here; but certain threads which run through many of them may be picked out.[19]

First, it is argued that the frictional problem of widespread public-sector action can only be resolved by some attempt to address the genuine claims and grievances of the workers involved, by establishing some mode of assessing pay and processing disputes.[20] Secondly, it is argued that the wider structural problem of incomes and inflation must be tackled by 'educating', involving, and informing workers in a process which enhances their understanding of the effects which the settlements in individual disputes may cumulatively have on the economy as a whole, and increases their involvement, both through local industrial democracy and, centrally, in the processes by which key decisions are taken.[21] Finally, it is suggested that the Government must always retain complete control and flexibility with regard to its legislative and economic programme, as perhaps it did not during the period of the social contract. This, it is said, would meet the political objection (whether from left or right) to the prospect of another social contract. It would also leave the Government in possession of the necessary sanctions and levers to deploy against the unions, if need be, in the shape not

---

[18] See Wedderburn (1982b: p. 8), (1985a: p. 55), (1984: p. 85).

[19] The two writers on whom this section draws who seem to have articulated the fullest approaches are Crouch, esp. (1983) and (1985), and McCarthy, esp. (1981), (1985), (1986), and (1987).

[20] See e.g. McCarthy (1985: p. 45); cf. SDP (1986: ch. 4). This debate was at the nub of the ambulance workers' dispute of 1989–90, with many regarding not the pay *claim*, but the creation of a pay *formula* which would among other things obviate the need for industrial action in future years, as the key demand.

[21] On these themes, see esp. Crouch (1982b: p. 217), (1983: pp. 133–6), (1985), and many others such as Wellington (1968: p. 326), England and Weekes (1985: p. 430).

of legal restrictions on industrial action, but of controls over union involvement in its counsels and over social, economic, and legislative plans, such
as public spending programmes and employment protection laws which
the unions seek (Crouch 1983: pp. 135–6; McCarthy 1981: pp. 111–16, 1986:
pp. 14–17).

These, in briefest outline, are some of the ways by which it has been
suggested that the frictional, structural, and political aspects of the strike
problem might be tackled without direct resort to legal restrictions. The
essence of the case which they make against restrictions on industrial action,
is that they are unneccessary (to the success of reforms based on non-legal
sanctions) and, in any case, not possible (because of the pragmatic
arguments). However, in the 1980s this last limb of the argument appears
severely to have been weakened. Although the argument that *any* restrictions
on industrial action would prove unworkable was no doubt fortified by the
experience of 1971–4,[22] and forcefully restated, as has been seen, by one camp
in the responses to the 1981 Green Paper, the account of subsequent events
which was offered in earlier chapters suggests that in today's conditions a
Government may show considerable sensitivity to such arguments, without
ruling out progressive restrictions on industrial action: indeed it may be
guided by them in shaping those restrictions. This means that, although the
arguments cautioning against legal attempts to mould the collective
bargaining system itself no doubt still retain their force, the pragmatist case
as a whole now faces the danger of falling at the earlier hurdle relating to
industrial action. Even where proposals for reform of the system are accepted
and pursued, therefore, restrictions on strikes may well be envisaged alongside, whether at the outset, or in the event that proposed non-legal measures
fail.[23] The main burden of argument against such supplementary restrictions
will then continue to rest with the democratic condition.

In summary, the core of the voluntarist tradition can be seen in terms of a
strong preference for the absence of legal restrictions on strikes, motivated by
support for the matching power argument and the democratic condition; but
given the existence of frictional, structural, and political stresses not
anticipated thirty years ago, the debate has moved on to the question of how
far restrictions on industrial action which are narrower than the settlement of
1906 might remain compatible with these goals. For those who do not
maintain that anything less than unrestricted legality short of violence spells
the demise of these values, consideration of restrictions aimed at alleviating
one or more of the dimensions of the perceived strike problem becomes a
logical step. Such an approach does not therefore necessarily entail a
wholesale rejection of voluntarism, for it might accept the voluntarist's

[22] Cf. Prondzynski (1985: p. 177).
[23] Cf. even Donovan's concession on legal enforcement of collective agreements noted at n. 8
above.

arguments as giving rise to a general presumption in favour of non-intervention, but one rebuttable in certain instances. The criterion by reference to which action is singled out for legal regulation might look to either frictional, structural, or political effects, or to some combination of these. As has been noted, traditional labour law gave little express attention to the latter two, so critiques which focus chiefly on the first of these might seem the closest to 'home' to which to turn next.

## (3) ATTACKING FRICTIONAL EFFECTS

Given that all strikes cause *some* frictional damage, and that how this is felt varies greatly according to one's relation to the dispute, it is not surprising that almost every piece of industrial action creates concern in some quarters about its frictional effects, nor that proposals for tackling these effects differ widely according to the perspective adopted by their source. Nevertheless, the voluntarist perspective looked at the picture as a whole, and concluded that overall levels of disruption were and could be kept sufficiently low to remain tolerable. As has been seen, however, in recent times increasing attention has been focused on the particularly severe disruption which can be caused in *individual* disputes, especially in the public services. Of course there has for many years been *some* legislation aimed at this sort of problem on the statute-book, but the doctrine of collective *laissez-faire* was apparently never intended to challenge the continuance of restrictions on industrial action by groups such as the police and armed forces, nor of executive powers for coping with national emergencies.[24]

Acceptance of such provisions has always involved a concession by voluntarists, but one never regarded as very serious, for perhaps several reasons. As has been seen, the need for some *limited* restrictions on industrial action was never ruled out by their position, and these provisions obviously addressed dramatic crises which could be hoped rarely to materialize. Further, the frictional harms contemplated were of the gravest kind: in effect the provisions envisaged situations where the distinction between economic and physical harm was itself in any case liable to break down, and voluntarists never sought to accord protection to anything involving the latter. Also, whatever its practical difficulties, the emergency powers legislation at least expressed a preference for the strategy of substitution for striking workers, which, while no doubt undermining the effectiveness of industrial action, did not entail a direct ban upon it. Kahn-Freund thought it could 'hardly be called an excessive interference with industrial relations' (1954a: p. 25).

Factors such as these may all help explain Donovan's (with one dissenter) neutral stance towards sections 4 and 5 of CPPA 1875 which, while

---

[24]  For the full details see Morris (1986: chs. 2 and 3); see too Ewing (1988c) on the debates in the wake of the general strike.

criminalizing some action according to its frictional effects, were limited to specific services, or to the gravest effects, and could be complied with by the giving of contractual notice, whereafter industrial action would be lawful (Donovan 1968: paras. 823–47). What is rather at issue in the modern debate is the need for a measure which more generally restricts peaceful industrial action by reference to its potential to cause serious frictional harms, according to some less stringent test. There is of course already some precedent for this too in the shape of the 'emergency procedures' in the IRA 1971 which turned on whether in the Secretary of State's view, certain harms were threatened if the dispute went ahead, harms which were rather more varied and less specific in their definition than anything previously seen.[25] However, as was noted earlier, in particular in chapter six, the modern debate has not looked to the discredited IRA style approach. Instead, restriction of frictional effects in public services by more general and less direct means has been suggested. Writers like Lords Wedderburn and McCarthy are prepared to accept the idea of no-strike agreements in essential services, provided that these are not imposed or legally binding (Wedderburn 1981: pp. 735–7; McCarthy 1985: p. 44, 1987: pp. 29–30); but others have argued that, if the basic cases for reducing levels of conflict and for maintaining levels of pay in the public services are accepted, then use of legal sanctions generally in relation to these services becomes a possible element in a strategy designed to ensure successful attainment of those goals. The SDP's 1986 proposals suggested how such an approach might work; the basic structure of immunities would remain, but enjoyment of the protections would depend upon certain conditions first having been met. Such an approach is highly flexible and can be used in conjunction with no-strike agreements, pay guarantee systems, independent arbitration, enhanced procedure agreements, or any combination of these.[26] The conclusions of some, that wider legal restrictions than presently exist must be ruled out altogether, and that no-strike agreements are unlikely to get off the ground,[27] might be open to reconsideration were a Government genuinely willing to hold out so many carrots.[28]

Preservation of essential services is the obvious priority target for those concerned about the level of frictional harms. The other leading target has been secondary action. That this criterion should so persistently and consistently have been alighted upon by those who are concerned about frictional harms requires some explanation, particularly in view of the fact

[25] IRA 1971 Part VIII.

[26] The SDP's proposals canvass most of these possibilities. See SDP (1982: pp. 37–45); SDP (1986: pp. 6–11). Their documents also open with characteristic affirmations of the basic voluntarist values.

[27] See Morris (1986: ch. 7).

[28] Cf. the SDP's acknowledgement that effective public-sector pay comparability arrangements would involve Governments accepting the obligations and restraints which they entail: SDP (1986: p. 7).

that, as will be argued in a moment, it is beset with its own difficulties. The general source of this concern may be the notion that, whatever specific controls there may be on the gravest harms threatened by public-service disputes, a legal regime which embodies no *general* controls on the extent of the frictional harms caused by industrial action, must be unsatisfactory.[29] That view can be set in the light of an aspect of the matching power argument to which attention has already been drawn. If it is correct that the strength of that argument varies on a case by case basis, then it might be argued that there will not only be cases where the union is too weak to benefit from matching power, but also those where it is too strong to need to draw on its power to its full extent. In such a case, matching power becomes an argument which actually dictates a *restriction* upon the union's ability to impose frictional harms.[30] Without such a restriction, it is argued, a powerful union may be able to escalate the effects of industrial action almost without limit, however 'excessive' its demands. As the Prior administration put it in 1980, an unrestricted immunity may be both 'unnecessarily and dangerously wide'.[31]

This view therefore couples a deeper anxiety about frictional effects with its own conception of the legitimate *social* goals of labour. It recognizes that labour does need to be able to use some autonomous sanction to match the power of capital,[32] but it firmly rejects the traditional voluntarist view as to the point at which that balance should be struck. There is no particular way to resolve disagreements which stem from a difference of underlying values, and voluntarists have also been attacked for too readily assuming that collective bargaining, even when unrestrained, achieves a balance favourable or acceptable to workers,[33] but given the view that the point of balance *is* to be found somewhere in the middle ground between no restrictions and a total ban on industrial action, the task then becomes to find a legal test capable of striking the appropriate balance. Given the impossibility of measuring the actual amount of economic harm caused by each dispute, and setting a limit upon this, the test of secondary action may be the most readily applicable proxy in the middle ground. It is a well-recognized strategy by which a union can spread the amount of frictional harm caused by its action, and superficially appears to correspond to the commercial distinction between different employers and, so it seemed in the 1970s, to the legal distinction between commercial and employment contracts, which had been seized upon as a historic symbol of an acceptable compromise.

---

[29] Correspondence in *The Times* (12 Feb. 1980), shortly before the secondary action working paper appeared, conveys the wide symbolic importance attached to the issue.

[30] For this view, see esp. Phelps Brown (1986: p. 52).

[31] Working Paper on Secondary Action, *The Times* (20 Feb. 1980: para. 7).

[32] Cf. the introduction to the 1981 Green Paper, which makes such an acknowledgement: DE (1981*a*: ch. 1).

[33] This debate is represented in the exchange between Clegg (1975) and Hyman (1978).

Yet, even if it can be implemented and applied in law (a task which the earlier account suggests may be trickier than might at first appear), it was suggested in chapter three that this kind of test is unlikely to achieve a consistent or coherent balance between the union's need to exert a matching power on the employer, and the Government's desire to achieve reasonable containment of frictional harms, at whatever level it is thought appropriate to pitch each of these requirements. On the one side, such a restriction is unlikely to restrain union power where it is thought to be most superfluous; indeed, it may tend to do just the opposite, for the general pattern seems to be that, whether the dispute be big or small, the need to call for secondary action is essentially a sign of union weakness, not strength.[34] On the other side, the extent of frictional harms caused by a dispute will not correlate in any systematic way with the use of secondary action for frictional harm is generally suffered by the customers and suppliers of the primary employer in any event. A primary dispute in a major industry may have a far more substantial impact on the community than many much smaller disputes in which secondary action is employed[35]—action which aims simply to duplicate the harm which the secondary employer would in any case have suffered as a side-effect, had primary action in fact been more effective.[36]

Other, more specialized, proposals for tackling frictional harms have been put forward, which do not depend upon the enactment of general legal restrictions. In particular, a number of suggestions have been made for redistributing the economic cost of frictional harms. The broadest scheme envisages redistribution of the costs across the whole community by means of a national strike compensation fund.[37] Such a proposal might be supported by the argument that if strikes are a necessary element of an institution, the maintenance of which is generally in the public interest, then it is only just that the public as a whole should bear that social cost.[38] Rather more narrowly based is the redistribution among employers achieved by mutual strike insurance along the lines proposed by the CBI in the early 1980s.[39] Narrowest of all, perhaps, is the right of lay-off of the type canvassed by the EEF which, in conjunction with the use of *force-majeure* clauses in business

[34] Cf. McCarthy (1985: p. 25); Kahn *et al.* (1983: ch. 4).

[35] Cf. the EEF's perspective on the essential services problem, discussed in chs. 5 and 6 above.

[36] For both types of criticism, see Kahn-Freund and Hepple (1972: pp. 31–4), and cf. also the discussion in ch. 3 above of the difficulties experienced in determining what the appropriate commercial relation between the primary and secondary employers should be. The Labour Party's policy-review proposals in Labour Party (1989: p. 25) perfectly illustrate the attraction of the notion that there must be some general limits on frictional harms, the difficulties of giving that notion any coherent or logical expression, and the consequently obscure and unsatisfactory principle generated by the tension between the two.

[37] See Forde (1984: pp. 46–9).

[38] Cf. England's (1976: p. 587) parallel argument that individual workers should not therefore be penalized for taking part in strikes.

[39] See the discussion in ch. 4 above.

contracts, redistributes the loss to a firm's customers, suppliers, and employees.[40]

These proposals illustrate the diversity of possible theoretical solutions to the problem of frictional harms, and the way in which the most ideal solution can take a very different form according to the perspective from which the problem is viewed. Clearly, from any one particular point of view, any scheme of 'self-help' which does not need legal proceedings to be effected, and shuffles off the economic costs of industrial action on to other parties, is bound to look attractive. However, the factional nature of such solutions is probably the chief reason why they have had difficulty in commanding very widespread support. In addition, they implicitly assume the perception of an underlying community of interest between those among whom the burdens are to be redistributed, which seems to run counter to the competitive spirit of decentralized and diversified capitalist market economy.[41]

Further, by defusing the impact of industrial action on the employer, such solutions tend to undermine the strength of the union's autonomous sanction, without offering any substitute.[42] A yet more imaginative approach to frictional harms, which does attempt to pay due heed to the union's need for an effective sanction, is discussed by Wellington.[43] In a 'non-stoppage strike' the Government intervenes to prevent a dispute which might cause undue harm to customers and suppliers, but both employers and workers suffer financial penalties—payable to central funds—until the dispute is settled. These penalties aim to duplicate the balance of economic pressure exerted on the respective parties in the course of an actual strike, whilst not being so severe as to discourage the continuance of work and production altogether. There are many obvious problems with, and objections to, such a scheme, as Wellington himself discusses,[44] and it is hard to imagine a Government seriously contemplating introducing it on a general basis; but a more informal practice which bears some similarities to it has been described by Morris. Her research into the conduct of disputes in the NHS revealed the 'joint regulation' approach, whereby, for example, unions agree to maintain levels of emergency cover, in exchange for management restricting admissions of less serious cases.[45] Such deals allow the union to demonstrate the reality and effectiveness of its industrial muscle in pursuit of its claims, whilst achieving the shared goal of avoiding the most serious disruptions to the service. Morris concludes that, in the present climate at least, joint regulation

[40] See the discussion in ch. 5 above.

[41] An important factor may be the lack of strong solidaristic structure within British employers' organizations. On this see Clegg (1979: pp. 93–4).

[42] On the tactical aspects of the EEF proposal, see the discussion in ch. 5 above. On those of mutual strike insurance, see Chiplin and Doherty (1980: pp. 2 and 9).

[43] See Wellington (1968: pp. 291–3).

[44] Ibid. pp. 293–4.

[45] See Morris with Rydzkowski (1984) and Morris (1986: ch. 6); 'Joint regulation' should be distinguished from unilateral self-restraint by labour, involving no special co-ordination with employers.

may be the best way of minimizing the harms caused by essential service disputes (1986: pp. 205–6).

## (4) STRUCTURAL EFFECTS, ANTI-INFLATION STRATEGIES, AND INCOMES POLICIES

As long as it is believed that high wage settlements contribute to inflation, and that the threat or use of industrial action contributes to high wage settlements,[46] the demands of anti-inflation strategies will tend to point in the direction of some statutory restriction of industrial action. As Lord Wedderburn points out, although in the past we have had incomes policies supplemented by criminal sanctions, they were never integrated into the general system for dealing with industrial conflict itself. An important aspect of this was the fact that the settlement criteria laid down by various incomes policies were never automatically fed into the mechanisms for voluntary state-assisted dispute resolution, which, as we have seen, were such a key element in the voluntarist approach.[47] However, once it is held that there is a need for the state to have a say in actual levels of settlement, the logical progression towards such a step may be hard for a Government to resist, particularly if proposals which aim by non-legal methods to bend the results of collective bargaining towards incomes policy norms do not succeed.[48] Nevertheless, for those who profess support for the maintenance of the voluntarist ethos, it is a decisive step to take. The SDP's 1986 proposals, for example, were notably equivocal about the terms of reference of arbitrators which 'would include the national interest as defined by Parliament at the time . . . ' although '. . . the arbitrators would be independent and free to make their own judgements in the public interest.'[49] Professor Meade, a sometime adviser to the SDP, has gone rather further. His proposals, at their most advanced, envisage a system of wages tribunals, competent to adjudicate upon any proposed settlement, chiefly by reference to its likely effect on levels of employment. A variety of sanctions would aim to encourage compliance with tribunal awards, including removal of immunities in respect of industrial action which opposes an award.[50]

Structural approaches can operate at the micro level in a variety of ways. Christopher Dow, a former executive and adviser at the Bank of England, analyses the elements of the economic benefits and costs of strikes to both employers and employees (1986: pp. 9–12). He concludes that at present the

[46] None of the pro-voluntarist writers encountered would want to argue that in a capitalist environment there is not *some* conflict involved here.

[47] See Wedderburn (1986b: pp. 354–62 at 356); Dickens (1987: pp. 112–13).

[48] See particularly Wellington (1968: pp. 324 ff.).

[49] See SDP (1986: p. 8).

[50] See Meade (1982: pp. 115–18) and (1985: pp. 25–34); in the full-blown version of Meade's proposals not only would immunities be forfeit, but further sanctions would aim to deter industrial action or breach of awards by strikers, strike organizers, and, indeed, employers.

balance tends to favour brinkmanship or actual industrial action by the union, but argues that quite modest restrictions on industrial action would tip the balance the other way, making such tactics no longer 'cost effective'. It is not clear, though, how or how closely he envisages that the legal form of such changes could be linked to their intended effect.

It may be too simple to dismiss proposals such as these as 'attempts to silence by adjudication the inconveniences of conflicts of industrial unrest',[51] not least because proposals such as Meade's and Dow's concentrate more on structural than on frictional harms;[52] nevertheless, there is a logical enough tendency for those who regard it as possible to say in normative terms which social goals are justifiable in terms of their structural effects, also to see the need to take industrial action as entirely superfluous. For in such a system, the court or tribunal could essentially take on an arbitral role, adjudicating on the merits of the dispute itself. Thus, Lord Donaldson, following his experience at the helm of the NIRC, continued to support the idea of a court which would tell the parties and the public who was right in a dispute, apparently including pay disputes, and concluded that the 'self-help' of industrial action would then become superfluous and could be abolished.[53] There is clearly enough an inherent and direct conflict between a fully-fledged faith in such arbitral models, and the values of the voluntarist system. Under the IRA itself, 'unfair industrial practices' included not only action proscribed because of its frictional effects, but also action taken in areas where the Act provided its own adjudicative process for resolving the dispute.[54] In fact the positive adjudication approach might in theory be applied to proscribe industrial action in support of any practice assessed to be on balance more structurally harmful than beneficial. Writers like Phelps Brown have clearly been tempted by such an approach in theory (1986: p. 304), but would be more willing than perhaps Lord Donaldson to admit that the obstacles to implementing it in practice would be simply too great.

Certainly, the structure of the legal framework necessary to implement this type of approach would be remarkably different from anything seen in British labour law before or after 1979. As Kahn-Freund observed:

It needs emphasis that our law knows of no administrative procedure to scrutinize the permissibility of hostile action in labour relations. Our criteria are the crude and mechanical criteria of the common law as mitigated by statutes (1968: pp. 64–5).

[51] Wedderburn (1984: p.79) referring to the proposals of Meade and of Lord Donaldson, discussed below.
[52] Both are evidently also concerned about frictional harms, but see their contributions as economists as being directed towards the structural problem as they each see it: see e.g. Meade (1981: p. 78); Dow (1986: pp. 3–8).
[53] See Donaldson (1975a: p. 192), (1975b: p. 68), and (1984).
[54] Notably the recognition procedure: IRA 1971 s. 54. Even when this was replaced by a voluntary procedure in 1975, Lord Denning for one continued to regard availability of a procedure and use of industrial action as mutually exclusive alternatives: see *ANG* v. *Wade* [1979] IRLR 201 at paras. 37–8; and cf. Mr Prior's early thoughts on the SLADE problem discussed in ch. 2 above.

The courts could not trace the limits of lawful action 'in the light of national necessities . . . '

. . . because they have no evidence before them on the general economic and political implications of the action they have to judge. In such cases there is no representative of the public interest in the English courts, only private interests are represented, and an interest which is not represented in a court cannot be considered and does not exist for the purpose of the proceedings (1969: p. 134).[55]

So, the plans of those who see the support of sophisticated structural policies as their main goal could hardly be implemented by means of mere modifications to the structure of torts and immunities. Economists like Meade and Dow see little in common between the approach of the post-1979 legislation and their own ideas. Dow regards the changes since 1979 as useful for their likely general progressive effect but 'not such as greatly to curb the power of unions to disrupt the working of the economy, nor what are argued to be the inflationary consequences of present arrangements (1986: p. 2). Meade recognizes that the precision of his test, which demands that wages be set in each firm at levels which maximize employment, means that '[t]here is no reason to believe that any single general set of rules (such as those in the Employment Act of 1980) could possibly give the correct answer in all cases' (1982: p. 93).

## (5) THE RELEVANCE OF POLITICAL EFFECTS

Critiques of the political and constitutional implications of social contract-type arrangements do not automatically suggest the need for any particular changes in industrial-conflict law. Rather, they simply urge that such arrangements be abandoned, whether by Governments or by union leaders, or by both: the essence of the recommendation is the same, whether it comes from left or right, a fact exploited by Mr Prior in the late 1970s.[56] Where the criticisms come from the right, restrictions on industrial action introduced for other reasons will no doubt be welcomed as assisting the alleviation of the problem: Brittan, for example, argues that strikes in essential services are a particular concern, not only because of their frictional effects, but because the need to tackle or avoid such effects is apt to become the chief motivator of political decisions relating to such services (1977: p. 196). Generally more extensive restrictions may be pushed through if the Government does not feel impelled to build its policies upon any basis of consensus;[57] but can any more specific connection with industrial-conflict law be formed?

[55] Cf. Rideout (1982: p. 51). The exclusive right of the Attorney-General to move the court in the public interest was asserted as a 'fundamental principle' by Lord Wilberforce in *Gouriet* v. *UPW* [1977] 3 AER 70 at 80a–b; compare the Court of Appeal's crude attempt at a 'public interest' doctrine in *APB* v. *TGWU* [1989] IRLR 305.

[56] See the discussion in ch. 2 above; for more sophisticated possible solutions to what he sees as the clash between 'parliamentarianism' and 'functionalism', see Moran (1977: ch. 9).

[57] Cf. Neal and Bloch (1983: pp. 10–12) on the 'myth of consensus'.

Some argue that the trade-disputes immunities are the specific source of union power—including power over Government—and must be repealed wholesale. This argument is considered elsewhere.[58] More popular is the argument that political strikes, particularly when they defy an elected Government, are illegitimate and should be unlawful. This argument was considered in chapter five. As we saw both there, and earlier in this chapter, the voluntarist view of the economic basis of the right to strike accepts that (if it could be found) action with a purely political object should be unlawful, but this is in effect because such action is regarded as going beyond the scope of the *social* justification of union activity.[59] However, as we also saw earlier, the term may be deployed in outlining a more restrictive view of what amounts to legitimate union activity, where the underlying Governmental cause of concern can be expressed in terms of frictional, structural, or political effects, and may indeed also have been the subject of other more direct measures. If anything less than the idea of a political right to strike— that is, a right which transcends the purposes for which it is used—is argued for, the use of the notion of political strikes may therefore signify no more than one of a number of arguments about social, frictional, structural, or political effects, which are better restated expressly.[60]

## (6) THE REGULATORY STRATEGY

So far, the discussion has looked at approaches to the different harmful effects which industrial action is perceived to cause, which seek to neutralize, defuse, or redistribute particular effects, or simply to outlaw action which causes them. A more fundamental approach involves attempts to manipulate or regulate the very processes by which industrial action is called, supported, or sustained, in an effort to pre-empt the undesired effect altogether. As has been seen, this was the principal technique adopted in the 1984 and 1988 Acts, which as well as introducing balloting requirements in the field of industrial conflict, imposed detailed and monolithic electoral systems for the choosing of unions' executive committees, and established a requirement of periodic balloting for political funds. Although ostensibly presented as measures which aimed to give unions back to their members, it was argued that these provisions had the main objective of stifling and inhibiting the conduct of industrial action, by mobilizing the forces of dissenting union members to greatest effect. This policy was detected too in the variety of other internal controls introduced by the 1988 Act.

The experience of the late 1980s suggests that the regulatory strategy can be a particularly hazardous and problematic one. By definition, its success at

---

[58] See discussion in ch. 5 above and section (7) of this chapter below.

[59] Thus Kahn-Freund (1954a: p. 124) suggested that the problem touches 'the borderline of what can legitimately be called "industrial relations"'.

[60] Cf. Rees (1982); Fox (1985a: ch. 7).

influencing external effects will depend upon the ability of its sponsor correctly to predict the likely impact of the measures in question on the internal functioning of the organization, and difficulties encountered in the dismal swamp may necessitate a potentially endless round of amendments and refinements to the regulatory framework. In addition, the intervention in the internal affairs of ostensibly private voluntary organizations which such strategies inevitably involve, demands some political justification in a liberal system, which may be difficult to supply where the concerns behind such a move are in fact of the external type. It is perhaps for both of these reasons that, as a technique for controlling the *external* effects of industrial action, the regulatory strategy does not bulk large in the wider debates and discussions of the 1980s. The promise of some form of regulation concerning ballots before industrial action in the proposals of the Labour and Social Democratic Parties, is rather more the product of a belief in the appeal of this particular version of *internal* democracy to union members.

To the Conservative Governments of the 1980s, the coincidence between a perceived mood among union members, an environment thought to render the strategy effective, and the political constraints on a too rapid implementation of a policy of pure restriction, meant that the regulatory strategy offered a potential ultimately too great to be ignored, whatever the hazards. For those less concerned with any political constraints on movement down the road of restriction, however, it may look like something of a distraction. It is this more absolutist approach which is characteristic of the New Right.

## (7) THE NEW RIGHT

Once thought of as a fringe, if not a lunatic fringe grouping, the 'New Right' have received rather more serious attention in recent years. Critics like Lords Wedderburn and McCarthy claim to detect their direct influence on the labout laws and wider industrial relations policies of post-1979.[61] Some supporters of the Governments of the period have made similar claims. There is certainly a case for regarding the New Right as a distinct and radical 'school', and their opportunities to be of influence with Government since 1979 as greater than ever before.[62] But what are the implications of their theories for labour law and the legal regulation of industrial conflict in particular? In seeking to provide an answer to that question, we are immediately faced with a difficulty of some importance. This arises from the fact that the New Right embraces a surprisingly disparate and diverse group of thinkers. As Gamble has pointed out, the chief thing which unites the

---

[61] See McCarthy (1985: pp. 5–6); Wedderburn (1984: pp. 78 ff.), and further discussion in ch. 11 below.

[62] There is a vast literature. As well as the work of the original authors discussed, this section draws on Bosanquet (1983); Gamble (1979), (1985: ch. 5), (1986), and (1988b); Butler (1983); Plant (1983); and others.

members of the New Right—and justifies their being grouped together at all—is their *rejection* of the package of political and economic ideas associated with the so-called post-war consensus. Beyond that, there are considerable differences within the school regarding the policies which should be pursued instead.[63] Nevertheless, to the extent that New Right thinkers are broadly in agreement about what was wrong with the voluntarist approach to labour law, we can establish the basic principles of their approach to each of the types of effect of union activity.

*Social Effects.*    The New Right deny that the activities of trade unions, and in particular collective bargaining, have in the past achieved or are inherently capable of achieving any benefits for trade-union members. On the contrary, it is argued, they may well have impoverished working people, and have certainly because of their other harmful effects impoverished the nation as a whole.[64] In any event, argues Hayek, the social goals to which trade unions purport to aspire are in fact misguided and selfish, for 'social justice' is a 'mirage' and the only real justice is that meted out by the unhampered operation of market forces free from collective or any other interference.[65] Here, New Right views bear a striking, if a little disconcerting, similarity to those of traditional voluntarists, for both concentrate their focus on the importance of the *framework* within which the allocation of rewards is determined—by essentially market processes. On both views, attempts at planning of incomes, however well-intentioned, are to be distrusted.[66] The all-important difference, of course, is that for voluntarists a market in which the free exercise of collective forces is suppressed is 'rigged' (Wedderburn 1985a: p. 43), whereas for the New Right the suppression of such forces is regarded as essential for the market to work properly.

*Frictional Effects.*    The New Right, not surprisingly, share the view that frictional effects are in themselves wholly undesirable, and they are implacably committed to the elimination of violence, coercion, and intimidation wherever these may be found to be present. But their negative view of the social effects of industrial action and collective bargaining, and their view of the working of market forces, particularly in relation to the movement and allocation of capital, lead them to conclude that the major if not only 'victims' of industrial conflict are workers themselves.[67] This may in part explain why frictional effects as such do not rank very highly on the New Right's agenda for action. Two more specific factors may also be mentioned. The first

---

[63] See Gamble (1988b: ch. 2) who draws a general distinction between a liberal and a conservative tendency in New Right thought.

[64] The case is presented in detail in Hutt (1975).

[65] A useful synopsis of Hayek's views on this is Butler (1983: ch. 4).

[66] Cf. the TUC's comment in its evidence to Donavan that '[n]o state, however benevolent, can perform the function of trade unions in enabling workpeople themselves to decide how their interests can best be safeguarded' (TUC 1968: p. 140).

[67] See Hayek (1960: ch. 18); Friedman and Friedman (1980: ch. 8).

derives again from the New Right preoccupation with the *rules* of the market rather than any particular outcomes. If the rules are set correctly then instances of conflict must be accepted as part of the competitive process. The second derives from the New Right's much greater concern with political and structural effects: the frictional costs of even a major national strike may be small when compared with the structural harms which can be caused by conceding or compromising the issue in dispute (Hutt 1975: p. 105).[68]

*Structural Harms.*   The New Right consider that trade-union activity causes major structural damage to the economy. In general terms it is said to block the smooth operation of market forces, leading to inefficient allocation of resources and consequent loss of consumer satisfaction and inhibition of the creation of wealth. In addition, while unions cannot themselves create inflation by 'wage-push', they may attain sufficient power to be able to 'force' Governments to adopt the political expedient of increasing the money supply—in effect resorting to inflation—in order to satisfy their demands.[69] This last view can also be seen as an aspect of the wider New Right critique of the political and constitutional effects of union activity.

*Political Effects.*   Implacably opposed to any form of 'pluralist' or 'pressure group' model of national politics, the New Right argue against the legitimacy of any influence which diverts Governments from the pursuit of the 'national interest'. Their critique therefore entails not just a 'free economy' but also a 'strong state'.[70] This argument therefore completes the New Right critique of collective bargaining, adding to their earlier exposé of the matching power argument a firm refutation of that based on the values of democratic pluralism. Indeed for some, the whole present system of Parliamentary democracy falls inevitably into question in view of the scope which it offers for disrupting the long-term course of economic policies pursued in the national and not the sectional interest.[71]

What are the implications for industrial-conflict law? Hayek's prescription has remained consistent and clear: salvation for Britain will not come unless or until the trade-disputes immunities are repealed in their entirety, for these are in his view the clear source of the unions' economic and political powers.[72] The simple logic underlying this conclusion is certainly not hard to

---

[68]  Cf. the well-publicized remark by Mr N. Lawson that expenditure on the miners' strike of 1984–5 'in narrow financial terms' represented 'a worthwhile investment for the nation'. See OR HC vol. 65 cols. 306–7 (31 July 1984). Contrast Dow (1986: pp. 10–11) who argues that the typical private firm usually stands to lose more from a strike than from a settlement.

[69]  See e.g. Hayek (1984); this of course assumes the 'monetarist' belief—most closely associated with Friedman—in an intimate and unique link between changes in the money supply and inflation.

[70]  This point is elaborated in Gamble (1979) and (1988*b*); cf. Crouch (1982*b*: p. 210).

[71]  The case is put in Brittan (1977: pp. xi–xii and ch. 19). Hayek (1982: ch. 17) makes detailed proposals for an alternative system of government.

[72]  See Hayek (1984: pp. 58 and 64); cf. Hutt (1975: pt. IV, ch. 4).

grasp, for complete exposure to the common law would have the practical consequence of rendering all collective action unlawful.[73] Nevertheless, we must approach it with some caution. By strong contrast with Hayek we may turn to Friedman, who places a low level of priority upon changes in the law, and suggests that economic recovery may well be achieved without the need to take such drastic steps.[74] His view of the sources of trade-union power may seem more sophisticated than Hayek's: that it is more likely that it is inflation coupled with official support that gives rise to strong unions than the other way around.[75] By taking control of the money supply and reducing the public sector, the 'union problem' can be reduced 'without very great difficulty'.[76] But Hayek's case for repeal of the immunities rests in strong measure as well on a *political* rather than an *economic* argument: that the immunities represent an illegitimate form of law, conferring selective privileges on one section of the community alone. This argument is, however, difficult to sustain under close examination[77] although the critique of 'privileges' no doubt forms a useful rhetorical plank for anyone wishing to attack the immunities.

If Hayek seems unsophisticated and Friedman uninterested, there are other New Right authors to whom we can turn for further enlightenment on the legal implications of their thought. Indeed, the 1980s saw a steady flow of papers from writers strongly identified as New Right, issued under the auspices of bodies with equally unmistakable credentials, such as the IEA. Nor do any of these authors fail to pay homage to Hayek or to acknowledge his inspiration; and most pay at least lip-service to his demand for the repeal of all immunities. But when it comes to the presentation of a more specific blueprint for industrial conflict and trade-union law, the lack of consensus among New Right thinkers becomes more prominent. This is a matter to which we will return in chapter eleven, but for the present, two examples from the period between the 1984 and 1988 Acts will suffice. By 1986, there was some anxiety among the Government's more right-wing supporters that the 1984 Act might prove to be the final step in the step-by-step reform of labour law. Accordingly, in May 1986, the I.o.D. published a paper by Dr Charles Hanson, entitled *Trade Union Reform—The Next Step*. This built upon Hanson's earlier assessment of the legislation of 1980–4, which had appeared by way of a postscript to Hayek's most recent work of labour market analysis.[78] Not surprisingly, these documents argued that the Government had gone in the right direction but not far enough, and that in seeking the 'ultimate objective' towards which the step-by-step process

[73] A fact acknowledged in the 1981 Green Paper (DE 1981a: p. 11).
[74] This is also a long-held view: see Friedman (1951: p. 233) and (1981).
[75] See generally Friedman (1951: esp. at pp. 222–3) and Friedman and Friedman (1980: ch. 8).
[76] Friedman quoted in the *Listener* (12 Mar. 1981).
[77] See the discussion in ch. 5 above.
[78] See Hanson (1986) and (1984) respectively.

should be working, one needed to look no further than Hayek. But Hanson concentrated his specific proposals for reform in two areas: the removal of remaining protections for secondary action, and further measures on essential services. Here, he suggested a combination of techniques: the removal of immunities, no-strike agreements, and possibly even the offer of some unspecified *quid pro quo* (Hanson 1984: p. 77, 1986: pp. 8–16).

Others cast their net rather wider. In April 1986, a month before the appearance of Hanson's proposals, the IEA published a paper by Shenfield entitled *What Right to Strike?* This contained some fourteen diverse proposals for legislative action (Shenfield 1986: pp. 45–9). These amounted to a curious mixed bag, some proposals seeming quite mild or even reflecting the already existing state of the law.[79] However, a recurring theme and a revealing one, was that a wide range of practices might be tolerated provided that they arose in the correct way. The 'law of the market' resting as it does on the central classical notion of freedom of contract,[80] Shenfield was prepared to tolerate closed shop, lawful secondary action, and other arrangements, with the important proviso in all cases that they be achieved 'subject to contract' (1986: pp. 45–9). In Shenfield's parlance this meant that the arrangements in question must have been achieved in the form of a binding contract, negotiated in the appropriate market conditions, and to the breach of which the 'usual' contractual remedies will apply.[81]

In this respect, the form of Shenfield's proposals provides a striking illustration of one of the implications of the New Right's concern with form to the exclusion of substance. It hints also at another more general implication of the arguments of the New Right for the formation of legislative policy. Because New Right arguments tend to point to aspects of the general legal framework rather than particular practices or arrangements, they are of limited utility if it is particular practices or arrangements which the legislature itself wishes to attack. To put it another way, implementation of New Right reforms may not of itself ensure that particular practices are indeed eliminated. Conversely, while Governments may wish to rest their general legislative approach on broad propositions such as that trade-union power is in general or in particular areas too great, for the New Right, however, the formal position remains that trade unions cannot in themselves be regarded as a good or bad thing:[82] it is simply the legal framework itself which may be open to criticism. In fact it is not uncommon to find writers associated with the New Right expressing a commitment to the notion of an

---

[79] See the commentary by Grunfeld appended to Shenfield (1986: at pp. 50–9).

[80] For an assessment of the correspondence of the idea underpinning classical contract theory and those of Hayekian style market economists, see Atiyah (1979: ch. 14 at pp. 402–4). See also Collins (1986: ch.1).

[81] In effect this means that the freedom is left to employers to enter into such arrangements with their employees if they so choose.

[82] The New Right priority placed upon individual liberty compels recognition of the liberty to associate in a trade union should the individual so desire.

indepedent trade-union movement as an important feature of a 'free society'.[83] Nevertheless, the New Right vision of what it is appropriate for free trade unions actually to *do* is a singularly limited one. They can be a 'sounding board for Government' and a 'friendly society' for their members (Hoskyns 1982); they can be a convenient mechanism through which employees reach collective decisions on those matters which the employer is happy to leave up to their choice, for example, in choosing between an available wage increase and non-cash benefits (Hayek 1960: p. 276; Hutt 1975: p. 74); they can perform an 'entrepreneurial' function, helping their members to work the labour market, by giving them training and gathering and disseminating information about openings and opportunities for relocation (Shenfield 1986: pp. 7–8). They can do all of these things 'provided neither they nor large employing organisations such as the Government played any role in wage and salary determination!'[84]

Shenfield's paper also put forward a New Right view on the legal position of the individual strike participant. Voluntarists used to give less attention to this tricky issue, in essence because it seemed invariably to be the case in a dispute that, as the CBI told Donovan, 'the main interest of the employer is in resumption of work and preservation of goodwill' (CBI 1965: para. 170); but now that permanent mass dismissal is reappearing as a viable employer sanction, voluntarists are logically enough beginning to argue the case for an 'immunity' in this area as well.[85] For the New Right, however, the only 'right to strike' is the right of the individual to withdraw his labour by resigning and offering it elsewhere in the market. It follows, argues Shenfield, that strikers cannot claim a continuing right to their jobs, as against whether the employer or scab labour. So the employer must be entirely free to dismiss and replace them without redress (1986: pp. 46–7).

As the comparison between these two papers suggests, there is no clear and agreed blueprint for industrial-conflict law reform offered by the New Right, beyond a shared critique of what was wrong with the voluntarist approach, and a shared endorsement of the theoretical Hayekian ideal of a complete removal of all immunities. Within the confines of these two basic parameters it is hardly surprising to find that almost any proposed measure which would restrict the lawfulness of industrial action, will in principle find favour with almost any New Right author. But the specific agenda of proposals regarded as the priority for legislative action differs considerably from one writer to the next. The general observation of Gamble seems to be particularly apposite in the field of industrial conflict, namely that what the New Right offer to government is

less a blueprint than a pool of ideas which [are] available to ministers either to justify policies or to seek new solutions (Gamble 1988b: p. 35).

[83] See e.g. Hanson (1978: p. 25); Hoskyns (1985: p. 21), who numbers freedom of association among the 'real' protections available to employees, as opposed to the right to strike.
[84] Marris (1981) (exclamation in the original).
[85] See e.g. Ewing (1986: pp. 149–53); Wedderburn (1987: pp. 16–17); Napier (1987).

# (8) CONCLUSIONS: SOME LESSONS FOR POLICYMAKING ANALYSIS

Chapter eleven offers a concluding assessment of the policies and influences underlying the new legislation. What guidelines and lessons can we take from this chapter to that task? A few can be suggested at this point. Others will be developed further in chapter eleven itself.

First, our survey suggests that it may be unwise automatically to associate particular types of legislative provision or modes of legal regulation with particular economic or political theories, ideologies, or strategies. Satisfaction with the absence of severe legal restriction may denote sympathy with Kahn-Freund or with Friedman. A preference for extensive removal of the immunities may indicate support for Hayek or for Meade. Support for certain specific measures of restriction may come from almost any camp pitched within the middle ground. This aspect provides, it is suggested, further justification for this book having looked beyond the statutory surface of the new law. At the same time, however, a grasp of some of the more theoretical academic positions complements this approach and provides a wider base from which to assess the Government's own statements regarding their objectives than a detective-like examination of the primary sources alone is likely to provide. For given that the adoption of a specific measure may indeed be open to a range of possible explanations, some wider criterion may be required in order to assess which of these—including the one offered by the Government itself—seems to be the most plausible or coherent.

The survey also suggests the importance of bearing in mind the simple practical matter of *priorities*. For it is a characteristic of much of the academic work, and particularly the pressure group proposals, that each tends to approach the subject with its own particular area of concern foremost in mind. What for some are crucially important problems may for others appear merely to be side issues, without there being much disagreement about the nature of the basic problem in each case. Writers who hope to have some influence on the course of actual policy debate are bound to set out what seem to them to be the most immediate areas of concern, whatever the strict implications of the more general theoretical underpinning of their views. The relative balance between theoretical underpinning and other more immediate influences on policy in the legislation of the 1980s is something which will be explored further in chapter eleven.

# [11]
# Concluding Assessment

## (1) INTRODUCTION

This chapter presents a concluding assessment of the new regime, in particular building upon the initial assessments of each measure put forward in earlier chapters, in the further light of chapter ten. As was noted in chapter one, a forceful and detailed critique of the legislation has been built up by a number of other commentators, which argues that it is to be most illuminatingly analysed and understood by reference to the tenets of the New Right, and in particular the ideology of Hayek. This chapter will accordingly develop the present writer's own assessment of the 1980s legislation from the starting-point of a consideration of this 'New Right thesis'. First, the core of the thesis itself is briefly stated; then the record of the 1980s is examined more closely against this bench-mark, initially by way of a general survey, and then in respect of each piece of legislation in turn. The chapter concludes with an appraisal of the strengths and weaknesses of the New Right thesis, which leads to the key conclusions of this book.

## (2) THE NEW RIGHT THESIS

Undoubtedly the leading and most thorough exponent of the New Right thesis is Lord Wedderburn, who built up the case in a series of publications throughout the 1980s.[1] The richness and range of Wedderburn's argument could not be fairly summarized or captured here; nevertheless, three key elements in the argument can be identified. By the mid-1980s, two central and recurring propositions had been established. First, the legislation of the 1980s was said to reflect a crucial break with past policy as, for the first time since the war, Government could be seen to be pursuing an industrial relations law policy 'integrally geared into its overall economic policies' (Wedderburn 1985a: p. 36). However strong a preoccupation anti-inflation and incomes policies may have been for previous administrations, yet the two streams had never before met. Now they flowed as one. Secondly, a common thread was identified running through the changes in industrial-conflict law, namely that

[1] See esp. Clark and Wedderburn (1983); Wedderburn (1984); (1985a), (1985b), (1986b: pp. 68–96), (1989b).

the collective strength of workers is to be limited by the boundaries of the employment unit (p. 43).

The third element in the argument was the identification of the ideology underpinning these developments. At an early stage the New Right were identified as the crucial body of influence, but the roll-call of influential names was a long one, and included a number of figures outside of the New Right.[2] By the end of the 1980s, however, Hayek had been identified as the single most important figure, and in 'Freedom of Association and Philosophies of Labour Law' (Wedderburn 1989b), the most comprehensive exposition of the thesis yet, Lord Wedderburn sets out the case for the proposition that

the character of labour legislation since 1979 can be better understood—and its future course probably better predicted—by reference to [the] framework set up by Hayek than to any other (p. 15).

In chapter ten, it was suggested that the work of the New Right, including that of Hayek, can be analysed in its application to industrial-conflict law by resolving the argument into three phases. First, an elaboration of the basic tenets of the New Right approach reveals a comprehensive rejection of the voluntarist analysis, and the conclusion that the effects of union activity are in all cases only harmful. This leads naturally to the second stage, which is the generalized demand for the repeal of all immunities. The third stage is the elaboration of a more detailed blueprint for trade-union law, where New Right authors seem to differ more widely in the approaches taken. Wedderburn follows broadly the same approach in his dissection of the writings of Hayek, and it is his conclusions at the third stage which are of greatest significance, for in a work of Hayek written some thirty years ago, he finds a programme which has 'a familiar look' and represents 'an approximation of the agenda for the British legislation of 1980–88' (p. 34). Hence the challenging conclusion that

The philosophy of Hayek and its importance for the new labour law has gone too long unemphasised, especially by those of us whose first task is to analyse and explain the legislation. It does not explain everything, but it illuminates much (p.37).

Let us then turn to take up this challenge, first by considering the legislation and the period of its enactment as a whole, and then by looking more closely at each instalment in turn.

## (3) THE NEW REGIME—AN OVERVIEW

If we take Government statements and pronouncements as our starting-point, the signs that the Hayek thesis may in general terms be vindicated look

---

[2] Names identified in Wedderburn (1984) include Minford, Hayek, Brittan, Meade, Donaldson, Tur, Roberts, Friedman, and Hutt.

promising. Mrs Thatcher is a self-confessed 'great admirer' of Hayek,[3] and Mr Nigel Lawson, the key architect of the economic policies of the 1980s, has endorsed the association with Hayek's name.[4] He has also set out the key components of the economic policy which the Government claimed to be pursuing from 1979, in impeccably New Right, and particularly Friedmanite, terms. At the macro level the aim was to take control of the rate of growth of the money supply; at the micro level the object was to free up the workings of the labour market, particularly at the bottom end, the overall strategy having the overriding priority goals of conquering inflation and improving competitiveness and efficiency.[5]

How accurate a picture that in fact represents of the economic policies pursued during this period is a judgement which we can leave to the economists; but it is worth noting that many have noticed from the mid-1980s onwards, a distinct loss of Governmental enthusiasm for orthodox monetarism, as, notwithstanding the variety of ways in which it was open to measurement, the money supply proved to be a persistently untameable beast.[6] Nor should we presume that a programme of restriction of the law of industrial conflict is itself automatically indicative of the influence of New Right economic theory. As was suggested in chapter ten, the notion that there is *some* degree of tension between the conduct of free collective bargaining and the pursuit of anti-inflation strategies is now widely shared, and restrictions on industrial action accordingly form an element of many such strategies. Certainly, the adoption of such a programme cannot be taken necessarily to signify the influence of the monetarist view, expounded particularly by Friedman, that union activity merely transmits, rather than initiates, inflationary forces, for as Mayhew observes, 'whatever view of the inflationary process is taken, a reduction of trade union bargaining power would weaken any initiatory or transmission effect of unions' (1983: p. 159). Indeed, as was also noted in chapter ten, Friedman himself sets little store by restrictions on unions' ability to call industrial action, and sees no need for draconian measures of this kind. As for Hayek, the legislation self-evidently does not meet his demand for a total repeal of the immunities, and he continued to voice a sense of urgency about the matter throughout the 1980s.[7]

Of course, it could be argued that the programme of the 1980s represents a determined series of steps towards the realization of Hayek's ideal, albeit that, ten years on, this has not yet been achieved. But even if the step-by-step approach has marched in the *direction* preferred by Hayek, such an analysis ignores how at odds as a *strategy* is step by step with the fundamental

---

[3] See OR HC vol. 1000 col. 756 (10 May 1981); Cosgrave (1978: pp. 86–7 and ch. 5).

[4] Lawson (1980: pp. 2–3), where Friedman is also cited with approval.

[5] See Lawson (1980), (1981), and (1984).

[6] See e.g. Robinson (1986: ch. 16); MacInnes (1987: ch. 1); Gamble (1988a: pp. 32–3).

[7] See e.g. *The Times* (9 May 1985).

approach which Hayek urges. For Hayek, solving the 'union problem' is *the* key to economic recovery, and the trade-disputes immunities are *the* source of union power. Furthermore, early on he concluded that 'A monetary policy that would break the coercive power of the unions by producing extensive and protracted unemployment must be excluded, for it would be politically and socially fatal' (1960: pp. 281–2). Instead, he urged a very specific strategy in the 1980s: a complete all-in-one repeal of the immunities, immediately followed by a monetary clamp-down to end inflation. Only the short sharp shock of one followed by the other could and would work.[8] But in steadfastly pursuing the step-by-step approach, the 1980s Governments effectively consistently rejected any such apocalyptic solution as itself potentially politically fatal, a view which, as we have seen, had obvious enough roots in the fate of the IRA. Furthermore, alongside the gradual introduction of labour laws, there were pursued a range of policies aimed at encouraging the fragmentation and decentralization of collective bargaining, against the backcloth of growing unemployment, which was permitted to rise indefinitely. This wider picture suggests that on the question of the origins and nature of union power, the Government may have paid rather more attention to Friedman's view that it is not primarily the legal framework, but economic and political conditions that are most important in determining trade unions' strength. That indeed is a view widely shared across the political spectrum, from Friedman through to Kahn-Freund, who throughout his work stressed the secondary nature of law as a social force,[9] and to the extent that the union movement was generally more quiescent for much of the 1980s, this has been widely attributed much more to factors such as the growth in unemployment than to changes in industrial-conflict law.[10] That approach is also relevant to our understanding of why, although some begged the Government to introduce tougher laws while the unions were weak, other more far-sighted employers urged that, precisely because union power might revive in changed future conditions, excessive restrictions could prove to be a long-term error.[11]

Where at this general level the 'Hayek thesis' is perhaps most commanding is in the way that it draws attention to the very thing which, as we have seen, unites the New Right, namely their *rejection* of the post-war consensus and the voluntarist tradition. The 'traditional analysis' is throughout Wedderburn's argument counterpoised against the analyses of Hayek and the new legislation. But correct as it surely must be to say that in the 1980s the 'old arguments' have in many quarters 'lost their magic' (Wedderburn 1989*b*:

[8] See esp. his letter to *The Times* (13 June 1980). Hoskyns and others urged the short sharp shock strategy in the late-1970s, but lost the argument to Prior: see Whitehead (1985: pp. 371–2); Hoskyns (1988).

[9] See e.g. Kahn-Freund (1977: esp. at pp. 3 and 10).

[10] See Mayhew (1985: p. 66); Hall (1986: ch. 5); McBride (1986: esp. p. 336); Moran (1986); Evans (1987: pp. 422–9).

[11] See e.g. *Management Today* (Jan. 1984: p. 3).

p. 36), this is not the same as to say that all the new arguments must inevitably be regarded as having the same character and pedigree. As the decade wore on, the rhetoric of ministers on industrial relations law became, as we have seen, increasingly unequivocal and explicit, with the absolute priority given to the individual over the collective being fervently avowed in 1987 and 1988, and the combined thrust of the legislation only fully explicable by reference to an underlying objective of simply minimizing the incidence of lawful and effective industrial action. But if the Thatcher Governments' rejection of voluntarism and its values is clear enough, how far can the programme in fact pursued be regarded in its particulars as following a New Right or Hayekian blueprint? To answer that, we need to look more closely at Hayek's work and at the elements of the legislative programme.

## (4) THE NEW RIGHT THESIS AND THE LEGISLATIVE PROGRAMME

In chapter ten it was suggested that, when it comes to a detailed legislative programme, there is no clear consensus among New Right thinkers. In one sense this is not surprising: if what is in principle thought to be essential is a complete and immediate removal of all immunities, then no step short of this is likely to have any greater appeal from the point of view of principle than any other. In his writing and interviews of the 1980s, Hayek has no agenda to offer to the British Government other than the persistent repetition of his basic demand. But Hayek—a man born in the last century—has been writing about 'labour unions' for a long time, and Lord Wedderburn argues that for a more detailed agenda we should go back to *The Constitution of Liberty*, written in 1959. In the chapter of this book devoted to the unions, it is argued, we find in outline the agenda of 1980–8: controls on 'picketing in numbers', secondary action, and the closed shop, and further protections for non-unionists (Wedderburn 1989*b*: p. 34, citing Hayek 1960: ch. 18). But how clear and detailed a blueprint was this? We should arguably be cautious about attaching excessive weight to a too close analysis of this chapter. There is little if any evidence to suggest that Hayek's understanding of British labour law has ever extended beyond a very basic grasp of the framework of the Trade Disputes Act 1906. Ewing has recently also stressed the importance of Hayek in relation to the new laws. But as he convincingly argues, Hayek's remarks in *The Constitution of Liberty* suggest that Hayek was woefully ignorant of British law at the time on matters such as picketing and the closed shop. Indeed, as Ewing also points out, it is not even clear that in this work Hayek is consistently thinking of Britain—or any particular country (1988*b*: esp. at pp. 144–6).

The explanation surely is that Hayek has never had any clear or detailed prescription for British industrial-conflict law beyond the insistence that immunities be abolished, and common-law regulation reinstated. The references to picketing, the closed shop, and so forth, are put forward as *illustrations* of how Hayek believes that unions abuse the power which the existence of immunities gives to them. Indeed, the essence of what unions do is in Hayek's view always reducible to the same thing, namely the 'coercion' of non-union workers. All union activity is interpreted as different manifestations of this, so that picketing becomes by definition the coercion of non-members to strike, secondary action by definition the coercion of non-members to accept union membership or union rates, and so forth. Just as the analysis of both the nature and the source of union power offered in *The Constitution of Liberty* and elsewhere is monolithic, so the solution, however expressed, is always the same:

The mere withdrawal of the special privileges either explicitly granted to the unions or arrogated by them with the toleration of the courts would seem enough to deprive them of the more serious coercive powers which they now exercise (Hayek 1960: p. 278).

The specific measures which would be required in any given country to reinstate the principles of free association in the field of labor will depend on the situation created by its individual development . . . [but the changes required] involve no more than that they be made to submit to the same general principles of law that apply to everybody else (p. 279).[12]

If we turn to consider each piece of legislation more particularly, the Hayekian explanation alone appears clearly to be insufficient. The assessment offered earlier of the 1980 Act suggests that it cannot be readily understood in purely economic or structural terms; rather, its measures were aimed at a well-defined set of perceived mischiefs, and more generally at striking a symbolic balance within a framework which gave at least some credence to voluntarist arguments. For Mr Prior, general structural harms were best tackled through the educative and annual economic assessment approach, in which union leaderships would play an important part. In fact, while he differed sharply from them on the matter of frictional harms, Mr Prior's approach to the *structural* problem had much in common with that of many contemporary pro-voluntarists, as discussed in chapter ten, a fact which highlights the detached way in which his views in the two areas were shaped. Wedderburn acknowledges that Prior shared at least *some* common ground with traditional voluntarists, and suggests that it was only in 1982 'that traditional analysis gave way finally to the thrust of the Hayek philosophy (1989*b*: p. 30).

Turning then to the 1982 Act, although it was noted that there was an important shift in Government rhetoric at this time, towards the language of the labour market and of economic analysis, we also saw how the majority of the actual changes which that Act introduced reflected traditional concerns going back over many years—concerns not inevitably linked to any precise

[12]  See too Hayek (1959: pp. 47–8).

economic theory of the type allegedly pursued in the 1980s.[13] Perhaps rather more clearly than the 1980 Act, the 1982 Act's redefinition of a trade dispute reflects a distinct conception of the legitimate *social* goals of industrial action, outside of which the frictional harms alone provide sufficient grounds for its restriction. The repeal of section 14 of the 1974 Act, the pivotal provision of the 1982 Act, and arguably of the whole corpus of legislation, was, it was suggested here, first and foremost dictated by the perceived need to ensure a framework within which the combined restrictions of the 1980 and 1982 Acts would be effectively operable and enforceable. The ideological significance of the repeal—whether for the followers of Hayek or for the unions—was secondary to that—and indeed still regarded in 1982 as politically potentially hazardous. Further, it was suggested that, while laying the ground for a greater incidence of conflict and litigation than was contemplated in 1980, the 1982 Act was still framed with a view to encouraging continued compliance with the law. Although the Government was, as we have seen, at this time increasingly preoccupied with disputes which presented a threat to its structural policies, rather than with the still overwhelmingly more common phenomenon of unofficial action, it was clearly not in this period in any way committed to the idea of facing out all conflict in these areas rather than making any structurally damaging concessions.[14]

The 1982 Act was perhaps a case of legislation rhetorically presented in a certain ideological package in order to achieve a desired political impact. An important task for Mr Tebbit and for this Act was to be seen as in all respects marking a significant change from the approach of Mr Prior, and the pursuit of a much more hostile and confrontational stance with the unions; but the underlying reality was, for all the undoubted restrictiveness of the measures, a package still tempered by cautious pragmatism and guided by the principles of step by step. If the New Right offered a 'pool of ideas' and rhetoric with which to marry up these disparate characteristics of the legislation, then so much the better.

What of the 1984 and 1988 Acts, and the policy of regulation, particularly through the use of ballots, which they pursue? It seems hard to see how these techniques can be fitted into the New Right scheme of things. Trade-union democracy is not a topic on the New Right's agenda. This fact is not so surprising, given the minimal impact of unions' activities in their ideal world, whether internally or externally, and the profound scepticism of many New Right authors about the benefits of democratic processes. In fact, the 1984 and 1988 Acts follow an alternative strategy to the New Right prescription of ever further restriction of industrial action, the Government in this second phase instead taking the political opportunity of the short cut of internal

---

[13] It is worth restating, for example, that a broad agenda for the 1982 Act measures may be found in *Fair Deal at Work* (CPC 1968).

[14] An illuminating comparison is between the approaches taken to disputes with the miners in 1981 and 1984–5.

regulation, to undermine industrial action and weaken the power of the union's threat in the collective bargaining process, by mobilizing the forces of dissent within the union movement itself.[15] The earlier assessment in chapters six to eight certainly suggests that the 1984 and 1988 measures sought both to pre-empt frictional harms and to damp down the structural impact of individual settlements, but also that the pursuit of those aims through the medium of the populist appeal to individual trade unionists can only be explained in the context of a unique configuration of political and economic circumstances at a particular time.

If we look to Hayek, we find once again that, for reasons which have been suggested, trade-union democracy, ballots, and elections, simply do not feature on his agenda, any more than the concerns addressed by measures contained in the 1988 Act. However, Lord Wedderburn argues that at least two features of the 1988 Act are distinctively Hayekian. The first is the way in which section 1 gives members the right to restrain industrial action which is unballoted, whether or not it would involve the commission of a tort. Thus 'it is not the unlawful act but the group pressure, the collective organization *itself*, that is the target. The link with Hayek', it is suggested, 'is immediate' (Wedderburn 1989*b*: p. 24).[16] But it is arguably the very feature of the structure of section 1 to which Wedderburn points, that suggests that it is in fact out of keeping with a purely Hayekian approach. For Hayek, as we have seen, regulation by the general principles of the common law, equally applicable to all persons, is all-important, and this points against the creation of 'special' rights and remedies to restrain industrial action, and in favour of the simple repeal of immunities. We also saw in earlier chapters how for its own political reasons, the Government in the early 1980s systematically pursued a strategy of simply opening up existing common-law rights. Yet with the 1984 and 1988 Acts the rhetoric claiming the continuance of that approach became rather less convincing, and section 1 of the 1988 Act is a clear example of a provision which in fact created a new statutory cause of action to supplement the common law, placed into the hands of union members—something which Hayek would arguably consider to be neither appropriate nor necessary.

The second specific provision of the 1988 Act which is said to have a particularly Hayekian pedigree is section 3, creating the new right not to be unjustifiably disciplined (Wedderburn 1989*b*: pp. 24–6). Once again, the basic proposition—that section 3 elevates the individual position absolutely above that of the collective—is indisputable. But is the mode of its operation characteristically Hayekian, as Lord Wedderburn suggests? We should be cautioned by the fact that among the opponents of section 3 were a remarkably wide range of organizations and individuals normally sympathetic to

---

[15] Clark and Wedderburn (1987: p. 183) acknowledge the 'tendency towards juridification' in the 1984 Act and the overall mixed experience of the 1980s.
[16] Emphasis in the original.

the Government, including some well to the right of the political spectrum.[17] What upset such people was not as such that section 3 permits the individual to trump the pressures of the collective, but more the fact that it does so by encouraging the member to dissent from within the union, rather than to leave. In the New Right's ideal world, we may recall, with their immunities gone, and their powers and role emasculated, unions would become 'genuinely free' associations, unable to 'coerce' individuals, who would be free to leave a union whose rules or organization did not appeal. However, the Government's strategy in 1988 was, as we have seen, based on the different approach of harnessing and mobilizing dissident members as a weakening force *within* unions. For this purpose, dissidents were to be encouraged not to leave, but through section 3 and other measures, and with the assistance of the new Commissioner, to stay and exercise their voice.

A number of writers have argued that the 1980s saw the significant marginalization in the policy development process, of the traditional pressure groups and of the civil service. It is often also suggested that into their former positions of influence have moved a much narrower group of individual 'policy advisers', and the new breed of right-wing research and policymaking organizations.[18] Whatever may be true of other areas of policy, any such change appears only to have had a limited impact in the field with which we are concerned. In general, it was frequently noted in earlier chapters that the Government's New Right critics, forceful and loud in their demands though they were, were at each stage of the step-by-step process, one, if not several, steps ahead of the Government itself, or simply out of step with it altogether. Indeed, in the mid- to late-1980s, the single thing which all New Right critics most consistently and strongly urged the Government to do—to introduce direct restrictions on strikes in essential services—was the thing which the Government steadfastly refused to do; and the central strategy instead pursued by the Government in this period—of regulation, particularly through the use of ballots before industrial action—was rejected by New Right critics as a 'merry-go-round' and a 'fruitless process' (Mather 1987: p. 6).

Thus, at the beginning of 1988, as another Employment Bill approached the statute-book, the Government's two most articulate and potentially influential New Right critics joined forces in an attempt to steer it back on to the 'right course'. In *Striking out Strikes*, published by the IEA, Hanson and Mather warned of the dangers of adhocery and pragmatism, detectable in the step-by-step approach, and of the fact that 'the hard core of immunity remains' (1988: pp. 26 and 76). The ballot process was criticized because it 'undoubtedly lends a spurious legitimacy to [industrial] action'. There was 'little logic for encouraging strikes following a ballot and discouraging other

---

[17] For a selection of different quotations, see the speech of Mr Meacher at OR HC St. Cttee. F 4th sitting (24 Nov. 1987) cols. 113 ff.; see too Hanson and Mather (1988: pp. 74–5).

[18] See e.g. Taylor (1982*b*: p. 184); Lewis and Wiles (1984: pp. 71 ff.).

strikes', especially in the public services, and the ballot 'is of no relevance to the economic issues leading to or stemming from the decision to strike' (pp. 76–7). Indeed, Hanson and Mather suggested that the step-by-step programme now be pushed forward to a rapid completion. A White Paper should lead to an Employment Bill no later than October 1989, consolidating previous legislation, and withdrawing immunities in the field of essential services. This would then leave the way clear following a general election, for a short bill in 1992–3 'repealing all the trade union immunities which remained' (pp. 91–2).[19]

The review of developments since 1988 contained in chapter nine, however, suggests instead a continuation of many previous trends and characteristics. The 1990 Bill's specific provisions on industrial conflict represent a continuation of the strategies of both restriction and regulation, guided in their particulars by the developments of the most recent and prominent disputes. The broad thrust of the measures is as ever firmly in the direction of further severe curtailment of the right to strike, while yet the most ardent critics on the right seem destined once again for disappointment.[20] Indeed, in January 1990, even before the start of the Bill's passage through Parliament, the newly appointed Employment Secretary, Mr Michael Howard, showed no inclination to reopen the question of restrictions on essential services, following the negative outcome of Mr Fowler's review; and even suggested that the 1990 Act will mark the end of this long programme of legislation,[21] reaching the statute-book just around the tenth birthday of the Act of 1980.

## (5) THE NEW REGIME: CONCLUDING ASSESSMENT

A summary of the main implications of this further appraisal by reference to the New Right/Hayek thesis, of the industrial-conflict legislation of the last decade, provides the starting-point from which to develop the essential conclusions of this book. It has been suggested that, whilst drawing attention to some vitally important aspects, the New Right thesis provides an insufficient basis alone for our analysis of this legislation, in four broad respects.

First, the thesis overestimates the degree of sophistication and cogency of the New Right position. It attributes a more detailed programme to Hayek

---

[19]  See too Roberts (1987: pp. 16–18) again calling for action on essential services.

[20]  Hanson and Mather (1989: paras. 13 and 18–24) reiterated their demands on strikes in essential services as a first step to the abolition of all immunities, and criticized proposals for restrictions on unofficial action. The I.o.D. (1989) called again for action on essential services in responding to the Green Paper on unofficial action.

[21]  The publication of the 1990 Bill brought indications that amendments on essential services would be tabled by back-bench Conservative MPs: see *Guardian* (27 Dec. 1989). For Mr Howard's comments, made against the backcloth of widespread public hostility to the Government's handling of the ambulance workers' dispute, see *Financial Times* and *Guardian* (5 Jan. 1990).

than he clearly articulates, and assumes a degree of consensus among his supporters which appears to be lacking. Secondly, the thesis neglects how at odds with the preferred strategy of Hayek were the step-by-step programme and the industrial relations and economic backcloth against which it was unfolded; and it underplays the extent to which the Government's strategy consistently failed to implement key elements of the programmes put forward by Hayek's disciples. Thirdly, the analysis assumes too readily that particular types of provision have an unmistakable ideological pedigree. In relation to the 1980 and 1982 Acts in particular, it therefore takes insufficient account of their peculiar origins and influences, which suggest that they were less the product of a detailed ideological blueprint, and more the result of the continual development and refinement of Conservative concerns over the period from 1974 onwards, which drew its shape both from traditional broad preoccupations,[22] and from the more specific *ad hoc* developments of the time, subject at all times to the influence of pragmatic and political concerns. Finally, the thesis pays inadequate attention to the diversity of techniques open to a Government determined to legislate in this field. Having regard in particular to the 1984 and 1988 Acts, it therefore tends to underrate the significance and character of the policy of regulation, through ballots and other techniques, which this phase of the legislation pursued.[23] In doing so, it fails to acknowledge just how different that policy is from the preferred approaches of the New Right, whether as expressed by Hayek or by his acolytes. Once again, this means that insufficient recognition is given to the particular configuration of political circumstances which gave rise to the strategy, and encouraged its pursuit.[24]

Of course, in developing the analysis along these lines, we must not lose sight of the basic fact that the changes introduced since 1979 have been massively restrictive of the ability of workers and their unions to engage in effective and lawful industrial action. And it is when we turn back to the broader canvas that the New Right thesis provides its strongest and most vital insights. It confronts us with what the step-by-step process might otherwise tend to obscure, namely the sheer cumulative severity of the changes introduced since 1980, and the progressively clearly and uncompromisingly articulated rejection of voluntarism and its values over the period. The New Right thesis remind us too of the absence of any new statutory protections, in

---

[22] The preoccupations in question were, as has been seen, invariably those of the Government itself, and others tended to make little headway where Government did not happen to share their concerns.

[23] For further discussion of the balance and interplay between 'deregulation' and 'regulation' in the post-1979 laws, see Lewis (1986) and Hendy (1989: pp. 22–3). The variety and complexity of techniques used is also indicated in the shifting focus of the industrial-conflict laws between individual organizers, trade unions, and individual participants in industrial action, as occasion seemed to demand.

[24] Non-legislative techniques, such as the positive encouragement given to right-wing breakaway, and 'new realist' unions and associations, as a further means of fragmenting worker opposition, are also important here.

a decade which saw important new developments and extensions of the economic torts, as the peeling back of the immunities increasingly exposed the state of the common law to the fresh eye of the courts, making it increasingly difficult to conduct a lawful dispute, even when complying with the new legislation to the letter;[25] and it highlights the increasingly implausible and untenable rhetoric which argued that the 1984 and 1988 Acts entailed the protection and strengthening of the interests of trade-union members. Finally, whatever may be the best precise analysis of the economic policies pursued in this period, and albeit that economic policy was not a simple or sole determinant of the industrial-conflict laws, yet still the restrictive thrust of those laws drove firmly with the grain of economic policy.[26]

It is also worth stressing that the New Right thesis looks to analyse the nature and impact of the full range of legislation introduced over the last decade, and not merely that of the industrial-conflict laws. Again, the cumulative impact and implications of a body of measures which has transformed almost every area of labour law, may all too easily be neglected by lawyers engaged in the analysis of any one particular area of the changes. As the ILO Committee of Experts has commented in a recent report:

Whilst it is true that most of the legislative measures . . . are not incompatible with the requirements of [ILO Convention 87], there is a point at which the cumulative effect of legislative changes which are in themselves consistent with the principles of freedom of association may nevertheless, by virtue of their complexity and extent, constitute an incursion upon the rights guaranteed by the Convention.[27]

In giving us in particular, these essential insights and reminders, and for the sheer vigour and passion which it restores to a debate which has frequently sidetracked and flagged over the course of recent years, the New Right thesis contributes some basic and essential elements to our understanding of the industrial-conflict laws of the last decade. But the picture which it alone provides is not sufficient. In particular, there are two broad and central conclusions to be derived from the study undertaken in this book, which it is suggested must be added to the analyses offered elsewhere.

First, to an appreciation of the differences between the pre- and post-1979 periods which have been exhaustively highlighted in the literature, it is essential to add an understanding of the extent to which in this field, the broad preoccupations of the post-1979 Governments were essentially the same as—or a continuation or development of—those of the Governments

---

[25] For a recent illustration of the problems, compare the approaches of Millett J, CA, and HL in *ABP* v. *TGWU* [1989] IRLR 291 (Ch. D.), 305 (CA), and 399 (HL). See further ch. 9, text to nn. 9 and 10 above. The closest the 1980s Governments came to tackling this problem was in the 1981 Green Paper's discussion of 'positive rights'.

[26] For an analysis of the full range of labour and employment law measures introduced since 1979, and their relationship to Mrs Thatcher's 'economic experiment', see Ewing (1989).

[27] ILO Committee of Experts *Observation 1989* on Convention 87, para. 3(*g*).

which immediately preceded them. The formal, and only briefly interrupted, continuity in the character of the framework of industrial-conflict law prior to 1979, and its progressive reconstruction subsequent to that date, should not be permitted to conceal the tensions between that framework and the pursuit of Government policies in other areas, which grew continuously through the 1960s and 1970s. It was this wider phenomenon which had generated the progressive breakdown over the period of the voluntarist consensus which had among other things sustained the abstentionist framework of labour law, a breakdown which, barely beneath the surface of Government rhetoric, was all but complete by 1979. The crucial development after 1979 was, then, the increasing readiness of Governments to resolve and overcome this tension by a progressive rejection and abandonment of the rhetoric, tenets, and objectives which were essential parts of the voluntarist consensus, most importantly perhaps, the commitment to full employment, and the belief in a need to involve trade unions—in one way or another—in the pursuit of economic and other key Government policies. It was this increasingly articulated and embraced *rejection* of the voluntarist consensus, as the decade wore on, which correspondingly increasingly liberated the Governments from the constraints of any commitment to the continuation of the approach to industrial-conflict law with which the consensus had been associated. It should be noted, however, that this was indeed the working out of a gradualistic process, with ministers throughout the period continuing to see it as an essential political requirement to maintain a commitment to a basic core right to strike, both in their rhetoric (however increasingly hollow), and in the preservation of the 'hard core' of trade-disputes immunities (however increasingly confined and inadequate).[28]

It should be noted also, that what this progressive abandonment of previous tenets therefore denoted was an essentially negative phenomenon: it represented not the development but the *dissolution* of a guiding theory about the role of trade unions, collective bargaining, and the right to strike, a process which unwound the ties around the hands of Governments, when fashioning their policies. It did not, however, also positively and inexorably determine precisely what those policies should be. Thus, whilst post-1979 administrations could increasingly be seen as sharing with the ideologues of the New Right a rejection of the ideals of voluntarism, that points only to a part—albeit an essential one—of the conditions which gave rise to the legislation which was in fact introduced. The second key conclusion is then that the legislation cannot be seen simply as the product of a New Right or Hayekian blueprint. Instead, to complete the picture it is essential to add, as has been attempted here, a more direct and detailed analysis of the shifting problems and preoccupations, priorities and political considerations, tactics

---

[28] Cf. Ewing (1989: p. 16), commenting that 'despite its radical rhetoric, in reality the government has not had the courage of its convictions. The restoration of a common law regime has been only partial.'

and techniques, which determined the various measures which the Governments in fact considered it expedient to introduce at each stage. Indeed, given that the abandonment of voluntarism was both gradual and incomplete, the story has frequently been one of a close interplay between such positive impulses and negative constraints.

We may conclude then with a reply to the basic question with which we began. How has the rapid and far-reaching revolution in our industrial-conflict law over the last decade come about? Three broad strands have been found woven together in the legislation. First, the broad commitment of the Conservative Governments, as with their predecessors, to the running of a capitalist market economy, and hence to tackling the developing problems of that economy in the Britain of the changing post-war era; a commitment which of itself was increasingly and widely believed to necessitate intervention with respect to free collective bargaining and the unfettered right to strike. Secondly, the progressive abandonment of any formal or actual commitment to the tenets of the voluntarist consensus, thus increasingly, although never completely, clearing away the obstacles to the implementation of whatever new industrial-conflict laws were deemed appropriate. Finally, the more specific and complex patchwork of influences which dictated the laws which were in fact introduced. Whilst the second strand strikes an unmistakable ideological chord, for those who yearn to extract some simple common theme underlying the third, it is perhaps to be found, if at all, not in the lofty realms of ideology, but in the altogether duller world of politics.

# Bibliography and References

*Unless otherwise stated, the place of publication is London, or in the case of Macmillan, London and Basingstoke.*

ACAS—see Advisory Conciliation and Arbitration Service.

Advisory Conciliation and Arbitration Service (1981), *Annual Report 1980*, HMSO.

—— (1982), *Annual Report 1981*, HMSO.

—— (1987), *Annual Report 1986*, HMSO.

—— (1988), *Annual Report 1987*, HMSO.

—— (1989), *Annual Report 1988*, HMSO.

AIB—see Association of Independent Businesses.

AIMS of Industry (1979), September, *Freedom Prosperity and the Trade Union*, AIMS.

Arnold, G. (1981), *The Unions*, Hamish Hamilton.

Association of Independent Businesses (1979), September, *Changes in Industrial Relations Legislation: Response to HM Government's Proposals*, AIB.

Atiyah, P. (1967), *Vicarious Liability in the Law of Torts*, Butterworths.

—— (1979), *The Rise and Fall of Freedom of Contract*, Oxford: Clarendon Press.

—— (1985), 'Common Law and Statute Law', 48 *MLR* 1.

—— (1987), *Pragmatism and Theory in English Law*, Stevens.

Auerbach, S. (1987), 'Legal Restraint of Picketing: New Trends; New Tensions', 16 *ILJ* 227.

—— (1988), 'Injunction Procedure in the Seafarers' Dispute', 17 *ILJ* 227.

Barnes, D., and Reid, E. (1980), *Governments and Trade Unions*, Heinemann/PSI.

Bassett, P. (1986), *Strike Free*, Macmillan.

Beaumont, P. (1982), 'Strikes and the Public Sector: The Position in Britain', 4/2 *Employee Relations* 23.

Behrens, R. (1977), *The Conservative Party in Opposition*, Coventry: Lanchester Polytechnic.

—— (1980), *The Conservative Party from Heath to Thatcher*, Farnborough: Saxon House.

Bellace, J. (1981), 'Regulating Secondary Action: The British and American Approaches', 4 *Comparative Labor Law* 115.

Benedictus, R., and Newell, D. (1981), 'Green Paper on Industrial Conflict Law', 10 *ILJ* 119.

Benn, T. (1981), 'The Trade Unions in the 1980s', in his *Arguments for Democracy*, Harmondsworth: Penguin.

Bennion, F. (1983), *Statute Law*, 2nd edn., Oyez Longman.

—— (1985), 'Mass Picketing and the 1875 Act', *Criminal Law Review* 64.

Bercusson, B. (1977), 'One Hundred Years of Conspiracy and Protection of Property: Time for a Change', 40 *MLR* 268.

Biffen, J. (1976), *A Nation in Doubt*, CPC.

BIM—see British Institute of Management.

Bosanquet, N. (1983), *After the New Right*, Heinemann.

Bowers, J., and Auerbach, S. (1988), *A Guide to the Employment Act 1988*, Blackstone Press.

British Institute of Management (1979), December, *Response to DE Discussion Documents*, BIM.

Brittan, S. (1977), *The Economic Consequences of Democracy*, Temple Smith.

Brown, W. (ed.) (1981), *The Changing Contours of British Industrial Relations*, Oxford: Blackwell.

Brownlow, J. (1980), 'The South Yorkshire Steel Strike', *Police* 20 June.

Butler, E. (1983), *Hayek*, Temple Smith.

CBI—see Confederation of British Industry.

CCO—see Conservative Central Office.

Centre for Policy Studies (1975), *Why Britain Needs a Social Market Economy*, foreword by Sir Keith Joseph, CPS.

—— (1980a), 12 September, *Give the Picketing Code the Sanction of Law*, Trade Union Reform Committee, CPS.

—— (1980b), November, *Liberties and Liabilities: The Case for Trade Union Reform*, Trade Union Reform Committee, CPS.

Chafee, Z. (1930), 'The Internal Affairs of Associations not for Profit', 43 *Harvard Law Review* 993.

Chiplin, B., and Doherty, N. (1980), 'Strike Insurance for Employers', April, 136 *Lloyds Bank Review* 1.

Clark, J. (1985), 'The Juridification of Industrial Relations: A Review Article', 14 *ILJ* 69.

—— and Wedderburn, Lord (1983), 'Modern Labour Law: Problems, Functions and Policies', in Wedderburn, Lewis, and Clark (1983) *qv*.

—— —— (1987), 'Juridification—a Universal Trend? The British Experience in Labour Law', in G. Teubner (ed.), *Juridification of Social Spheres*, Berlin: Walter de Gruyter.

Clegg, H. (1975), 'Pluralism in Industrial Relations', 13 *BJIR* 309.

—— (1979), *The Changing System of Industrial Relations in Great Britain*, Oxford: Blackwell.

Clutterbuck, R. (1978), *Britain in Agony*, Faber and Faber.

Coates, K., and Topham, A. (1986), *Trade Unions and Politics*, Oxford: Blackwell.

Collins, H. (1986), *The Law Contract*, Weidenfeld & Nicolson.

Confederation of British Industry (1965), First Memorandum of Evidence to the Donovan Commission, published in *Selected Written Evidence* (1968, HMSO).

—— (1978), September, *British Means Business 1978*, CBI.

—— (1979a), September, *Proposed Industrial Relations Legislation: CBI Memorandum of Views*, Social Affairs Directorate, CBI.

—— (1979b), *Summary of Views of Member Employers' Organisations on the Government's Working Papers on Amendment of Industrial Relations Law*, Social Affairs Directorate, CBI.

—— (1980), February, *Trade Unions in a Changing World: The Challenge for Management*, CBI.

—— (1981), June, *Green Paper on Trade Union Immunities: Response from Confederation of British Industry*, Social Affairs Directorate, CBI.

—— (1983a), March, *Green Paper on Democracy in Trade Unions: Response from Confederation of British Industry*, CBI.

*Confederation of British Industry*, (1983*b*), September, *Proposals for Legislation on Democracy in Trade Unions: The CBI's Response to the Government's Consultative Document*, CBI.

—— (1984), *The Trade Union Act 1984: A Practical Guide to the Law*, CBI.

—— (1989*a*), *Government Green Paper: Removing Barriers to Employment, The CBI's Response*, CBI.

—— (1989*b*), December, *CBI Response on Green Paper: Unofficial Action and the Law*, Employment Affairs Directorate, CBI.

Conservative Central Office (1976), *The Right Approach: A Statement of Conservative Aims*, CCO.

Conservative Political Centre (1968), *Fair Deal at Work*, CPC.

Conservative Trade Unionists (1987), *Trade Unions and Their Members: Observations and Views of the Conservative Trade Unionists National Committee*, CTU.

Cosgrave, P. (1978), *Margaret Thatcher*, Hutchinson.

CPC—see Conservative Political Centre.

CPS—see Centre for Policy Studies.

Craig, F. (ed.) (1975), *British General Election Manifestos 1900–1974*, Macmillan.

Crouch, C. (1982*a*), *Trade Unions: The Logic of Collective Action*, Fontana.

—— (1982*b*), *The Politics of Industrial Relations*, 2nd edn., Fontana.

—— (1983), 'Industrial Relations', in J. Griffith (ed.), *Socialism in a Cold Climate*, Unwin.

—— (1985), 'Conditions for Trade Union Wage Restraint', in L. Lindberg and C. Maier (eds.), *The Politics of Inflation and Economic Stagnation*, Washington, DC: Brookings Institution.

CTU—see Conservative Trade Unionists.

Daniel, W., and Millward, N. (1983), *Workplace Industrial Relations in Britain*, Heinemann.

Davies, P. (1979), 'Arbitration and the Role of Courts in the United Kingdom', 3 *Comparative Labor Law* 31.

—— and Anderman, S. (1974), 'Injunction Procedure in Labour Disputes II', 3 *ILJ* 30.

—— and Freedland, M. (1979), *Labour Law: Text and Materials*, 1st edn., Weidenfeld & Nicolson.

—— —— (1983), *Kahn-Freund's Labour and the Law*, 3rd edn., Stevens.

—— —— (1984*a*), *Labour Law: Text and Materials*, 2nd edn.

—— —— (1984*b*), 'Labour Law', in J. Jowell and J. McAuslan (eds.), *Lord Denning: The Judge and the Law*, Sweet & Maxwell.

DE—see Department of Employment.

Denning, Lord (1983), *The Closing Chapter*, Butterworths.

DEP—see Department of Employment and Productivity.

Department of Employment (1979), February, *The Economy, the Government and Trade Union Responsibilities* (Joint government/TUC statement), HMSO.

—— (1980), 22 January, *Memorandum on Trade Union Immunities*, printed in Select Committee on Employment (1980*b*) *qv*.

—— (1981*a*), *Trade Union Immunities*, Green Paper Cmnd. 8128, HMSO.

—— (1981*b*), 23 November, 'Proposals for Industrial Relations Legislation', reprinted in the Select Committee on Employment's *First Special Report Session 1981–82*. 2 Dec. 1981 (HC 85) HMSO vii–xiv.

244    Bibliography and References

Department of Employment (1983*a*), January, *Democracy in Trade Unions*, Green Paper Cmnd. 8778, HMSO.

—— (1983*b*), July, *Proposals for Legislation on Democracy in Trade Unions*, HMSO.

—— (1984), *A Guide to the Trade Union Act 1984*, HMSO.

—— (1986), *Building Business . . . Not Barriers*, White Paper Cmnd. 9794, HMSO.

—— (1987), February, *Trade Unions and Their Members*, Green Paper Cmnd. 95, HMSO.

—— (1988), *Draft Statutory Code of Practice on Trade Union Industrial Action Balloting*, DE.

—— (1989*a*), March, *Removing Barriers to Employment*, Green Paper Cmnd. 665, HMSO.

—— (1989*b*), October, *Unofficial Action and the Law*, Green Paper Cmnd. 821, HMSO.

—— (1990), *Code of Practice Trade Union Ballots on Industrial Action*, HMSO.

Department of Employment and Productivity (1969), *In Place of Strife: A Policy for Industrial Relations*, Cmnd. 3888, HMSO.

Dicey, A. (1885), *Introduction to the Study of the Law of the Constitution*, 10th edn., 1959 Macmillan.

—— (1914), *Law and Public Opinion in England*, 1963 edn., Macmillan.

Dickens, L. (1987), 'The Advisory Conciliation and Arbitration Service: Regulation and Voluntarism in Industrial Relations', in R. Baldwin and J. McCrudden, *Regulation and Public Law*, Weidenfeld & Nicolson.

Donaldson, J. (1975*a*), 'Lessons from the Industrial Court', 91 *LQR* 181.

—— (1975*b*), 'The Role of Labour Courts', 4 *ILJ* 63.

—— (1984), Speech to EEF reported in *The Times*, 15 February.

Donovan, Lord (1968), *Report of the Royal Commission on Trade Unions and Employers' Associations*, Cmnd. 3623, HMSO.

Dorfman, G. (1983), *British Trade Unionism against the Trades Union Congress*, Macmillan.

Dow, C. (1986), 'Trade Unions and Inflation', 159 *Lloyds Bank Review* 1.

Drake, C. (1985), *The Trade Union Acts*, Sweet & Maxwell.

Dunedin, Viscount (1906), *Report of the Royal Commission on Trade Disputes and Trade Combinations*, Cmnd. 2825, HMSO.

Dunn, S., and Gennard, J. (1984), *The Closed Shop in British Industry*, Macmillan.

Durcan, J., McCarthy, W., and Redman, G. (1983), *Strikes in Post-War Britain*, Allen & Unwin.

Edwards, P. (1982), 'Britain's Changing Strike Problem', 13/2 *Industrial Relations Journal* 5.

EEF—see Engineering Employers' Federation.

Elias, P., and Ewing, K. (1982), 'Economic Torts and Labour Law: Old Principles and New Liabilities', 41 *CLJ* 321.

—— (1987), *Trade Union Democracy Members' Rights and the Law*, Mansell.

Engineering Employers' Federation (1979*a*), March, *Guidelines on Collective Bargaining and Response to Industrial Action*, EEF.

—— (1979*b*), 17 August, *Representation on Picketing*, EEF.

—— (1981–2), miscellaneous circulars to members, memoranda, and press releases relating to 'lay-off' proposals, EEF.

Engineeering Employers' Federation (1983*a*), March, *Response to Green Paper 'Democracy in Trade Unions'*, EEF.

—— (1983b), September, *Response to Government's Proposals for Legislation on Democracy in Trade Unions*, EEF.

—— (1984), *Employers' Guide to the Trade Union Act 1984*, EEF.

—— (1987a), *Response to the Green Paper 'Trade Unions and Their Members'*, EEF.

—— (1987b), December, *Proposal for a Code on Industrial Action Balloting*, EEF.

—— (1989), November, *Response to Green Paper 'Unofficial Action and the Law'*, EEF.

England, G. (1976), 'Loss of Jobs in Strikes: The Position in England and Canada Compared', 25 *ICLQ* 583.

England, J., and Weekes, B. (1985), 'Trade Unions and the State: A Review of the Crisis', in W. McCarthy (ed.), *Trade Unions*, 2nd edn., Harmondsworth: Penguin.

Evans, S. (1983), 'The Labour Injunction Revisited', 12 *ILJ* 129.

—— (1987), 'The Use of Injunctions in Industrial Disputes May 1984–April 1987', 25 *BJIR* 419.

Ewing, K. (1979), 'The Golden Formula—Some Recent Developments', 8 *ILJ* 133.

—— (1985), 'The Strike, the Courts and the Rule-Books', 14 *ILJ* 160.

—— (1986), 'The Right to Strike', 15 *ILJ* 143.

—— (1988a), 'Rights and Immunities in British Labour Law', 10 *CLLJ* 1.

—— (1988b), 'Trade Unions and the Constitution: The Impact of the New Conservatives', in C. Graham and T. Prosser (eds.), *Waiving the Rules: The Constitution under Thatcherism*, Milton Keynes: Open University Press.

—— (1988c), 'The Death of Labour Law?', 8 *OJLS* 293.

—— (1989), 12 October, *Economics and Labour Law in Britain: Thatcher's Radical Experiment*, John Alexander Weir Memorial Lecture.

—— and Napier B. (1986), 'The Wapping Dispute and Labour Law', 45 *CLJ* 285.

Flanders, A. (1970), *Management and Unions*, Faber.

—— (1974), 'The Tradition of Voluntarism', 12 *BJIR* 352.

Forde, M. (1984), 'Bills of Rights and Trade Union Immunities: Some French Lessons', 13 *ILJ* 40.

Fosh, P., and Littler, C. (eds.) (1985), *Industrial Relations and the Law in the 1980s*, Aldershot: Gower.

Fox, A. (1985a), Man Mismanagement, 2nd edn., Hutchinson.

—— (1985b), *History and Heritage*, Allen & Unwin.

Fredman, S., and Morris G. (1988), 'Civil Servants: A Contract of Employment?', *PL* 58.

Friedman, M. (1951), 'Some Comments on the Significance of Labor Unions for Economic Policy', in D. McWright (ed.), *The Impact of the Union*, New York: Harcourt Brace.

—— (1981), interview, *Listener*, 12 March.

—— and Friedman, R. (1980), *Free to Choose*, Secker & Warburg.

Frodsham, A. (1981a), article, *Guardian*, 8 April.

—— (1981b), article, *The Times*, 25 November.

Gamble, A. (1974), *The Conservative Nation*, R&KP.

—— (1979), 'The Free Economy and the Strong State: The Rise of the Social Market Economy', *Socialist Register* 1, Merlin Press.

—— (1980), ch. 2 of Z. Layton-Henry (ed.), *Conservative Party Politics*, Macmillan.

—— (1985), *Britain in Decline*, 2nd edn., Macmillan.

Gamble, A. (1986), ch. 1 of R. Levitas (ed.), *The Ideology of the New Right*, Cambridge: Polity Press.

—— (1988*a*), 'Economic Decline and the Crisis of Legitimacy', in C. Graham and T. Prosser (eds.), *Waiving the Rules: The Constitution under Thatcherism*, Milton Keynes: Open University Press.

—— (1988*b*), *The Free Economy and the Strong State: The Politics of Thatcherism*, Macmillan.

—— (1989), 'Privatization, Thatcherism, and the British State', 16 *JLS* 1.

Gardiner, G. (1981), *The Next Employment Bill: Agenda for Action*, Bow Publications.

Geary, R. (1985), *Policing Industrial Disputes*, Cambridge: CUP.

Gennard, J. (1977), *Financing Strikers*, Macmillan.

Goodman, G. (1979), *The Awkward Warrior*, Davis-Poynter.

Gordon, C. (ed.) (1983), *Erskine May's Treatise on the Law, Privileges, Proceedings and Usage of Parliament*, 20th edn., Butterworths.

Gregory, R. (1984), 'Conservative Democracy and Union Power: The Trade Union Bill 1983', 244 *Contemporary Review* 181.

Griffith, J. (1974), *Parliamentary Scrutiny of Government Bills*, George Allen & Unwin.

Grunfeld, C. (1966), *Modern Trade Union Law*, Sweet & Maxwell.

—— and Bloch, L. (1986), *Law Reform and the Mining Dispute 1984–85*, I.o.D.

Gwynn, S., and Tuckwell, G. (1917), *The Life of Sir Charles Dilke*, Murray.

Hain, P. (1986), *Political Strikes*, Harmondsworth: Penguin.

Hall, P. (1986), *Governing the Economy*, Cambridge: Polity Press.

Hanson, C. (1978), 'Collective Bargaining: The Balance of Market Advantage', in *Trade Unions: Public Goods or Public 'Bads'?*, IEA Readings no. 17, IEA.

—— (1984), 'From Taff Vale to Tebbit', postscript to Hayek (1984) *qv*.

—— (1986), *Trade Union Reform—the Next Step*, I.o.D.

—— and Mather, G. (1988), *Striking out Strikes*, Hobart Paper 110, IEA.

—— —— (1989), 12 June, *Submission to the Department of Employment in response to the Green Paper 'Removing Barriers to Employment'*.

Hartley, J., Kelly, J., and Nicholson, N. (1983), *Steel Strike*, Batsford.

Hayek, F. (1959), 'Unions, Inflation and Profits', in P. Bradley (ed.), *The Public Stake in Union Power*, Charlottesville: University of Virginia Press.

—— (1960), *The Constitution of Liberty*, R&KP.

—— (1976), 'The Mirage of Social Justice', in Hayek (1982) *qv*.

—— (1982), *Law, Legislation and Liberty*, R&KP.

—— (1984), *1980s Unemployment and the Unions*, 2nd edn., IEA.

Hendy, J. (1989), *The Conservative Employment Laws: A National and International Assessment*, IER.

—— McCarthy, Lord, and Wedderburn, Lord (1989), *Ballots on Industrial Action— the Draft Code of Practice*, IER.

Hepple, B., and Brown, W. (1981), 'Tasks for Labour Law Research', 1 *LS* 56.

Heydon, J. (1978), *Economic Torts*, 2nd edn., Sweet & Maxwell.

Hickling M. (1967), *Citrine's Trade Union Law*, 3rd edn., Stevens.

Hirschman, A. (1970), *Exit, Voice and Loyalty*, Cambridge, Mass.: Harvard UP.

Holmes, M. (1983), 'Trade Unions and Governments', in H. Drucker (ed.), *Developments in British Politics*, Macmillan.

—— (1985*a*), *The Labour Government 1974–1979*, Macmillan.

—— (1985*b*), *The First Thatcher Government 1979–1983*, Brighton: Wheatsheaf Books.

Honeyball, S. (1989), 'Employment Law and the Primacy of Contract', 18 *ILJ* 97.

Hoskyns, J. (1982), 'The Corrupting Power of Immunity', *The Times*, 2 September.

—— (1985), *An Agenda For Change*, I.o.D.

—— (1988), letter, *Guardian*, 19 September.

Howard, M. (1983), 'The Right to Refuse to Strike', *Daily Telegraph*, 5 October.

Howe, G., Joseph, K., Prior, J., and Howell, D. (1977), *The Right Approach to the Economy*, CCO.

Hurd, D. (1979), *An End to Promises*, Collins.

Hutt, W. (1975), *The Theory of Collective Bargaining 1930–1975*, IEA.

Hutton, J. (1984), 'Solving the Strike Problem: Part II of the Trade Union Act 1984', 13 *ILJ* 212.

—— (1985), 'Ballots before Industrial Action', 14 *ILJ* 255.

Hyman, R. (1978), 'Pluralism, Procedural Consensus and Collective Bargaining', 16 *BJIR* 16.

—— (1984), *Strikes*, 3rd edn., Fontana.

—— (1987), 'Trade Unions and the Law: Papering Over the Cracks?', 31 *Capital and Class* 93.

—— (1989*a*), *The Political Economy of Industrial Relations*, Macmillan.

—— (1989*b*), *Strikes*, 4th edn., Macmillan.

Inns of Court Conservative and Unionist Society (1958), *A Giant's Strength*, IOCCAUS/Christopher Johnson.

Institute of Directors (1979*a*), July, *Response to the Working Papers on Proposed Industrial Relations Legislation*, I.o.D.

—— (1979*b*), *Trade Union Power: A Case for Reform?*, papers delivered at a conference on 5 December 1979, I.o.D.

—— (1980), March, *Response to the Working Paper on Secondary Industrial Action*, I.o.D.

—— (1981), June, *Trade Union Law and the Pursuit of Prosperity—the Next Step*, Industrial Relations Committee, I.o.D.

—— (1983), April, *Democracy and Competitiveness—Further Steps Towards Trade Union Reform*, I.o.D.

—— (1984), position paper *Settling Disputes Peacefully*, I.o.D.

—— (1985), *Settling Disputes Peacefully II—Procedure Agreements*, I.o.D.

—— (1987), April, *Response to the Green Paper Trade Unions and Their Members*, letter to Paymaster General, I.o.D.

—— (1989), 30 November, *Green Paper: Unofficial Action and the Law*, letter to Mr Fowler, I.o.D.

Institute of Personnel Management (1979), September, *Comments on DE Working Papers for Consultation on Proposed Industrial Relations Legislation*, IPM.

—— (1988), *Comments on the Employment Bill, 1987*, IPM.

IOCCAUS—see Inns of Court Conservative and Unionist Society.

I.o.D.—see Institute of Directors.

Jacob, J. (1986), 'Sequestration for Contempt of Court', 39 *CLP* 219.

Jeffery, K., and Hennessy, P. (1983), *States of Emergency*, R&KP.

Johnson, N. (1985), 'The Employment Committee 1979–1983', in G. Drewry (ed.), *The New Select Committees*, Oxford: Clarendon Press.

Joyce, P., Woods, A., and Hughes, G. (1984), 'Trade Union Law in Action: A Transition Period', 14 *Kingston Law Review* 60.

Kahn, P., Lewis, N., Livock, R., and Wiles, P. (1983), *Picketing: Industrial Disputes Tactics and the Law*, R&KP.

Kahn-Freund, O. (1954a), 'Legal Framework', in A. Flanders and H. Clegg (eds.), *The System of Industrial Relations in Great Britain*, Oxford: Blackwell.

—— (1954b), 'Intergroup Conflicts and Their Settlement', reprinted in Kahn-Freund (1978) *qv*.

—— (1959), 'Labour Law', reprinted in Kahn-Freund (1978) *qv*.

—— (1966), 'Reflections on Legal Education', 29 *MLR* 121.

—— (1968), *Labour Law: Old Traditions and New Developments*, Toronto/Vancouver: Clarke, Irwin & Co.

—— (1969), 'Industrial Relations and the Law—Retrospect and Prospect', 7 *BJIR* 301.

—— (1970), 'Trade Unions, the Law and Society', 33 *MLR* 241.

—— (1977), *Labour and the Law*, 2nd edn., Stevens.

—— (1978), *Selected Writings*, Stevens.

—— (1979), *Labour Relations: Heritage and Adjustment*, Oxford: OUP.

—— (1981), *Labour Law and Politics in the Weimar Republic*, ed. R. Lewis and J. Clark, Oxford: Blackwell.

—— and Hepple, B. (1972), *Laws against Strikes*, Fabian Society.

Kerr, A. (1980), 'In Contemplation or Furtherance of a Trade Dispute . . . ' *DULJ* (Oct.) 59.

Kidner, R. (1975), 'Picketing and the Criminal Law', *Criminal Law Review* 256.

—— (1982), 'Lessons in Trade Union Law Reform: The Origins and Passage of the Trade Disputes Act 1906', 2 *LS* 34.

—— (1986), 'Sanctions for Contempt by a Trade Union', 6 *LS* 18.

Labour Party (1989), *Meet the Challenge Make the Change: A New Agenda for Britain*, Labour Party.

Lawson, N. (1980), *The New Conservatism*, CPS.

—— (1981), *Thatcherism in Practice: A Progress Report*, speech of 14. Jan. published as HM Treasury Press Release.

—— (1984), *The British Experiment*, Mais Lecture, 18 June, published as HM Treasury Press Release.

Leggatt, A. (1979), *Report of Inquiry into Certain Trade Union Recruitment Activities*, Cmnd. 7706, HMSO.

Lewis, N., and Wiles, P. (1984), 'The Post-Corporatist State?', 11 *Journal of Law and Society* 65.

Lewis, R. (1976), 'The Historical Development of Labour Law', 14 *BJIR* 1.

—— (1979), 'Kahn-Freund and Labour Law: An Outline Critique', 8 *ILJ* 202.

—— (1983), 'Method and Ideology in the Labour Law Writings of Otto Kahn-Freund', in Wedderburn, Lewis, and Clark (1983) *qv*.

—— (1986), 'The Role of the Law in Employment Relations', in id. (ed.), *Labour Law in Britain*, Oxford: Blackwell.

—— (1988), *Strike-Free Procedures: Are They What They Seem?*, Warwick Papers in Industrial Relations 20, Coventry: University of Warwick.

—— Davies, P., and Wedderburn, Lord (1979), October, *Industrial Relations Law and the Conservative Government*, Fabian Society.

—— and Simpson, R. (1981), *Striking a Balance?*, Oxford: Martin Robertson.

—— —— (1982), 'Disorganising Industrial Relations: An Analysis of Sections 2–8 and 10–14 of the Employment Act 1982', II *ILJ* 227.

Lightman, G. (1987), 'A Trade Union in Chains: Scargill Unbound—The Legal Constraints of Receivership and Sequestration', 40 *CLP* 25.

Lloyd, J. (1985), *Understanding the Miners' Strike*, Fabian Society.

—— and Adeney, M. (1986), *The Miners' Strike 1984–5: Loss Without Limit*, R&KP.

McBride, S. (1986), 'Mrs Thatcher and the Post-War Consensus: The Case of Trade Union Policy', 39 *Parliamentary Affairs* 330.

McCarthy, Lord (W.) (1981), 'Socialism and Incomes Policy', in D. Lipsey and R. Leonard (eds.), *The Socialist Agenda: Crosland's Legacy*, Jonathan Cape.

—— (1985), *Freedom at Work: Towards the Reform of Tory Employment Laws*, Fabian Tract 508, Fabian Society.

—— (1986), *Freedom, Democracy and the Role of Trade Unions in Modern Industrial Society*, Jim Conway Lecture, 12 November.

—— (1987), 'The Case for a More Balanced Framework of Labour Law', in *The Future of Labour Law: Two Views*, Warwick Papers in Industrial Relations 14, Coventry: University of Warwick.

Macfarlane, L. (1981), *The Right to Strike*, Harmondsworth: Penguin.

MacInnes, J. (1987), *Thatcherism at Work*, Milton Keynes: Open University Press.

McKendrick, E. (1986), 'Trade Unions and Non-Striking Members', 6 *LS* 35.

McNee, D. (1980), Written and Oral evidence reported in Home Affairs Committee, *5th Report Session 1979–80, The Law Relating to Public Order*, Vol II (HC 756), HMSO.

Marris, R. (1981), 'Why the SDP Should Abolish the Right to Strike', *The Times*, 5 October.

Martin, R. (1985), 'Ballots and Trade Union Democracy: The Role of Government', in Fosh and Littler (1985) *qv*.

Mather, G. (1987), 'The Future Shape of Labour Legislation', in *The Future of Labour Law: Two Views*, Warwick Papers in Industrial Relations 14, Coventry: University of Warwick.

Maudling, R. (1978), *Memoirs*, Sidgwick and Jackson.

Mayhew, K. (1983), *Trade Unions and the Labour Market*, Oxford: Martin Robertson.

—— (1985), 'Reforming the Labour Market', 1 *OREP* 60.

Meade, J. (1981), 'The Fixing of Money Rates of Pay', in D. Lipsey and R. Leonard (eds.), *The Socialist Agenda: Crosland's Legacy*, Jonathan Cape.

—— (1982), *Stagflation Volume I: Wage-Fixing*, George Allen & Unwin.

—— (1985), *Wage-Fixing Revisited*, IEA.

Middlemas, K. (1983), Articles in *New Statesman*, 10 and 17 June.

Miers, D., and Page, A. (1982), *Legislation*, Sweet & Maxwell.

Miller, K. (1982), 'Factory Occupations in Scotland', 11 *ILJ* 115.

Millward, N., and Stevens, M. (1986), *British Workplace Industrial Relations 1980–1984*, Aldershot: Gower.

MMC—see Monopolies and Mergers Commission.

Monopolies and Mergers Commission (1989), *Labour Practices in TV and Film Making*, Cmnd. 666, HMSO.

Moran, M. (1977), *The Politics of Industrial Relations*, Macmillan.

Moran, M. (1979), 'The Conservative Party and the Trade Unions Since 1974', 27 *Political Studies* 38.

—— (1986), 'Industrial Relations', in H. Drucker *et. al.* (eds.), *Developments in British Politics*, Macmillan.

Morris, G. (1986), *Strikes in Essential Services*, Mansell.

—— with Rydzkowski, S. (1984), 'Approaches to Industrial Action in the National Health Service', 13 *ILJ* 153.

Murray, L. (1980), article, *The Sunday Times*, 10 August.

Napier, B. (1987), 'Strikes and the Individual Worker—Reforming the Law', 46 *CLJ* 287.

Neal, L., and Bloch, L. (1983), March, *The Right to Strike in a Free Society*, Trade Union Reform Committee, CPS.

—— —— and Grunfeld, C. (1984), May, *Essential Services—Whose Rights?*, Trade Union Reform Committee, CPS.

O'Higgins, P. (1976), 'The Right to Strike: Some International Reflections', in J. Carby-Hall (ed.), *Studies in Labour Law*, Bradford: MCB Books.

Phelps Brown, E. (1986), *The Origins of Trade Union Power*, Revised edn., Oxford: OUP.

Plant, R. (1983), 'The Resurgance of Ideology', in H. Drucker (ed.), *Developments in British Politics*, Macmillan.

Pollock, F. (1908), *Law of Torts*, 8th edn., Stevens.

Prior, J. (1976), article, *The Times*, 15 June.

—— (1977*a*), letter, *Financial Times*, 30 May.

—— (1977*b*), article, *Guardian*, 14 December.

—— (1977*c*), interview, *Guardian*, 15 September.

—— (1979*a*), interview, *Business Week*, 16 April.

—— (1979*b*), 'Some Reflections on Industrial Relations', *IRJ* Autumn 9.

—— (1979*c*), interview, *Personnel Management*, 16 July.

—— (1980), written memorandum to the Select Committee on Employment published in id. (1980*c*) *qv*.

—— (1985), interview, *New Statesman*, 13 December.

—— (1986), *A Balance of Power*, Hamish Hamilton.

Prondzynski, F. Von (1985), 'Conclusions: The Changing Functions of Labour Law', in Fosh and Littler (1985) *qv*.

Purcell, J., and Sisson, K. (1983), 'Strategies and Practice in the Management of Industrial Relations', in G. Bain (ed.), *Industrial Relations in Britain*, Oxford: Blackwell.

Raz, J. (1979), *The Authority of Law*, Oxford: Clarendon Press.

Rees, W. (1982), 'Frames of Reference and the "Public Interest"', in Wedderburn and Murphy (1982) *qv*.

Rideout, R. (1979), 'Power, Pickets and the Closed Shop', 32 *CLP* 199.

—— (1982), 'Arbitration and Public Interest: Regulated Arbitration', in Wedderburn and Murphy (1982) *qv*.

Roberts, B. (1987), *Mr Hammond's Cherry Tree: The Morphology of Union Survival*, Occasional Paper 76, IEA.

Robinson, D. (1986), *Monetarism and the Labour Market*, Oxford: Clarendon Press.

Rubin, G. (1985), 'Strike Ballots and the Trade Union Act 1984', *JBL* 326.

SDP—see Social Democratic Party.

Select Committee on Employment (House of Commons) (1980*a*), *Minutes of Evidence Session 1979–80, 27 Feb. 1980*, HC 462–ii, HMSO.

—— (1980*b*), *Minutes of Evidence Session 1979–80, 20 Feb. 1980*, HC 462–i, HMSO.

—— (1980*c*), 13 November, *Second Special Report Session 1979–80*, HC 848, HMSO.

—— (1981), 21 July, *Second Report Session 1980–81*, including oral and written evidence taken by the committee and appendices, HC 282, HMSO.

—— (1982), *Minutes of Evidence Session 1981–82, 3 Feb. 1982*, HC 153–iii, HMSO.

—— (1983), *Minutes of Evidence Session 1982–83, 2 Mar. 1983*, HC 243–i, HMSO.

Shenfield, A. (1986), *What Right to Strike?*, IEA.

Simpson, R. (1983), 'A Not so Golden Formula: In Contemplation or Furtherance of a Trade Dispute after 1982', 46 *MLR* 463.

—— (1986), 'British Labour Relations in the 1980s: Learning to Live With the Law', 49 *MLR* 796.

—— (1989), 'The Summer of Discontent and the Law', 18 *ILJ* 234.

Singer, P. (1974), *Democracy and Disobedience*, Oxford: OUP.

Sked, A., and Cook, C. (1984), *Post-War Britain*, 2nd edn., Harmondsworth: Penguin.

Smart, B. (1985), 'The Right to Strike and the Right to Work', 2 *Journal of Applied Philosophy* 31.

Social Democratic Party (1982), *Industrial Relations I: Trade Union Reform*, Policy Document no. 8, SDP.

—— (1986), *Industrial Relations: A Fresh Look*, Consultative Paper, SDP.

Soskice, D. (1984), 'Industrial Relations and the British Economy, 1979–1983', 23 *Industrial Relations* 306.

Summers, C., Wellington H., and Hyde, A. (1982), *Cases and Materials on Labor Law*, Mineola, NY: Foundation Press.

Taylor, R. (1982*a*), 'The Trade Union "Problem" Since 1960', in B. Pimlott and C. Cook (eds.), *Trade Unions in British Politics*, Longman.

—— (1982*b*), *Workers and the New Depression*, Macmillan.

—— (1984), 'In Place of Strife', *Management Today* January 50.

Tebbit, N. (1981), 23 November, Memorandum to the Select Committee on Employment reproduced in their *First Special Report Session 1981–82, 2 Dec. 1981*, HC 85, HMSO.

—— (1982), oral evidence to Select Committee on Employment (1982) *qv*.

—— (1983), 'Industrial Relations in the Next Two Decades: Government Objectives', 5/1 *Employee Relations* 3.

Trades Union Congress (1968), 93–238 of *Royal Commission on Trade Unions and Employers' Associations—Selected Written Evidence*, HMSO.

—— (1981*a*), *Beat the Act*, Workbook on the Employment Act 1980, Education Service, TUC.

—— (1981*b*), oral evidence to Select Committee on Employment (1981) *qv*. 170 ff.

—— (1981*c*), *Conference Report 1980*, TUC.

—— (1982), *Report by the TUC General Council*, adopted at Wembley conference, April 1982, TUC.

—— (1983), May, *Hands up for Democracy*, TUC.

TUC—see Trades Union Congress.

Tur, R. (1982), 'Trades Unions at the Crossroads: The Legitimacy of Industrial Action', in Wedderburn and Murphy (1982) *qv*.

Undy, R., and Martin, R. (1984), *Ballots and Trade Union Democracy*, Oxford: Blackwell.

—— Ellis, V., McCarthy, W., and Halmos, A. (1981), *Change in Trade Unions*, Hutchinson.

Wallington, P. (1983), 'The Employment Act 1982 Section 9—a Recipe for Victimisation?', 46 *MLR* 310.

Webb, S. (1906), memorandum appended to Dunedin (1906) *qv* 18.

—— and Webb, B. (1920), (first published 1897) *Industrial Democracy*, Longman.

Wedderburn, Lord (K.) (1965), *The Worker and the Law*, 1st edn., Macgibbon and Kee.

—— (1969), 'Conflicts of "Rights" and Conflicts of "Interests" in Labour Disputes', in B. Aaron (ed.), *Dispute Settlement Procedures in Five West European Countries*, Los Angeles: University of California.

—— (1974), 'The Trade Union and Labour Relations Act 1974', 37 *MLR* 525.

—— (1978), 'The New Structure of Labour Law in Britain', 13 *Israel Law Review* 435.

—— (1980), 'Industrial Relations and the Courts', 9 *ILJ* 65.

—— (1981), written and oral evidence to Select Committee on Employment (1981) *qv*.

—— (1982a), *Clerk and Lindsell on Torts*, 15th edn., ch. 15, Sweet & Maxwell.

—— (1982b), 'Introduction: A 1912 Overture', in id. and Murphy (1982) *qv*.

—— (1984), 'Labour Law Now—A Hold and a Nudge', 13 *ILJ* 73.

—— (1985a), 'The New Policies in Industrial Relations Law', in Fosh and Littler (1985) *qv*.

—— (1985b), 'The New Politics of Labour Law', reprinted in W. McCarthy (ed.), *Trade Unions*, 2nd edn., Harmondsworth: Penguin.

—— (1986a), 'Labour Law Research in Britain', in S. Edlund (ed.), *Labour Law Research in Twelve Countries*, Stockholm: Almquist and Wiksell.

—— (1986b), *The Worker and the Law*, 3rd edn., Harmondsworth: Penguin.

—— (1987), 'Labour Law: From Here to Autonomy?', 16 *ILJ* 1.

—— (1989a), 'The Injunction and the Sovereignty of Parliament', 23 *The Law Teacher* 4.

—— (1989b), 'Freedom of Association and Philosophies of Labour Law', 18 *ILJ* 1.

—— and Murphy, W. (eds.) (1982) *Labour Law and the Community*, IALS.

—— Lewis, R., and Clark, J. (eds.) (1983), *Labour Law and Industrial Relations Building on Kahn-Freund*, Oxford: Clarendon Press.

Weekes, B., Mellish, M., Dickens, L., and Lloyd, J. (1975), *Industrial Relations and the Limits of Law*, Oxford: Blackwell.

Wellington, H. (1968), *Labor and the Legal Process*, New Haven: Yale UP.

Whitehead, P. (1985), *The Writing on the Wall*, Michael Joseph.

Wigham, E. (1982), *Strikes and the Government 1893–1981*, Macmillan.

Wilkinson, T. (1987), *A Guide on Workplace Balloting*, IPM.

Younson, F. (1984), 'Who's Been Using the Law in Industrial Disputes?', *Personnel Management* June 32.

# Index